William Cook is the author of *Ha Bloody Ha – Comedians Talking* and *The Comedy Store – The Club That Changed British Comedy*.

He has worked for the BBC and written for the *Guardian*, the *Mail on Sunday* and the *New Statesman*. He is also the editor of the hugely successful *Tragically I was an Only Twin: The Complete Peter Cook*.

GOODBYE AGAIN

The Definitive Peter Cook and Dudley Moore

EDITED BY WILLIAM COOK

arrow books

Published by Arrow Books in 2005

1 3 5 7 9 10 8 6 4 2

Copyright © 1963, 1971, 1976, 1977, 1980, 1987, 2002, 2004, Lin Cook and
Martine Avenue Productions Inc.
Royal Box from Beyond the Fringe © 1963, Alan Bennett, Lin Cook, Jonathan
Miller, Martine Avenue Productions Inc.
Bo Duddley © 2004, Essex Music (from Chapter 2)
Goodbye © 2004, Essex Music (from Chapter 9)
Introductions copyright © William Cook, 2004

First published in the United Kingdom in 2004 by Century

Arrow Books Limited
The Random House Group Limited
20 Vauxhall Bridge Road, London, SW1V 2SA

Random House Australia (Pty) Limited
20 Alfred Street, Milsons Point, Sydney,
New South Wales 2061, Australia

Random House New Zealand Limited
18 Poland Road, Glenfield
Auckland 10, New Zealand

Random House (Pty) Limited
Endulini, 5a Jubilee Road, Parktown 2193, South Africa

The Random House Group Limited Reg. No. 954009

www.randomhouse.co.uk

A CIP catalogue record for this book
is available from the British Library

Papers used by Random House are natural, recyclable products made from wood
grown in sustainable forests. The manufacturing processes conform to the
environmental regulations of the country of origin

ISBN 0 09 947256 2

Printed and bound in Great Britain by
Bookmarque Ltd, Croydon, Surrey

Acknowledgements

Grateful thanks to the following institutions, which first recorded, broadcast or published much of this material: broadcasters and producers – ABC, ATV, the Australian Broadcasting Commission, the BBC, ITV and Network Nine Television; record companies – Atlantic, BBC Worldwide, Capitol, Decca, EMI, Essex Music, Island, Laughing Stock, Parlophone, Pye Cube, Springtime and Virgin; publishers and periodicals – Mandarin, Methuen, Samuel French, Souvenir Press, and the *Radio Times*. Grateful thanks, too, to Anne Bancroft, Rodney Bewes, John Cleese, Brian Murphy, Anna Quayle and John Wells who helped to perform some of this material. Grateful thanks also for their help in compiling this collection to the following institutions: the BBC, Carlton Television and Martine Avenue Productions Inc. And grateful thanks, too, for all their help, to the following individuals: Julian Alexander, Peter Bellwood, Alan Bennett, Hannah Black, Mark Booth, Michael Burrell, Brian Dallow, Dick Fiddy, Bruce Hunter, Jonathan Miller, Geoffrey Strachan, Kate Watkins, Roger Wilmut, Alice Wilson, Cy Young – and, above all, Lin Cook and Rena Fruchter, without whom this book never would have been published.

Contents

Introduction   1

Chapter One *Beyond the Fringe*   23
Royal Box; Bloody Rhondda Mine; Dudley Moore's Postscript;
Peter Cook's Postscript

Chapter Two *Not Only . . . But Also . . .*   38
Prospective Son-in-Law; The Most Boring Man in the World
Competition; Italian Restaurant; The Music Teacher; Bo Duddley;
The Fairy Cobbler; Swinging London

Chapter Three *Goodbye Again*   70
The Masked Phantom; Long Distance; Sherlock Holmes
Investigates; War Correspondent; Aversion Therapy; Herman
Hermitz Reports; That Rebellion Thing; Plunger Jarvis; Insurance
Salesmen

Chapter Four *Not Only . . . But Also . . . (Again)*   118
The Glidd of Glood; The Piano Tuner; The Scriptwriter; In the
Club; Permission to Marry; Lengths; Conman; The Lunch Party;
The Making of a Movie; Pseudolene; Shirt Shop

Chapter Five *Behind the Fridge*   170
Foreign Office; Party Political Broadcast; Conservative;
Prestissimo; Peter Cook by Dudley Moore; On Location; Soap
Opera; Speech Impodiment; Dean of University

Chapter Six *Derek & Clive*   204
The Worst Job He Ever Had; Squatter and the Ant; Winkie Wanky
Woo; Bo Duddley (Again); Top Rank; Cancer; Back of the Cab; I
Saw This Bloke; Endangered Species; Politics; The Worst Jobs They
Ever Had; General Eisenhower; Vietnam; A Million Pounds; Top
Rank (Again); The Worst Jobs They Ever Had (Again)

Chapter Seven *Pete & Dud*   256
The Fork Idiom; By Appointment; Christmas; Diseases; Music; In
Heaven; The Unexplained; The Beeside; In Prison; At the Doctor's;
At the Gym; A Spot of the Usual Trouble; Dreams; Double O Dud;
Racial Prejudice; Bestseller; The Art of Seduction; Women's Rights

Chapter Eight *Sir Arthur Streeb-Greebling*   352
Tailor Shop; The Frog & Peach; The Funnel-Web Spider;
Terminated Interview

Chapter Nine *Goodbye-ee*   370
The Tower of London; Madame Tussaud's; Horse Guards Parade;
One Leg Too Few; Goodbye-ee

Notes   384

Introduction

This is the story of an extraordinary relationship – a friendship, a partnership, almost, at times, a marriage. Like a lot of love affairs, it didn't last for ever, but over twenty years, this true romance spawned some of the funniest sketches ever written. And over eighty of these sketches are gathered together in this volume.

This book is called *The Definitive Peter Cook and Dudley Moore*, but it's really a little less, and a lot more, than that. Less, because Cook and Moore created far more comedy than you could ever squeeze into a single volume – more, because this comprehensive collection doubles as a diary of their daily lives. From the precocious satire of *Beyond the Fringe* to the boozy obscenity of *Derek & Clive*, their comedy was a sort of autobiography – and that's what makes it so enthralling, even on those occasions when it doesn't actually make you laugh out loud.

Although you'll need to search pretty far and wide to find a sketch of theirs that won't amuse you, Cook and Moore didn't just set out to make people laugh. Not that they approached their work with some pompous sense of higher purpose – far from it. Their humour was wonderfully free from political polemic or didactic cant. Like all the best writers and comedians, their main motivation was simply to amuse themselves. It's this indifference to polite taste, this refusal to pander to their punters, which makes their humour seem so intimate – even after forty years. It's not like watching a public performance – it's more like eavesdropping on a private conversation. They aren't talking to us – they're talking to each other, and allowing the rest of us to listen in. Their writing was always personal, and so were their performances – which is why fans of theirs who never knew them (like me, and millions like me) often end up calling them Peter and Dudley, or Pete and Dud, rather than Cook and Moore.

A quarter of a century since they went their separate ways, amid the sort of acrimony that only soulmates share, Peter and Dudley are still commonly – and quite rightly – regarded as the greatest double act that Britain has ever produced. Today, it's hard to imagine modern comedy without them. If you're a fan of *Monty Python* or *The Comic Strip*, *The Fast Show* or *The Office*, then whether you know their work or not, you're a fan of Cook and Moore.

Before Peter and Dudley got together, comic sketches were usually seen as forgettable fillers between the dancing girls of West End revue. Peter and Dudley didn't look down on this music-hall tradition. Both men had a soft spot for dancing girls, on the boards and in the wings, but that didn't prevent them taking a genre previously dismissed as Shaftesbury Avenue frippery and transforming it into a proper art form that was populist, and intelligent too. Their brilliant BBC series, *Not Only . . . But Also . . .*, was sophisticated AND accessible – a radical departure in an age when TV was still strictly segregated into highbrow culture and lowbrow light ent.

Peter and Dudley broke down that old class barrier between art and entertainment. Of all the great British double acts, the only pair that really bear comparison are Morecambe and Wise. From the fifties to the eighties, Eric and Ernie bridged the gap between variety and television, but they were still a fairly conventional front-of-curtain duo. By comparison, a lot of Peter and Dudley's work was positively avant-garde. It didn't always work, but it was never boring – and never again could class-bound critics dismiss comedy out of hand. Anyone could see that Peter and Dudley were infinitely smarter than an awful lot of actors. No one could write them off as just another pantomime turn.

Like Eric and Ernie, Peter and Dudley's comedy was unique yet universal – universal in that it could be understood by virtually anyone, unique in that you couldn't imagine it being done by anybody else. In *Derek & Clive (Live)*, they inspired alternative comedy. With *Beyond the Fringe*, they entertained the Queen, the Prime Minister and the President of the United States. Eric and Ernie never really cracked America. Peter and Dudley did. And they had something else that Eric and Ernie never had, and never even aspired to. They weren't only extremely funny. They were extremely sexy, too.

Before Peter and Dudley came along, sex appeal was something home-grown comedians simply didn't go in for. Frankie Howerd, Tommy Cooper, Arthur Askey – none of these comics were sexy, at least not in the way that Peter and Dudley were. Peter had the three Bs (Brains, Beauty and Breeding), while Dudley had something even more elusive – that seductive *je ne sais quoi* which is the hallmark of every leading man. Their *Beyond the Fringe* colleagues, Alan Bennett and Jonathan Miller, more than matched their intellect, but they couldn't hope to compete with them in this particular field of expertise. As Miller said on *The South Bank Show*, Dudley had 'an almost pagan, Pan-like capacity to enchant ladies'. Peter, too, was in a league of his own – able to captivate men as well as women. 'He was devastating to the girls,' confirms his Footlights and Establishment colleague, John Fortune. Making audiences laugh *and* swoon is a pretty potent combination. British comedy had never seen anything like it. It was like trading in George Formby for the Rolling Stones.

Like a lot of the best double acts, they could hardly have been less alike. Peter's father was a diplomat; Dudley's, an electrician. Peter grew up in twee Torquay, on the English Riviera. Dudley grew up in dreary Dagenham. Peter went to Radley, one of the best public schools in the country. Dudley went to the local grammar. 'We were diametrically opposed in everything,'[2] said Dudley, but there was one thing they did share – a sense of humour. Even offstage or off-camera, they were always improvising. As Barry Humphries says, 'it was impossible to get a word in'.[3] Intimate, intuitive, almost telepathic, this instinctive bonhomie brought them together, and eventually pulled them apart.

Such intangible empathy was just about the only thing they had in common. Even physically, they were poles apart. Peter was over six foot tall, lithe and athletic. Dudley was barely five, and far from sprightly. 'I spent the first seven years of my life siphoned off in hospital beds and wheelchairs with a club foot,' he remembered, in the year he traded in his comic partnership with Peter for a new career as a Hollywood movie star. 'I had special boots and – like Rumpelstiltskin – the only way I could express my rage was by stamping on the floor until it collapsed and gave way.'[4]

This physical disparity was reflected in their comedy. Peter was a wit, Dudley was a clown, and it was the differences between them that made them such a perfect pairing. Their incompatibilities enhanced the comedy they shared. With their contrasting physiques and backgrounds, they could satirise every age and social bracket. Their caricatures straddled the generation gap, as well as the class divide, from posh codgers like Sir Arthur Streeb-Greebling to proletarian adultescents like Pete and Dud or Derek and Clive.

Peter was a natural-born writer and Dudley was a natural-born actor, but they probably never would have worked together if it hadn't been for *Beyond the Fringe*, that graduate riposte to the undergraduate revues of the Edinburgh Festival Fringe. However, even their Oxbridge backgrounds were notable for their differences. Peter advanced from Radley to Cambridge more or less as a matter of course, and took to daily life at Pembroke College quite easily. Conversely, Dudley's advancement from Dagenham County High School to Magdalen College, Oxford, was so unusual that the headmaster awarded a half-day holiday to the entire school. Dudley felt equally unusual when he got there. 'I felt dwarfed by the social ease of the people who'd come from public schools,' he recalled. 'I couldn't stand the sound of their voices – they seemed so in charge of themselves.'[5]

However, there was one area in which Dudley was infinitely better educated and more self-assured than Peter, and that was music. Dudley went to Oxford on an organ scholarship and his amazing musicality gave their partnership a melodious quality that Peter's more literate humour always lacked. Despite the lyrical beauty of his writing, and his fluency in three foreign languages – French, German and Spanish – Peter was triumphantly tone deaf. Dudley, on the other hand, was a bona fide maestro, who could have enjoyed a brilliant career as a classical or jazz musician rather than a comic actor – and maybe would have been happier if he had. As Jonathan Miller said, Cuddly Dudley 'secreted music like sweat'.[6] And this melodic perspiration didn't just lubricate his piano playing. In a typical Cook and Moore sketch, the concepts are mainly Peter's, but the rhythm is all Dudley's.

Peter's fingerprints are all over these sketches. Dudley's are often hard to find. However, appearances can be deceptive. Most writing partnerships consist of an innovator and an editor. The innovator has the ideas, but it's the editor who nails them down. Dudley modified the inconsistencies in Peter's inspired conceptual leaps, and brought his surreal flights of fancy back down to earth. Even when they're improvising, Peter plays the melodies, while Dudley plays the bass line, without which the entire composition would unravel.

As a virtuoso jazz pianist, Dudley understood the delicate balance between composition and improvisation. Too much composition can be dull, but too much improvisation spells chaos. Dudley's steady stage skills gave some dramatic structure to Peter's free-flowing wit, in much the same way that, on the piano, his left hand provided a harmonic framework for his free-flowing right. Between them they combined spontaneous and scripted comedy better than any other domestic double act, before or since. Improvisation was an essential ingredient, but writing and rehearsal were just as vital. When they did no preparation whatsoever, the results were rarely up to much. Even on their *Derek & Clive* LPs, which revelled in disorder, the funniest sketches were the ones they'd written in advance.

This combination was the result of a particular writing and performing style – half rehearsed, half off the cuff. Peter and Dudley wrote together by improvising into a tape recorder, refining their duologues over a series of several takes. The final take was typed up as a conventional script, which Dudley learned by heart. When they subsequently filmed the sketch, in front of a studio audience, Dudley would recite his lines from memory. Peter, on the other hand, relied on idiot boards and inspiration, improvising to his heart's content while Dudley kept the storyline on track. It wasn't terribly fair on Dudley, giving him most of the work and less of the glory, but as long as they stuck with this winning formula, it worked a treat.

Consequently, the broadcast versions of these sketches are often markedly different from the original scripts, and where both versions still exist, there's the enjoyable dilemma of deciding which one to print. Usually, I've favoured the broadcast version, if I could find it, but there are some super scripted jokes, which fell by the wayside in performance, and remained unheard by anyone, apart from the secretary who transcribed the tape. Sometimes, it seemed a shame not to include a few of these forgotten gags, so I've used the odd scripted version, even though it meant excluding some equally good impromptu jokes from the final cut. As you'd expect, it's Peter's lines that tend to deviate between the scripted and broadcast versions, while Dudley's remain fairly consistent from take to take.

So was the writing half and half? Not quite. Dudley's contribution to the partnership has always been underestimated, but Peter was still the driving force behind most of the stuff they wrote. Dudley wrote virtually no sketches on his own, but to get a truer idea of his input, you only have to look at Peter's writing before they got together, and after they fell apart.

Before he teamed up with Dudley, in 1960, Peter's output was prolific. 'His imagination was like a machine that had got out of control,' says George Melly[7]. Peter wrote twenty-three sketches for *Pop Goes Mrs Jessop*, often cited by those who saw it as the funniest Cambridge Footlights show of all time. He also wrote thirteen sketches for a West End revue (*Pieces of Eight*, with Kenneth

Williams) while he was still an undergraduate, and ten more for the sequel (*One Over the Eight*, with Williams again) shortly after he came down. However, even though his solo compositions are audaciously funny, there's nothing remotely real about the characters. They're merely ciphers for Peter's other-worldly wit. No wonder they only sustain the audience's interest for a few minutes, before their abstract humour fizzles out. Brilliant though it is, there's nothing here that compares with the sustained kitchen sink realism of Pete and Dud, or even the rambling nihilistic naturalism of Derek and Clive.

After their partnership ended, in 1979, during the ill-fated recording of their final LP, *Derek & Clive – Ad Nauseam*, Peter only occasionally reached the comic heights he'd scaled so regularly with Dudley. He wrote some fine sketches in the eighties and nineties, but it was only a fraction of what he'd written in the sixties and the seventies. And it's significant that, like his earlier work with Dudley, what Peter got around to writing in his later years was also frequently written with other people, like Peter Fincham, John Lloyd, Bernard McKenna and Rory McGrath. Throughout his life, Peter needed someone else to bounce off, and the person he bounced off best was Dudley.

If Dudley's role in the writing process tends to be underrated, his role as a performer was even more central to their joint success. It's very revealing to watch Peter in his later years, performing with other people. Even with famous comics like John Cleese or Rowan Atkinson, or old Footlights pals like John Bird and John Fortune, the sketches simply aren't as funny as they were with Dudley. Clive Anderson played the straight man in Cook's swansong on Channel 4, and Chris Morris played a similar supporting role in his finale on Radio 3. Both of them put in fine performances, and drew even finer performances from Peter. Yet even when he was merely reading scripted questions from a clipboard, Dudley still did it better.

It was the same story before Peter and Dudley got together. Peter wrote their most famous sketch, 'One Leg Too Few', when he was still a teenager – years before he met Dudley. Yet of all the sketches in *One Over the Eight*, Kenneth Williams' West End revue, Williams liked it least of all. It was Dudley's performance, as the one-legged optimist auditioning for the role of Tarzan, that transformed it into a comic classic. So what was it about Dudley's acting that made Peter's comedy come alive?

Dudley's greatest asset as an actor was his humanity. Offstage or off-camera, Peter could be an adorable companion – but onstage or on-camera, he was often difficult to warm to. Audiences admired him. Other comedians were in awe of him. However, his acting was often aloof and disengaged, like the characters he played. 'Peter has a kind of madness on stage,' said Alan Bennett, recalling their time together in *Beyond the Fringe*. 'His performance would often be quite dangerous, on the edge of embarrassment.'[8] 'Peter's accuracy is the genuine accuracy of recording a slightly schizophrenic thought process,' agreed Jonathan Miller. 'He's an accurate observer of mad thought.'[9] This was fascinating and very funny, but only in small doses. Dudley brought a reassuring sanity to Peter's distant acting, and allowed him to stretch his short sketches into longer, more realistic routines.

However, even with Dudley's easy realism to dilute it, Peter's schizophrenic acting style still felt awkward outside the safe confines of the sketch format, as he discovered to his cost when he graduated to leading roles in feature films. At heart, Peter was most comfortable performing surreal monologues in a live setting, ably supported by an adept feed. This was not a problem in the theatre, where Peter always triumphed, but on TV or in the movies, a little ad hoc surrealism goes an awfully long way. Audiences need someone to sympathise with, as well as someone to marvel at. Peter was the one they marvelled at, but the one they sympathised with was Dudley.

Unlike Peter, Dudley was a realistic, naturalistic actor – and unlike Peter, his acting had that integral warmth which all the biggest movie stars share. Peter's speciality was the comedy of cruelty, but without anyone to feel for, audiences were cast adrift. Dudley didn't just provide a target for Peter's comic spite, he provided a focus for spectators' sympathies. Onstage, as well as backstage, Dudley was twice as lovable as anyone you could think of, and so

Peter being beastly to Dudley was twice as painful – and twice as funny – as Peter being beastly to anyone else.

For such a gifted performer, Dudley was a remarkably unselfish actor – possibly because his greatest gift (his music) lay elsewhere. Even in *Arthur*, his biggest box-office hit, he shares the laughs around. It was John Gielgud, not Dudley, who got the Oscar for that movie. In *'10'*, he makes Julie Andrews look sexy, and Bo Derek sound urbane. Even in his Hollywood flops (and there were a fair few of those), other actors spoke warmly about working with him. Dudley always made his co-stars shine, often at his own expense, and Peter was no exception.

Like Michael Caine, Dudley appreciated that on-screen, if not onstage, less is usually much more. Peter was a comic soloist by inclination, and so other people often found it hard to share his limelight – not because he was a prima donna, but because his comedy was so unusual. Only Dudley, with his combination of talent and humility, could set up Peter's punchlines, stand back and let them breathe. Peter said funny things but Dudley did funny things, which is why he fared so much better in the movies. The reason they worked so well together was that they weren't chasing the same laughs.

Of course, Dudley didn't do too badly out of Peter, either. When they were first introduced in *Beyond the Fringe*, alongside Alan Bennett and Jonathan Miller, Dudley was (justifiably) sure of his musical ability but (unjustifiably) unsure of his ability as an actor. While Peter held court at his Establishment Club, Dudley played the piano in the basement (though this proved to be a much better way of picking up women than prancing about onstage). When Dudley invited Peter to join him in *Not Only . . . But Also . . .*, he was still a musician first and a performer second – by his own private estimation, as well as in the public eye. 'Peter was incredibly prolific, and it gave Dudley an enormous security,'[10] says Dick Clement, who produced the second series. After a decade performing together, and sharing the writing credits on numerous sketches which had been initiated by Peter, Dudley felt confident enough to pursue a solo Hollywood career. It was Dudley's increasing confidence, as much as Peter's increasing drinking, which altered the balance of their partnership, and brought it to a close.

Thankfully, while it lasted, it was a partnership which produced a rich body of work, much of which is included here: two major stage shows (*Beyond the Fringe* and *Behind the Fridge*); four TV series (three *Not Only . . . But Also . . .* for the BBC, plus *Goodbye Again*, for ITV); three *Derek & Clive* LPs (the first of which, at least, is an iconoclastic classic); plus a handful of movies, ranging from the sublime (*Bedazzled*) to the disastrous (*Derek & Clive Get the Horn*). There could have been a lot more (and by rights there really should have been) but in terms of quality, if not quantity, they did more in twenty years than most comics manage in a lifetime. For all but the most obsessive fans, this selection should be more than enough to see you through.

Naturally, reading Peter and Dudley's work is no substitute for watching it, but seeing them in action is easier said than done. Scandalously, the BBC wiped most of *Not Only . . . But Also . . .*, along with countless other TV classics, as part of a general policy of recycling old master tapes. You can still buy a video of the series (aptly entitled *The Best of What's Left of Not Only . . . But Also . . .*, released in 1990) selected by Peter and Dudley from surviving footage, but though it features several of their finest sketches, it's more of an aperitif than a main course. Some of the sketches the BBC erased survive in various audio formats, but many of them have been deleted, or scattered far and wide. Others still exist thanks to the efforts of foreign broadcasters, who bought the rights to the series, and subsequently took better care of it than the BBC. Two Australian specials, made by Peter and Dudley down under, have also survived. Brief clips from these shows sometimes surface in documentaries, but they've never been released commercially – although with their location footage, Antipodean versions of otherwise extinct sketches and even several cameos by Barry Humphries (one of Peter's Establishment Club protégés) they'd make a super DVD. Likewise, *Goodbye Again* survives intact, yet it has languished unseen in the archives for over thirty-five years.

Indeed, when it comes to Peter and Dudley's work, the general rule of thumb seems to be that the better it is, the more of it has been eradicated and the more difficult the remainder is to find. Naturally, with so many of their best sketches lost for ever, the survival of anything they did together is a bonus, but the imbalance of their surviving work isn't just frustrating for their diehard fans – it also distorts their reputation. While Pete and Dud enthusiasts scour the charity shops for discarded cassette tapes and LPs, the complete works of *Derek & Clive* are available on CD from every high-street record shop. Now, you can debate the merits of *Derek & Clive* until the (fucking) cows come home, but if you've heard all that stuff and not a lot else, you're bound to end up with an extremely lopsided view.

This book is a bid to redress that imbalance. Even if, like me, you yearn to see these sketches, as well as reading them, it should give you a much better idea of what Peter and Dudley did together – onstage and on TV. I was pleasantly surprised by how well these sketches translated in print. Mind you, with their popular appeal *and* their erudite Oxbridge educations, it should have come as no surprise that their work proved so readable. What's more surprising is that, despite a public profile bordering on pop stardom, for a long time it wasn't even considered worth writing down.

The reason for this is that Peter and Dudley were comedians, and until very recently, comedy wasn't considered to have any literary merit. Unlike so-called serious drama, it was merely something you used once or twice then threw away. This attitude was epitomised by the BBC, who even mislaid the scripts of the first series of *Not Only . . . But Also . . .* Sketch comedy was merely regarded as one more end-of-the-pier amusement, like conjuring or ventriloquism. In *Derek & Clive*, Peter and Dudley satirise those hypocritical snobs who criticised their swearing while praising playwrights like Harold Pinter for using similar swear words in his plays. Ironically, on the printed page, a lot of these sketches read a lot like Pinter (Pete and Dud would have been perfect in Pinter's two-hander, *The Dumb Waiter*) and a generation later they're finally receiving some of the same acclaim.

Of course, these pieces weren't originally meant to be read, but re-enacted – yet you could say the same of Shakespeare, and that's never stopped people reading his work, with only a vague idea of how it was first performed. And although they inevitably lose something in the transition from tape to type, other qualities come to the fore. The Pete and Duds seem more poetic, the Derek and Clives even bleaker, and you needn't worry about catching Peter and Dudley on an off day (or an off decade). In this book, you can picture them playing each sketch at the peak of their powers.

As their TV career progressed, Peter and Dudley became increasingly adventurous, and some sketches (especially those with lots of characters and locations) are too visual to transcribe successfully into print. I've included a couple, to show how their work developed, but stage directions are a bore to read. Pieces with lots of dialogue and not much action tend to transfer best. It's these theatrical sketches, performed in front of a studio audience, which bore the brunt of the BBC's parsimonious cull, while the more cinematic pieces, filmed without an audience in a variety of exterior locations, were shot separately on film, and so tended to survive. Scripts of their filmed sketches are often a poor substitute for the real thing, whereas the scripts of their studio sketches are often the only thing that's left.

For the last fifteen years of Peter's life, Peter and Dudley did virtually no work together, and it's impossible to talk about their partnership without talking about the hows and whys of this virtual divorce. As with most separations, it wasn't a mutual decision. It was Dudley who made the break and Peter who was hit hardest. 'He [Dudley] gave and gave until there was nothing left to give,' said Alexander Cohen, who produced the American runs of *Beyond the Fringe* and *Behind the Fridge* (or *Good Evening*, as it was called in America). 'You could hardly call that abandonment, but I think that's how Peter viewed it.'[11] And Eric Idle agrees. 'When Dudley went on to become a film star, I think Peter felt very abandoned.'[12]

As with most break-ups, there was more than one reason for the final split. The practical reason was Dudley's decision to remain in America after the end of the long-running *Behind the Fridge* to be with his new wife, the American actress Tuesday Weld, and their new baby. However, Dudley's motivation for staying in the US was emotional, too. Peter had always felt at home in buttoned-up, self-deprecating, class-bound Britain. It was what his comedy was all about. Dudley, on the other hand, felt far more comfortable in America. Like him, it was frank, aspirational and comparatively classless. And there were creative differences, too. To put it bluntly, he'd had enough of doing sketches, and he'd had enough of doing them with Peter.

Like the abusive but faithful husband of a gentle yet wayward wife, Peter seemed to sense the end was nigh. 'It's like a marriage,' Dudley told Michael Parkinson, in one of their 'never a truer word' attempts to laugh off the explosive mechanics of their partnership. 'How is it like a marriage?' asked Parkinson. 'We're getting divorced,' quipped Peter.[13] Yet the split, when it came, was more final and total than Peter had expected.

Peter's drinking probably hastened Dudley's departure, and maintained his absence from the fold, but even if Peter had been tee-total, Dudley probably would have gone his own way in the end. Dudley wanted to play himself in proper movies, rather than playing the fool in Peter's fantasies. Peter liked playing caricatures. He wasn't so keen to play himself. Peter and Dudley had appeared together in several films (*The Wrong Box*, *The Bed Sitting Room*, *Monte Carlo or Bust*) but none of them had seduced the critics or – more important – the box office. They'd made one great movie together, *Bedazzled*, but that hadn't received the recognition it deserved, and in *The Rise and Rise of Michael Rimmer*, Peter proved beyond all reasonable doubt that he was not a natural movie actor. 'I can't act,' he admitted in an interview with Mavis Nicholson. 'I'm just very self-conscious and I just feel a prat.'[14]

In fact, Peter was being rather hard on himself. He could act, just not in the conventional way that Hollywood requires. He was perfectly good at saying his own lines. He simply wasn't all that good at saying other people's, unless he was playing eccentric arche-types, preferably in surreal fantasies like Jonathan Miller's *Alice in Wonderland* or Rob Reiner's *The Princess Bride*. 'Cookie was the best sketch actor that I ever saw but I don't think he was anything like as good when he was trying to be absolutely real and portray real emotion,'[15] says John Cleese. Film acting requires real emotion, or at least a passable imitation of it, and this was one impersonation that Peter could never carry off. From now on, his stop-start movie career was limited to brief cameos. 'At one time I had the idea of doing romantic leads,' he told the *Mirror* in 1980, the year Dudley played the romantic lead that spelt the end of their double act. 'But I looked such a berk I couldn't carry on.'

Dudley's unaffected acting style, on the other hand, was perfectly suited to mainstream movies. And although his elevation from character actor to sex symbol was a revelation to virtually everyone, including Dudley, the potential was always there. Peter tended to win most of the plaudits for their TV sketch shows, but Ken Annakin, who produced and directed them both in *Monte Carlo or Bust*, considered Dudley to be the more talented of the pair. In the sixties, Peter was supposed to be the new Cary Grant. By the eighties, that accolade had become Dudley's. 'I wasn't surprised,' said Alan Bennett. 'My only surprise was that they hadn't got on to him sooner.'[16]

In the sixties, Peter was the dominant personality in the partnership. Dudley admitted that he followed Peter around like a chihuahua. When Gerald Scarfe drew their portrait, he depicted Dudley as Peter's glove puppet. By the seventies, however, Dudley had become confident enough to say to Michael Parkinson, 'I'm not quite the servile little creep that I used to be.' As long as there was something in it for both of them, their alliance endured, but most relationships, however intimate, are contracts based on mutual need, and this one was a case in point. During the sixties, Dudley needed Peter as much as Peter needed Dudley. By the seventies, their talents, and their futures, lay in different fields, and subsequently in different countries, too.

A short two-man sketch is the essence of comedy – humour stripped to its bare essentials, the purest and most perfect form of dramatic comic art. Sadly, most people tend not to see it that way. In terms of status (as opposed to talent), movies are at the top of the career ladder and sketches near the bottom. Of course, the idea of ranking completely separate genres in the same showbiz league table is ridiculous – but it remains the industry standard, on both sides of the pond. Peter's last sustained piece of work, and also one of his finest, was for radio – the best broadcast medium for his humour, and also the least prestigious. Aptly, it was called *Why Bother?*.

Dudley's talents led him down an entirely different path. His amiable acting promised him a glowing future in the sort of mainstream American movies for which Peter's acerbic screen persona was utterly unsuited. Dudley's gift was for romantic comedy, and in the first few years, his Hollywood career soared. 'He always was the second banana to Peter and being accepted as leading man all of a sudden I think was something he relished and cherished,'[17] says his agent, Lou Pitt. However, it only lasted a few years.

In 1979 Dudley starred in '*10*', and in 1980 he starred in *Arthur* – two massive hits, in successive years. In 1981, he was rated the third biggest movie star in America. Only Burt Reynolds and Clint Eastwood were bigger. However, in Hollywood, you're either hot or you're not – there are no in-betweens. Once Dudley had climbed that summit, the only way was down. His next movie, *Six Weeks*, for which he wrote the score as well as playing the lead, was given a kicking by the critics, and hardly helped at the box office by the studio's decision to release the film at Christmas (it was about a terminally ill child). 'That was his greatest disappointment throughout his entire career,'[18] says Pitt.

Despite the smaller disappointments that followed, Dudley continued to make big money and even win awards. In 1983, *Unfaithfully Yours* landed him a $2.5 million fee (a hundred times what he got for his first US film, *Foul Play*, only five years earlier) and in 1984, he won a Golden Globe for *Micki + Maude*. Yet only a few years after *Arthur*, it seemed he could sense the best was over. 'Steve Martin, Eddie Murphy and Bill Murray must have been off form this year,' he quipped, as he collected his prize. His self-deprecating acceptance speech proved prophetic. The next year, he was paid $4 million to play an elf in *Santa Claus*, but *Arthur 2: On the Rocks* didn't match the magic of the original (talk about a title tempting fate) and as for the rest of his career – well, how many other Dudley Moore films can you name? 'Look at the careers of most actors,' Dudley told the *Mail on Sunday* in 1995. 'If they're lucky, they're top banana for five years, no more. I was tops for around two years. And then, one morning, you wake up and find you've been shifted onto another list. You're no longer an A list actor. You're now on the B list – and falling.'

Peter's work post Dudley was, through his own choice, more sporadic, although his long periods of inactivity were punctuated by spectacular hits. For a few years, however, it seemed as if Dudley could do no wrong, and inevitably, the perennial talking point was whether Peter envied Dudley's triumphs. This is the sort of goading that British newspapers have always gone in for, and as the owner of *Private Eye*, Peter knew such mischievous speculation was simply par for the course. Usually, Peter was a model of diplomacy. 'Of course I miss him,' he told the *Sun*. 'I'm really very fond of the little sod.' Yet occasionally he dropped his guard, and gave the papers the sort of imprudent quote they craved. 'I'm not jealous of Dudley,' he quipped. 'Perhaps if I had been born with a club foot and a height problem I might have been as desperate as Dudley to become a star in order to prove myself.'[19] In the past, in fact, Peter had frequently called Dudley a club-footed dwarf. 'He complained to me that in Hollywood he's surrounded by fools and sycophants who laugh at everything he says,' said Peter. 'I reminded him that when he was living here he was surrounded by intelligent people who kept telling him what a toad he was!'[20] However, these dark comic insults, which had once sounded daring and iconoclastic, now appeared sour and out of sorts. 'The two of them spent a lot of time together, they wrote an awful lot of material, they made albums, so you get to know somebody really, really well,' says Pitt, 'so I'm sure he was disappointed and hurt.'[21]

In fact, Peter was probably more irritated by the invidious prob-ing of the papers, but movie stardom really is a kind of royalty, and anyone who doesn't pay homage can easily seem bitter and resent-ful. Far more damning than these habitual quips was Peter's admis-sion that he hadn't actually seen *Arthur*. He'd decided to wait until it was on TV, he told the press, but in the end he'd opted to watch a football match on the other channel instead. Still, you could hardly blame him for not tuning in. 'Dudley credits Peter with giving him the character of Arthur,'[22] said his long-term girlfriend Susan Anton. Far from being churlish, perhaps Peter was wise not to watch. 'Peter always longed for that type of show business success,'[23] says Jonathan Miller. Alan Bennett agrees. 'Peter was the only one of us who really wanted the fame.'[24] Maybe they're quite right (they're in a pretty good position to judge), but look at it this way – if your business partner decided to go it alone, and promptly became one of the world's biggest movie stars, how would you feel? The question people always ask is, 'Did Peter envy Dudley?' The question people ought to ask is, 'Who on earth wouldn't?'

Everyone makes cruel comments about the people they love the most. Thankfully, most of these comments are forgotten. Peter's are remembered, partly because he was famous, and partly because even when he was being cruel, he couldn't help being funny. 'I can be verbally very vicious,' Peter admitted to Russell Harty, in the mid seventies. 'I can be extremely nasty. In my personal life, I've often come up with what might be called a biting remark. Once, I said to my wife Judith, about a year ago, which I thought was quite funny at the time, I said, "You know nothing – keep it to yourself."'[25]

Peter's bad behaviour is generally blamed for the break-up, but although his savage jokes and heavy drinking must have been mighty hard to bear, Dudley wasn't the easiest person to live with, either. One of his therapists described him as a gentle man in a rage (a description that could also have applied to Peter) and towards the end of the partnership, at least, he gave as good as he got. 'I think the hurt thing with Dudley and Peter worked both ways,' says Joe McGrath, who produced the first series of *Not Only . . . But Also . . .* and directed the London run of *Behind the Fridge.* 'I think that Peter hurt Dudley quite a lot in the early days and later on too, but I think when it got later in their relationship, Dudley could hurt Peter just as much as he hurt him.'[26]

Peter was often cruel to Dudley's face, but he frequently praised him behind his back. Compared to Dudley, said Peter, even comics like Spike Milligan and Peter Sellers seemed like interlopers. Maybe if he'd saved a few of these compliments for Dudley, rather than squandering them on reporters, their relationship would have lasted. But effusive Americanisms were never Peter's style, and even if he'd been the perfect gentleman, would Dudley have stuck around? 'I experience relationships eventually as a form of death,' said Dudley. 'I run like a fool who feels that he will die from a sort of strangulation.'[27] As he told the *Daily Mail* in 1972, 'I want to be loved and yet, my God, I am terrified of somebody loving me.' Admittedly, he was talking about marital relationships, not professional ones, but Peter and Dudley both joked that their partnership was a sort of marriage. 'Those two had a real romance going,' says Dudley's old friend, the advertising director Francis Megahy. 'It had its ups and downs, but it was a romance all the same.'[28]

Eventually, thanks in no small part to the diplomatic efforts of Peter's third wife, Lin, Peter and Dudley achieved a cautious yet heartfelt reconciliation, aided by the happenstance that as Dudley's film career dwindled, this former child prodigy returned to his first love – music. Piano playing, said Leslie Bricusse, was the thing that made Dudley tall. 'I think Dudley is only really alive when he's at the piano,' concurred his friend and musical partner, Rena Fruchter, with whom he worked on Music For All Seasons – a charity that takes live music to places where people are confined, from hospitals to prisons to children's homes. 'There's an intensity and caring about his music that doesn't exist anywhere else in his life. Only through music is he able to show real emotion and achieve genuine happiness. And when he's involved in it, there's nothing else that's really important.'[29] Maybe once you've been the world's third biggest movie star, it's hard to maintain an intimate relationship with anyone, whether they envy you or not.

In fact, the rancour that infected this partnership was fed by something even more virulent than envy. The fact of the matter is, there's a sadomasochistic strain in most double acts – and this one was even more sadomasochistic than most. In *Not Only . . . But Also . . . Down Under*, Peter plays a chief executive who interviews Dudley over dinner, and empties several plates of food over his head. In the *Not Only . . . But Also . . .* Christmas Special, Peter plays an aristocratic huntsman who pursues Dudley across a moor with a pack of hungry hounds. This sort of ritual humiliation is the basis of a lot of double acts, but in most other double acts, it's more evenly spread. Oliver Hardy belittles Stan Laurel, but he also endures his fair share of pratfalls. Dudley, on the other hand, was the butt of almost all the jokes. Like a married couple, Peter and Dudley knew all too well how to hurt each other, because they knew each other so well. 'No wonder we're breaking up,' says Peter, in *Derek & Clive Get the Horn.* 'Breaking up is so easy to do,' replies Dudley, sensing exactly where to stick the knife.

This shift in status even affected the dynamics of their Pete & Dud alter egos, as they proved in a bizarre bit of role-playing, half fact, half fiction, for the benefit of readers of the *Daily Mirror.* 'What aspects of the thespian arts are you currently engaged in, Dud?' asks Pete. 'Or, to put it another way, what is a small, stunted, ugly Dagenham git like you doing here in the living temple to the likes of Gloria Swanson, Mary Pickford, Rudolph Valentino and Fatty Arbuckle?' 'I'm glad you asked me that question,' replies Dud. 'I'm filling out my time being a multimillionaire, having earned a bit of pocket money for jumping up and down on top of Bo Derek, in a film called *'10'* to the music of some bloke called Bolero.'[30]

Two TV interviews with Mavis Nicholson, conducted sixteen years apart, provide a fascinating record of their split. For more than a decade, their shared sense of humour had hidden the fundamental differences between them – but as in any marriage, incompatibility, like the truth, will out. 'I think we are terribly opposite,' Dudley tells Mavis, in 1973, 'opposite to the point where it becomes difficult to communicate.' 'It's like the worst kind of polite marriage,' adds Peter. 'Neither of us is really any good at coming out with what we think.'[31] 'Have you had a trial separation?' she asks them, in 1989. 'No,' replies Peter. 'An acrimonious divorce.'[32]

And yet their lives still seemed to run in parallel, even an ocean apart. As Peter once wrote to Dudley, in America, 'I worry, you worry; I move to Hampstead, you move to Hampstead; I get divorced, you get divorced.' And like a doting wife, Dudley understood Peter's outrageous outbursts better than anyone, and generally accepted them for what they were – the quirk of an imagination incapable of passing up a brilliant joke, however much it might smart or sting. 'Peter has a desire to shock like a flasher on Hampstead Heath,' said Dudley. 'He wants to see the lady indignant but without any interest in molesting her.'[33] Dudley racked up four marriages to Peter's three, but they both had two children (sons for Dudley, daughters for Peter) and both died relatively young, neither of them reaching the statutory threescore years and ten. Dudley at least made it into his mid sixties. Peter didn't even live to collect his London Transport bus pass.

Dudley is still famous in America for '10' and *Arthur*, just as Peter remains an individual icon in Britain, on account of his solo career. However, as these memories recede, it's the sketches they did together that remain sharpest in the mind's eye. In caps and macs as Pete & Dud, as trampolining nuns in *Bedazzled*, or setting new world records for swearing in *Derek & Clive* – this is the stuff that refuses to fade away. Like Lennon & McCartney, Peter and Dudley both gave the other something they lacked. Like Paul McCartney, Dudley made Peter's work feel softer. Like John Lennon, Peter gave Dudley's work more bite. And that's why, like Lennon & McCartney, they hit the mark far more consistently together than they ever did apart.

When Peter died, in 1995, of a gastrointestinal haemorrhage, Dudley was bereft. The first thing he did was to phone Peter's answering machine, just to hear his voice again – an act of undying love, if ever there was one. 'There's a hole in the universe,'[34] he said. Now there really was no way back. The magic was gone for good. Dudley died seven years later. His final years were blighted by progressive supranuclear palsy, a neurological disease which affects eye movement, speech and balance, giving the erroneous impression, to those who did not know him, that he was often drunk. God, it seems, has a sense of humour every bit as sick as Derek & Clive's.

'Like all the best double acts, theirs was a love affair,' wrote

Howard Jacobson, after Dudley's death in 2002. 'Did you see that film footage of Jerry Lewis breaking down in a limousine, remembering his days with Dean Martin? Did you see Ernie Wise on television after the death of Eric Morecambe? Widows, both of them, their grief unbearable to behold. But Peter Cook and Dudley Moore seemed to be entwined ever tighter still. And that was because Dudley Moore appreciated Peter Cook's genius to the depth of his soul, got him as no one would ever get him again. And the sign of that appreciation was his laughter, his failure, no matter how hard he struggled, to keep his face straight, his divine incapacity, once his partner was in full flight, to hold himself together.'[35] Peter loved making Dudley corpse, and audiences loved to watch them, and Dudley's poker face in *Derek & Clive Get the Horn* was a surefire sign that he'd fallen out of love with Peter – comedically, at least. Peter and Dudley never regained that gigglesome quality which made their sketches so special. That secret something had vanished, and they never got it back. But a decade later, if not onstage, then at least on the chat-show sofa, they were able to laugh and joke together like they used to.

'In an age where mediocrity is becoming the accepted standard, it is sad to note that some of the best films have never reached the screen,' wrote Peter and Dudley, in the opening paragraph of a sketch called 'The Epic That Never Was', only the first page of which survives. 'Bleeding chunks of celluloid still lie mouldering in studio vaults of major production companies – incomplete, discarded, rejected, forgotten.' Well, here they are, fresh from the vaults – some incomplete, some discarded, some rejected, some forgotten, plus some of the most celebrated sketches of the last fifty years. And in these bleeding chunks of celluloid, an extraordinary relationship endures.

Chapter One
Beyond the Fringe

Looking back on the comedy they shared, and the lives they led together, it's almost impossible to imagine Peter and Dudley as strangers. However, they probably never would have got together in the first place if it hadn't been for *Beyond the Fringe*. This show changed a lot of people's lives, none more so than Peter and Dudley's, and like a lot of life-changing events, its origins owed more to good luck than good judgement. Indeed, 'the moment when English comedy took its first decisive step into the second half of the 20th Century',[1] arose out of a parochial tussle between two rival factions at that annual luvvie jamboree, the Edinburgh Festival.

Since 1947, the Edinburgh International Festival of Music and Drama had been the summer highlight of the British arts calendar. However, during the fifties, the festival's highbrow plays and recitals, staged in Edinburgh's grand old theatres, had been increasingly upstaged by a growing crowd of less formal shows, mounted in more informal venues, collectively known as the Festival Fringe. By the end of the fifties, these artistic gatecrashers were fast becoming more newsworthy than the stars of the International Festival, and since the festival shut up shop around last orders every evening, late-night Fringe revues were especially popular. In 1960, the artistic director of the official festival, an Old Etonian and former Guardsman called Robert Ponsonby, resolved to beat these uninvited upstarts at their own game.

In 1959, Ponsonby had booked comical musical duo (Michael) Flanders and (Donald) Swann, and in 1960 he tried to book American jazz legend Louis Armstrong. When that fell through, he decided to stage a revue instead. 'I was tired of the Fringe continually stealing our thunder with brilliant revues,'[2] he said. Ponsonby wanted to mount a show that would be way beyond the capabilities of anyone on the Fringe. It was this audacious mission statement that gave this show its convoluted yet catchy title.

Back in 1960, comedy was still a class-bound business. Working-class comics like Ken Dodd and Tommy Cooper played the old variety theatres, while college troupes like the Cambridge Footlights and Oxford's Experimental Theatre Club had the run of the Festival Fringe. Ponsonby was an Oxbridge man, as was his young assistant, John Bassett. Bassett proposed a show that brought together the best Oxbridge comics of the last five years and Ponsonby approved.

Bassett's role as Ponsonby's assistant was another of life's little coincidences. His interview for the post had resulted in a dead heat with a rival candidate. Unable to choose between them, Ponsonby consulted his secretaries, who advised him to reject the other candidate, on account of his suede shoes. Ponsonby duly gave the job to Bassett, and invited him out to lunch to celebrate. Bassett arrived wearing a pair of suede shoes.

Bassett had recently come down from Oxford, where he'd played the trumpet in his own jazz band, the Bassett Hounds. They wore stripy blazers and straw boaters. The piano player was a pint-sized chap called Dudley Moore. He'd be perfect for *Beyond the Fringe*. Not only was he a brilliant musician, he was also an accomplished clown. And though he was now busy plying his trade as a jazz pianist in London, surely he could spare a week in August, for a fee of £100? Bassett sought him out. He could indeed. Dudley recommended a medieval historian called Alan Bennett, whose spoof sermons by banal Church of England vicars had been a hit in Edinburgh the previous summer, with the Oxford Revue. Now all Bassett needed was an equally funny pair from Cambridge.

Again, Bassett's decent education stood him in good stead. He'd been at school with a girl whose sister had married a young doctor called Jonathan Miller. Miller's starring role in the 1955 Footlights show had earned him the simplistic yet memorable accolade 'the Danny Kaye of Cambridge', and though he was now working full-time at London's University College Hospital, as a newly qualified house surgeon, he'd kept his humorous hand in with various appearances on BBC Radio and TV. Bassett collared Miller in the casualty department of UCH, still clutching a sterile dressing, and even though he subsequently claimed that he fiercely regretted this distraction, this reluctant comedian was persuaded to come to Edinburgh too. Dr Miller didn't just agree to come along. He also recommended the star of the latest (and greatest) Footlights show, *Pop Goes Mrs Jessop*. This remarkable young man had written most of that show, and the largest slice of Kenneth Williams' latest West End revue. Incredibly, he was still an undergraduate. His name was Peter Cook. Bassett's comic quartet was complete.

Even though he was still a student, Peter was already a professional sketch writer, on a retainer of £100 per week (more like £1,000 today). Consequently, his agent, Donald Langdon, didn't think all that much of *Beyond the Fringe*. 'Don't jeopardise your career by working with these three amateurs,' he told Peter. Luckily for his career prospects, Peter disregarded Langdon's advice, but Langdon did manage to negotiate a higher fee for his client. Langdon secured £110, which, after Langdon's 10 per cent had been deducted, left Peter with £99, a pound less than the others. 'The meek shall inherit the earth,' noted Dudley, sagely, still mindful of this episode a decade later.

Bassett invited his foursome to lunch at an Italian restaurant in Euston, near enough to UCH for Miller to nip out in his lunch hour. 'The first meeting was very apprehensive,' recalls Bassett. 'They all had an astonishing reputation within university circles and none of them was prepared to jeopardise it by cracking the first joke.'[3] Yet it didn't take Peter and Dudley very long to shed their apprehension, in contrasting styles that set the tone for their future partnership. Typically, Peter delivered an unstoppable barrage of invective, while Dudley imitated the stooping gait of Groucho Marx as he followed the waitresses through the swing doors and out into the kitchen. 'Dudley broke the tension,' remembers Bassett, 'and because it was very physical, and very endearing to see, suddenly the atmosphere became very warm, very friendly, and from then on the jokes just flowed thick and fast.'[4] Yet when Dudley suggested a sketch of his own – a mime about a violin that behaved like a baby – Peter dismissed it as a non-starter, and would often refer to it in the future, to put Dudley in his place. In that first meeting, the parameters of their partnership were established. Peter was the brilliant, intimidating wit, Dudley the lovable fool.

Consequently, Dudley contributed very little to the script of *Beyond the Fringe*. He reckoned Peter wrote about two-thirds of it, while Alan and Jonathan wrote the other third between them. Dudley's brief was to provide the score, but his parodies of famous composers were far more than mere curtain music. From 'Colonel Bogey' by Beethoven to 'Little Miss Muffet' by Benjamin Britten, they were arguably the most sophisticated feature of the entire show, and they bound the whole evening together. *Beyond the Fringe* would have been very thin without any of Peter's sketches, but it would have been very dry indeed without Dudley's erudite melodies. And in their own way, they were just as satirical as Peter's spoken pieces, especially his send-up of Peter Pears singing Britten's folk songs. Dudley later chose this as one of his Desert Island Discs. 'I do this out of absolute love and admiration for Britten and with no malice aforethought at all,' he told Roy Plomley. However, in the Beyond the Fringe programme, the number was called 'Little Miss Britten'. Unsurprisingly, Pears didn't like this title and never went to see the show. Dudley's music wasn't as shocking as Peter's monologues, but it still had bite.

In those days, any theatrical script had to be approved in advance by the Lord Chamberlain, but bizarrely, the censor's only objection was to some camp stage directions. 'Enter two outrageous old queens' was duly changed to 'Enter two aesthetic young men', presumably to protect the cast and crew from corruption. By modern standards, a far more daring item was 'Black Equals White', Peter's interview with Mr Akiboto Mbizu, leader of the Pan-African Folklore Party (played by Jonathan Miller), who has straightened his hair and whitened his skin so he can better represent the interests of his people by speaking to the white man on his own ground.

None of them were stars (not yet) and there wasn't a lot of advance publicity. On the first night, Edinburgh's Royal Lyceum Theatre was less than one-third full. However, the show went down a storm, and within days it was sold out, through word of mouth, with punters queuing for returns. 'You knew you were in the presence of something extraordinary,' recalls *Guardian* theatre critic Michael Billington, who saw the first night, as an Oxford undergraduate. 'You came out feeling physically slightly ill, because to laugh for that length of time is exhausting. And it was a shock, a slap in the face to all of us, because we'd seen nothing like this before.'[5]

The reason students such as Billington had seen nothing like it was because *Beyond the Fringe* was about real life and real people. The most notorious sketch was Peter's shocking impersonation of Macmillan, but there was more to it than that. Other revues were safe and self-referential, relying on cosy caricatures with no equivalents beyond the confines of the theatre. *Beyond the Fringe* was about people you really talked about, people you really knew. It wasn't about the fantasy land of Shaftesbury Avenue, with its greenroom jokes and backstage gossip. It was about the world you really lived in, and talked about every day.

The broadsheets were complimentary, but the first paper to stick its neck out was the less fashionable *Daily Mail*. 'The funniest, most intelligent and most original revue to be staged in Britain for a very long time,' wrote Peter Lewis, who went on to write for the BBC's ground-breaking satire show, *That Was The Week That Was*. 'Disregarding all the jaded trimming of conventional sketches, production numbers, dancing and girls, they get down to the real business of intimate revue, which is satire and parody,' he added. 'If the show comes to London I doubt if revue will ever be the same again.'

It did, and it wasn't. 'Satirical revue in this country has been, until now, basically cowardly,' wrote Bernard Levin in the *Daily Express*, reviewing the show's West End opening, at the Fortune Theatre in May 1961. 'First, it has picked on the easy targets. Second, however hard it hit the targets (and it rarely hit them at all, let alone in the middle), it left its audience alone, to leave the theatre as fat and complacent as it came in.' The year before, Peter had suggested calling the show *One of the Best Revues for Some Time – Bernard Levin*. Levin's real review was even better. 'It has no slick coffee bar scenery, no glib one-line blackouts, no twirling dancers in tight trousers, no sad ballets for fisherwomen in fishnet stockings,' wrote Kenneth Tynan in the *Observer*. 'English satire advances into the Sixties' read the headline above his rave. But just how satirical was *Beyond the Fringe*? Not terribly, if you go along with Bassett, who ought to know.

'We had no idea it was satire, and I think even to this day, Jonathan is very vehement that it certainly isn't satire,'[6] says Bassett, and Miller agrees – more or less. 'Having been praised for being satirical, I suppose we adopted it with some sort of enthusiasm and said, "Well, that's what we are." But of course we weren't at all. We were just mildly cynical.'[7] Satirical or merely cynical, the British public loved it, and so did American impresario Alexander Cohen. The next year, leaving a replacement cast in London, Peter, Dudley, Alan and Jonathan sailed to the United States.

If anything, *Beyond the Fringe* was an even bigger hit in America. 'In many respects, it was much more successful on Broadway than it had been in London,' said Jonathan Miller. 'We were rather surprised that people adored it in the United States.'[8] It stormed Washington, Boston and Toronto and ran for a year and a half on Broadway, repaying the confidence of its American producer, Alexander Cohen, who had refused to dilute this Anglocentric show for American consumption. 'Alexander Cohen took the absolutely correct view that it would become an immensely chic show in the

States, and the fact that it was English and we hadn't altered a word would be a sort of built-in snob merit,'⁹ said Peter.

The first-night notices bore him out. 'There is hardly a review this morning that is less than delirious,' recorded Alistair Cooke, of the opening night on Broadway. 'This tumult of acceptance is a puzzle to many shrewd theatre men here, who deplored the quartet's decision not to adapt their material to American themes or their strangulated tripthongs to the ears of a people to whom a vowel is a vowel is a vowel. But they make no concessions, a British trick Oscar Wilde discovered before them.'¹⁰

Cooke was spot on, as usual. Although a few topical references eventually crept into the script, the cast made no other concessions to any Americans whatsoever, not even the President of the United States. When they were invited to perform the show for John F. Kennedy, in the presidential splendour of the White House, Peter refused. If the President wanted to see the show, said Peter, he could come to the theatre. Incredibly, JFK did just that, even though he was really rather busy at the time, trying to avert the outbreak of World War III. Still, if you had tickets for *Beyond the Fringe*, there were some office chores that simply had to wait.

'It is astonishing that the show could have had so much effect, and yet the four participants were totally unaware of the effect they would have, and just fell into it backwards, and saw it as a nice way to pass a week and return with a hundred pounds in their pocket,'¹¹ says Bassett. In the end it passed several years, and earned them considerably more than a hundred quid apiece. So why was it such a success? Partly, it was sheer good fortune. As Eric Idle says, the show looked 'aggressively Sixties',¹² but its minimalist aesthetic was the result of economic necessity rather than radical chic. 'We resolved not to have scenery because we didn't have enough money to put it up, and then we suddenly realised there was a virtue in it,'¹³ revealed Jonathan. 'Part of the style of the show came from the lack of money,' agreed Peter. 'We'd have been delighted to have had a hundred chorus girls dancing about.'¹⁴ The same went for their matching monochromatic costumes, which predated the Beatles by several years. Yet these sets and costumes (or the lack of them) were merely window dressing. What made the show so special was the unique chemistry between them, which would have lit a fire in any time or place.

With his front foot in Shaftesbury Avenue, Peter was loath to be offensive, but Bennett and Miller had no such vested interests. This was simply a brief interlude before their real careers, or so they thought. For the first time in his life, Peter had come up against two creative and intellectual equals (Alan and Jonathan) plus a wonderful performer (Dudley) whose talents for music and clowning provided the ideal foil for his dry, cerebral wit. The four of them sparked off each other, and created a show that was even greater than the sum of its four parts. It was the perfect combination of complementary talents. 'They were fooling about on the stage in exactly the same way as they fooled about off it,'[15] said John Wells. It was as if they'd stepped out of a study bedroom, in mid conversation, and straight into the theatre. By the time the curtain fell, they had the world at their feet.

ROYAL BOX
(Fortune Theatre, London, 1961)

This elegant and understated sketch originated during Peter's Cambridge Footlights days, mocking Britain's unending obsession with the Windsors. The first two-hander that Peter and Dudley performed together, it made clever use of its theatrical setting, casting them as members of the audience. This ingenious device took a surreal turn when the Queen came to see Beyond the Fringe *in 1962. With her was the Lord Chamberlain, who still had the power to censor any 'invidious' public stage portrayal of 'a living person, or a person recently dead', or any drama he deemed 'indecent, blasphemous, or inciteful to crime'.[16] Did this show flout these draconian restrictions? Michael Frayn certainly thought so. 'Beyond the* Fringe *did breach the Lord Chamberlain's guidelines because it featured real political characters,'[17] he says. However, the only attempt at regal censorship didn't come from the Lord Chamberlain, or the Palace, but from the theatre's own management, who asked Alan Bennett to omit the word 'erection' from one of his monologues. Bennett 'priggishly' refused. 'I suppose I must be one of the few people who have said "erection" in front of the Queen,' he says. 'I wish I hadn't. I don't suppose either of us profited from the experience.'* [18]

(*Dudley is sitting in the stalls of the Fortune Theatre. Peter joins him.*)

PETER: No, I won't have a programme, thank you very much. Excuse me, is this P? Row P?

DUDLEY: Yes, P1, 2 and 3.

PETER: I'm P3.

DUDLEY: I'm P2.

PETER: I'm most frightfully sorry to come in late like this, but I couldn't get a taxi. You know how it is at this time of night.

DUDLEY: Oh yes, I know how it is. Well, you've only missed three and a half minutes of the overture. It's a seven-and-a-half-minute overture, actually.

PETER: You've seen this show before, have you?

DUDLEY: Oh yes, I've seen this show, let me see now, five hundred – no, I tell a lie – four hundred and ninety-seven times.

PETER: Four hundred and ninety-seven times! That must be some sort of a record. Are you that fond of the show?

DUDLEY: Oh no. It's not my sort of show at all, really.

PETER: Well, why on earth do you keep coming?

DUDLEY: Well, you see, it's the Royal Family.

PETER: The Royal Family? Are they in some way connected . . . ?

DUDLEY: No. No, you see, I read in the newspapers that the Royal Family was planning a visit to this theatre, so naturally I came along. You see, up there, that's what they call the Royal Box. But I don't know if you've noticed, there's no Royalty in it. No Royal People there at all. No Royal Personage actually gracing the Royal Box – unless, of course, they're crouching. But, I mean, that wouldn't be Royalty, would it?

PETER: Not crouching, no.

DUDLEY: No, not on the crouch.

PETER: Not on the crouch – they don't go in for that very much.

DUDLEY: Anyway, I was here last Tuesday, and guess who I saw?

PETER: Do you really want me to guess?

DUDLEY: Yes. Go on. Guess.

PETER: Arthur Tinty.

DUDLEY: Arthur Tinty?

PETER: It's just a guess. He sometimes comes to the theatre.

DUDLEY: Arthur Tinty? No, I can't say I saw Arthur Tinty.

PETER: Well, he probably wasn't here.

DUDLEY: I tell you who I did see. Arthur Grodes. But I can't say I saw Arthur Tinty.

PETER: Well, don't worry. He may not have been here.

DUDLEY: No. What's he look like?

PETER: Tinty? Well, he's very hard to describe, really. He has a typical Tinty look about him – average height, average build.

DUDLEY: I saw him, yes. So that's Arthur Tinty! But is he regal?

PETER: No. He's not regal, no.

DUDLEY: Noble?

PETER: Not noble, no.

DUDLEY: No, well, er . . . Anyway, I am hoping against hope that one night the Royal Family will turn up and make my having to sit through this rotten, awful show every night worthwhile.

PETER: Do you really mean to say you spend fifteen shillings every night just on the off chance you may catch a glimpse of the Royal Family?

DUDLEY: Well, they're not worth the pound.

BLOODY RHONDDA MINE
(Fortune Theatre, London, 1961)

There were actually only three Beyond the Fringe *sketches featuring Peter and Dudley as a duo, and this one is the least well known. It didn't make the New York run, and it's not even included in* The Complete Beyond the Fringe *(published by Methuen). Its combination of posh presenter (Peter) and ethnic musician (Dudley) reads like a dry run for Bo Duddley (see Chapter Two), and it's telling that here, as elsewhere, Peter's satirical targets were more often left than right.*

PETER (*in an impeccably posh accent*): Songs of sweat and sorrow – songs of the downtrodden industrial classes.

DUDLEY (*sings, unaccompanied, in an indignant working-class voice*):

> And twenty men did die that day
> Down bloody Rhondda Mine
> And my dear wife she cried lackaday
> As she stood in the weeping line
> And the bosses they did shout for joy
> As each corpse was brought up
> They said 'Oh damn the dead and gone,
> As long as we fill our cup.'
> They brought a dead man, laid him here
> With a dirty great gash behind his left ear
> I said to my wife as we stood by the mine
> 'I'm glad I weren't down there at the time.'

PETER (*posh but earnest*): Thank you very much indeed.

DUDLEY (*posh and breezy*): Thanks awfully! They're so wonderful, these mining songs, aren't they? Absolutely wonderful!

DUDLEY MOORE'S POSTSCRIPT
(1986)

Dudley wrote this piece for Methuen's Complete Beyond the Fringe, *first published in 1987.*

My memories of the first glimmerings of *Beyond the Fringe* are somewhat hazy. The first meeting we had seems to have achieved some notoriety in all of our minds, although I for the life of me cannot really remember too much about it . . . except that we were in a restaurant with John Bassett who initiated the whole idea with Robert Ponsonby. I remember feeling very small figuratively and physically at these first meetings. Jonathan was and is a powerhouse of enthusiasm and curiosity, coupled with a singeing slash of melancholia, which graces his face from time to time.

Peter Cook seemed to me a very urbane, relaxed, sophisticated young chap. Of course in many ways that assessment proved right, since Peter later established with great ease and aplomb the Establishment Club. In many ways I found Peter the most approachable and relaxed – of the four of us . . . including me, of course.

I don't recall much of the writing process . . . perhaps because I felt fairly futile in its creativity. However, I stayed in there, the actor-musician supplying a sense of diminution to the three other lads whose six-foot-twoness needed to have some sort of response, which I supplied with my almost eccentric five foot two.

The preparation for the show seems so murky now. The lighting man, I seem to remember, supplied us with a very practical and economical set. He lit it very well, not having to deal with too many sharp colours, since we were all dressed in grey worsted suits, white shirts and black ties. There was also an occasional dark grey sweater. We supplied props in a minimal way, which I think proved to be a very useful element in the show's success. For a long time revues had been very camp and overly colourful: our muted business suits maybe afforded a welcome contrast to the revue fare of Shaftesbury Avenue.

The work was done, much to my fairly disguised humiliation, since I was not able to participate in any way that could be hailed as helpful. I had to win my laurels eventually, it seemed, through my abilities as a performer – especially as a reactor, since most people who invented a line kept it! Therefore, I was a mildly mute person onstage while the others flourished their wares shamelessly! I think that my musical efforts were viewed somewhat patronisingly –

certainly with little comprehension – dare I say it . . . I was a rehearsal pianist.

I remember vaguely the night before the first performance at Edinburgh and the actual night itself. I had to construct a solo – we all had one solo during this shortened version of *Beyond the Fringe* – and I still hadn't got one that I felt was satisfactory. I decided to write a sonata movement, using one of the silliest songs that I knew and one of the greatest composers. It seemed to be a marriage which would give some spicy instances of satire. Thus, I chose the 'Colonel Bogey March' as used in the film *Bridge on the River Kwai* and worked it in the style of Beethoven. I did it very loosely in first-movement form (sonata form) and I remembered some time later in London, when my professor (Jack Westrup from Oxford) came to see the show and commented he was longing for a 'development section'! I had to point out that in the interests of comedic economy, no such luxury could be afforded. I composed this piece quickly and directly the night before the show and remember being somewhat delighted at the response of the audience . . . especially at an extended ending that aped the Beethoven ending of the Fifth Symphony. I improvised endless codas, to the delight of the audience it seemed, until one day the construction of the thing became thoroughly solid. Since then I have played that item to death many times!

They were exotic years and exotic experiences . . . I don't think I ever had such grand excitement. It was everything I had ever wanted . . . to be onstage in a revue. The response and environments could not have been better and I came back finally from America feeling that I had probably achieved everything I ever wanted to – until I found that the prospect of appearing on TV was possible. Peter and I in fact had been able to get a very good relationship going in the last year of *Beyond the Fringe* on Broadway. We had such a grand time that obviously the temptation grew to repeat the experience on television, which we eventually did in our programme *Not Only . . . But Also . . .* [see Chapter Two].

Alan Bennett and I had been very friendly at the beginning of the American run, having dinner every night at a place called

Barbetta's, which was just west of Eighth Avenue on 45th or 46th Street. Alan and I used to go to this restaurant, always greeted by the doorman, who had a very thick foreign accent – I don't quite know where he came from – with the immortal lines: 'Ah, Mr Moore, Mr Cook . . . *Behind the Fridge*.' Eventually, Peter Cook and I usurped this garbled title and used it for a subsequent two-man show which we did in Australia, New Zealand and England [see Chapter Five]. When we finally came to Broadway we changed the title to *Good Evening* and I'm happy to report we had a great success doing that show there too.

PETER COOK'S POSTSCRIPT
(1987)

Peter wrote this piece for the same Methuen edition, The Complete Beyond the Fringe.

I had never had it so good. As far as I was concerned, the wonderful old showbiz fraud had got it right. I had a flat in Battersea, a Hillman Convertible and the chance to show off every night. 'Don't jeopardise your career by working with these three amateurs' had been the advice of my agent who shall remain nameless (but Donald Langdon is pretty close).

It was a peculiar business assembling the show. Only Dudley and I seemed to want to do it; the other two were perpetually struggling with their consciences. Should Jonathan desert medicine for this frivolous pursuit? Would Alan forsake Oxford and Medieval History for the transient glamour of the Fortune Theatre? Would they ever make up their minds?

In the early days Alan was delightfully shockable. It gave me enormous pleasure to come up with some piece of smut and watch him writhe and moan in agony or amusement, stuffing his hand-kerchief into his mouth. This handkerchief technique must have had its uses. Sometimes it was employed to stifle his own laughter, at others to conceal his vexation. It was quite hard to tell whether he was having a fit of the giggles, or in an almost terminal state of irritation. Happily, he eventually became as filthy-minded as the rest of us. I look back on the show with nothing but pleasure. I can remember very few rows, though there was one occasion when Jonathan hurled a tea tray across the dressing room in a fit of pique with, I think, Alan. Possibly the latter had been chewing his handkerchief in an insolent manner.

At another time Jonathan became enraged at me. It was often my wont to interrupt the 'philosophy' sketch by staggering on as an ancient retainer to deliver some incongruous piece of news. One night Rachel Miller was backstage with their newborn son. Grabbing baby from the willing Mrs Miller, I wandered on saying: 'Excuse me, sir; your wife's just given birth to this,' to which I think Jonathan replied: 'Go away and put it in the fridge.' I thought this a highly successful piece of improvisation but at the interval Jonathan reprimanded me severely. 'You might have dropped it!' he said. Never having wittingly dropped a baby in my life, I felt a little aggrieved. (He was the one who was clumsy with props.) I seem to remember at a later date carrying Dudley on and saying: 'I've discovered this man in bed with your wife and so I shot him,' to which Jonathan rather cruelly replied: 'Oh well, just drop him anywhere.'

As the show went on, I began to enjoy the 'digressions' more than the written text. I particularly looked forward to Dudley interrupting the 'civil defence' sketch. The barmy ad libbed questions and answers, usually nothing to do with the subject, were the highlight of the evening for me. I think it was this kind of daft random backchat that led to the two of us working together on television. There is only one depressing side effect of rereading the text – I may have done some other things as good but I am sure none better. I haven't matured, progressed, grown, become deeper, wiser, or funnier. But then, I never thought I would.

Chapter Two
Not Only . . . But Also . . .

In 1964, the American production of *Beyond the Fringe* finally closed, after 669 performances, and Peter and Dudley returned to Britain. Dudley went back to playing jazz with the Dudley Moore Trio, moved into a flat in Mayfair, bought a black Maserati Mistrale, and was promptly offered his own music series, *Offbeat*, by the BBC. Jonathan Miller and Alan Bennett were also working for the Beeb. Jonathan had returned home in 1963 (his part was taken by the expatriate English actor Paxton Whitehead) and was now working for the BBC's highbrow arts show, *Monitor*. Alan, meanwhile, was working on the BBC's new satire show, *Not So Much a Programme, More a Way of Life*. Peter had written most of *Beyond the Fringe*. He'd performed its most famous set pieces. Yet he was the only member of the cast who hadn't landed a plum job with the BBC. Back in the West End, *Beyond the Fringe* was still going strong – but with a completely different cast.

Neither *Offbeat* nor *Monitor* would have been remotely suitable for Peter, but his absence from *Not So Much a Programme . . .* was rather ironic, to say the least. *Not So Much a Programme . . .* was the

BBC's sequel to *That Was The Week That Was*. This satirical smash hit was practically the only part of the satire boom that Peter hadn't had a hand in, but was the one that had become most established in the public eye. While Peter was busy in America, this show had captivated Britain. By the time he returned home, its anchorman, David Frost, had become the face of satire and Peter had more or less been forgotten – by the man in the street, at least. 'Nobody knew me from Adam,'[1] he said, with only a slight degree of exaggeration.

It was a graphic example of the growing power of television. David Frost could reach more people in a single TV transmission than Peter had reached in several years of daily performances on Shaftesbury Avenue and Broadway. With Frost now appearing in *Not So Much a Programme* . . . alongside several of Peter's other Footlights chums, including Eleanor Bron, John Bird and John Fortune, this trend looked set to continue. Without a BBC series to keep him busy, Peter turned his attention to *Private Eye*.

In 1962, Peter acquired a controlling share in the *Eye* for £1,500. It was a perfect match for Peter's satirical nightclub, the Establishment, which he'd launched the year before, and during the Profumo scandal of 1963 circulation climbed to 80,000. However, while Peter was in America, the Establishment folded, and the Great British public (or at least the Great British press) decided that the satire bubble had burst. The implications for a satirical magazine were ominous, but at least the closure of his Soho club left Peter more time for the *Eye*.

In Peter's absence, *Private Eye*'s circulation had shrunk to 20,000. Now Peter set about reviving it. He wrote some articles of his own and inspired countless others. He put another two thousand quid into the magazine, and persuaded celebrity pals like Jane Asher, Dirk Bogarde and Peter Sellers to become shareholders, at a cost of £100 apiece. He even organised bizarre publicity stunts, leading a march of readers from the *Eye*'s Soho offices to 10 Downing Street, in support of that spectacularly uncharismatic Conservative Prime Minister, Alec Douglas Home. Circulation recovered and eventually surpassed its previous peak. What had started out as the least prestigious part of Peter's satirical empire ended up as its sole surviving asset. For the rest of his life, Peter would sustain his role as Lord Gnome, *Private Eye*'s enigmatic hands-off proprietor and enthusiastic hands-on contributor. It was the only constant in his career, outlasting his partnership with Dudley. 'We were saved by the return of Peter Cook,'[2] said Willie Rushton, one of *Private Eye*'s original founders. His fellow founder, John Wells, agreed. 'There was such an unstoppable flow of ideas,' said Wells. 'He was tremendously inventive all through those first few years of *Private Eye*.'[3]

Peter kept his hand in as a performer, recording twenty monologues for ATV's *On the Braden Beat*, as E.L. Wisty – a character Peter described as 'a man on a park bench who talks endlessly about everything and knows nothing'.[4] However, although Peter's amateur philosopher became a nationwide hit, his attempts at writing something more substantial failed to get off the ground. With John Bird, he wrote a screenplay of Evelyn Waugh's great journalistic novel, *Scoop*, but this intriguing project never saw the light of day. A play he began writing on his own, set in a police station, also failed to materialise.

Peter and Dudley did a couple of things with the other *Beyond the Fringe*rs. In August 1964, the original foursome performed the show again, in front of a live audience – and the BBC cameras. The BBC finally broadcast their film of this performance in December 1964, more than four years after its premiere in Edinburgh, but by then this satirical quartet had disintegrated. An attempt to write a screenplay together came to nothing, despite what sounds like a vastly entertaining premise – dastardly Prussians cause havoc in Victorian England by planting a fifth column of fake Queen Victorias behind enemy lines. Miller, Bennett, Cook and Moore never worked together again, and their one brilliant stage show remains the sum total of their collective output. Its influence was out of all proportion to its compact size – as if *Monty Python's Flying Circus* had achieved the same impact with a single revue, rather than four TV series and four feature films – and it's tantalising to think what else might have been if this precocious troupe had stayed together.

Bennett and Miller went their separate ways, but Peter and

Dudley carried on working together. Peter asked Dudley to join him on a couple of *Private Eye* records (an EP called *Private Eye Sings* and an LP called *Private Eye's Blue Record*, featuring *Eye* stalwarts like John Wells, Willie Rushton and Richard Ingrams) and Dudley repaid the compliment – with interest – by asking Peter to join him on TV in *The Dudley Moore Show*.

This show owed its genesis to Joe McGrath, producer of such BBC programmes as Michael Bentine's *It's A Square World*. McGrath had also made a show for ABC Television featuring Dudley, and the two of them had stayed in touch. When the BBC asked McGrath to produce a one-off comedy special, he got in touch with Dudley, and suggested they do another show together. Dudley suggested they get in touch with Peter. NOT ONLY was he fun to work with, said Dudley, BUT he'd ALSO be a wonderful contributor. It was Dudley's endorsement that gave the show its eventual title.

For the time being, however, Peter was just one of several guest stars – and by no means the biggest. By far the most famous name was John Lennon, who had been persuaded to recite a couple of his nonsense poems on the show. McGrath filmed Lennon's performance on Wimbledon Common, sitting on a children's swing. Dudley did the pushing, but he pushed a bit too hard. John's contact lenses fell out and were lost for ever in the long grass – despite the efforts of the production team, who stopped filming to search for them. Lennon's £15 fee didn't even cover the cost of replacements, but although his performance left him out of pocket, he remained a fan of Cook and Moore. 'I really dig what you're all doing,' he told them, at a Chinese restaurant where they'd all gathered to celebrate the end of the show. Lennon became a friend, of Peter's in particular, and made a subsequent appearance in *Not Only . . . But Also . . .* , playing a doorman in the 1966 Christmas Special.

Peter was merely booked to write two sketches for the show, which he was due to perform with Dudley, but the sketches he delivered were two of the best he would ever write. In one, Dudley interviewed Peter as Sir Arthur Streeb-Greebling, a deluded upper-class idiot who had spent a lifetime trying – and failing – to teach ravens to swim underwater. In the other, Peter and Dudley played two equally deluded working-class idiots, swapping implausible stories about being pestered by amorous film starlets. This sketch in particular went down a storm, and the next morning, the Controller of BBC2, Michael Peacock, offered Dudley *and* Peter their own series. Peter ran down the corridor in delight. It was like being back at university, he said, but with bigger grants.

As far as the outside world was concerned, Peter was still only Dudley's guest, and the first episode was duly broadcast as *The Dudley Moore Show, Starring Not Only Dudley Moore But Also Peter Cook and John Lennon*. However, the title soon changed, to reflect the true balance of power, from Dudley's show to Dudley and Peter's show to Peter and Dudley's. *The Dudley Moore Show* became *Not Only Dudley Moore and Peter Cook* and eventually *Not Only Peter Cook and Dudley Moore*.

'In *Not Only . . . But Also . . .*, Dudley is clearly the junior partner,'[5] says Eric Idle, and Joe McGrath agrees. 'Dudley felt slightly in awe of Peter,' he says. 'They started off equal, but Peter was more equal than Dudley.'[6] Yet as the series developed, the inequality of that partnership began to change. Dudley said that Peter had seventeen ideas to every one of his, but although Peter was never short of great ideas, the ideas he had with Dudley tended to reach fruition, unlike quite a few of his solo schemes. Dudley was far more than just a straight man, but like Ernie Wise, he made his partner far more funny, far more often. Suddenly, Peter and Dudley had become a fully-fledged double act. 'There was nothing to indicate it was going to happen,' says Jonathan Miller. 'And yet when it did happen it seemed quite natural. Once you saw what they were doing together it seemed inevitable.'[7]

John Fortune called Peter and Dudley a classic double act, both physically and temperamentally, but the success of *Not Only . . . But Also . . .* wasn't entirely theirs alone. Joe McGrath's direction added greatly to the magic of the mix, and one of the greatest strengths of his production was its intimate theatricality. The show wasn't broadcast live, but it was virtually shot as such, with retakes reserved for only the biggest glitches. For once, the studio audience – all five hundred of them – actually felt like proper punters in a proper theatre, and, even more remarkably, so did the viewers at home. Tight schedules and low budgets added to the theatrical flavour. An absence of elaborate props, scenery or costumes created an informal spit-and-sawdust image, much as it had done in *Beyond the Fringe*.

Unlike *Beyond the Fringe*, *Not Only . . . But Also . . .* wasn't remotely satirical, but Peter and Dudley still wrote right up to the deadline, as if they were working on a topical show. 'We always had enough material for the show, but practically inevitably we'd change it,' said Peter. 'We'd become dissatisfied with the stuff we'd written, and do something at the last minute.' [8] And the stuff they did was both spontaneous and scripted. 'We didn't have scripts as such,' said Peter. 'We had a lot of headings. We'd rehearsed a lot, and we roughly knew what we were going to say, but not word for word. It came across as if we were improvising it, which was not strictly true.'[9]

The series went out fortnightly between January and April 1965. The public lapped it up, and so did the papers. From *The Times* to the *Sun*, Fleet Street was united in its praise – confirmation of the duo's classless appeal. 'Dudley can root out a lot of things from his working-class past, and I can root out a lot of things from my basically middle-class upbringing,'[10] observed Peter. And it wasn't just the press who liked it. Peter Sellers phoned Joe McGrath and practically begged him for a guest spot. McGrath and his colleague Bob Fuest wrote a couple of sketches for Sellers, who duly appeared alongside Peter and Dudley in the fifth episode of the series.

The BBC were similarly enthusiastic, taking the remarkable step of repeating the entire series on BBC1, only a month after it finished its first run on BBC2. 'It was a good thing, really, doing it first on BBC2,' said Peter. 'There was no pressure and very little publicity. Then it got repeated on BBC1 and everyone saw it.'[11] The show won awards and invitations flooded in, from an anti-apartheid gala to the Royal Variety show. The BBC commissioned a second series. If anything, it was even funnier than the first.

The second series went out on BBC2 a year later, from January to February 1966. This time the show was broadcast weekly, giving it more momentum, and the response was even more enthusiastic than before. Joe McGrath was now directing movies, so his place was taken by Dick Clement, most famous as the creator (with Ian La Frenais) of *Porridge* and *The Likely Lads*. 'It was a very, very happy partnership,' says Clement. 'The main drive of new ideas was more from Peter than from Dudley, but the combination of the two of them working things out together was perfect. Peter was very cerebral in many ways, and slightly cold, whereas Dudley was extremely warm, and so you put that together and you get a very potent combination.'[12]

The BBC were keen to capitalise on this potent combination (they repeated the second series on BBC1 between May and July in peak time on Saturday night), but like Joe McGrath, Peter and Dudley were now being wooed by a bigger screen. Between movies, they made a series for ATV in 1968, and a final series for the BBC in 1970. Yet they never quite scaled the heights of the first two series, which looked like the foothills of their partnership – but were actually its premature peak.

PROSPECTIVE SON-IN-LAW
(BBC2, 1965)

The first of many father-and-son sketches that Peter and Dudley did together. Peter is a middle-class, middle-aged father. Dudley is his young, working-class prospective son-in-law. Peter's wife, Beryl, is played by Anna Quayle, who went on to work with Eric Sykes in Spate of Speight.

BERYL: I'm sure you two will have an awful lot to say to each other, so I think I'll just leave you alone.
PETER: Yes. I'm sure you have lots of womanly work to do, Beryl.
(*Exit Beryl.*)
(*Dudley belches.*)

DUDLEY: Whoops. Better out than in, eh, squire?

PETER: Yes, Reg. Reg, would you like a little brandy?

DUDLEY: Lovely.

PETER: Armagnac – that's quite a nice little one. It's over 130 years old.

DUDLEY: Yeah?

(*Dudley pours himself a large brandy.*)

PETER: I think that's probably enough, Reg – probably see you through.

(*Dudley gives his brandy a sniff.*)

DUDLEY: Gone off a bit, hasn't it, squire?

PETER: No, Reg. Brandy, unlike the human body, tends to improve with age. (*Peter laughs.*)

DUDLEY: Quite a joker, aren't you, squire?

PETER: Yes, I like to think so.

DUDLEY: Cheers.

PETER: Er, cheers, Reg. I think it's probably time you and I had a little chat about this and that.

(*Dudley squeezes his palms together, emitting raspberry sounds.*)

PETER: There's a number of things I'd like to ask you . . . Er, how do you make that extraordinary noise?

DUDLEY: Well, you know, you get your palms together, and, you know, squeeze, you know.

(*Dudley squeezes his palms together again.*)

PETER: Yes. I imagine you must have very sweaty palms, from the noise.

DUDLEY: Careful, squire. I'll have to smash your face, you know? All right?

PETER: I understand from my wife, Beryl, that you've been seeing quite a fair amount of my daughter.

DUDLEY: That's putting it mildly, squire. I think I've seen the lot. I'm telling you, squire, your daughter is fantastic. She was like an animal, you know. You touch her elbows and she's away!

PETER: Er . . . she's a lovely little thing, isn't she? Reg, what I really wanted to know, as a father, was what exactly your intentions are towards my daughter.

DUDLEY: Fulfilled, squire. Cheers.

(*Dudley swigs his brandy.*)

PETER: Cheers, Reg. No need to keep saying Cheers every time you drink, you know.

(*Dudley starts squeezing his palms together again, making more raspberry sounds.*)

PETER: Reg, as you'll realise, my . . . I wish you wouldn't make that ghastly noise, Reg. As you'll realise, as a father, I have certain responsibilities towards my daughter, and I have to find out certain things about you. For example, where did you go to school? Not that it matters, but it is important.

DUDLEY: Well, I went to tech and then I was in nick for a year, on the moor.

PETER: On the moor? Some sort of Duke of Edinburgh outdoors scheme, was it? Climbing ladders and weaving ropes? That sort of thing?

DUDLEY: In the nick. You know, jug. You know.

PETER: Oh, in jail?

DUDLEY: Right.

PETER: Falsely imprisoned, I trust.

DUDLEY: No, no. No, I was beating this old lady over the head with a handbag, and I got caught.

PETER: You were obviously a grievously disturbed child.

DUDLEY: Yeah. I was minding my own business, beating this old lady up, and the law came up and disturbed me.

(*Dudley helps himself to some grapes, spitting out the pips as he eats them.*)

PETER: Yes. What I meant was, you . . . I wish you wouldn't keep spitting pips, Reg. Another thing I'd like to know is, where exactly did you meet Melanie?

DUDLEY: Who?

PETER: Melanie. Where did you meet her?

DUDLEY: Who's that?

PETER: Melanie. My daughter.

DUDLEY: Oh, is that her name? Melanie?

PETER: Yes.

DUDLEY: That's nice. I like that.

PETER: It's a lovely name, isn't it? You don't attend the Young Conservatives balls, do you?

DUDLEY: No. No, I met her in the Estrada, Edmonton.

PETER: Yes?

DUDLEY: I was down the one and nines, you know – watching *Apache River.*

PETER: Yes?

DUDLEY: And this bird comes down, you know. I thought, you know – hello, hello! Dolly-bird here! Bit of totty! You know.

PETER: Yes.

DUDLEY: And, you know, she comes in, sits beside me. Half a minute goes past and the knee's coming across, like that, right? And she leans across and whispers in my ear. She says, 'How would you like to have the most fantastic time you've ever had?' So I say, 'Right, darling!' Off we go in the car, off to Watford. I'm telling you, mate – way hay!

PETER: And this was, er, this was Melanie?

DUDLEY: This was Melanie, all right. Three days ago.

(*Dudley begins tapping glasses with a fork.*)

PETER: Reg, forgive me for asking this . . . For God's sake, don't keep tapping things! What sort of job . . . Would you like a grape? Here. What sort of job do you have? What do you do?

DUDLEY: I've got a newspaper round on Tuesdays.

PETER: Ah. How much does this bring in?

DUDLEY: Two and three, two and four – you know.

PETER: Two and four on a good week, and . . .

DUDLEY: Two and three on a bad week.

PETER: Two and three on a bad week. I can't quite see, Reg, exactly how you hope to keep Melanie in the style to which she has become accustomed on two and four a week.

DUDLEY: I thought she might, you know, lend a hand here and there.

PETER: Well, she's not qualified for any job, Reg.

DUDLEY: I think she's well qualified for everything, you know.

(*Dudley laughs lecherously.*)

PETER: Reg, where do you intend to live?

DUDLEY: Well, I mean, this is very nice.

PETER: It is very nice. You'd like to find somewhere similar to this, and, er . . .

DUDLEY: Nah.

PETER: Settle down.

DUDLEY: Nah, this is fine, here.

PETER: I don't think you entirely understand, Reg. We've a fairly small house, and we only have one bedroom, in which my wife and I live. I hardly see where you'd fit in.

DUDLEY: Well, I thought we might, you know, squeeze in, squire. After all, I mean, we're not prudes, are we, squire, you know?

PETER: Yes, we are prudes, Reg. At least, I am – I can't vouch for Beryl. I've never asked her, but I have every reason to believe that she is.

DUDLEY: If you ask me, squire, I reckon your Beryl's just a bit kinky.

PETER: Really? I don't think so, Reg.

DUDLEY: Yeah, when she was offering me the broccoli, it wasn't just the broccoli she was offering me – way hay!

PETER: Reg, why do you keep going way hay, and clapping and spitting grape pips? Is it absolutely necessary? Let me ask you one thing before you spit any more. When do you intend to marry my daughter?

DUDLEY: Get off! What?

PETER: Are you not intending to enter into the sacred vows?

DUDLEY: Nah. I thought, you know, I'd just get what I could out of her and yourself and bog off to Ireland.

PETER: What a refreshing attitude you've got to established values.

DUDLEY: Right.

PETER: Well, look here, Reg. I think I'll leave you for a moment. Leave you to your nuts, and, er, have a word with Beryl. You'll be all right in here?

(*Exit Peter.*)

BERYL (*to Peter*): Well, George, what's he like?

PETER (*to Beryl*): Well, he seems a nice enough chap – a bit shy.

THE MOST BORING MAN IN THE
WORLD COMPETITION
(BBC2, 1966)

'The Bore of the Year Awards' and 'Great Bores of Today' have been mainstays of Private Eye *for years. This is a sketch which shares the same comic root.*

PETER: Good evening, and welcome to the Albert Hall, where the eighteenth Most Boring Man in the World competition is just reaching its final stages. As you can well imagine, on this great occasion, there is an expectant thrush in the audience tonight, and a very lovely creature it is.

There is a very encouraging crowd here this evening. Last year, a somewhat disappointing response – over 375 people turned up. Today, only seventeen – a triumph, I think, for the organisers. Tonight, the judging panel consists of Alan Freeman, the vivacious Catherine Boyle, the positively blooming Percy Thrower and, to lend an international flavour, the delectable Jacqui Chan.

We've just witnessed the Mackintosh Parade of the five finalists. The judges have already seen over three thousand bores from all over the world. At this stage of the competition, the panel has a brief conversation with the five final bores. Points are awarded for Banality of Thought, Tedium of Movement, Dullness of Appearance and Torpor of Conversation. And this is what you're seeing now on your screens. We can see Mr Switzerland talking to the panel and I think by the look of it – yes, this is very exciting – he's doing very well indeed. I've never seen Katie Boyle looking so bored. Mr Switzerland is obviously a very strong contender for this much coveted title.

Very soon, the contestants will be changing out of their gabardine mackintoshes and into their more revealing blue serge suits. And I see Mr Switzerland has finished his conversation, and the panel are looking very bored indeed. And I think Mr Switzerland must be pleased with himself. Of course, he won't be allowed to smile. A smile would immediately penalise him.

The contestants will now begin their final parade in their blue serge suits. And let me see who we are going to have first. Here we have – ah yes, it's Mr Chile – it's Mr Chile who's the first to come out of the tunnel, wearing a very conservatively cut boring blue serge suit. Note the extremely lethargic way he moves. Now, a secret of a Great Bore is lethargic movement, and Mr Chile is world-famous for his tedious movement. There he goes. The panel are looking very bored.

Now our next contestant is – yes, Mr St Kitts. May I say how marvellous it is to see a really first-class coloured bore. In the past, the title has been an entirely white province, and it is very heart-ening to see that the coloured people can really match up to the white bores. Mr St Kitts won this title in 1961 and has written a book about it, which has sold three copies – *How I Bored My Way to the Top* by Ntoule Molaawaa – a very strong contender. And now, coming up the tunnel is one of the great bores of all time, one of the greatest bores the world has ever seen – Mr Free China, Ling Kwa Fey from Free China. He has a fund of tedious Chinese stories, which are really successful. I noticed Alan Freeman actually dropped off during one of the Chinese stories, and he must have picked up points there.

And now coming up the tunnel – oh yes, yes indeed – a tremen-dous ripple of indifference moves through the audience as we see Mr Switzerland – and finally, Mr UK. Well, what can you say? Here he comes. Elected Mr Droitwich in 1937, has never relin-quished the title, has bored his way around the world – Mr Edward Marle, the British Bore. And I know that everybody watching, and I hope there aren't many of you, will be hoping that Mr Great Britain can for the third time carry this world title. It will be an unprecedented thing if he was to win for the third time.

Well, you've joined me at a very exciting moment. These are Mr Freeman's pants, which have just been bored right off him by the British contestant. He must have picked up points there. Mr Droitwich – what a contender! There he goes, just round the rostrum, and our hearts go out to him.

Well, the actual boring is over, and now it's up to the panel to decide the winner. I see they're conferring, exchanging notes, and it is nice to see them all working again.

(*Peter is joined by Dudley as Edward Marle, aka Mr Droitwich, newly crowned as The Most Boring Man in the World.*)

PETER: Tonight, Mr Edward Marle, the World Bore of 1966, is with us in the studio. Mr Marle, how does it feel to have won the title for the third year running?

DUDLEY: Third year walking.

PETER: Third year walking. How does it feel? You must be tremendously excited.

DUDLEY: No, it bores the bloody pants off me, winning it time after time. It's like a drug. Every time I go in for it, I win. Bloody boring. And then I go in the next year.

PETER: Are you bored stiff?

DUDLEY: I'm bored flabby, rather. I mean, every time I know I've got the title in my grasp.

PETER: Was there any time during the proceedings that you felt in danger of losing the title?

DUDLEY: Well, yes. I had a very nasty moment in the second minute, when one of the judges showed a flicker of interest, so I quickly changed the subject of what I was talking about.

PETER: What do you normally talk about?

DUDLEY: Carpets, and how difficult it is to park in London. Well, I was on this and everybody started getting interested, so I changed to a discussion of paper. This really set them back.

PETER: How do you train for your boring?

DUDLEY: Well, I get up about four o'clock in the afternoon. I have a lukewarm cup of tea, and then I put the radio on, and I watch it with the sound turned down, and if I feel I'm getting a bit too lively, I pop up to the West End and see *The Mousetrap* and have a meal in an Eggburger, and that soon brings me down to earth, boy.

PETER: Yes. What did you feel about the other contestants? For example, Mr Free China. Do you think he's a potential threat for the future?

DUDLEY: Not really. He hasn't got this, you know, the, er, thing we British borers have got. I mean, apart from anything, he likes my jokes.

PETER: Could you tell us one of your jokes?

DUDLEY: Yes, I'll tell you one of my jokes. I go up to him and I say 'Hello Mr Free China! Got any free china?' And he laughs. And I know – right, he's out for a start, and it's one less in the way.

PETER: Yes, I see where you score, Mr Marle. It has been said that a bore reaches his peak at the age of forty-three. You are fifty-one. Do you think you're over the top?

DUDLEY: Oh no. I think I've got a few boring years in front of me, boy. I hope senility will overtake me soon, and a combination of senility and boredom is unbeatable.

PETER: Well, I think while people with the spirit of Edward Marle are abroad, we can look forward to a wonderful future in this country.

ITALIAN RESTAURANT
(BBC2, 1966)

(Peter is an Italian waiter in an Italian restaurant. Enter Dudley and his female companion)

PETER: Buona sera, signor, signora.

DUDLEY: Good evening.

PETER: You like to order already now?

DUDLEY: Yes, if we may order very quickly, because madam and I are in rather a hurry. We've only got about half an hour to catch a train, and I wonder if you could serve something up pretty sharpish.

PETER: What you like? A nice bit of spaghetti?

DUDLEY: No, I think not. We're decided, aren't we, darling? Two lasagnes. Nothing to start – just two lasagnes.

PETER: Two lasagnes.

DUDLEY: And a bottle, a carafe, of red. Is that all right with you, darling? Carafe of red.

PETER: No salad?

DUDLEY: No salad, no vegetables – no thank you very much.

PETER: Two lasagne . . .

DUDLEY: Carafe of red.

PETER: Carafe of red.

DUDLEY: And if it could be, you know, sort of very quick.

PETER: Very quick. Quick.

DUDLEY: Quick. Yes, yes – prestissimo.

PETER: Ah, you speak a little Italian! No, you speak a little . . . No, this is interesting for me, because I, um . . . I myself, I love English, because I wish to speak English, because I, um . . . from . . . You have been . . .

DUDLEY: Er, yes, I've been through . . .

PETER: And I come to England to learn speak English because I not a waiter. I don't wish to wait . . .

DUDLEY: No, no – of course not.

PETER: Because it is, you know, is not right for a man to be waiting.

DUDLEY: No, we don't want to wait either, do we darling?

PETER: And so I come to learn. I wish to tich.

DUDLEY: Yes . . .

PETER: I wish to, I wish to . . .

DUDLEY: Teach.

PETER: I wish teach, yes. I teach English because it is for my family. It better for tich than for wait.

DUDLEY: Than waiting. Yes, of course.

PETER: Wait I don't like.

DUDLEY: Yes, of course. No harm in filling in time, is there?

PETER: But I have not already, I am here ten years, but already I am learned for example, um . . . um . . . momento. How you say, is knife is right?

DUDLEY: Yes, yes – knife.

PETER: Knife and is frock.

DUDLEY: Fork.

PETER: Knife and frock.

DUDLEY: Fork. Frock is, um . . . what madam has on, a frock.

PETER: Aye, aye, signor. Frog. Frog.

DUDLEY: No, frog is, er . . . frog. No, no – frog is an animal.

PETER: Scusi, scusi.

DUDLEY: Yes. Oink, oink. Lives by ponds.

PETER: Frog is animal.

DUDLEY: Animal, yes. Frock is what one wears, and fork is what one . . .

PETER: Is knife and fork.

DUDLEY: Picks up Spaghetti Bolognese.

PETER: And spon.

DUDLEY: Spoon.

PETER: Frog, spon.

DUDLEY: Spoon – as in moon and June.

PETER: Frog, spon is right.

DUDLEY: Frog spawn, yes. No, no – that's . . . those are the eggs, aren't they?

PETER: It's eggs and it's glass.

DUDLEY: That's a glass, yes.

PETER: It's glass.

DUDLEY: Yes, glass.

PETER: Yes. In my book I'm reading is now the face and the body. For now, if I am right, you have a moment, is . . . is nose.

DUDLEY: Yes. Yes, well . . .

PETER: Is nose.

DUDLEY: Yes, nose. Nose.

PETER: Is nose, is ice.

DUDLEY: Eyes, yes.

PETER: Ice, is ice.

DUDLEY: Ice is water – very cold water.

PETER: Ice is water, and is mouse.

DUDLEY: Mouse is mouth. I mean this is a mouth. Mouse is a little animal.

PETER: Mouse is animal, a frog. Mouse is frog. Frog is mouse. Is frog a knife – fork, mouse, spoon.

DUDLEY: Yes – knife, fork . . .

PETER: Is frog spawn, is mouse spoon.

DUDLEY: Yes, they are all the same.

PETER: Is right. Is correct. Because I learn all the time, and is good to speak to someone who is speak well, from Oxford.

DUDLEY: Oh, yes.

PETER: Because it is so useful for me.

DUDLEY: But the thing is, we're in a bit of a hurry.

PETER: Si, thank you very much, is wonderful.

DUDLEY: So, you know, if you could, you know, get the food in pretty quickly, we'd be very grateful.

PETER: Ah, signor, no, I'm sorry, is a little late, because it is eleven o'clock, and eleven o'clock we close. We are clos-ed.

DUDLEY: Close. We are closed.

PETER: We are clos-ed.

DUDLEY: We are closed.

PETER: We are closed.

DUDLEY: Closed?

PETER: Buona sera, signor. I must catch my bus.

(Exit Peter)

THE MUSIC TEACHER
(BBC2, 1966)

(Dudley is playing the piano. A baby is crying)

DUDLEY: Pamela, keep that baby quiet! I can't hear myself bloody sing down here, girl!

(Enter Peter)

DUDLEY: Oh, Mr Stigwell!

PETER: Mr Blanfeddy?

DUDLEY: Yes, you phoned me a couple of days ago, wasn't it?

PETER: Yes, my secretary made an appointment.

DUDLEY: Yes, would you like to sit down? Can I take your coat and hat?

PETER: I think I'll keep it on. It's not exactly overheated in here, is it?

DUDLEY: Well, take a seat anyway.

PETER: Thank you. I understand you teach the piano. Do you?

DUDLEY: Yes I do, yes.

PETER: Could you teach me?

DUDLEY: Well, I've been teaching the piano for five years now. I don't see why you should be an exception. Have you had any musical training before now?

PETER: I've had no formal musical education, but I have a certain sort of instinctive feel for it. I'm a very rhythmical person. All my family are very rhythmical. My mother was very rhythmical before me. I know the basic things about the piano. The notes. The white ones – the black ones. The black ones play louder than the white, don't they?

DUDLEY: No, somebody's been leading you up the garden path there I think, a bit. You can get the same amount of volume out of the black and the white ones.

PETER: There must be some reason for them being black and white surely.

DUDLEY: Well, I suppose the same reason why some people are black and others are white, you know. There's no colour bar on the piano. The black and the white nestle here together.

PETER: I'm paying you to be a musical tutor, not a comedian. Can we start?

DUDLEY: Aye, aye. Well, there's one thing I ought to bring up – it's the sordid subject of money.

PETER: There's nothing sordid about money, Mr Blanfeddy.

DUDLEY: No, I suppose not, but I always get a bit embarrassed about it. The thing is, my lessons are a little expensive – seven and six an half hour.

PETER: I think I can run to that.

DUDLEY: That's alright, I didn't want to embarrass you later on.

PETER: No you won't. Right! Where shall we start?

DUDLEY: Well, I think first of all, learning the names of the notes is most important. For instance, this is sort of generally accepted as the sort of middle of the piano, you see. Middle C, then it goes up in alphabetical order – C, D, E.

PETER: Yes, I don't like that very much, Mr Blanfeddy. It seems a bit complicated starting in the middle. Couldn't we start at the end here – one, two, three, four, five, six, seven, eight, nine, ten, eleven, twelve – all the way up there. Then it'd be quite easy. You just shout out the numbers and I could poke my fingers in.

DUDLEY: You'd get yourself in a bit of a tangle, I think.

PETER: I don't think I would.

DUDLEY: It's a bit unorthodox.

PETER: It may be unorthodox, Mr Blanfeddy, but I'm in a bit of hurry. Let me explain one thing. Tuesday fortnight is my wife's birthday, and I'm very anxious to surprise her with a little sort of musical treat, and I thought it would be very nice if I could have learned something, and while she's having her birthday breakfast upstairs – champagne, flowers, cakes, that sort of thing – she could hear the music wafting up the stairs. There's one particular piece of music she's very fond of, which I'd like to get sort of mastered for then – Beethoven's Fifth. You're familiar with it, are you? Beethoven's Fifth thing?

DUDLEY: Beethoven's Fifth Symphony?

PETER: Yes.

DUDLEY: By Tuesday week?

PETER: Tuesday week, yes. If you could concentrate on that and get that out of the way, then we can go onto something else later.

DUDLEY: It would be very nice, but it'd be a bit of miracle if you could do that by Tuesday week. I mean I could probably get you Blackbird Gavotte with one hand under your belt by next Tuesday.

PETER: Mr Blanfeddy, I am not interested in Blackbird Gavotte with one hand under my belt by next Tuesday. I'm interested in Beethoven's Fifth Symphony. Let's get on with it. It's not going to be easy.

DUDLEY: Well, I don't know. It's a bit difficult, really. I mean, it's an orchestral piece, really. You need an orchestra for it.

PETER: I've got an orchestra Mr Blanfeddy. I bought one last Wednesday. Got them in a merger for tax purposes, and I'd like to play with the lads – you know, a nice group of people, a few harps, double basses, and things. I'd like to join in.

DUDLEY: It doesn't really matter if you've got the Welsh National Philharmonic in the back yard. It's not a piano concerto – it's a symphony. There's no piano part in it.

PETER: Mr Blanfeddy, if it's my orchestra, I would have thought I could come in with what instrument I like at what time I like. I'm sure they'll see it my way. We can put a piano in just like that.

DUDLEY: Mr Stigwell, I must tell you that, you know, some things are a little impossible.

PETER: Nothing is impossible, Mr Blanfeddy! Let me tell you a few things about myself. I was born with nothing in a minefield. I had a straw in my mouth and that was all. From that I've worked my way up to my current position. I'm a millionaire at thirty-one. I have the largest juice importing business in the world. And how did I get it? Through integrity, strength of mind and physical fitness. Don't tell me I can't master this.

DUDLEY: Well, Mr Stigwell, let me tell you that however rich you are, I can't accelerate the process of musical tuition.

PETER: How much money do you want?

DUDLEY: You can't, you can't, you can't buy musical talent like a pound of sausages.

PETER: How much money did you say you charged?

DUDLEY: Well, I charge seven and six an half hour.

PETER: I'll pay you fifty guineas a half hour. Let's get on with it.

DUDLEY: Mr Stigwell, I don't think you understand. I can't be bought. I'm not some sort of a musical harlot. Goodness! fifty guineas a half hour! Don't you think that isn't tempting now? I mean, I could be sunning myself in the Bahamas, couldn't I, for fifty guineas an half hour? Instead of living here on seven and six a half hour in a pokey two room flat in Upminster, with my wife and baby screaming upstairs half the bloody day. But there's such a thing, Mr Stigwell, as integrity. I don't suppose you've come across that in your chequered career have you? Look boy, if I pretended I could teach you Beethoven's Fifth by Tuesday week I'd be telling a lie, and I can't afford to do that. Not for financial reasons Mr Stigwell, but because of self-respect and that, my boy, is more valuable to me than fifty guineas an half hour. There you are, I've had my say. You might as well go now. We've nothing more to discuss.

PETER: First class, Blanfeddy. Nobody's spoken like that to me for years. I like your style. I like the cut of your jib. Integrity! That's a valuable thing and I'm willing to pay for it. I'll give you a hundred guineas an hour.

DUDLEY: That's more like it now, boy! That's right! You'll find the black notes play a bit louder than the white ones.

BO DUDDLEY
(BBC2, 1966)

Thankfully, this musical sketch has survived on film as well as audio, which is an added blessing since its undisputed star is Dudley's blues piano. The hopelessly patronising attitude of white, middle-class liberals towards black popular culture has never been more shrewdly parodied. Peter and Dudley revived it in New York a decade later, on their first Derek & Clive *LP, but its initial broadcast on BBC2, surrounded by the well-meaning arts programmes it lampooned, gave it an extra bite.*

PETER: Good evening. This evening we have taken our *Not Only . . . But Also . . .* cameras to the heart of London's West End where, at a nightclub, La Maison Sophisticate, we see the opening of the great coloured jazz singer, Bo Duddley.

(*Dudley sings a passionate twelve-bar blues, in a thick black American accent, raucously self-accompanied on the piano.*)

DUDLEY (*sings*):

> Mama's got a brand new bag, yeah!
> Mama's got a brand new bag, yeah!
> We're gonna groove it the whole night, baby!
> We're gonna groove it the whole night, baby!
> We're gonna work it out, baby! Ugh!
> We're gonna shake it tonight!
> Stretch out now, stretch out, baby!
> I hear you talking, I hear you talking now!
> You turn me on, baby, mm!
> You're burning up now, yeah!

PETER: Absolutely terrific!

DUDLEY (*suddenly posh*): Did you like it?

PETER: Yes, I thought it was tremendous. Now, Bo Duddley – or may I call you Bo?

DUDLEY: B. O. Call me Bo.

PETER: Bo, I think for the benefit of English viewers it would be a help if you could actually explain some of the lyrics. I think the slang is a little hard to understand. Could we go through the song verse by verse?

DUDLEY: Of course. I'd be delighted. (*Sings.*) Mama's got a brand new bag, yeah!

PETER (*repeats, deadpan*): Mama's got a brand new bag, yeah. This is fairly self-explanatory, isn't it? It's a simple story. Mama, the sort of Harlem mother, has gone out into the streets and she's seen this bag, which is very nice, and she's bought it, and that's it. She's got a brand new bag. What kind of a bag would that be?

DUDLEY: Well, of course in the old days it probably would have been a carrier bag. But in these days of scientific advancement it's probably a gaily coloured plastic bag.

PETER: A gaily coloured plastic bag, which she has bought, and it's brand new, and the song goes on . . .

DUDLEY: It goes on . . . (*Sings.*) We're gonna groove it the whole night long, baby!

PETER (*repeats, deadpan*): We're going to groove it the whole night long, baby. Now this presumably is a reference to the fact that the mother, having bought the bag, decides to make some indentations on it, to make some grooves on the bag – a sort of decorative pattern, presumably.

DUDLEY: It's a darkie decorative process.

PETER: Is it?

DUDLEY: Yes.

PETER: How is it done, the grooving?

DUDLEY: It's done with a groover.

PETER: With a groover?

DUDLEY: Of course, in the old days, when they used to have knife grinders and watermelon sellers in the streets, you used to have groovers. (*Sings.*) Mississippi Groover! (*Speaks.*) They used to call out, you know. Well, in fact it's now a purely domestic occupation.

PETER: It's done by the Mama.

DUDLEY: By Mama, by the darkie Mama. 'We're going to groove it the whole night long.'

PETER: It takes a long time?

DUDLEY: It takes a long time, the whole night long, baby. It's for the baby.

PETER: Is it the child's anniversary or something?

DUDLEY: Probably the child's anniversary, or the first tooth being cut – that sort of thing.

PETER: And so the bag is grooved by the mother all night long. It's a long process.

DUDLEY: Exactly. And it goes on . . . (*Sings.*) We're going to work it out, baby! Ugh!

PETER (*repeats, deadpan*): We're going to work it out, baby. Ugh. This is a little surprising, isn't it, that having grooved the bag she should then decide to work it out. Isn't that rather . . . ?

DUDLEY: Well, it's rather putting the chicken before the china shop, isn't it? Because she's grooved the bag and then suddenly she decides to work it out.

PETER: A little late.

DUDLEY: A bit too late there, isn't it?

PETER: Because the bag is already grooved. Far too late. She should have worked it out before she grooved it, shouldn't she? And this, presumably, is the explanation of the Ugh at the end.

DUDLEY: The Ugh! The exasperation. She goes on to say . . . (*Sings.*) We're gonna shake it tonight! (*Speaks.*) We're going to shake it tonight.

PETER: We're going to shake it tonight. Presumably in frustration at the fact that she's grooved the bag badly, without having worked it out properly, so in her frustration she shakes the bag – just shakes it all night.

DUDLEY: Out of exasperation. Then, of course, exhausted by all this, she goes on and says . . . (*Sings.*) Stretch out now, stretch out, baby!

PETER: Stretch out. She wants to stretch out and fall into a double bed.

DUDLEY: Fall asleep. And then, unfortunately, she says . . . (*Sings.*) I hear you talking, I hear you talking now!

PETER: What's that? The neighbours?

DUDLEY: The neighbours, chatting next door.

PETER: Through the paper-thin walls comes the sound of the neighbours talking, just when she wants to go to sleep.

DUDLEY: Exactly. And she goes on to say . . . (*Sings.*) You turn me on, baby, mm! (*Speaks.*) This is a sort of jive, jazz, boogie-woogie abbreviation of 'turn the light on for me, baby'. Turn for me – in parenthesis – the light on, baby.

PETER: Oh, I see. A sort of linguistic trick. Rather like the German, I out of the door go must.

DUDLEY: Exactly.

PETER: A similar sort of thing. A jive, boogie, Harlem thing, isn't it?

DUDLEY: Boogie, Harlem, darkie, jazz-rhythm thing.

PETER: And how does it go on?

DUDLEY: It goes on . . . (*Sings.*) You're burning up now, baby!

PETER: You're burning up now, baby?

DUDLEY: You're burning up now, baby. The baby's turned the lights on, fused the whole house and the wigwam is in flames. The whole igloo's set on fire.

PETER: You don't think any of these lyrics could be in any way connected with making love or sex?

DUDLEY: Oh, good lord, no. And anyway, I wouldn't sing that sort of garbage.

PETER: Well, to summarise, basically this is a simple story. The Mama has gone out into the gay, bustling streets of Harlem. She's seen a brand new bag. She's bought it, this gaily coloured plastic bag. She brings it home, spends the whole night grooving it for her child. Then she discovers she's grooved it badly. She hasn't worked it out. And so, in her rage, she shakes all night, attempts to go to sleep but the neighbours start talking. She asks her child to turn on the light, but she fuses it and the whole igloo or wigwam goes up in flames. And we're left with the underlying question – was it right for the mother to squander her money on these gaily coloured plastic bags? Wouldn't she have better spent it on rewiring the entire house? And isn't one left also with the question – should there be legislation to prevent the sale of these bags to people who aren't quite ready to use them? I wonder.

DUDLEY (*sings*): Mama's got a brand new bag, yeah!

THE FAIRY COBBLER
(BBC2, 1966)

This sketch featured in Peter and Dudley's 1966 Christmas Special, but there's nothing remotely festive about this disconcerting blend of Enid Blyton and Who's Afraid of Virginia Woolf?. *The storybook setting and Dudley's drag act give it a pantomime flavour, but these jolly details merely make the central marital spat more disturbing. Dudley corpses, as usual, but it's Peter who fluffs his lines – and for once, it's Dudley who has the upper hand. A Grimm fairy tale indeed –* Play For Today *meets* The Borrowers. The Elves and the Shoemaker *was never half as dark as this.*

(*An enchanted elfin cottage. Peter plays Marcel, the fairy cobbler. Dudley plays Melanie, his fairy wife.*)

PETER (*sings*): I cobble and I cobble, I cobble away, I am the fairy cobbler, I cobble and I cobble . . .

(*Enter Dudley.*)

PETER (*sings*): I cobble and I cobble and I cobble away, they call me the cobbler goblin, I cobble and I cobble and . . . Ah, hello, Melanie. I didn't hear you come in.

DUDLEY: No, I don't suppose you did, did you?

PETER: Did you have a good afternoon, dear heart?

DUDLEY: I think some of us had a rather better afternoon than some of us not a million miles away from here.

PETER: I hope you had a good afternoon, Melanie. I've been busy, as you can see, with all these fairy boots. There's been a lot of orders for fairy boots.

DUDLEY: Yes, those stupid little shoes of yours.

PETER: They're not stupid little shoes, Melanie. They're fairy boots, and what's more . . .

PETER/DUDLEY (*together*): They're our bread and butter.

PETER: You may laugh, Melanie. You may laugh.

DUDLEY: I don't need your permission to laugh, Marcel.

PETER: I'm not suggesting you need my permission to laugh, Melanie. I am merely pointing out that if it were not for these stupid little shoes, as you see fit to call them, were it not for these stupid little shoes, we would not be able to live in this lovely little toadstool and have all these things which make life so comfortable for both of us, dear.

DUDLEY: That make life all the more damp and poky for both of us, you mean. Why can't we live in a wonderful gingerbread house, like Goldilocks does?

PETER: You know very well I can't afford it on a cumbler's humble . . . a cobbler's humble wage.

(*Dudley gets the giggles.*)

PETER: No, you may laugh. A cumbler also has a humble wage, as well as a cobbler. He has a humbler wage than anyone else. I've never seen a humbler wage than a cumbler's. Anyway, we're not moving into a gingerbread house on my income. And if you don't like shoes, Melanie, my precious heart, then you should have pointed that out when you married me. I always have been a cobbler. I've always wanted to be a cobbler. I always will be a cobbler. I hope my children are cobblers, too. Cobblers, all through.

DUDLEY: Wonderful. What a prospect, spending the rest of my life with a bunch of cobblers. Don't you realise, Marcel, that under these gossamers there's a passionate fairy trying to get out? My goodness me, Marcel, why don't you take it upon yourself to tie me to a cowslip leaf and thrash the living daylights out of me?

PETER: Melanie, my dear, you're overwrought.

DUDLEY: Overwrought? I'm underwrought, if anything. When was the last time you wrought me? When you were drunk on cuckoo spit and dressed yourself up like a centipede.

PETER: Melanie, you're completely . . . Where have you been? Your gossamers, your lovely gossamer threads and wings! They're tattered and torn! Where have you been?

DUDLEY: Perhaps someone's been a little rough with me this afternoon.

PETER: What do you mean, Melanie?

DUDLEY: Well, perhaps something not dissimilar to a rude, naughty, eager water boatman has been scrabbling at my gossamers, has been showing me a thing or two, has been showing what a husband should be like.

PETER: Have you been out with the water boatman?

DUDLEY: Yes I have.

PETER: And was he – romantic?

DUDLEY: As a matter of fact he was.

PETER: Well, it's all very easy for a water boatman. All he has to do is scud over the water and sing Italian songs, while I have to do a job of work back home. It's all very well for the water boatman.

DUDLEY: Yes, well, if that's all you think a water boatman does, scud over the water, you should have seen him scud over me this afternoon.

PETER: Well, if that's how you want to spend your afternoons, Melanie, there's nothing I can do about it, is there?

DUDLEY: No. Of course there's nothing you can do. You can't stop me, can you? You can't stop me. Oh, Marcel, you're so pathetic. Don't you realise, Marcel, I've been unfaithful to you? Aren't you going to discipline me? Aren't you going to punish me? Aren't you going to be masterful?

PETER: You want me to be masterful?

DUDLEY: Yes I do.

PETER: You think I can't be masterful, I suppose?

DUDLEY: Yes.

PETER: Well, I'll discipline you all right.

DUDLEY: For once in your life . . .

PETER: You want me to dominate you?

DUDLEY: For once . . .

PETER: I'll be tough and firm with you. Don't you worry. Listen to this, now. Sit down, Melanie! Shut up and let me get on with my cobbling! How's that?

DUDLEY: Pathetic.

PETER: I'm sorry you feel that way.

DUDLEY: You're sorry I feel that way? How do you know how I feel? You haven't felt me for years. You're so pathetic. I've never heard anything of the sort in my life. My goodness, Marcel, why can't you rave a bit?

PETER: Why can't I rave a bit? I'm glad you asked me that. Has it ever occurred to you that perhaps I can rave a bit? But has it ever occurred to you that perhaps you don't bring out the raver in me? Perhaps you're so fat and sluggish and smelly and ghastly, you don't bring out the raver in me, with your tatty clothes. Perhaps some other fairy like Tinkerbell makes me rave like anything. You ask Tinkerbell whether I rave or not. You ask Tinkerbell whether I rave.

DUDLEY: Perhaps I've already asked her.

PETER: Oh? And what did she say?

DUDLEY: Oh, who's your lady friend? I'll tell you what she said. She told me how pathetic you were. She told me you made a pass at her in the fairy ring on midsummer's night, and you asked her up here to look at your cobblers last . . . cobblers first, if you ask me. Oh my God, she laughed so much, until her gossamers dropped. Tinkerbell laughed so much that she cracked her bell and couldn't tinkle for six months.

PETER: That's what Tinkerbell told you?

DUDLEY: Yes. That's what she told me.

PETER: That wasn't very kind, was it?

DUDLEY: No it wasn't very kind but it was no more or less than you deserve, Marcel – no more or less, cos you're such an ineffective, twitty, incompetent goblin. You're not a cobbler, not a sprite. You don't deserve the name of a – (*Peter seizes Dudley and shakes him.*)

PETER: That does it! That does it! You stupid fat cow! How do you think I like it, living with someone as fat and ugly? With your filthy hairy chest! I'm going to beat the living daylights out of you! I can't stand you, you filthy, dirty hag! Get upstairs! Get upstairs!

DUDLEY: Oh, that's more like my man! I'm going to go upstairs and put some pollen behind my ears and some elderflower wine between my toes. I'll be waiting for you, my dear.

(*Dudley goes upstairs.*)

PETER: Well, that seemed to get her going a bit. Now, if I can just get these twelve boots done, I'll be up in a couple of hours. (*Sings.*) I cobble all night, I cobble all day . . .

SWINGING LONDON
(BBC2, 1966)

PETER: Americans have become extremely interested in the phenomenon of Swinging London. We'd now like to show you a prize winning documentary made for Idaho television.

(*Peter plays American TV presenter Hiram J. Pipesucker, Dudley plays a groovy lavatory attendant, in an underground gents' toilet in the heart of Swinging Soho)*

PETER: Good afternoon, My name is Hiram J. Pipesucker. I'm from Idaho Television.

DUDLEY: Welcome to the Ad Lav Club, sir.

PETER: Thank you very much. Now, you must be Mr Druff.

DUDLEY: Oh, just call me Dan.

PETER: Thank you, Dan. Now, you're the owner of the club, I believe.

DUDLEY: That is correct.

PETER: Beautiful music I heard, coming down.

DUDLEY: Yes, just a little spot of Handel.

PETER: Now tell me, what gave you the idea of starting a sophisticated spot for lavatory lovers?

DUDLEY: Well, I'm glad you asked me that, Hiram. About four years ago, I spent a very boring five minutes in a government sponsored public convenience and I thought to myself, 'This is tatty – this is real tat.' I looked around and I thought, 'I don't know – the writing's on the wall for the old style lav,' and immediately I had this brainwave. I bought up these premises, I did them up as elegantly as I could, and by the first night I had ten thousand members hopping about the streets, shrieking to get in.

PETER: You became the 'in' spot. Now, tell me, Dan, who are your regulars, so to speak?

DUDLEY: Well, not to mention any names, the Rolling Stones, Lord Snowdon and Alf Ramsey often pop in here for a quick one.

PETER: How very exciting. Now, to what do you attribute the success of the Ad Lav club?

DUDLEY: Well, quite honestly, Hiram, I think that when people go out to the lav, they want something special. They want something out of the ordinary, something they wouldn't get at home, and here we try and provide extra special comforts – home comforts. As you see, the décor is very elegant.

PETER: Spectacular décor, certainly.

DUDLEY: And of course the atmosphere is something special again. And on top of it all, there's the host. I think, you see, people are after the personal touch. They're after a bit of privacy, and they're after a joke.

PETER: You provide the personal touch, and I believe you vary your lavatory music for whoever is coming down – to suit their mood, so to speak.

DUDLEY: That is correct. Whenever Noel Coward comes in here, we always go into A Room With A Loo.

PETER: I understand, yes. Yes, you make him feel at home.

DUDLEY: That's exactly the idea, yes. Sir Laurence Olivier came down here after the first night of his triumphant Othello, and I swung straight into a Black Bottom.

PETER: I wonder, Dan, could you tell me if you have been in any way affected by the credit squeeze? I know that up and down the country, businessmen have been forced to make drastic slashes.

DUDLEY: Well, no. In fact, I've been very unaffected by the squeeze, Hiram. In fact, I am hoping to expand. I'm about to open branches up and down the country. By 1970, I hope to be in control of a huge lavatory chain.

PETER: A gigantic lavatory chain, covering the face of England – that's the exciting prospect held out by young Daniel Druff, here at the Ad Lav club in the heart of London. Now Dan, if you have a few moments, I wonder if you could show me a little more of your beautiful city . . .

Chapter Three
Goodbye Again

Peter and Dudley's small-screen triumphs made them a bankable commodity on the big screen, and in 1966 they appeared together in a British movie called *The Wrong Box*. Directed by Bryan Forbes, based on a yarn by Lloyd Osborne and Robert Louis Stevenson, this old-fashioned farce also featured Michael Caine, Tony Hancock, John Mills and Ralph Richardson, plus Peter and Dudley's *Not Only . . . But Also . . .* guest star, Peter Sellers.

Despite its starry cast, *The Wrong Box* wasn't a great success, but Cook and Moore did enough to attract the attention of the acclaimed American film director Stanley Donen. Donen's credits included *Singing in the Rain* and *Seven Brides for Seven Brothers*, but this celebrated blockbuster-maker was still blown away by *Not Only . . . But Also . . .* 'I remember watching it religiously and thinking it was the funniest, cleverest, most pointed material I'd seen,' he says. 'I thought they were so gifted that I simply picked up the telephone and tracked them down and said, "Would they meet with me? Would they like to make a movie?"'[1] That movie was *Bedazzled*. It was the only time Donen had contacted two performers and asked them to work with him, simply on the strength of a performance. Donen's enthusiasm was reciprocated by Peter and Dudley. The budget was relatively modest – only $600,000 – but all three of them were so committed, they waived any sort of salary.

Peter and Dudley were contracted to make *Bedazzled* together, but even though they were both cast in leading roles, Peter resolved to write it alone. This was surely a mistake. Peter spent more than a year on the script but, for once in his life, if anything he worked too hard. On the big screen, Peter's bon mots lacked the bathos Dudley usually gave them, and even though Dudley's delivery was as endearing as ever, Peter seemed distracted and remote. Peter said they were both overawed. Dudley said Peter's writing was gawky. In a way, they were both right. The film has a jerky, disjointed feel at odds with Donen's slick track record. But although this odd, staccato style is partly due to Peter's lifelong diffidence as a film actor (Dudley's fluid acting is difficult to fault), the main reason for its relative failure was that Peter had written a brilliant stage play wrapped up in an awkward screenplay. There are too many words for the screen, and not enough action. People stand around talking, rather than doing anything. In the theatre, Peter's natural home, it would have played like a dream.

Peter's script was a cheerful but remarkably intelligent update of *Faust*, with Peter as a mischievous rather than evil Devil. Dudley plays a pathetic short-order chef, flipping burgers in a Wimpy bar, hopelessly infatuated with his grumpy waitress – a superbly unappealing portrayal by Peter's old Footlights co-star Eleanor Bron. There are also entertaining cameos by several of the Seven Deadly Sins, including Barry Humphries as Envy, and Raquel Welch as (Lillian) Lust – a woman so alluring that Dudley had to wear three pairs of underpants in the bedroom scene, to constrict any involuntary passions that might arise. Peter wanted to call the movie *In Raquel Welch*, so the posters would read 'Peter Cook and Dudley Moore *In Raquel Welch*'. It might have made a better title than *Bedazzled*, which flouts the first rule of film titles: tell the punters what the film's about.

The names of Peter and Dudley's characters were also both injokes. Peter's Devil is called George Spiggott, after the one-legged

Tarzan in their sketch, 'One Leg Too Few', while Dudley's chef is called Stanley Moon, a name mistakenly ascribed to Dudley by the absent-minded John Gielgud (Gielgud and Dudley's cinematic paths would cross again thirteen years later, when Gielgud won an Oscar playing Dudley's butler in *Arthur*). Egged on by Spiggott, Moon trades his soul for seven wishes, each of which he wastes trying to win Margaret's empty heart. Moon tries every conceivable trick (fame, fortune, brains, beauty), transforming himself into a man of means, a man of letters, a pop star and, finally – accidentally – a lesbian nun. In each wish, Spiggott finds a way to cheat Moon of his heart's desire – prompting a series of theological and philo-sophical debates, which aren't only amusing, but also surprisingly thoughtful and profound.

Peter's satanic persona gave him licence to rage demonically (and comically) against all his contemporary pet hates, while Dudley's put-upon romantic lead was a dry run for greater glories still to come. Yet *Bedazzled* was too esoteric and Anglocentric to be a smash hit in the States. *Time* magazine said Peter and Dudley had failed to grasp the basic difference between a four-minute sketch script and a 107-minute feature film, but for Peter and Dudley's British fans *Bedazzled* probably wasn't sketchlike enough. Their TV heroes surely would have made a bigger splash with *Pete & Dud – The Movie*. Significantly, *Bedazzled* fared far better on the Continent, where audiences hadn't seen *Not Only . . . But Also . . .* 'I saw it in Rome, dubbed into Italian,' recalled Peter. 'It was fabulous in Italian. I had the most wonderful voice.'[2]

However, such Continental novelties were scant consolation for the film's comparative failure in Britain and the States. Peter had written a super script, albeit for the wrong medium. Dudley had demonstrated his talent as a downtrodden leading man. At least Dudley would eventually get another chance to prove his poten-tial. Peter's greatest movie, however, had come and gone. Even more galling, the passage of time, which erodes the reputations of all but the greatest movies, has done nothing to diminish *Bedazzled*, and everything to enhance it. Half a lifetime since it was made, *Bedazzled* has belatedly been recognised as a flawed but brilliant masterpiece, whose cult status is still growing, while most successful films of that era are long forgotten. Its many fans range from Mel Smith in Britain to Chevy Chase in the States, who called it one of the funniest movies he'd ever seen. Yet, although Peter was never short of compliments from friends and colleagues, mainstream popularity is what matters in the movies, and the backhanded compliment of the recent remake came several decades too late.

Peter and Dudley appeared in a few more films soon after, but none of them really compensated for the tepid reaction to *Bedazzled*. *The Bed Sitting Room* is a surreal, post-apocalyptic black comedy, adapted from a stage play by Spike Milligan and John Antrobus, set in the aftermath of a nuclear holocaust. Peter and Dudley played two policemen, who spend most of their time in a hot-air balloon. During their last day on location, in a visionary metaphor for their respective future film careers, the balloon abruptly fell to earth, landing Peter in hospital, while Dudley walked away unharmed. Peter and Dudley also played two army officers in Ken Annakin's sequel to *Those Magnificent Men in their Flying Machines*. In America it was called *Those Daring Young Men in their Jaunty Jalopies*. In Italy, it was called *Quei temerari sulle loro pazze, scatenate, scalcinate, carriole*. In Britain, it was called *Monte Carlo or Bust* – a pithier title, but one that sorely tempted providence. This road-race caper wasn't too badly treated by the critics, but it was not a commercial hit.

In the summer of 1968, after these mixed fortunes at the movies, they resumed their television partnership, not with the BBC but for ITV. They made three one-hour shows that year, and another one the year after, under the umbrella title *Goodbye Again*. Unlike *Not Only . . . But Also . . .* , the entire series is still intact, safely stored away in Carlton's vaults. And unlike *Not Only . . . But Also . . .* , some of it actually reads better than it plays on-screen.

There were several reasons for this mismatch, none of which really show up in the scripts. Unlike the subtle, multiple settings of *Not Only . . . But Also . . .* , each episode of *Goodbye Again* was mainly shot on one large realistic set. The sets for *Not Only . . . But Also . . .* were like stage sets, almost abstract in their simplicity. The sets for *Goodbye Again* were more cinematic, and similarly restrictive. Bizarrely, each set took its cue from the theme of that week's Pete and Dud sketch – a jail in the first show, a hospital in the second and a gymnasium in the third. However, most of the other items in each episode bore no relation to Pete and Dud's chosen subject, and the results were rather incongruous, to say the least. This might not have mattered quite so much if every episode had opened with Pete and Dud, but their flat-cap duologues were reserved for the second half of each programme, and consequently the first half of each show had a slightly unreal ambience, as if the cast had taken a wrong turn in the corridor, and wandered on to a different set.

Even if the production standards had been faultless, an hour is an awful lot of comedy on anybody's TV set, and Peter's humour in particular had always been at its best confined to a series of short sprints. 'Most of my ideas are only worth about five minutes,'[3] he once said. The first series of *Not Only . . . But Also . . .* comprised seven forty-five-minute episodes, the second series comprised seven thirty-minute episodes, and watching *Goodbye Again* a generation later, it feels as if there are six half-hours in here, fighting to get out. But although these problems were painfully apparent in the broadcasts, they're virtually invisible in these selected scripts. If you sat down to watch (or read) *Goodbye Again* expecting another *Not Only . . . But Also . . .* , you'd probably be a bit disappointed. Yet since it's languished in an archive for a quarter of a century, forgotten by virtually everyone, apart from Peter and Dudley's most ardent fans, chancing upon its unfamiliar pleasures is actually a wonderful surprise.

THE MASKED PHANTOM
(ATV, 1968)

PETER: Good evening. Tonight in Worldnewspectoramaprobe, we examine the controversial sport of wrestling. Last week, I went down to the Shoreditch gymnasium to see the Masked Phantom in training . . .

(Cut to the Shoreditch gymnasium)

PETER: Well, here I am at the Shoreditch gymnasium, and we're about to see a practice bout between the Masked Phantom, who is just over here behind me, and looking very confident – a very fit, compact and agile fighter. His opponent tonight is an extremely dour and tough northerner from Scunthorpe, the Scunthorpe Strangler. I'm just going to try and get a word with them before the fight begins . . .

(The bell rings. The wrestlers start fighting)

PETER: I think I'll probably leave now, and let them get on with it . . .

(The Scunthorpe Strangler picks up Peter, and hurls him out of the ring. The Masked Phantom wins the ensuing bout, and joins Peter for an interview)

PETER: Speculation has been raging up and down the country as to the true identity of this ferocious fighter. Tonight, for the first time in the history of the universe, the Masked Phantom rips off the mask and reveals his true identity.

(The Masked Phantom removes his mask, revealing the familiar features of Dudley)

DUDLEY: *(very camp)* Hello.

PETER: Good evening, Phantom.

DUDLEY: I wish you'd call me Tom.

PETER: Tom, wrestling's a pretty rugged sport. What made you go into it?

DUDLEY: I think really to prove myself as a man, you know. The whole Sir Francis Chichester, Round The Horn bit, you know.

PETER: I understand – to prove yourself as a man. Are these fights in any way ever fixed?

DUDLEY: *(increasingly effete)* Well, I can't speak for my colleagues in the profession, but speaking purely personally, you know, I go in that ring to be champ. I go in there to win. I become like some ferocious beast, you know – like some savage monster. I pull that mask over my head and something goes pop in my mind. And then something comes over me.

PETER: The mask, presumably?

DUDLEY: Right first time, cheeky chops. Whereas in real life, look at me now. Gentle, sensitive person – wouldn't hurt a fly.

PETER: Well, we have a chance to test the sincerity of the Phantom's words, as I happen to have a fly with me here in the studio, which I'm going to place in front of him and judge his reactions. Phantom, a fly for you.

(*Peter takes a small box from his pocket, and passes it to Dudley*)

DUDLEY: A fly for you and a fig for me.

(*Dudley opens the box*)

DUDLEY: What a beauty! What a lovely creature! I think you're very cruel, keeping him cooped in here like that. (*To the fly*) Off you go, Ferdinand! (*To Peter*) Honestly, you are awful!

PETER: Proof positive, I think, of the Phantom's sincerity.

DUDLEY: If I may interrupt here, excuse me, but as Goethe, the great German poet said, *die Liebe ist Alle* – all you need is love, baby.

PETER: You mention Goethe. What are your favourite kind of books?

DUDLEY: Er, leather bound ones, mainly. You know, I love old things. Any old thing appeals to me. It's what they say about me down the gym, anyway.

PETER: Have you any interests outside the ring?

DUDLEY: My goodness gracious me, yes I have! Oh, yes! The people look at me and, you know, all they see is a great hunk of flesh. You know, I get branded as a wrestler, whereas in fact I'm interested in anything you care to mention – ceramics, pottery, sculpture, music, dancing, theatre. You name it, and I love it.

PETER: You mention theatre. What sort of roles do you see yourself in?

DUDLEY: Ooh, you're going to get me going, aren't you? Well, nothing ventured, nothing gained. I know I'm stretching my neck out, but I love Shakespeare. You know, whatever anybody says about him, I adore that man. I'd love to have a go at his King Lear, for instance.

PETER: You see yourself as King Lear?

DUDLEY: Well, shall I say I feel it here within me, you know. But all I need is a good director to coax it out. I think, oh what's his name? Come on, mutton head! Peter Brook! Peter Brook could get a wonderful Lear out of me. He could get a wonderful anything, you know. I only wish I'd put myself up for Oedipus.

PETER: You're interested in the Greek theatre, too?

DUDLEY: (ecstatic) The Greek theatre! I've loved the Greek theatre ever since Never On A Sunday. All that music and dancing, the philosophy – I love it!

PETER: Have you been to Greece recently?

DUDLEY: I only put a little body oil on before the show. Does it show?

PETER: I meant the country.

DUDLEY: Oh, I thought you meant grease! I'm sorry! I'm miles away!

PETER: Outside all your interests such as the theatre and ceramics, I understand you're also something of a singer.

DUDLEY: Yes, I've waxed my first disc, actually, just recently.

PETER: And I believe that, rather unusually, you accompany yourself on your own body.

DUDLEY: Yes, I call it deep singing. It's actually just an extension of Paganini's dictum. You know, the great violinist, Paganini.

PETER: Yes.

DUDLEY: He used to say, 'Whenever I make love to a lady, I like to think I'm playing the violin.'

PETER: I wonder if you could give an example of your singing now?

DUDLEY: I'd be delighted. I'll just whip my cosie off.

PETER: Right. Here, accompanying himself on his own body, in O For The Wings of A Dove, the Masked Phantom.

DUDLEY: Don't laugh, now.

(sings) O for the wings, for the wings of a dove

Far away, far away would I roam

(speaks, to Peter) I feel a bit thin without the backing behind, but that's the sort of thing.

PETER: I think it's very promising, and I'm sure we all wish the Masked Phantom an immense hit with his first record.

DUDLEY: You're very sweet, thank you.

LONG DISTANCE
(ATV, 1968)

This Restoration comedy of free love and costly transatlantic trunk calls is a fascinating period piece, which flaunts several of television comedy's most sacred conventions. Neither of these characters is remotely likeable, neither of them gets the comeuppance they deserve, and the audience is left stranded – not knowing when to laugh, or even whether to laugh at all.

However, despite these innovations (or, more probably, because of them) it's a riveting two-hander, enlivened by the sort of naturalistic acting you rarely see lavished on a short comic sketch, especially not on ITV. Dudley's persuasive portrait of an adulterous husband provides a foretaste of his future movie roles – and remarkably for a man whose acting was often dismissed as tense and stilted, Peter's portrayal of his sneaky sidekick is equally realistic. There's nothing awkward about Peter's performance here, and you'd be hard pushed to predict which of these men would become a Hollywood star in ten years' time. In the cynicism of its denouement, and its disinterest in chasing laughs, 'Long Distance' anticipates the gloomy malice of Peter and Dudley's stage show, Behind the Fridge. *Why on earth should sketch shows always be laugh-out-loud funny? Why not make a sketch show whose wit was too bleak for belly laughs? On this evidence, why not indeed?*

(Peter and Dudley, two self-assured, successful young men, return from a fashionable restaurant to Peter's similarly fashionable apartment.)

PETER: Would you like a drink?
DUDLEY: Yeah, I'll have a lager or a Coke or something fizzy.
PETER: Would you like some ice in it? It's a bit warm.
DUDLEY: If you don't mind.
(Peter fixes Dudley a drink.)
DUDLEY: Here, by the way, can I make a phone call?
PETER: Where to? Timbuktu?
DUDLEY: No, Mexico.
PETER: Mexico? On my phone?

DUDLEY: Well, no. I've booked a call on my number this morning, and it should be coming through about now.

PETER: So you want it to come through here?

DUDLEY: Yeah. Is that all right?

PETER: So it's to avoid your going home and taking it there?

DUDLEY: Exactly.

PETER: And I won't have to pay for it?

DUDLEY: Exactly.

PETER: Exactly.

DUDLEY: Wonderful arrangement.

(*Peter hands him a drink.*)

PETER: There you are. One nasty fizzy lager.

DUDLEY: Thank you very much indeed.

(*Dudley picks up the phone and begins to dial.*)

PETER: Calling Penny?

DUDLEY: Who else, ducky?

PETER (*sarcastic*): Your one true love.

DUDLEY: Why not? (*To the operator.*) Hello, bookings? This is Kensington, 2902. I made a call this morning, about eleven o'clock, from Swiss Cottage 9100, to Mexico . . . Yes, the number is Acapulco 748 269 . . . erm . . . (*To Peter.*) What was it?

PETER: I don't know. It's your girlfriend. Napoleon's birthday plus one – is that it?

DUDLEY: (*struggling to hear the operator*): Shut up.

PETER: The end of the war plus two . . .

DUDLEY: Shut up, shut up! (*To the operator.*) 341, extension 27 . . . Yes . . . And it was a person-to-person call from David Moon to Penny Garland . . . Yes . . . Well, it should be coming through now, yes . . . right . . . No, I'm not the subscriber on this line. He's the subscriber . . .

PETER: He's the subscriber and you're paying for it.

DUDLEY (*to the operator*): Peter Ray is the subscriber.

PETER: And you're paying for it.

DUDLEY (*to the operator*): Yes, the Swiss Cottage number takes the bill, OK? Thank you very much.

(*Dudley hangs up.*)

PETER: You're wonderfully definitive on the phone. I'll say that for you.

DUDLEY: You can say that. Yes, indeed.

PETER: What's she doing over there?

DUDLEY: Oh, she's modelling bikinis for a colour supplement.

PETER: Who with? Who's she out with?

DUDLEY: She's with that photographer, Terry – you know.

PETER: What? The one with the pink trousers?

DUDLEY: Yeah. Not much trouble there, I don't think.

PETER: No trouble at all, I shouldn't think. How long's she been away?

DUDLEY: She's been out there about two weeks. She's got another week to go.

PETER: Have you been making use of your bachelor freedom?

DUDLEY: Let me put it this way. The time has not exactly been without its compensations.

PETER: Who was it last night?

DUDLEY: D'you remember that girl Julie, from Portuguese Airlines?

PETER: The one with five cats?

DUDLEY: Oh, unbelievable. Really. Ridiculous.

PETER (*sarcastic*): I imagine your relationship with her in no way alters your very deep personal feelings for Penny. I shouldn't think that for a moment, would you?

DUDLEY: You're quite right, as a matter of fact. Look, by the way, when the call comes through, I'd be obliged if you don't fall about laughing when I say that last night we were out at Rossano's Restaurant.

PETER: Were we really?

DUDLEY: Yes, having dinner together – you and I.

PETER: Oh, yes. So we were.

DUDLEY: Last night.

PETER: I remember it.

DUDLEY: Sunday night.

PETER: Yes, I remember it. Yes.

DUDLEY: And we were with . . . erm . . .

PETER: We weren't with anybody. Don't bring anybody else in, for goodness' sake. It'll be a right muddle.

DUDLEY: No. Right. Yeah.

PETER: So we had a quiet business dinner, talked about boring things, came home and went to bed.

DUDLEY: Mmm.

PETER: Is that it?

DUDLEY: Mmm.

PETER: Is she very suspicious?

DUDLEY: No. It's just that I sound guilty when I'm on the phone to her.

PETER: You sound guilty?

DUDLEY: Yeah.

PETER: D'you think it's anything to do with the fact that you *are* guilty? Could they possibly be linked together, do you think?

DUDLEY: I don't think there's any link at all, no.

(*The telephone rings.*)

DUDLEY: Hold on.

PETER: Ah! love beckons!

(*Dudley picks up the phone.*)

DUDLEY: Kensington 2902 . . . Yes, thank you. (*To Peter.*) Watch it. (*Into the telephone.*) Hello?

PETER: Hello!

DUDLEY (*on the phone*): Hello, Penny?

PETER: Hello, darling!

DUDLEY (*to Peter*): Shut up, I can't hear her. (*On the phone.*) Penny?

PETER: Yes!

DUDLEY (*on the phone*): Penny, I can hardly hear you!

PETER: I can hear you!

DUDLEY (*to Peter*): Shut up, I can't hear the girl! (*On the phone.*) Penny, I can hardly hear you! . . . I know it's a bad line, but I can't get another one. I've been trying to get this one all day . . .

(*Peter does his utmost to distract Dudley, making incriminating noises, turning up the record player, whispering sweet nothings in his ear.*)

DUDLEY: (*to Peter*): Shut up! I can't hear the girl! (*On the phone.*) How are you, anyway? . . . I just wanted to say I miss you very much . . . (*Shouts.*) I said I miss you very much! . . . I'm not shouting, it's just that you didn't hear me the first time, so I said it a bit louder the second time, and it's a very resonant room . . . Yeah . . . How is it out there, all right? . . . How's Terry, eh? . . . Has he made a pounce yet? Hammering on the door at four in the morning in his pink trousers, yeah? . . . Anyway, I just wanted to say I love you . . . (*Shouts.*) I love you! . . . L – leather, O – ovaries, V – vanity, E – eczema, I love you! . . . I'm not angry! I can hardly bloody hear you! . . . I can't exactly be intimate with Peter grinning across the way, three thousand miles of Atlantic in between . . . Of course it's a Kensington number because I'm at Peter's. I'm not at Swiss Cottage, our own number . . . No, I've transferred it here . . . There's nobody else here except Peter! There's not a party going on! He's put the record player on.

(*Dudley tries to fend off Peter's advances.*)

DUDLEY (*to Peter*): Stop it! She thinks there's a bird! You speak to her! Tell her it's you!

(*Dudley passes the phone to Peter.*)

PETER (*on the phone, in a shrill falsetto*): Hi there, Penny. It's good to talk to you. You've got nothing to worry about. What David and I have is purely physical . . .

DUDLEY: It's a pound a minute, mate.

PETER: (*on the phone, reverting to his normal voice*): No, Penny, it is me. It's Peter. It's not David imitating Peter. It's Peter.

DUDLEY: And this is David.

PETER: (*on the phone*): This is Peter, this is David, speaking to you from over the Atlantic.

DUDLEY: Together.

PETER: (*on the phone*): Sorry about that. I was a bit drunk, that's all. How are you? . . . Oh well, you know, very dull over here. Rotten weather. We went out to dinner this evening, as indeed we did, er, last night. We went to, um, Rossano's . . . Yeah, it was quite nice. A bit, you know, dull. Anyway, he misses you very much. I've never seen him looking so, you know, woebe-gone. He's a real ghost of his former self. Anyway, he wants to talk to you so I'll hand you back to him. See you when you get back, eh? All right? Bye-bye.

(*Peter passes Dudley the phone.*)

DUDLEY (*to Peter*): Wonderful performance. (*On the phone.*) All right? . . . Yes . . . What d'you mean I don't talk to you the way Peter does. He doesn't have to live with you, does he? . . . Gawd blimey! . . . Yeah, it was very nice . . . Yeah, we were at Rossano's last night, Sunday night . . . Yeah, I know Rossano's is closed on a Sunday night . . .

PETER: Her time, her time! Six hours!

DUDLEY (*to Peter*): Oh, yes! (*Into phone.*) No, but you're six hours behind us, you see.

PETER: Exactly. Lunchtime is her dinnertime.

DUDLEY (*into phone*): Yeah, when I said we were at dinner at Rossano's, we were at lunch – your dinnertime!

PETER: Her dinnertime, our lunchtime.

DUDLEY (*into phone*): Well, Penny darling – Penny, you either believe me or you don't, darling.

PETER (*falsetto*): I don't believe you.

DUDLEY (*to Peter*): Shut up! (*On the phone.*) No, we're still talking, thank you very much, operator. Hello? We're still talking . . . Operator, I don't need to be told from you what to say to the girl. I'll say what I like, operator . . . Get off the line, you Mexican bint! Who won the World Cup, eh?

PETER: Who's that?

DUDLEY (*to Peter*): It's the Mexican operator on the line.

PETER: Hey, you're sure it's not Terry?

DUDLEY (*into phone*): Hold on. (*To Peter.*) What?

PETER: You're sure it's not Terry in the room with her, doing his Mexican bit? He does a Mexican accent.

DUDLEY (*into phone*): Penny! Is that Terry in the room there with you, doing his Mexican operator's voice? . . . Is he in there with you? . . . You sound a bit tense . . . Not very convincing . . . Yeah, I bet he's in there . . . Yeah, fine! Same to you, darling . . . Yeah? Oh, I might see you in a week's time and I might not!

(*Dudley slams down the phone.*)

PETER: How did it go? All right?

DUDLEY: Great! Marvellous! Fifty quid! Fifty quid to know that

that Terry is in the room with his pink trousers on, about to take her off to a Mexican siesta!

PETER: It's wonderful how the phone brings you closer together, isn't it? Marvellous thing.

DUDLEY: Two weeks away, two weeks away from me – she can't be faithful. She has to grab the first thing that falls into her lap – marvellous, innit?

PETER: That Terry does very well, doesn't he?

DUDLEY: Yeah. He pretends he's a poof and makes it a challenge to their powers of feminine persuasion.

PETER: Well, as long as it works, ducky – that's what I say.

DUDLEY: Oh, yeah. Fine, they –

(*A buzz on the intercom.*)

DUDLEY: That must be the girls!

PETER: Aha! (*On the intercom.*) Is that the delicious Ingrid?

DUDLEY: And is that the sensual Barbara?

PETER (*on the intercom*): Come on up, girls. We're ready for you. OK? See you. (*To Dudley.*) Hey, put a record on.

DUDLEY: Right.

(*Dudley puts a record on the turntable – the Beatles'* Rubber Soul.)

DUDLEY: Here, can I borrow some of your aftershave?

PETER: Yeah, and take the phone off the hook. We don't want any more of that trouble, do we?

SHERLOCK HOLMES INVESTIGATES
(ATV, 1968)

Dudley plays Doctor Watson to Peter's Sherlock Holmes, in this adept Arthur Conan Doyle parody, which predated their Hound of the Baskervilles *movie by almost a decade. And by common consent, there are probably more laughs in this brief sketch than there were in that entire film. Peter's Holmes is an acute pastiche of Basil Rathbone, and Dudley's matter-of-fact Watson is his perfect foil. If only they'd maintained these conventional playing styles in the subsequent feature film, then their movie-making partnership might not have shuddered to such an untimely halt. Peter opted for a Jewish Holmes and Dudley for a Welsh Watson, and 'Sherlock Holmes Investigates the Case of the One-Legged Dog' remains a cinematic mirage – a tantalising trailer for the great Cook and Moore movie that never was.*

(*The scene: a wooded river bank. Watson is fishing. Holmes is playing the violin.*)

WATSON (*voice-over*): Undoubtedly, one of the most mysterious episodes during the course of my acquaintance with Sherlock Holmes was the curious case of the one-legged dog. For the first time I can recall, Holmes seemed baffled, and with some difficulty I persuaded him to take a few days off in the country. Travelling light, with a violin and a crate of cocaine, we camped comfortably by the banks of the River Stron, a pleasant little tributary of the Striddle. The country air, however, did very little to calm the restless mind of my eminent companion. I had never seen the greatest thinking mechanism in the history of Europe so absorbed in the icily calm process of ruthless mental analysis.

HOLMES (*shouts*): Who did it? Who bloody did it? Don't sit there, Watson, you great boring fat toad of a doctor! Do something!

WATSON (*voice-over*): I was used to Holmes's erratic outbursts of emotion, caused in no small way by the three bottles of an excellent Château Blanc de la Touche consumed in a huff before lunch. I resumed fishing with the quiet satisfaction of having been completely humiliated.

(*An unseen hand hurls a dagger at Watson. It embeds itself in his chest, but Watson remains oblivious.*)

WATSON (*voice-over*): It was at that moment that something struck me.

HOLMES: Tell me, Watson – did you detect the sound of something going . . .

(*Holmes reproduces the sound of the dagger exactly.*)

WATSON: Yes, I took it to be the sad cry of some lonely marsh bird.

HOLMES: If I'm not much mistaken, Watson, you're mistaken. What you in fact heard was the sound of the trajectory and impact of a small Bavarian hunting knife, manufactured in Munich in the spring of 1833 by the firm of Grosselweik & Sons.

WATSON: Don't be preposterous, Holmes. Don't be preposterous.

HOLMES: Preposterous perhaps, my dear Watson, but if you examine the left-hand side of your ribcage, with particular attention to the gap between your third and fourth ribs, I think you'll find the object in question.

WATSON: Good heavens, Holmes! You're incredible!

(*Watson removes the dagger – there is a letter attached to it.*)

WATSON: Holmes, there must be some mistake – this letter is for you.

(*Watson passes him the letter.*)

WATSON (*voice-over*): He opened it.

(*Holmes opens the envelope and hands the letter back to Watson.*)

WATSON: Now what?

HOLMES: Read it.

WATSON: Right. (*Voice-over.*) I read it.

HOLMES: Aloud. To me.

WATSON (*reads*): 'Dear Sherlock Holmes and idiotic accomplice . . .' (*Voice-over.*) A reference I took to be to myself. (*Reads.*) 'If you wish to find the body of young Daisy Adler, don't for goodness sake go to Cotley Spinney, where it most assuredly is not. Yours sincerely, a one-legged dog.' (*Voice-over*) An immense feeling of relief seized me. At least one hiding place had finally been ruled out. (*To Holmes.*) Well, that's a start, Holmes. At least we know we needn't bother to go to Cotley Spinney.

HOLMES: Not so fast, Watson.

WATSON: Why not? I mean, if there's one fellow who knows where the body's not, it's the one-legged dog.

HOLMES: And don't you think that's precisely the reaction our adversary is hoping for? In my view, Watson, Cotley Spinney is the one place that we shall find the body. Come, Doctor.

(*Holmes and Watson advance through the wood. Holmes strides down the woodland path, playing the violin as he goes, while Watson struggles through the bushes.*)

WATSON (*voice-over*): I took the sensible precaution of threading my way through the dense undergrowth, whilst my intrepid companion strode noisily along the open pathway, playing the mad scene from Verdi's *Il Doctori et Stupido*. I must confess I was puzzled by his behaviour.

HOLMES: Come out of that shrubbery, Watson. Don't you see it will afford you no protection? It's the one place our friend, the enemy, will be looking. His suspicions will scarcely be aroused, however, by the sight of two ordinary wayfarers playing the mad scene from Verdi's *Il Doctori et Stupido*.

(*We see a man hammering a sign reading 'Not This Way' to a tree.*)

HOLMES: Did you hear the sound of something going . . .

(*Holmes reproduces the sound of the hammer exactly.*)

WATSON: Yes I did. I took it to be the persistent tapping of our industrious little English friend, the woodpecker.

HOLMES: I think you are mistaken, Watson. The sound you heard was, in fact, made by a small Bavarian hammer, manufactured in the spring of 1833, by Grosselweik & Son of Munich.

WATSON (*voice-over*): I realised for the eight millionth time that I was in the presence of a genius of the first water and a violinist of the second water. (*Reading the sign on the tree.*) Well, not this way then, Holmes.

WATSON: But precisely this way!

(*We hear the sound of a man shouting woof, woof.*)

HOLMES: Our one-legged canine adversary! If I'm not mistaken, the grave of the unfortunate Miss Adler will not be far.

WATSON (*voice-over*): We entered Cotley Spinney cautiously. Suddenly, Holmes pounced.

(*Holmes picks up some leaves and examines them with his magnifying glass.*)

WATSON: What is it, Holmes?

HOLMES (*deep in thought*): Leaves. Dead leaves.

WATSON (*also deep in thought*): Leaves, dead leaves. Leaves . . . dead leaves! Dead leaves, Holmes! Dead leaves! Leaves, dead leaves! Dead leaves – Daisy Adler!

HOLMES: No. Dead leaves.

WATSON (*voice-over*): I had to demur to Holmes's superior analysis. We sat for a moment of quiet rumination on a leafy hillock.

(*HOLMES and WATSON sit on a leafy hillock, oblivious to the female corpse, half buried beside them.*)

WATSON (*voice-over*): I asked him a question that was uppermost in my mind. (*To Holmes.*) Holmes, what is that sinister ticking noise I hear? (*On the tree beside them is a cuckoo clock.*)

HOLMES: It sounds to me like some form of primitive explosive device, of the type manufactured in Bavaria in the spring of 1833 by Grosselweik & Sons of Munich, powered, I should say, by a water driven cuckoo clock and, by the increased tempo of the mechanism, due to explode in approximately thirty seconds.

WATSON (*voice-over*): I was much calmed by Holmes's explanation, but a further distraction was in store.

(*A bell rings. Watson opens his Gladstone bag and pulls out a telephone.*)

WATSON: Excuse me, Holmes. (*Into phone.*) Doctor Watson here . . . Oh, I see. Well, give her plenty of hot water, and for goodness' sake keep pumping.

(*Watson picks up his Gladstone bag and dashes through the forest. The cuckoo clock cuckoos and explodes.*)

WATSON (*voice-over*): As I left Holmes, I thought I heard the joyous cry of the first cuckoo of spring.

WAR CORRESPONDENT
(ATV, 1968)

(*Peter plays Gavin Thread, a well-spoken war reporter*)

PETER: Hello, this is Gavin Thread, reporting to you from the battle-scarred field outside the rebel held town of Semantics.

Fierce hand to mouth fighting has been going on here for several weeks and the situation is a trifle confused, to say the least, but I've got reason to believe that a small brigade of the Hungerford Light Infantry is holed out just behind me – there, on the left – and I'm going over there, just now, to have a word with them, to clear up exactly what the situation is.

(*Oblivious to the shells exploding all around him, Gavin Thread prances through a hail of bullets, and reaches a shallow trench full of soldiers*)

PETER: Hello, I'm Gavin Thread from English television. Who's in charge here?

DUDLEY: Sergeant McPepper here.

PETER: Oh, hello Sergeant! (*Peter's pleasantries are rudely interrupted by a flurry of gunfire*) I'm sorry, are there people out there?

DUDLEY: There's an enemy sniper, you see, holed up in a small house over there.

PETER: Oh, I see – over there.

DUDLEY: Aye.

PETER: How long has he been in there?

DUDLEY: He's been in there approximately two years.

PETER: Two years? As long as that?

DUDLEY: And we're going to flush him out today.

PETER: This is mortar fire, is it, coming over at the moment?

DUDLEY: Yes.

PETER: I wonder if you could tell us something about this mortar fire and how it affects morale and so on. Want to say something about it for the viewers?

DUDLEY: I'd prefer to . . .

PETER: Into that camera, over there.

DUDLEY: Oh, good evening. I'd prefer to launch the attack while there's the slightest element of surprise, still. So, Gavin, if you wouldn't mind, you and the viewing millions, I'd like to get Operation 100% Successful, as we call it, underway.

PETER: That's a very good name. There's just one thing I wondered. There's a bit of cloud going under the sun at the moment. It's very difficult for the camera boys to sort of pick up in this murky light. Do you think we could delay it just a few seconds, so we could get a better shot?

DUDLEY: Well, we were hoping to use the gloom to infiltrate under maximum cover, you see.

PETER: I see. Well, it's your war. You get on with it however you like. I mean, just carry on as if I wasn't here.

DUDLEY: Right. Arkwright! Get in your position and wait for my signals.

PETER: I wonder if I could just have a word with Arkwright. (*To Private Arkwright, aka Rodney Bewes*) Before you go, Arkwright, I just wondered if I could ask you a couple of questions. Tell me, is this your first sniper flushing?

PRIVATE ARKWRIGHT: Oh, no – it's not me first flush. I've flushed before. But it's certainly my first time on television.

PETER: Not been on television before?

PRIVATE ARKWRIGHT: No. Is it really on television?

PETER: Yes, you're on now. That's the camera, over there. You can look into it.

PRIVATE ARKWRIGHT: Oh, that's fantastic, isn't it? I can't believe it!

PETER: It's true.

PRIVATE ARKWRIGHT: I can't believe it!

PETER: How do you feel about it?

PRIVATE ARKWRIGHT: Well, I've not been on before. I mean, you feel a bit of a fool, don't you? I expect you feel a bit of a fool, don't you?

PETER: You'll soon get used to it. You'll find techniques to overcome it. You've got a little bit of shine on your nose. If I could just powder it up, like that.

(*Peter powders Private Arkwright's nose*)

PRIVATE ARKWRIGHT: I've been a bit poorly, actually, Gavin.

PETER: Have you?

PRIVATE ARKWRIGHT: Yes. I've had the flu, actually.

PETER: I thought you looked a bit rheumy eyed. Have you got anything you'd like to say to the friends at home?

PRIVATE ARKWRIGHT: (*stage struck*) What? To the, er . . .

PETER: To the people there? Would you like to say something?

PRIVATE ARKWRIGHT: Well, er, nah!

PETER: Well, just a short message. Come along.

PRIVATE ARKWRIGHT: Well, all right. Um . . . Hello Mum, hello Dad, hello Daphne. It won't be long now. Hello Auntie Elise, and a big hello to Mr Deacon and family, the newsagent at the corner of Hollybrush Road. Oh, that's advertising, isn't it? I shouldn't have . . .

PETER: Don't worry. It's quite all right. It's your first time on television. I understand.

PRIVATE ARKWRIGHT: Well, and I'd also like to say hello to Mrs Wainwright and her daughters, Beryl, Daphne and Doreen, and Mrs Clisby. Hope you're better, Mrs Clisby.

PETER: So do I, and . . .

PRIVATE ARKWRIGHT: And could we have for us all Engelbert Humperdinck singing The Last Waltz?

DUDLEY: Shut up, that man! Come on, get going!

PETER: And tell me, sergeant, have you got any requests you'd like to make?

DUDLEY: Yes I do, but I don't think it's suitable for family audiences.

PETER: This war fire is certainly very accurate, isn't it?

DUDLEY: Certain is, aye.

(*Dudley advances into battle*)

PETER: Of course. (*To Private Forsythe, aka Brian Murphy*) Forsythe, just before you go, I wonder if I could have a word with you. How is the state of morale in the platoon, and, in particular, what do you think of your platoon commander?

PRIVATE FORSYTHE: Well, to be perfectly candid, I mean, strictly off the record, I reckon he's dia-bleeding-bolical.

PETER: Really?

PRIVATE FORSYTHE: Yeah. I mean he's got no tactical sense, has he? The men can't stand him. I mean, what he knows about sniper, er, sniper . . .

PETER: Flushing?

PRIVATE FORSYTHE: Flushing, yeah! I mean, that could be written on a gnat's backside.

PETER: Yes, right. Controversial views. I'm now going to put them to Sergeant McPepper himself. (*To Dudley*) Sergeant, I've just been talking with Forsythe over there, and he told me, completely off the record, of course, that he has no confidence in your tactical skill or your command. What is your reaction to this kind of criticism?

DUDLEY: Gavin, completely off the record and in total confidence, of course, my considered response to your interesting question is shut your face or I'll stuff your teeth down your windpipe!

PETER (*to camera*): Well, naturally nerves become extremely frayed. (*To Dudley*) Now, sergeant, I notice you put Arkwright over on the left, and you sent Forsythe over on the right. Now, is this just random – or is this a plan of some kind?

DUDLEY: Arkwright's going out on the left to draw the enemy fire. Forsythe and people are going on the right with us to form a classic Alamein pincer movement, to expose the enemy's flank.

PETER: It sounds a very good plan, and I for one can't understand why Forsythe isn't confident in it. Now, tell me, when does the attack take place?

DUDLEY: In approximately twenty seconds.

PETER: Twenty seconds. Well, at this tense moment, I'm going to try and get a word with the sniper, before he's actually flushed out.

(*Peter dashes over to the sniper's hideout*)

DUDLEY: Come back here, you Sassenach git!

PETER: Well, here I am at the enemy's hideout. Just going over to try and get a word with him if I can. Hello, enemy sniper? Are you there? Are you in there? Ah, he seems to be down here. Well then, enemy sniper, how do you feel about being flushed out?

(*The sniper says something completely indecipherable and untranslatable*)

PETER: Well, he sounds very confident, but I wonder if he'll be quite so confident when I tell him about Sergeant McPepper's brilliant plan. Enemy sniper, do you realise that while your attention is being diverted on the left by Forsythe and his platoon,

Arkwright and his lot will be forming a classic pincer movement in the style of Alamein? How do you feel about that?

(*The sniper says something else completely indecipherable and untranslatable and then 'thank you very much*')

PETER: Now back to Sergeant McPepper. (*To Dudley*) Well, I just had a word with the sniper, and I told him your plan, and he seemed not to like it a bit.

DUDLEY: You told him the plan, did you Gavin?

PETER: Yes, I told him the plan and he was thoroughly disconcerted.

DUDLEY: Well, Gavin, in addition to revealing our position here, you've also made it completely impossible to catch that enemy sniper we've been after for the last two years.

PETER: I'm terribly sorry. How silly of me. It's my first war. I don't really know what I'm up to. What are you going to do now?

DUDLEY: Well, Gavin, I think, in the circumstances there's only one thing I can do, and that is take this revolver . . .

PETER: Oh yes, I know those. My father had one to shoot rabbits.

DUDLEY: Take this revolver and point it at your chest, pull the trigger, and thus resulting, Gavin, love, in your instantaneous demise.

PETER (*to camera*): A summary execution – an ugly factor in any war, but one which is increasingly understandable in situations such as these. (*To John Wells*) Johnny Sound, can you cope with an explosion at close quarters?

JOHNNY SOUND: Can you give us a level?

PETER: Just shoot up in the air, would you, sergeant?

(DUDLEY fires a shot into the air)

JOHNNY SOUND: Yes, that's fantastic. If you could do it a bit more off mike.

DUDLEY: I'll do it a bit more off mike and a bit more on Gavin, if you see what I mean. (*Hysterical, to himself*) I mustn't break. I must not break!

JOHNNY SOUND: Death of Gavin Thread, slate 44, take one. Action!

(*Dudley shoots Peter*)

PETER: This is Gavin Thread signing off and saying I won't be with you next week, or any other week for that matter.

AVERSION THERAPY
(ATV, 1968)

Peter always relished playing psychiatrists, despite (or perhaps because of) his scepticism about psychoanalysis. Dudley, naturally, was very well versed in the role of libidinous patient.

PETER: Right you are, Sonia. Would you send in the next patient please?

SONIA: This way, Mr Wetherskill.

(*Enter Dudley.*)

PETER: Ah, Mr Wetherskill. Come in, five guineas, sit down, ten guineas, how are you, fifteen guineas.

DUDLEY: I'm very well, thank you.

PETER: Well, you may be physically very well, but obviously you've got some sort of a problem, otherwise you wouldn't have come to see me.

DUDLEY: Yes, true enough.

PETER: Good, well, I like you to be very open, very frank with me. Treat me as if I was your oldest friend.

DUDLEY: Well, in that case I'll get straight down to it. I've been married for seven years.

PETER: Seven years. Really. Oh dear. Yes, it's a terribly dangerous period, isn't it – seven years? Did you see that wonderful motion picture? What was it called? *The Seven Year Marriage Bug*, was it?

DUDLEY: *The Seven Year Itch*?

PETER: *The Seven Year Itch*. What wonderful entertainment it was, about a basically very tragic subject. Basically very tragic, but most amusing.

DUDLEY: Yes, I loved it enormously. Well, this is the thing, you see. I've been married for seven years, and I've got a wife and two lovely children.

PETER: A wife and two lovely children. Do you mind if I take notes during the conversation? It'd be a great aid to me.

DUDLEY: Not at all.

PETER: A wife and two lovely children, yes.

DUDLEY: And the thing is, for the last four years I've been having an affair with my secretary, Jane.

PETER: You've been having an affair for four years with your secretary, Jane. And you're married to this woman . . .

DUDLEY: Mary.

PETER: You're married to this woman, Mary, and you've been having an affair with Jane. Yes, I understand.

DUDLEY: Well, the thing is, you see, she's a very attractive girl, my secretary.

PETER: Jane. Very attractive girl, is she?

DUDLEY: In fact, I've got a photograph of her here.

PETER: Oh, you've got a photograph. Oh, I'd love to see that, if you have it.

(*Dudley passes Peter a photograph.*)

PETER: Oh, my goodness me, yes. She's a very attractive girl, Jane. I can understand any able-bodied man having an affair with this, yes. She's a delicious piece of crumpet, I think the modern slang is. Superbly well proportioned, yes.

DUDLEY: But the thing is, you see, what is difficult to explain is that my wife is equally as attractive, and I'm head over heels in love with her.

PETER: With your wife?

DUDLEY: Yes, and this is the awful thing, you see.

PETER: I wonder if you have a photograph of your wife I could see. Would that be possible?

DUDLEY: You want to see a photograph of my wife?

PETER: I'd love to see a picture of your wife, yes.

DUDLEY: Well, if it's absolutely necessary.

PETER: Yes, well it would help me a great deal to see a picture of your wife and compare it.

(*Dudley passes Peter another photograph.*)

PETER: Thank you very much. I see. Oh yes.

(*Peter compares the two photographs.*)

PETER: And this is your secretary, Jane.

DUDLEY: That's my secretary, Jane.

PETER: And this is your wife, Mary.

DUDLEY: Agh!

PETER: Yes. This one is Jane and this one is your wife.

DUDLEY: Agh!

PETER: Mr Wetherskill, I couldn't help noticing that when I showed you the picture of your wife, Mary, you emitted what can only be described as a spontaneous scream.

DUDLEY: Yes, you see this is the awful thing, but every time I see my wife, I scream. I don't know what it is. It's something . . .

PETER: Something involuntary. You scream whenever you see your wife, and this, I imagine, to a certain extent, is undermining the marriage relationship.

DUDLEY: To a large extent. I mean, I can only say things to her from another room, you see, really.

PETER: Yes, this is stopping you getting terribly close.

DUDLEY: It is, yes.

PETER: And you want to bring this affair with secretary, Jane, to an end.

(*Peter shows Dudley the photograph of Jane.*)

PETER: And get on to a firm marital basis with your wife, Mary.

(*Peter shows Dudley the photograph of Mary.*)

DUDLEY: Agh! Yes, I wish you wouldn't do that.

PETER: I'm sorry. I'll keep her to myself in future. Right, well, I don't see why this shouldn't be done. One method, of course, would be deep psychoanalysis – delving deep into your past to discover the subconscious reasons why you scream when you see your wife. For example, it might be possible that when you were a child in your pram, a thrush may have popped into the pram and pecked you on the cheek, causing you to scream, and you might subconsciously associate the thrush with your wife, Mary. Has she got a very long nose?

DUDLEY: No, it's not very sharp, she hasn't any feathers, doesn't eat worms – that sort of thing.

PETER: No, it was purely an example, Mr Wetherskill. But this is a very lengthy process, seventy-five guineas, so I would suggest a somewhat more radical way of rooting this problem out, and in particular I would suggest a course of aversion therapy.

DUDLEY: Aversion therapy?

PETER: Aversion therapy.

DUDLEY: What does that entail?

PETER: Well, it entails this – it's a process which I pioneered myself, in the United States of America, with great success. I had particular success with the famous cowboy film star. Do you remember him – Roy Mix?

DUDLEY: Oh yes, what a performer!

PETER: He was in a terrible state, you see, because he had a wife and two lovely children, like yourself, but unfortunately, on the set, he had become infatuated with his horse, Trigger. He'd become madly infatuated with his horse – a magnificent animal.

DUDLEY: A wonderful beast.

PETER: A magnificent animal, and he was living in the stables with Trigger. And he came to me, wanting to get back to his wife, but unable to, because of his infatuation. And I prescribed a course of aversion therapy, and the method was this – I flashed up a picture of his horse, Trigger, on the screen, and then I hit him round the head with a cricket bat. And then I flashed up a picture of his wife on the screen, and gave him some strawberry yoghurt, to which Roy, like so many of the Hollywood greats, was addicted.

DUDLEY: Yes.

PETER: And very rapidly, he began to associate pain with his horse, Trigger.

DUDLEY: The cricket bat.

PETER: The cricket bat, precisely. And pleasure with his wife.

DUDLEY: Strawberry yoghurt.

PETER: Yes. And very soon, he went right off his horse, and back on to his wife. The only trouble was, it rather marred his screen career because the public weren't quite ready for the sight of Roy Mix careering round the prairie on his wife's shoulders, you see. It made it a little tricky for him, but I think a happy marriage is worth so much more than all the glitter and gloss and tinsel of show business.

DUDLEY: Oh, certainly, yes.

PETER: If we just turn the chair round, like that, you see, and then I'll feed these two pictures of your wife and your secretary into the slide machine, and now all I'm going to do here, don't be alarmed, is to plug you in. There you are, nicely plugged in. Now, let me explain. When I flash a picture of your secretary up on the screen, you will sensate – or rather feel, I use the word sensate advisedly, and wrongly, indeed – you will feel a mild electric shock. Nothing fatal, but nevertheless . . . It seems to amuse you.

DUDLEY (*corpsing*): It does, yes.

PETER: A mild electric shock, and you will begin to associate pain with your secretary, Jane. In fact, I'd like you to say the words – pain, Jane.

DUDLEY: Pain with Jane, on the main, er, mainly . . .

PETER: Precisely, yes – and completely wrong. Well, are you ready for a picture of your secretary? Here comes your secretary, and . . . come along, Jane. There we are, and . . .

(*A buzzer sounds.*)

DUDLEY: Agh!

PETER: That's right. Pain with Jane, pain with Jane. And here comes Jane again.

(*A buzzer sounds again.*)

DUDLEY: Agh! Agh!

PETER: I think that's probably enough of Jane. Now I'd like to put up a few pictures of your wife Mary on the screen, and I'd like you to associate her with pleasure. And I was wondering if any of these particular comestibles appealed to you – these sort of choc ices and lollies and things like that.

DUDLEY: Well, I'm very partial to Turkish delight.

PETER: Turkish delight, right. Whenever I flash a picture of your wife up on the screen, I'll give you a little bit of Turkish delight as a reward. Are you ready?

DUDLEY: Yes.

PETER: Here comes your wife, up on the screen. Think of the pleasure as your wife comes up on the screen.

DUDLEY: Agh!

(*Peter shoves some Turkish delight into Dudley's mouth.*)

PETER: And munch into that lovely Turkish delight. And now here comes Jane again. Pain, pain, pain with Jane.

(*A buzzer sounds.*)

DUDLEY: Agh!

PETER: And now here comes Mary again, your lovely wife.

DUDLEY: Agh!

(*Peter shoves some more Turkish delight into Dudley's mouth.*)

PETER: And tuck into that lovely Turkish delight. Oh, what pleasure, pleasure, pleasure, pleasure, pleasure. Well, I think that's probably enough treatment for the first week. I think after about six weeks, you should be well on the way to a cure. It's delicious, isn't it?

DUDLEY: It is delicious, but the point is . . . (*He corpses.*)

PETER: The point is that you're spluttering, Mr Wetherskill.

DUDLEY: It's got so much powder on it. When do I start screaming at my secretary?

PETER: It may mean that you will start screaming at your secretary, but I don't think that really matters. I mean, that's what secretaries are there for. (*Screams.*) Sonia!

(*Enter Sonia.*)

PETER (*to Sonia*): If you'd fix up an appointment for Mr Wetherskill at the same time next week? Would you do that? Thank you very much. (*To Dudley.*) Very nice to meet you. I'm so glad the treatment has gone so well, and that will be a hundred and seventy-five guineas.

DUDLEY: Agh!

(*Peter shoves some more Turkish delight into Dudley's mouth.*)

PETER: Pleasure, pleasure, pleasure. It really is very good. One could become addicted to this stuff, you know.

HERMAN HERMITZ REPORTS
(ATV, 1968)

Peter plays Herman Hermitz, an earnest German news reporter presenting an earnest German news report about the causes of violence in modern Britain.

HERMAN HERMITZ: Violence is very much in the air these days. What is the cause of violence? Why is it on the increase? In order to find out the answer to some of these questions, I spoke to some of the people who are directly involved. I talked first to a young man who is a convicted soccer hooligan – his name, Ted Stagger.

(*Enter Dudley as Ted Stagger, a football fan with a thick London accent*)

HERMAN HERMITZ: Ted, tell me – what drives you to this violence at football matches?

TED STAGGER: Well, I normally take me dad's Vauxhall – or else I nick the nearest vehicle.

HERMAN HERMITZ: What I was meaning was, what are the causes of these fracas on the terraces in which you are involved?

TED STAGGER: Well, of course now you're asking about the fracarse on the terraces. Well, I'll tell you straight off – I do not start the fighting myself.

HERMAN HERMITZ: You mean you are provoked?

TED STAGGER: I never retaliate unless provoked, right? Take last Saturday, for instance. In the stand, I'm waiting for the football match to start. Very patient. Quiet. A small, quiet, dangerous Hitler type bloke comes and stands beside me, blatantly flaunting a rosette purporting to be representative of the visiting team of thugs who are about to sully the verdant pitch of the eleven good men and true of Stoubridge United.

HERMAN HERMITZ: This is your team, Stoubridge United?

TED STAGGER: Yes. (*He chants*) S, T, O, U, B, R, I, D . . . (*He blows a raspberry*) G, E. (*He sings*) We are the champions!

HERMAN HERMITZ: I'm sure you are. What did you do then?

TED STAGGER: Faced with this indisputable act of aggression, I done what any normal red blooded supporter of Stoubridge would do. I asked him politely for a light, and while his hands were in his pockets, I laid one on him, didn't I? Bang bang, bang bang bang! We are the champions!

HERMAN HERMITZ: So without this provocation, no violence would have occurred?

TED STAGGER: No. I mean, I never start fights. I only finish them. (*he chants*) S, T, O, U, B, R, I, D . . . (*he blows a raspberry*) G, E.

(*Exit Dudley, singing*)

HERMAN HERMITZ: Thank you, Ted Stagger. I wonder if we can learn something about violence in human beings by studying violence in the animal kingdom? Professor Lubowksi in his book on aggression has pointed out through his experiments that spiders are often driven to fury by certain colours. For example, the blue bottom of a bluebottle fly will cause a spider to go mad with rage. Perhaps some crowd hostility towards the police can be explained in these terms. More likely, it can't. Nevertheless, I spoke to Inspector Knacker of the Yard about it.

(*PETER plays Inspector Knacker, standing outside a jeweller's shop, oblivious to the robbery that is in progress behind him*)

INSPECTOR KNACKER: You know, I think the only way we're going to be able to cope with this problem – and let's face it, it is a problem, it's a big problem and we've got to face it, let's face it fair and square in the face – if we're going to face this problem of the rising tide of crime and violence, I think we in the police have to be eternally vigilant. I think vigilance is the watchword here. If we aren't vigilant, then we aren't going to detect the crimes. And if we don't detect the crimes, we can't find out who did it. After the vigilance, of course, comes the digulence. We've got to be digulent, going round from house to house, searching the house, looking for fibres in the pockets, vacuum cleaning the bodies, inspecting the teeth, seeing if the teeth tally with the bullets found in the corpse – this type of thing. Modern forensic medicine, wristwatches, hovercraft, two way radio – one way to the police. But of course, even with all these modern aids, we still rely on you, the general public, going out and committing the crimes. Then there'd be nothing at all for us to do. Thank you. Goodnight.

HERMAN HERMITZ: Strong views from the police. I then decided to ask an ordinary member of the public her views on violence.

(*Dudley plays an ordinary member of the public, a housewife in a headscarf and pinafore, speaking in a working-class falsetto accent*)

ORDINARY MEMBER OF THE PUBLIC: My husband, Ronald, is a manure spreader, and of course when he comes home, his clothes are very filthy, and he only has to come through the door and I go . . . (She sniffs) . . . And I know he's about. And a couple of spoonfuls of our stuff in the wash makes it come out beautiful and clean.

HERMAN HERMITZ: Look, I was asking you about violence, madam.

ORDINARY MEMBER OF THE PUBLIC: Oh yes, that's the one with the hole, isn't it? I can't tell it from butter.

HERMAN HERMITZ: Thank you so much, madam.

ORDINARY MEMBER OF THE PUBLIC: Thank you.

HERMAN HERMITZ: I decided to give up speaking to ordinary members of the public, and I talked instead to Justin Honeyblade, one of London's leading male models, who has strong views on the subject.

(*Dudley plays Justin Honeyblade, a posh, effete male model, being made up for a photo shoot*)

JUSTIN HONEYBLADE: I'm quite convinced that violence is a product of frustration. I mean if one is some sort of spiv in a boring, dismal job, then of course one's going to need an outlet and veer towards this violence thing. (*To make-up artist*) Sorry, sweetie. Shall I do it? (*To the camera*) I think it's frightfully important that one finds a satisfying, meaningful, absolutely fulfilling type of work. (*To make-up artist*) Johnny, sorry. (*To the camera*) And then, of course, the whole problem never arises, does it?

HERMAN HERMITZ: Justin Honeyblade sees the answer in creative outlets for young people. I spoke next to Mrs Agnes Chadawade, a lady magistrate of many years experience.

(*Peter plays Agnes Chadawade, an elderly, upper class, softly spoken woman*)

AGNES CHADAWADE: Hello. I've been in probation work for forty years and, do you know, whenever I have one of those strapping young thugs up before me I feel an overwhelming desire to communicate, to get through to them. It seems so tragic to me to send one of these young, healthy boys down to a borstal institution where they're only going to meet and rub shoulders with hardened criminals. So what I usually do is sentence them to about six months light dusting round at my house. There's two of the lads now, chintzing up the bedroom. I think it does them good and I know it's getting me somewhere.

HERMAN HERMITZ: A worrying problem in some parts of the country is the undoubted increase in so-called senile delinquency. Old people, frustrated perhaps by their dismal and drab surroundings, are seeking excitement in a life of crime. I asked two such persons, the notorious Fred and Deirdre Nimble, what led them to this kind of antisocial activity.

(*Dudley plays Deirdre Nimble, in a wheelchair, dressed like an elderly version of Faye Dunaway in the 1967 feature film Bonnie And Clyde. Peter plays Fred Nimble, an old man dressed as Warren Beatty in the same movie. Despite these American antecedents, they speak in broad London accents*)

FRED NIMBLE: Well, it's all the young people's fault, isn't it? I mean we're only following their example. You see, they're wandering round, getting all the publicity, loads of money and their Carnaby fashions and everything like that, smoking LSD. Well, it's high time the old people had a bit of fun, isn't it Deirdre?

DEIRDRE NIMBLE: What?

FRED NIMBLE: I said isn't it Deirdre?

DEIRDRE NIMBLE: Oh, yes.

FRED NIMBLE: I mean you're always reading about some young thug getting hold of an old lady, smashing her down and nicking her handbag. It's high time we nicked their handbags, isn't it?

DEIRDRE NIMBLE: What?

FRED NIMBLE: Nicked their handbags.

DEIRDRE NIMBLE: No, I haven't got any knickers in my handbag. I'm wearing both pairs, cos it's rather chilly.

FRED NIMBLE: Yes, course it is, love – very chilly. (*To Herman*) Forgive her, Eamonn, but old Ironside's been a bit deaf in the last decade. She's not too well.

DEIRDRE NIMBLE: Yes, I heard every word you said, mate.

FRED NIMBLE: She hears what she wants. Let's face it, she hears what she wants.

HERMAN HERMITZ: I asked them to recount some of their latest crimes

FRED NIMBLE: Ah well, of course the last big job we done was the Peckham Hospital tooth snatch. It was a classic crime. (*To Deirdre*) Remember that? Tooth snatch? (*To Herman*) We got information, you see, from the other tea leaves and underworld contacts and that, that there was a sizeable hoard of teeth out there. So we went down there, disguised as out patients – as invalids. I took along me crutch. You see me crutch there? It's an exploding crutch. (*Peter holds up the crutch – there is a gun barrel at the end of it*) I only had to go boom-boom-boom, boom-boom-boom and everybody's dead. It's a wonderful weapon. You just bang 'em away like that. Anyway, while Deirdre diverted the doctors' attention with one of her coughing spasms . . . (*Dudley coughs*)

FRED NIMBLE: . . . Very similar to the horrible noise she just made then, I made off. I made off with the teeth. And we got a sizeable hoard, didn't we. Still got the teeth.

DEIRDRE NIMBLE: Still got some in my blouse, if you'd like to see any.

HERMAN HERMITZ: I assured them that I had sufficient teeth myself already, and wished this disgusting old couple a fond goodbye.

FRED NIMBLE: Goodbye mate. Very nice talking to you.

DEIRDRE NIMBLE: Goodbye. Lovely to see you.

FRED NIMBLE (*To Deirdre*): Here, grab hold of this.

(*Peter hands Dudley his exploding crutch. They turn the corner and are gunned down by the police, like Bonnie & Clyde, in a hail of bullets*)

HERMAN HERMITZ: The lesson surely is plain. Crime and violence can never pay, unless of course you happen to be making a TV film about it, like myself, in which case you get about 500 guineas. Goodnight.

THAT REBELLION THING
(ATV, 1968)

John Cleese saw Beyond the Fringe *in Cambridge as a twenty-one-year-old student. Seven years later, having played a waiter in* Not Only . . . But Also . . . , *he played a butler in this father-and-son sketch. Cleese went on to appear with Peter on TV in* Peter Cook & Co, *at the movies in* Yellowbeard *and* The Rise and Rise of Michael Rimmer, *and onstage in Amnesty International's* Secret Policeman's Ball. *'Put him in front of an audience, and something almost paranormal happened,' wrote Cleese. 'He'd just sit there on his bench and start talking, and after a few seconds perfectly sane, sensible people would start moaning and pawing the air and emitting strange wounded-animal noises. And he would drone on and on, with celestial timing, looking like a huge demented vole, creating physical pain and irrepressible joy.'[4] Swap the words 'sit there on his bench and start talking' for 'sit at the piano and start playing' and you could be talking about Dudley.*

(Peter plays Sir Giles, a posh, self-assured middle-aged businessman. A telephone rings. Enter the butler, Gatiss, played by John Cleese, carrying the telephone on a tray. Peter clicks his fingers. John puts the telephone on the table. Peter clicks his fingers again. John lifts the receiver, and passes it to Peter.)

PETER: Thank you, Gatiss.
(Exit John Cleese.)
PETER *(into the telephone)*: Hello. Sir Giles. Yes, one million pounds – that's my final offer . . . I'm sorry, I can't go any higher. One

million pounds – take it or leave it . . . Very well. One million pounds, one and eleven pence – you've got a deal . . . Operator? Operator, would you get me New York, please . . . No, on the telephone – I don't want to buy it . . . Thank you. Would you call me when you've got a line? . . . Yes, it's very urgent. Thank you.

(*Peter hangs up. A knock at the door.*)

PETER: Come in.

(*Enter Dudley. He plays Edward, a much younger man than Sir Giles, more casually dressed, and with a London accent.*)

DUDLEY: Hello, Father.

PETER: What was that?

DUDLEY: I said hello.

PETER: No, you said something after that. You said hello, something or other.

DUDLEY: Yes. Hello, Father.

PETER: Hello Father? Oh, you must be . . . um . . . you must be . . . um . . .

(*Peter clicks his fingers, trying to recall his son's name.*)

PETER: Ed . . . Ed . . .

DUDLEY (*mimicking him*): Ed . . . Ed . . . Ed . . .

PETER: Ed . . . Ed . . . Edward! Edward, my son, how are you? What can I do for you?

DUDLEY: I've come to say goodbye.

PETER: I thought you just came in to say hello. You came in and said, 'Hello, Father.'

DUDLEY: That's right. I came in to say hello, and follow that up with goodbye. I'm off.

PETER (*blasé*): I see. Well, goodbye, nice to meet you. Hope you're going well . . . Um, just before you leave, is there any particular reason for your going so suddenly? I mean, you've been with us a long time, haven't you?

DUDLEY: Twenty-five years, to be exact, Father.

PETER: Twenty-five years! Is it as long as that? My goodness, it seems just like yesterday you were a toddler!

DUDLEY: Seems like twenty-five years to come that I've been cooped up in this rotten place. I might as well not exist as far as you're concerned. Well, I've had enough. I'm going away. I'm off. And I'm going to get married.

PETER: Going to get married, are you, Edward? Don't you remember me telling you, never get married before you're thirty years old?

DUDLEY: Well, maybe that's the precise reason why I'm getting married at the age of twenty-five.

PETER: Oh, I see. It's a sort of rebellion thing, is it?

DUDLEY: Sort of rebellion. Yeah.

PETER: Sort of rebelling against me . . .

DUDLEY: That's right.

PETER: . . . And everything I stand for.

DUDLEY: That's right, yes.

PETER: Yes. Why are you talking in this rather extraordinary working-class accent?

DUDLEY: Cos I can't stand the way you talk, you upper-class git.

PETER: Ah, the rebellion thing all over again.

DUDLEY: Yeah. That's right.

PETER: Didn't you used to be a lot taller?

DUDLEY: Yeah, I used to be six foot four – but as I can't stand upper-class gits, I went on a crash diet and got myself down to five nothing.

PETER: Ah, bless me, that reminds me of me when I was your age. My father was five foot one. I couldn't stand the way he looked or anything about him. Got myself stretched up to six foot two. You're a real chip off the old block. Have a brandy before you go. Come on.

DUDLEY: No thank you.

PETER: Have a brandy, have a –

DUDLEY: I don't want anything you have to give me, Father.

PETER: I like your spirit, son. I'll let you know, laddie – the only thing I've ever wanted is for you to be completely happy.

DUDLEY (*sarcastically*): Oh, that twice, all of that, yeah.

PETER: It's true. It's true. I'm sorry it's taken twenty-five years to get across to you, but it's true nonetheless. You know, I sometimes feel that, as a father, I may have tended to be a little remote at times.

DUDLEY: You're very good with the telephone, though – aren't you, Father? Very good with that.

PETER: Very good with the telephone, Edward. Very good with that – very good with business. But when it comes to matters more delicate, such as human, um . . . human . . .

DUDLEY: Feelings, Father? Is that the word you're groping for?

PETER: Human feelings, yes, I'm not quite so good at those. But if you've found some young girl and you're in love with her and you're going to get married, well, I just . . . (*He pats Dudley.*) . . . I just hope you'll be very happy.

DUDLEY: You know I wish I could believe that, Father – I really do. Honestly.

(*The telephone rings. Peter picks up.*)

PETER (*into the telephone*): Is that my call to New York? Cancel it, would you please? I've got something more important to do. Thank you.

(*Peter hangs up.*)

PETER: You can believe it, Edward, because it's true.

DUDLEY: But they wanted you on the blower, Father.

PETER: On the what?

DUDLEY: On the telephone.

PETER: I told them I had something very much more important to do, Edward, concerning you. Namely, that if you're setting out on the rocky road to matrimony, I'd very much like to meet this young girl.

DUDLEY: Well, I mean . . . if I thought there was any point in bringing her up, I would have done so, wouldn't I?

PETER: There is a point, Edward – because if you bring her up, I can meet her. If you don't bring her up, I can't meet her. I'd like to meet her, so if you'd bring her up, I can meet her.

DUDLEY: You really want to meet her?

PETER: I'd really like to meet her, Edward. Is she . . . is she . . .

DUDLEY (*incredulous*): Downstairs? Yeah.

PETER: Good lad. (*Into the telephone.*) Gatiss? Would you show the young lady up, please? Thank you.

(*Enter John carrying a man-sized wooden box. He puts it on the floor and exits.*)

DUDLEY (*speaking posh*): Thelma, darling – this is Father. Father, this is Thelma – my fiancée.

PETER (*to the box*): How do you do? (*To Dudley.*) Is there any chance at all I could have a peek at her? Look into the box at all?

DUDLEY: Certainly, yes.

(*Dudley fetches a chair. Peter stands upon it.*)

DUDLEY: Mind how you go.

(*Peter opens the top of the box and looks inside.*)

PETER: Hello? Thelma? Where are you?

DUDLEY: Thelma, darling – would you put the torch on?

PETER: Thank you very much. That's much better. How are you keeping? Lovely weather we've been having. This sun is doing a lot of good for the wheat. So I'm told in any case . . . Um, well, I'm sure you've got lots of things to get on with in there. I won't take up any more of your valuable time. Very nice to see you. Good.

(*Peter closes the box and clambers down.*)

PETER: Well, Edward, my lad, I think you've done very well for yourself. She's a beautiful little thing.

DUDLEY: I think she's an absolute sweetie.

PETER: Terribly, terribly nice. She seems very quiet.

DUDLEY: She's a bit, you know, shy, sensitive – that sort of thing.

PETER: I think it's much better to have a quiet wife who knows her place in the house rather than one of those awful, neurotic scream-ing ratbags who goes around shouting about women's rights the whole time. Know what I mean?

DUDLEY: Couldn't agree more.

PETER: What about the wedding? What arrangements have you made?

DUDLEY: A very quiet wedding, I think – you know.

PETER: Going to have the vicar lowered in the top, are you?

DUDLEY: Yes, I think so.

PETER: Reverend Spendal's very good value. You thought about the honeymoon at all? Got yourself a double box, maybe?

(*Edward looks bashful.*)

PETER: I like your style. There's just one thing before you two young lovebirds dash away into the night. It'd be awfully nice if Thelma could have a word with your mother.

DUDLEY: Do you think Mummy would like to see her?

PETER: I think they'd get on like a house on fire. (*Into the telephone.*) Gatiss, show my wife in, would you please? There's a good fellow. (*To Dudley.*) Well, cheers!

(*Peter and Dudley drink. John brings in a second man-sized box.*)

PETER: Marcia, my darling, come along in. There you are. (*To Dudley.*) Kiss your mother, Edward.

DUDLEY: Hello, Mummy.

(*Dudley kisses the second box.*)

PETER: Marcia, this is Thelma. Thelma, this is Marcia. Well, I think we might as well leave the little ladies to have a bit of a chinwag. You know what they are. I'm glad you got rid of that ghastly accent. It never really suited you.

DUDLEY: No.

PLUNGER JARVIS
(ATV, 1969)

(*Peter is a traditional circus impresario with an implausible false moustache. The setting is a traditional circus Big Top*)

PETER: Next act please.

(*Enter Dudley, accompanied by a glamorous sequined assistant*)

PETER: How d'you do. Your name?

DUDLEY: My name is Plunger Jarvis and this is Estelle, my exquisite assistant, direct from a sensational season at the Moulin Rouge.

PETER: I understand you have an act which might interest us here.

DUDLEY: I most certainly do, yes. The name Plunger Jarvis is of course a bit of a giveaway. As you may infer from same, I plunge.

PETER: You are a *plongeur*.

DUDLEY: *Je suis un plongeur*, as the French would so aptly dub me.

PETER: Could you describe your act?

DUDLEY: I could and will. Firstly, Estelle, my exquisite assistant, blindfolds me – no mean moment in itself.

PETER: I imagine not.

DUDLEY: I imagine not. Then I climb to the top of a 500 foot pole and dive head first into this bucket of petroleum, which has been ignited by the exquisite Estelle.

PETER: You dive 500 foot into a bucket of flaming petroleum?

DUDLEY: I plunge into this flaming bucket.

PETER: Well, it sounds like the sort of act which might interest us. Could I see it?

DUDLEY: Most certainly you can. Estelle, the blindfold.

(*Estelle blindfolds Dudley*)

PETER: This, I imagine, is what you call the boring part of the act.

DUDLEY: This is the bit you have not been waiting for.

PETER: Yes. Ladder, please.

DUDLEY: Bucket, Estelle.

(*Estelle brings a rope ladder and a bucket*)

PETER: Thank you.

DUDLEY: Ta. Right. I shall now get up it.

(*Dudley climbs the rope ladder*)

DUDLEY: Ooh, blimey!

PETER: You're very agile on the ropes, I must say.

DUDLEY: I should coco, yes.

PETER: It must take a lot of training.

DUDLEY: It takes a lot of straining, too. (*out of shot*) These 200 foot poles you've got aren't my style, you know. I like the 500 foot-ers, you know.

PETER: Prefer a bigger one, do you?

DUDLEY: Oh yes.

PETER: I'm sure we can get one in for you.

DUDLEY: Blimey, me ears are popping a bit up here. Right! Estelle, would you place the bucket in position, my dear?

(*Estelle positions the bucket*)

DUDLEY: Ta. Two inches to your left, sweetheart. Thank you. Now, ignite the petroleum. Give the signal to the timpanist. (*Drum Roll*) Plunger Jarvis is plunged!

(*A deafening crash. Enter Dudley, with his head inside a smouldering bucket*)

PETER: Plunger, may I call you that? I want to tell you, that's a sensational act.

DUDLEY: Thank you.

PETER: As far as I'm concerned, you can start work tomorrow. What do you say to two hundred pounds a week?

DUDLEY: No.

PETER: It's a special act, Mr Jarvis. I agree with you there – three hundred pounds a week.

DUDLEY: Not interested.

PETER: Breaks my heart to do this, really breaks my heart, but I am willing to offer you three hundred pounds a week, and that's my final offer.

DUDLEY: Stuff it.

PETER: Mr Jarvis, I must have you. This act is really sensational. I'm willing to pay you more than any other performer in the history of the circus. Seven hundred and fifty pounds a week and an air-conditioned caravan – what do you say to that?

DUDLEY: I say get lost.

PETER: Mr Jarvis, I don't understand your attitude. You come in here all eager. I offer you more money than any performer in the history of the world. What's made you change your mind?

DUDLEY: Well, to tell the truth, it's the first time I've tried it, and I don't fancy it very much.

INSURANCE SALESMEN
(ATV, 1969)

A traditional turn from the Anne Bancroft special, with Peter and

Dudley cast as colleagues rather than adversaries. Perhaps they should have employed more guest stars. With someone else to gang up against, they spark off each other rather well. And although she's merely treading water, Bancroft radiates dramatic class, even in a pleasant piece of nonsense such as this. She'd recently had her greatest hit, The Graduate, *but here she seems far too young for Mrs Robinson. Bancroft was only in her mid thirties when she played Dustin Hoffman's middle-aged lover, and when she performed this sketch, her fortieth birthday was still a few years away. Richard Attenborough called her the greatest actress of her generation, and her husband, Mel Brooks, was one of Peter's favourite comics. 'A beautiful and talented woman who can lift your spirits just by looking at you,' said Brooks. She certainly lifted this sketch.*

(Anne Bancroft is relaxing in her sumptuous open-plan living room. Peter and Dudley appear outside the French windows.)

PETER: Are you Mrs Weeks?

DUDLEY: Yes is the correct answer, and it entitles you to let us in. (*Anne lets them in.*)

PETER: Thank you very much.

DUDLEY: Oh, blimey! Look at this then! Very nice place you got here – very costly trappings.

PETER: Tastefully put together, innit? Very tasteful. Those curtains must have set her back a bit, I'd say.

ANNE: Is there anything I can do for you gentlemen?

PETER: Well, it's more a case of what we can do for you, innit?

ANNE: No, I meant exactly who are you?

DUDLEY: Very profound questions, Mrs Weeks.

PETER: Ooh, that is a deep one. That is a deep one!

DUDLEY: Who are we, why are we, what's it all about, Alfie?

PETER: One of the big philosophical problems of our time, Mrs Weeks.

ANNE: No, no. I meant exactly what is your business?

DUDLEY: Reasonable enquiry, George.

PETER: Fair question, fair question. We are representatives of the Pioneer Insurance Company, which was founded well over ten minutes ago.

DUDLEY: Our card, Mrs Weeks.

ANNE: Oh, I see. Well, I'm sorry to disappoint you, but my husband and I are really fully insured.

DUDLEY: Well, that depends what you mean by fully insured, doesn't it?

ANNE: Oh. Well, I mean that our policy covers every contingency, except of course acts of God.

PETER: Well, let me ask you, are you covered against acts of Cedric?

ANNE: I don't know what you mean.

DUDLEY: She don't know what you mean, George.

PETER: She don't know what I mean. All right, let me explain. Supposing one day, God forbid, some lunatic were to come in here, start setting fire to your costly Chippendales and slashing your Picasso with a fish knife.

ANNE: Who on earth would do a thing like that?

PETER: Cedric. You see, the trouble with Cedric is he's uncontrollable. I think you'd bear me out here, wouldn't you, Cedric?

DUDLEY: I'll bear you out on this.

PETER: Unconbloodytrollable, Cedric. I'm the only one who can sort of keep him in order. If I hadn't said to him, just before we come in, I said, 'Don't set light to her Chippendales! Don't slash her Picasso!' he'd be at it now, slashing all over the place, banging things around.

DUDLEY: I'd have got hold of your precious vases like this . . .

(*Dudley picks up a vase and drops it. It shatters.*)

DUDLEY: . . . And dropped them.

PETER: Just like that. Dropping them on the floor like that.

DUDLEY: I'd have been doing that if my brother had not expressly forbade the aforesaid perpetrations.

PETER: You see, the trouble is he's a loony.

DUDLEY: Yeah.

PETER: A loony. Psychopath was the word Dr Henderson used, just before Cedric bunged him in the deep freeze.

ANNE: Well, why don't you gentlemen come back later and discuss this with my husband?

PETER: Ah, well, now, that's the thing. Your husband, you

see, he's been a bit tied up at the office, ain't he?

DUDLEY: I roped him to the duplicating machine.

ANNE: The duplicating machine?

DUDLEY: They'll be two of him by the time he gets back.

ANNE: I think I'm going to go and make a telephone call.

PETER: Don't you shift your elegant self, m'lady. Cedric! What kind of a gentleman are you? Get the lady the phone!

DUDLEY: George, I'm sorry. How remiss of me.

PETER: Good heavens, I do apologise for this. He's a bit of a tearaway. (*Dudley rips the telephone out of the wall socket.*)

PETER: There we are. We'll soon have it over here.

(*Dudley hands him the phone.*)

PETER: Thank you very much. Now then, let's get the number for you. Would you believe it? Line's gone dead.

DUDLEY: Stone me! Bloody GPO!

PETER: Just the sort of situation you must dread. Cut off from the outside world like this. Ooh, I don't envy you in a situation like that.

ANNE: Oh, really?

PETER: No. Let me tell you about Pioneer Insurance. All right?

ANNE: Well, I really do think we have enough insurance.

PETER: Let me tell you about it. Look, let me ask you a question. For example, are you insured against attacks by horrible hairy tarantula spiders?

ANNE: Oh, we don't have any tarantulas in England.

PETER: Did you hear what she said?

PETER/DUDLEY (*together*): No tarantulas in England?

DUDLEY: I've got thousands back at my place, lady.

PETER: He's got hundreds of them back at his place. Now, supposing one night, God forbid, you were lying in the bath.

DUDLEY: In the bath.

PETER: Lying in the bath there, all quiet, soaping yourself nicely. Suddenly, one of these horrible hairy little monsters comes creeping up your drain and jumps on your neck.

DUDLEY: Now, we at Pioneer Insurance are geared for this

contingency. You see, we could fit you out with an anti-tarantula warning system second to none.

PETER: Nobody else makes them. We could come in here, for five thousand pounds, we could get all the equipment in – trip wires, pressure pads, infra-red lamps, cotton wool under the sofa, all that kind of stuff. But what I would recommend – I think Cedric would go along with me here.

DUDLEY: I'd go along with you here, George.

PETER: What I would recommend is our personal security system, whereby, for a consideration – five thousand pounds – we move into an upper chamber and exercise twenty-four-hour surveillance against tarantula attack, or any other contingency.

ANNE: Like what?

PETER: Well, let's take the obvious one. 2b, Cedric.

DUDLEY: 2b.

PETER: 2b or not to 2b, as they say. 2b. You're sitting at home, you see, quietly watching television, all snug with your husband, everything like that, just quite quietly. Suddenly, an orang-utan what's been bitten by a mad dog sees the light on, comes in and starts seizing hold of your cushions.

(*Dudley, doing an uncanny impression of an orang-utan, proceeds to tear up her cushions.*)

PETER: There, seizing hold of it, you see. Tearing it apart, pulling all the feathers out, everything like that. Well, under our system, Cedric and I will be downstairs in a flash with our anti-orangutan spray. All right Cedric, that's enough, thank you. That will do, thank you. The lady's allergic to feathers! Enough!

ANNE: Well . . .

PETER: It's good, innit?

ANNE: Well, I think that this insurance would be very advantageous. Yes, I'll just go and get my chequebook.

PETER: Well, it's in your interests, innit, lady. We wouldn't do it otherwise. It's only in your interests.

ANNE: Oh yes, of course. I mean, supposing that a rogue elephant, blinded by the London fog, came in through those French windows and started jumping on my piano.

DUDLEY: Something you must live in daily fear of.

ANNE: Oh, I do.

PETER: Well, under our system, Cedric and I would be out in the drive, reasoning with it in elephant language.

(*Dudley trumpets like an elephant.*)

PETER: That is elephant language for 'Mrs Weeks is not at home. Why don't you try next door, Jumbo?'

ANNE: Well, I think this is a wonderful idea!

DUDLEY: I'd go along with you there, Mrs Weeks.

ANNE: Good! Now, when would you like to move in?

PETER: Well, let me see, you give us your cheque for five thousand pounds, Cedric and I nip back to the headquarters at Willesden, get all the equipment, we should be back here in about, well, half an hour?

ANNE: Half an hour, yes, good. Of course, then you will untie my husband from the duplicating machine.

DUDLEY: Yeah, both of him.

ANNE: That's very cute, Cedric, very cute.

DUDLEY: Thank you very much.

ANNE: Well, shall I show you to your quarters?

PETER: Oh, that's very civil of the lady, isn't it?

DUDLEY: Yes, thank you very much indeed.

ANNE: I'll ring for the maid.

(*Anne pulls a cord. Peter and Dudley fall through a trapdoor.*)

ANNE: Well, thank goodness I had that bear trap installed.

Chapter Four

Not Only . . . But Also . . . (Again)

After the relative disappointment of *Goodbye Again* between 1968 and 1969, Peter and Dudley's third (and final) series with the BBC in 1970 represented a return to form – if not triumphant, then certainly a step up from their brief dalliance with ATV. It didn't quite measure up to their first two series, but against any other yardstick, it was a considerable success. This was all the more remarkable, given the conditions under which it was made. The producer, Jimmy Gilbert, had barely a month to prepare a series comprising seven forty-five-minute episodes, with one week of rehearsal and one week of filming between each fortnightly transmission.

Dudley was otherwise engaged, playing the lead in a West End production of Woody Allen's *Play It Again Sam*, and making the series in what should have been his spare time added up to a very gruelling schedule. He was onstage six nights a week, plus Saturdays and Wednesday matinées. The only day he could do studio recordings or location shoots was Sunday – his one free day from the theatre. Some locations were out of town (like the title sequence shot on the *Ark Royal*) and consequently required an overnight stay.

Peter's career was suffering from the quite opposite problem. His latest film – *The Rise and Rise of Michael Rimmer*, a political satire about an opinion pollster turned dictator, played by Peter – had been shelved by the studio until after the forthcoming general election. If Rimmer had been released before the election – which the Tories won, against the odds, just as the film predicted – it would have had a lot more bite. Instead, it proved to be the last leading role Peter ever played in the movies. Against this troubled backdrop, Gilbert worked wonders to produce such a successful series. Not that there's an awful lot of it left to see. Only the location footage, shot on film, escaped the BBC's parsimonious passion for recycling. Virtually everything they filmed in the studio was destroyed. Mercifully, the scripts survive, and the best of them are reproduced here.

This series saw a shift in the balance of power between these partners. Dudley was no longer merely Peter's fall guy. Sometimes, on-camera and behind the scenes, he even got the upper hand. 'Gradually, Dudley developed far more of a role in the writing,'[1] revealed Peter, a decade later. It was a role that differed markedly from his own. 'I tend to flutter off very quickly and improvise, and ignore illogicalities,' said Peter. 'I'd rather get through a whole sketch quickly, and then come back and deal with whatever is wrong. Dudley began, when we had an idea, to examine what was logically incorrect, right at the beginning. I would regard this as pernickety, and he would regard it as logical. So the writing process became slower.'[2] But it also became more solid, and on Dudley's sturdier foundations, Peter could build longer, more sustained sketches than before. 'Peter has this extraordinary seam of invention,' explained Dudley. 'I perhaps have a slightly stronger feeling, though, for the emotional content and architecture of a sketch.'[3] However, there wasn't much time for architecture once this series got under way. Peter and Dudley spent a fortnight writing the script for the first show, but on the first day of rehearsal, that was all they had. Gilbert shut them in a room with a tape recorder, into which they improvised fresh sketches. His secretary then transcribed the tapes as they came in. Gilbert later likened this process to the improvised scripts of Mike Leigh, but Leigh surely never cut it quite so fine as this. Typically, the scripts for the filmed sketches weren't ready until the day they were shot. Even the score of Dudley's Beethoven skit didn't arrive until the day. Dudley said he could only work to deadlines, and Peter was much the same. As Gilbert says, they worked very hard once they got started, but getting started could be a problem. They liked to leave it late, and they left the writing for this series later than any other.

The item that got them out of jail was 'Poets Cornered', a sort of highbrow forerunner to *Tiswas*, in which guest stars were suspended above vast vats of green gunge and forced to make up instant rhymes to save themselves from a sticky dunking. Cornered poets included Ronnie Barker, Alan Bennett, Barry Humphries, Spike Milligan, Frank Muir, Denis Norden and Willie Rushton. Sadly, every instalment was deleted, and since it was all improvised, there's not even anything in the surviving scripts. By all accounts, it was hilarious, but it was also immensely useful. Firstly, it was a regular feature that required no advance preparation whatsoever – a bonus in a series so short of writing time. Secondly, with his finger on the gunge button, Gilbert could vary the length of the contest, depending on whether the rest of the show was running under or over time.

The series was broadcast between February and May 1970 on BBC2, and repeated on BBC1 between September and October the same year. For these repeats, Gilbert trimmed each episode down to half an hour from the original three-quarters, cutting out all the guest musicians (including Yes and Joe Cocker) and was delighted with the leaner result. 'The last TV series seemed textually messy,'[4] remarked Peter a few years later. In the circumstances, it was a wonder there had been any text at all.

In 1974, Gilbert was hired by the BBC to direct Peter and Dudley in some new links for a compilation of old *Not Only . . . But Also . . .* material, and discovered that most of his series (and much of McGrath's and Clement's) had already been wiped. One dreads to think what twaddle the Corporation taped over it. The only reason the film footage survived was because Gilbert stumped up a £60 storage fee to stop it being destroyed.

The last programmes to bear the *Not Only . . . But Also . . .* brand name were a couple of Antipodean specials, recorded in Australia in January 1971. These two half-hour shows included a number of new sketches, some featuring that restless Australian native, Barry Humphries. There were also several remakes of old favourites – a blessing, since some of the originals have subsequently been destroyed. The shows were broadcast by the Australian Broadcasting Commission in February and repeated on BBC1 in June under the title *Pete and Dud Down Under*. In September, Peter and Dudley returned to Australia to do a two-man stage show. It was supposed to last five months. In the end, it would keep them occupied, on three continents, for the next four years.

THE GLIDD OF GLOOD
(BBC2, 1970)

Peter was always swift to acknowledge his debt to the doyens of Victorian nonsense verse, Edward Lear and Lewis Carroll. In the first series of Not Only . . . But Also . . . , *Peter and Dudley dramatised one of Lear's poems, 'Incidents in the Life of my Uncle Arly', with Peter playing Uncle Arly. In the second series, they filmed Carroll's 'The Walrus and the Carpenter' from* Alice's Adventures in Wonderland. *Dudley played the Walrus and Peter played the Carpenter, in a minimalist rendition that anticipated Jonathan Miller's bold BBC adaptation of the novel (with Peter as the Mad Hatter) later that year. There are dashes of Lear and Carroll in much of Peter's solo work, especially his early monologues, but no other sketch pays more direct homage to that genre than this mock-heroic poem – a 'Jabberwocky' style doggerel which bears comparison with 'The Owl and the Pussycat', or anything in* Through the Looking-Glass.

'The Glidd of Glood' was borrowed from Peter's never-to-be-finished book of children's verse – and if this remnant is anything to go by, it's a great shame it remained incomplete. The influence of Carroll is

impossible to ignore, but it's still an original and idiosyncratic piece, which made a striking piece of film – not laugh-out-loud funny, but riveting nonetheless. Peter played the Glidd of Glood, dressed only in brown paper, plied with brandy by producer Jimmy Gilbert to keep out the winter cold. Dudley played Sparquin, the court jester, and the suitably bleak setting was Bodiam Castle – a windswept ruin on the south coast.

The Glidd of Glood would wander nude throughout his spacious
   castle
So everyone could plainly see his huge brown paper parcel

In this the Glidd kept carefully hid his jewels, gold and crown,
Tied to his wrists with bits of string – he never put it down

There's never been a man so mean – he didn't mind the cold
When clothes grow old their value goes – unlike a piece of gold

And when the Glidd got into bed, he'd cuddle with his treasure
And kissed his parcel constantly – this was his only pleasure

His servants all were quite appalled of everything he did
But no one dared to say a word – they feared the cruel Glidd

For he could kill a man at will – his power was absolute
And every night, at half past eight, they'd smile and kiss his foot

'Oh Glidd of Glood, you are so good, as any Gloodite knows'
They whispered this each time they kissed his gnarled and grimy
   toes

And when they ate it was their fate to sit with him at table
And look as grateful as they could – but very few were able

To save on food he fed them wood, mixed up with grains of rice
On Sundays, as a special treat, he served them boiled mice

When in the mood, the Glidd of Glood would have a bit of fun
With Sparquin, the court jester, a man of eighty-one

Who'd say 'I say, I say, I say – who does not love our Glidd?
I beg you, stand and raise your hand' – but no one ever did

'We love him so because we know that nowhere could we find
A man so generous and true, so gentle and so kind

Oh lovely Glidd, we love you so – I kiss your knee, I suck your
    toe
Oh lovely Glidd, don't ever go'

And then the Glidd would sternly bid them drink the moral
    toast
With water from a plastic cup, one-quarter full at most

The Glidd of Glood thought he saw God, one dark and stormy
    night,
A figure with a green moustache, and clad in shrouds of white

'You ghastly Glidd,' the vision said, 'Get on your knees and pray,
If you want to enter paradise, you give all your wealth away'

'What? All of it?' replied the Glidd – 'my crown and jewels as
    well?'
'Yes, all of it, you greedy twit – or else you'll burn in hell'

In wild despair, with many a tear, the Glidd undid the strings
And handed over jewels and crown, and all his precious things

The sobbing Glidd returned to bed, to moan and weep and fret
And when the sun came up at dawn, his sheets were soaking wet

His morning tea arrived and he shrieked as he seized the cup
'Fetch me Sparquin here at once! I need some cheering up!'

'I fear he's gone,' replied the man – 'he caught the morning
    flight,
He left behind this green moustache, and long white nighty'

And here's a note that Sparquin wrote – it seems a little odd
It says 'Goodbye, you greedy Glidd,' signed Sparquin, alias God

The Glidd fell ill, a sudden chill, and very soon he died
The funeral was a gay affair, and not a Gloodite cried

They drank and sang, the church bells rang, and then there was
    a dance
No flowers decked his grave save one, signed 'Sparquin, South of
    France'

And here's the moral of this tale of greed and gross deceit
If God asks you for all your cash, do ask for a receipt

THE PIANO TUNER
(BBC2, 1970)

(Dudley is tuning a piano. Enter Peter)

PETER: Hello darling.
DUDLEY: Hello sweetheart.
PETER: Oh, sorry – I thought . . . I thought for a moment you
    were my, er, wife.
DUDLEY: No, I'm not.
PETER: I mean, I didn't think you were my wife, but, um, I expected
    my wife to be in.
DUDLEY: Er, no – I'm the piano tuner, and your wife, er, said she
    was just going to see her mother, who's got a touch of the flu.
PETER: Oh, I see . . . Oh, there's a lot of it about, isn't there?

DUDLEY: Oh, there's a lot of flu about – and there's a lot of 'it' about.
(*Dudley laughs*)
PETER: Quite a lot of flu about, as you say.
DUDLEY: And a lot of 'it' about. 'It.'
(*Dudley laughs again*)
PETER: I've just got a bit of prep to correct, and you just carry on.
DUDLEY: Yes, your wife said you were a Latin master.
PETER: Yes, down at the local primary. I teach Latin.
DUDLEY: I couldn't stand my master when I was a lad. Oh, he was a . . . he was a right twit. He used to make us sing this rotten song about prepositions – taking the ablative. Oh, I couldn't stand him. Anyway, I suppose things have changed now.
PETER: Yes, we have rather more advanced methods of teaching nowadays.
DUDLEY: I should hope so. Your wife's a very attractive lady, if I may say.
PETER: My wife?
DUDLEY: Very attractive.
PETER: Well, I'm glad you thought so. Thank you very much.
DUDLEY: Yes. Seemed to me a very artistic type.
PETER: Yes, she is, actually. She's got all sorts of, um, er, interests. See those flowers over there?
DUDLEY: Yes, beautifully arranged. I noticed she has artistic hands.
PETER: Yes, she arranged those, and that's really why I got her the piano, you know, to give her an interest – something to do in the afternoon.
DUDLEY: Yes, I suppose anyone would get bored with just doing the housework.
PETER: Well, that's what I thought.
DUDLEY: Every woman gets the urge for a bit of outside interest. So you're safer keeping her here in the house. I mean idle hands turn to mischief, don't they?
PETER: Oh, that wasn't really the reason why I got her the piano. She has, you know, a lot of interests, in fact, you know. She's learning the piano, as I say, and she goes to the WI quite a lot, you know.

DUDLEY: Oh, what does that stand for?

PETER: WI – Women's Institute.

DUDLEY: How funny – silly, really. When I saw the initials WI on your wall diary every Wednesday and Friday, I didn't think of Women's Institute. I thought of a friend of mine, er, Willy Ivanoff. I don't know if you know him?

PETER: No, I don't.

DUDLEY: He's a fiery Russian character – plays the piano like a maniac. He's got very big hands and plays like a demon – fingers like hammers.

PETER: I haven't come across the gentleman.

DUDLEY: I was round his place tuning his piano. Apparently, the other night he was half way through A Night On The Bare Mountain and his sustaining pedal fell off.

PETER: Sorry to hear that.

DUDLEY: Funny it's the same initials.

PETER: Not all that funny. Could be West One.

DUDLEY: I always remember reading my ex wife's diary – RSPCA every Wednesday and Friday afternoons.

PETER: Your wife was an animal lover, was she?

DUDLEY: Well, in a manner of speaking, I suppose. She was certainly a lover and certainly a lover of animals. RSPCA turned out to be Rodney, Sidney, Percy, Cedric and Arthur. Bloody pop group. Arthur was the drummer. She was mesmerised by his maracas. She ran off with them. Bloody groupie.

PETER: Oh, I'm very sorry to hear that about your marriage.

DUDLEY: All that I can say, I hope your marriage has a better start.

PETER: Well, I'm very lucky in that, you know, I trust Vera implicitly, and she trusts me, and we're very happily married.

DUDLEY: Yes. I think the trouble with women, though, is, you see, that they need a bit of variety – rather like a piano. You know, one day they need the light touch of a Mendelssohn – and the next day, they need the big bang of a Beethoven. Just like a piano, they like to be tuned very regularly – kept up to concert pitch and as many hands over their keys as possible.

PETER: Yes. Well, I don't think your experience is altogether the same as mine.

DUDLEY: I don't suppose it is. You must have had quite a party a couple of days ago, didn't you?

PETER: We had a small sort of wine and cheese gathering, yes.

DUDLEY: Well, I thought so. You've got a bit of Cheddar stuck on your middle C, here – and there's a Twiglet sticking out one of your sound holes.

PETER: Oh dear.

DUDLEY: Yeah. Have a good time, did you?

PETER: Yes, it was a very nice evening.

DUDLEY: Yes, I can just see your wife raving around, dancing exotically to the Stones and the Cream.

PETER: No, it was really just people sitting down, talking – no dancing, as such.

DUDLEY: Yeah. I reckon your wife looked attractive though, didn't she? She looked very attractive this afternoon, I can tell you.

PETER: So you've already told me, yes.

DUDLEY: She looked a treat. My God, she was got up to the nines! Looked as though she was going to a film premiere, rather than your mother. Thigh length boots, micro skirt, see through blouse, Indian headband.

PETER: What did you say?

DUDLEY: See through blouse, Indian . . .

PETER: My wife was wearing a see through blouse?

DUDLEY: Yes.

PETER: I've never seen her in a see through blouse.

DUDLEY: Well, maybe she's keeping it as a surprise for you – or someone else. Might just have been to cheer your mother up. But mind you, it's the sight of pert nipples as a flu cure that's news to me.

PETER: Are you absolutely certain my wife was wearing this rather explicit costume?

DUDLEY: Oh yes. She looked very tantalising. Oh, I hope she got to your mother all right. I mean, you never know – dressed up the way she was, to kill, something might have happened to her.

She could have just sort of gone out the door, crossed the road, fallen under a West Indian. You never know what could happen.

PETER: It might actually be a good idea if I rang my mother in law, just to check up how she was.

DUDLEY: Yes. Just see if Vera arrived there OK in one piece.

PETER: Yes, well I'll just give her a tinkle.

(*Peter picks up the telephone and dials*)

PETER (*on the phone*): Hello, Mama . . . Yes, it's Peter speaking . . . I was just ringing up to see how you were . . . Oh, good . . . On the mend . . . I hope you're up and about soon . . . Is Vera still with you? . . . Oh, good . . . Fine, thank you . . . Bye.

(*Peter hangs up*)

PETER (*to Dudley*): Yes, she got there safely.

DUDLEY: Oh, I see. You had a word with Vera, did you?

PETER: No, I had a word with her mother.

DUDLEY: You didn't actually exchange words with Vera?

PETER: No, I spoke to her mother, who said Vera was there.

DUDLEY: Oh yes, the familiar story – mother hen protecting her brood.

PETER: What do you mean?

DUDLEY: Well, I mean you didn't actually speak to Vera, did you?

PETER: No, I spoke to her mother.

DUDLEY: My mother-in-law used to back my wife up every inch of the way. Still, it's your life. I rang twelve times. She said Sonia had popped down to the launderette. Two-legged launderette called George Wrigley. Not that your wife would do anything like that.

PETER: No, of course not – she's very different. I can't think why she was wearing this rather peculiar costume you mention.

DUDLEY: Does seem a bit on the extreme side, doesn't it?

PETER: Yes. In this cold weather, she might . . . Actually, what I might do is just ring up again, because I ought to tell Vera, you know, what I'm doing, when I'm going to be back. I've got this meeting this evening. So I'll just give them another ring.

(*Peter picks up the telephone again and dials*)

PETER (*on the phone*): Oh, Mama . . . Yes, yes – it's me again . . .

I'm just really ringing up to see if you were any better than you were two minutes ago – and is Vera there? . . . I see . . . She's just left . . . Yes.

DUDLEY: What was she wearing?

PETER: I beg your pardon?

DUDLEY: What was she wearing?

PETER: Well, I hope you get better – and what was she wearing? . . . A beige coat?

DUDLEY: Oh dear.

PETER: Thank you . . . Yes . . . No, that's quite all right . . . Thank you . . . Great . . . Woolly, beige coat . . . Thank you very much . . . Yes . . . Well, I hope you haven't got the sort of flu that turns you blind . . . There is some kind of flu about which turns you blind . . . Unable to see things . . . Completely well . . . and no doubt I'll see Vera soon . . . Probably popped into the WI for a moment, has she? . . . Yes, well goodbye.

(*Peter hangs up*)

DUDLEY: Bloody women. I've seen so many good men ruined by women. I was ruined by my old woman – bloody slag, dirty bag.

PETER: Well, I've got to be off now, because I've got this meeting with the NUT.

DUDLEY: NUT?

PETER: National Union of Teachers. We meet quite often – trying to get a pay increase.

DUDLEY: Oh, yes. Yes, well you deserve all you can get, sir.

PETER: And perhaps you'll tell Vera, if and when she comes in, exactly where I've gone, and to expect me when she sees me.

DUDLEY: Yes, I will. Don't you worry, sir. Good luck.

(*Exit Peter, Dudley plays the piano, Enter Vera, Peter's wife, demurely dressed in a beige wool coat*)

VERA: Oh, hello. Is my husband here?

DUDLEY: No, he just popped out, actually.

VERA: Oh yes, he's got a meeting tonight.

DUDLEY: Yes, with the NUT, as he called it – something about getting a rise. Suppose he's a big one for this union business.

VERA: Well, he goes down there quite regularly, yes.

DUDLEY: Sure he does. Yes, oh, talking of the NUT, there were calls for your husband just after he went out – Natalie, Ursula and Theresa.

VERA: Did they leave any message?

DUDLEY: They said they'd see him at the Union. Could be bring a bottle? Good-looking bloke, your husband, isn't he? Suppose it's the Latin temperament that gives him that sparkle in his eye. He went out looking rather attractive. Had all this sort of beaded suede stuff on – psychedelic T shirt and these Indian moccasins, tight velvet trousers, smelling of incense and, er, none of my business mind you, but . . .

THE SCRIPTWRITER
(BBC2, 1970)

This was one of Dudley's favourite sketches (and one of producer Jimmy Gilbert's too) and although the idea of writers and producers haggling over swear words may seem far-fetched, it's actually based on a real meeting, in which tits and bums were traded like percentage points in a showbiz contract. Peter and Dudley sidestepped the Corporation's self-censorship by adopting an ingenious ruse employed by hagglers throughout the ages. Instead of trimming their four-letter quotient in advance, they deliberately overloaded their work with bad language, so their subsequent concessions actually reduced the number of rude words to the requisite amount. A similar ruse was used by Johnny Speight, who provided the inspiration for Dudley's part. For the benefit of younger readers, Speight's great sitcom, Till Death Us Do Part, *was about an East End bigot called Alf Garnett (immortalised by Warren Mitchell) whose racist rants were inevitably peppered with terms like 'bloody' and 'bugger'. Compared to the sort of phrases blokes like Garnett really use, Mitchell's language was actually quite restrained. Yet back then, the BBC was still in the business of teaching people how to speak, rather than reflecting how they really spoke*

– and despite the popularity of his creation, Speight had plenty of linguistic battles with the suits upstairs. 'You can't say "bloody" this many times,' they told him. 'You've already said "bum" five times.' 'All right,' said Speight. 'I'll drop one "bloody" if you'll let me have another "bum".'⁵ And it wasn't just the management who were squeamish about these Anglo-Saxon idioms. When Gilbert's secretary typed up the script, she substituted 't*ts' for 'tits', proving that BBC executives weren't so out of touch with public opinion, after all. How times (and tastes) change. It all seems terribly mild by modern standards, and positively polite compared to Peter and Dudley's foul-mouthed alter egos, Derek & Clive.

(Peter, Head of Light Entertainment, is in his office at the BBC. Enter a cockney scriptwriter called Johnny, aka Dudley.)

PETER: My dear Johnny, come on in.

DUDLEY: Yes, I'd like a drink. Large Scotch and sherry, please.

PETER: Johnny, I want to tell you straight away, this is one of the funniest scripts I've ever read. It's witty, it's visual – but above all, it's damned funny.

DUDLEY: And it's got something to say. That's the point. It's got social comment about the bloody world we live in. Cheers!

PETER: This is what makes it so uniquely yours. Like all great comedy, it involved the audience. We want to do it, and, by God, we will do it. It's terrific. Terrific.

DUDLEY: But?

PETER: But what, Johnny?

DUDLEY: You were about to say 'But . . .'

PETER: No, I wasn't. I think it's terrific, but . . .

DUDLEY: There you go.

PETER: Now, Johnny, you know perfectly well the BBC has been a pioneer in the field of controversial comedy – *TW3*, *Steptoe*, *Till Death* . . .

DUDLEY: What are you trying to say?

PETER: I'm just trying to say the BBC has led the way. You've got twenty-seven bloodys in your script and I'm not worried.

DUDLEY: It reflects life, dunnit? I use bloody the whole bloody time.

PETER: Of course. Now the only thing that worries me about your script is the number of bums you have.

DUDLEY: What's the matter with that? I've got thirty-one bums in the script. They're all there for a dramatic, accumulative purpose. I mean, bums exist. You've got a bum.

PETER: I'm not trying to pretend that I don't have a bum, but what I do ask is whether a family audience wants to have a barrage of thirty-one bums fired into their living room at eight o'clock in the evening. My feeling – and I could be wrong – is that we're not ready to crash through the bum barrier yet.

DUDLEY: Yes, but only a year ago, Kenneth Tynan said –

PETER: I know perfectly well what Kenneth Tynan said, but that was a live, unscripted programme over which we had no control. I'm afraid we've never allowed a bum to get through until after eleven in the evening, and then only in a serious medical context.

DUDLEY: What miracle happens at 10.59 that suddenly takes the sting out of a bum?

PETER: I know it's illogical, Johnny. I'm willing to fight tooth and nail for your bums. We'll keep as many as possible. We'll have to lose a few. But there is one word in your script which you use several times that I'm even more worried about, and that's your colloquial word for a woman's chest.

DUDLEY: You mean my comedic use of the word tits?

PETER: Now that is a word you could use on a nature programme to describe the bird of the same name, or even in the phrase tit for tat, but not in the way you use it. Now, Johnny, I think you'd lose none of the humour if you dropped them completely.

DUDLEY: They're a vital part of the vernacular. If I drop them, I wouldn't be true to myself as a writer. The whole point of the script would be lost if you snipped out the bristols.

PETER: Now you've put your finger on it, Johnny. I think I could get a few bristols across without too much trouble.

DUDLEY: But bristols don't have the impact of tits.

PETER: You could use other rhyming slang, like sans or fainting.

DUDLEY: Sans or fainting? What are you talking about?

PETER: San Moritz. Fainting fits.

DUDLEY: That'll really get 'em going when this big bird goes by and the fella says, 'I wouldn't mind getting my sinkings round them faintings.'

PETER: Sinkings?

DUDLEY: Sinking sands – hands. Look, this isn't just a comedy – it's a social document. It mirrors the whole cosmic spectrum of our Zeitgeist.

PETER: Exactly. Your material is indestructible. You don't need to fall back on a bum or a thingamabob for a laugh.

DUDLEY: I'm not falling back on them. I'm using them as a comment. I mean you've got to have a go in life, haven't you? Those bums are more than just bums. They're used in a symbolic way. The bum represents the workers' struggle with his past.

PETER: Johnny, I realise how important these bums are to you.

DUDLEY: Not to mention the tits.

PETER: Yes, not to mention them. Now, as I respect you as a writer, I'm prepared to go out on a limb and allow you all of your twenty-seven bloodys, let's say seven bums and, because it's you – I wouldn't do this for anybody else – as a special concession – and I'm really putting my head in the noose here – you can have one tit.

DUDLEY: Not even a pair?

PETER: Sorry, Johnny.

DUDLEY: Look, tell you what I'll do. I'll lose ten bloodys if you give me two more bums and an extra tit.

PETER: Right, that leaves you seventeen bloodys, eight bums and a pair of doodahs.

DUDLEY: Hold on. How many bloodys are there to a bum?

PETER: Let's say ten.

DUDLEY: Right, let's see. I can lose that one. Ten bloodys in the pub sequence – that gives me an extra bum to play with. But I think the scene in the launderette cries out for another tit.

PETER: So that's a deal. Seven bloodys, seven bums and three of the other.

DUDLEY: I raise you one bum.

PETER: You're really pushing me into a corner. But what's the point in letting one bum stand between us. Another bum it is. I'll whip the script off to Sooty this afternoon.

IN THE CLUB
(BBC2, 1970)

Usually, it was Peter who made Dudley corpse, but on this particular occasion it was the other way round. Producer Jimmy Gilbert recalls Peter cracking up completely during the shooting of this sketch.

(Peter and Dudley are two very drunk toffs, having enjoyed a very large – and largely liquid – lunch at a gentlemen's club called Blunts.)

PETER: I really must thank you for a most delicious meal.

DUDLEY: The duck was absolutely delicious, wasn't it?

PETER: Superb. I love the way it just lay there on a plate and allowed you to eat it – very civil.

DUDLEY: There's nothing worse than a duck that flies up in your face every time you try to put your fork in it.

PETER: There's nothing I enjoy more than a good bit of duck of an evening, a glass to drink and some decent conversation.

DUDLEY: I think the tragedy – apart from this wine going down my suit – the tragedy of modern life, you know, is that most people have lost the art of conversation.

PETER: Completely lost it. I mean, ordinary people at work – I don't know what they do. What do they work at these days?

DUDLEY: I don't know. Sell lamp-posts?

PETER: Sell lamp-posts or redecorate sheep or whatever it is. They come home from their work, plonk themselves down in front of the television, and don't say a blind word.

DUDLEY: Yes, I refuse to have a television in the house.

PETER: Quite right.

DUDLEY: I've put it down the end of the lawn, near to the elder-berries. Of course, Cynthia's glued to it every night.

PETER: Well, it's a woman's medium, isn't it? Would you like another drop of wine?

DUDLEY: I'd love some.

PETER: What do you prefer? Red or white?

DUDLEY: I don't mind. It doesn't really matter. I'm colour-blind.

PETER: Another drop of rosé. Haines! Haines, would you get us another bottle of rosé? At the double, there's a good chap.

DUDLEY: Wait a minute. Haines, would you make it a barrel? Saves him nipping backwards and forwards. Oh blast, I've missed my mouth again.

PETER: Do you keep missing your mouth? Look, if it's any help in pinpointing it, your mouth is positioned almost directly beneath your nose.

DUDLEY: Well, that's the trouble. I can't see it. My nose gets in the way.

PETER: I have the same trouble. You would have thought that almighty God in His almighty wisdom – is that what He's called?

DUDLEY: Almighty God, yes.

PETER: You would have thought that almighty God in His almighty wisdom – let's grant Him that – would have had the decency and sense to make the nose go inwards, so you'd know where your bloody mouth was! Extraordinary business, really.

DUDLEY: Do you remember this club in the old days?

PETER: I'll never forget it. In the thirties and the forties and the ones.

DUDLEY: I remember you could come in here and mix with liter-ary circles.

PETER: Wonderful conversationalists, all of them.

DUDLEY: You could come in here any day and find Augustus John rubbing shoulders with Anona Winn.

PETER: Is she still with Godfrey?

DUDLEY: I hope so.

PETER: Because I didn't get a card from her this year. I was a bit upset.

DUDLEY: Augustus John was a wonderful character.

PETER: Wasn't he a wonderful character, Augustus John? Beautiful body.

DUDLEY: Superb draughtsman.

PETER: Wonderful draughtsman. I remember, he used to come into the club and lie down by that crack under the door, and within seconds we had a wonderful fug up in the club.

DUDLEY: I beg your pardon?

PETER: Fug up in the club. He'd kept it warm, keep the draughts out.

DUDLEY: I do have one quibble with him, though. That portrait he did of me, you know.

PETER: It wasn't very flattering, was it?

DUDLEY: It wasn't. It made me look absolutely blotto – pissed as a newt.

PETER: I beg your pardon? I must ask you to withdraw that phrase!

DUDLEY: What phrase?

PETER: What you just said about being P.I.S.S.E.D. as a newt. I've studied newts all my life! I've worked with them, I've lived with them. I don't know if you've read my book on the newt?

DUDLEY: *My Life With Newts?*

PETER: *My Life With Newts.* And in all that time I've never seen a single newt touch a drop of alcohol.

DUDLEY: What about married newts?

PETER: Married or unmarried, the newt is a very abstemious animal, and every newt I've ever known has been as sober as a judge.

DUDLEY: I must ask you to withdraw that remark!

PETER: I will.

DUDLEY: Every judge I have ever known has been pissed as a newt!

PETER: They have a very heavy onus on their shoulders. Imagine having to weigh up in your own hands, in the scaly hands of justice, whether a man be sent to Alcatraz for five hundred years' solitary confinement, or just have his licence endorsed.

DUDLEY: It's a terrible decision. I mean, you can understand why they take to drink.

PETER: I can understand it. Mind you, I yield to nuns.

DUDLEY: There's no point in fighting them.

PETER: I yield to none in my admiration for the British judicial system. It's the finest we have in the country.

DUDLEY: I couldn't agree more. I think we're running out of wine a bit.

PETER: What? For God's sake! Haines!

DUDLEY: Where the bloody hell's the wine?

PETER (*to Haines*): Will you stop touching that awful feathered alligator over there and come over here?

DUDLEY: The service has really gone down since the War.

PETER: Yes, it's dropped off.

DUDLEY: I'm sorry to hear that.

PETER: But there's one thing I wanted to ask you while Haines is getting the wine. I hope you won't mind me asking because it's rather a personal question.

DUDLEY: I've just swallowed a black mamba. You want to ask me a personal question? Please do. I won't be offended.

PETER: I've wanted to ask you this for many years but I held back because I don't want to hurt you.

DUDLEY: What are friends for if they can't ask each other personal questions?

PETER: What are friends for? And you promise you won't be offended if I ask?

DUDLEY: Absolutely not.

PETER: Who the bloody hell are you?

DUDLEY: That's a bit of a tricky one. Look, I'll tell you what I'll do. I'll sleep on it and I'll see you here same time tomorrow and I'll try to come up with something.

PERMISSION TO MARRY
(BBC2, 1970)

Another father and son sketch, with Peter as the father and Dudley as his son.

(*A knock at the door*)

PETER: Bloody timber beetles.

(*Another knock at the door*)

PETER: Get out! I mean come in.

(*Enter Dudley*)

DUDLEY: Father?

PETER: Father? Don't you even bother to say how's your father these days? Don't you youngsters have any respect? What do you want? More money?

DUDLEY: No, father. It's just that I'm planning to get married this Saturday, and I wanted you to be the first to know.

PETER: Haven't you told the girl yet?

DUDLEY: Of course I have.

PETER: Good, good. I think she ought to be in on it at the planning stages.

DUDLEY: Father, I just want to get your permission.

PETER: Permission, is it? How old are you, laddie? Out with it!

DUDLEY: Sixteen.

PETER: Sixteen years of age, that is? Only 16 years old, and you want to get married? Do you know what my reaction is to that bit of news?

DUDLEY: No, father.

PETER: I'll tell you what my reaction is. My reaction is Ha. Or possibly Psh. Somewhere between Ha and Psh.

DUDLEY: Given that your reaction is somewhere between Ha and Psh, I take it you have no objection?

PETER: What I want to ask you is this – at 16, do you really think you're mature enough, emotionally and spiritually, to deal with the profound complexities of a meaningful marital relationship?

DUDLEY: You think you have those qualities, father?

PETER: Yes, but it's taken me years to get there.

DUDLEY: Father, is throwing crockery at mother last night part of this emotional maturity?

PETER: My dear boy, I was not throwing crockery at your mother. I was aiming it at a fly on the wall that your mother asked me to remove.

DUDLEY: Why did you say, 'Take that, you stupid bitch'?

PETER: I was addressing this remark to the fly, which I had reason to believe was female, and, being momentarily stumped for the right word for a female fly, I called it a stupid bitch.

DUDLEY: You went on to say, 'Why the bloody hell did I marry you?' Was that another passing remark to the fly, father?

PETER: In the heat of the moment, one often says things to flies one later regrets. You know as well as I do, I wasn't married to that fly. I'll admit it – I was intent on saying the most wounding thing I could to it.

DUDLEY: You then hit mother over the head with a golf club.

PETER: Well, the fly was obviously humiliated by my remark about never wanting to marry it, and in a fit of jealousy made a beeline for your mother's forehead. I had no option but to strike while the iron was hot.

DUDLEY: That sounds very reasonable, father.

PETER: Look laddie, I don't want to be a dog in the manger, but for your own sake, I think I ought to know who this young girl is.

DUDLEY: I think you've met her, father.

PETER: I may have met her father, but I don't think I've met her.

DUDLEY: Sally and I have been living upstairs in this house for the last three years.

PETER: That girl upstairs, the one who's always in the bathroom when I need a shave? I thought she was the au pair girl.

DUDLEY: She's not.

PETER: And you've been living together in the same room? You might have told me. I thought all that noise at night was mice in the rafters. I've had the pest people round eight times in the last week. Anyway, how old is this young sprig you've shacked up with under my own nose?

DUDLEY: She's seventeen, father.

PETER: Seventeen? Oh, my god. Do you realise you're marrying an older woman? Have you really considered the fact that when you're 54, she'll be . . . What will she be? Er, 16 plus 28, take away the number you first thought of . . . I'll just get this down on a map.

DUDLEY: She'll be 55, father.

PETER: You might be a bright young lad, but don't try to teach your father mathematics. Now then, the square on the hypotenuse equals the sum of the three sides of a triangle . . . Anyway, when you're 54, she'll be somewhere between 54 and 60.

DUDLEY: Fifty-five, father.

PETER: I think you're forgetting one thing. A woman tends to age more quickly than a man – not that you'd know that, you young snippet. Listen, I'm not trying to put you off the girl. The thing that worries me is your lack of experience. I've read too many tragic stories in Marjorie Proops' column about the inexperienced lover on his wedding night.

DUDLEY: Father, Sally and I have been living together for three years. All we want to do is to get married.

PETER: Well, on your own head be it. Only one thing, laddie – I don't know if you believe in the supernatural, but during the War, a group of us were holding out in a bar in Tunisia – enemy everywhere – completely surrounded, and Brigadier Squatter Madras came up to me and said 'Edward, if you ever have a son aged 16 who comes in one afternoon and asks if he can marry a girl called Sally who's a year older and they've been living under your roof for three years anyway, for God's sake don't say yes.' Four days later the poor blighter bought it – blown up by an unexploded lager. And so it's really against my better judgement, but if you want to drive your father insane, your mother into the grave, and insult the dead into the bargain, by all means go ahead.

DUDLEY: Thank you father, I will.

PETER: But when you're 98 and you're wife's, er . . .

DUDLEY: Ninety-nine.

PETER: Ninety-nine, and I'll be, er, 180, don't come crying to me and saying 'you're right, dad. I wasn't ready for marriage.'

LENGTHS
(BBC2, 1970)

This sketch was inspired by the frenetic chaos of Jimmy Gilbert's production office – typing and retyping scripts, booking guest stars and locations – chaos caused in no small part by Peter and Dudley's indifference to impending deadlines. Gilbert and his secretary shared the same phone line, so they colour-coded their telephones – something Peter used as the basis for this piece. Remarkably, it took Peter and Dudley less than an hour to put together.

(*Peter and Dudley sit in an office, reading newspapers. The phone rings.*)

PETER: Oh, there's a call coming through on Green, Reg.

DUDLEY: Oh, that'll be Alan from Sales if it's on Green.

PETER: Alan from Sales? Would you like to take it?

DUDLEY: No, that bloke gets up my nose. I don't want to talk to him.

PETER: Oh, I'll take it. Otherwise, he'll hang up. You know Alan.

DUDLEY: Yes.

(*Peter picks up the phone.*)

PETER (*on the phone*): It's George here. Hello, Alan.

DUDLEY: Who is it?

PETER: It's Alan, Sales.

DUDLEY: Oh, Alan on Green.

PETER: Yes. (On the phone.) Hello, Alan. What are you talking about? No, we haven't got the lengths. What? You've not got them? (*To Dudley.*) He's not got the lengths.

(*Dudley picks up his phone.*)

PETER (*on the phone*): Reg is coming on Green, Alan.

DUDLEY (*on the phone*): Alan, I've got one thing to say. The lengths go through Admin, not via us. Thank you.

(*Dudley hangs up.*)

PETER (*on the phone*): Look, I'm sorry, Alan. It's not our fault. No, it should have gone right through Admin straight through to you. Yes, well, it's not really our department, but we'll look into it and I'll get back to you on Blue. No, I can't really talk, cos he's here. Yes, I love you too. Right.

(*Peter hangs up.*)

DUDLEY: Now how could he have not got the lengths?

PETER: I don't know. He says he hasn't got the lengths. I'd better get on to Bernard right away.

DUDLEY: Bet Daphne's cocked it up again.

PETER: Oh, Daphne's very suspect.

(*Peter picks up the phone.*)

PETER (*on the phone*): Sylvia, get me Bernard, would you please? . . . On Green . . . Bernard, it's George here. Sorry to trouble you, but we're in a bit of trouble re these lengths. I've got Alan on my back. They've been through Transit Control and on to Admin, but they haven't been roneoed and there's no dockets.

(*Dudley picks up the phone.*)

DUDLEY (*on the phone*): Er, Bernard, it's Reg here. Sorry to interrupt.

PETER (*on the phone*): It's Reg on Green, Bernard.

DUDLEY: (*on the phone*): Yes. I've just had a look through here at what we've got, but there's nothing at all. We haven't got a trace of a docket, either. Unless we have a docket, we can't move.

(*Dudley hangs up.*)

PETER (*on the phone*): Can't move without a docket, Bernard. Understand me, we've got valued clients in here all the time. Look, I'll get on to Dorian.

(*Dudley picks up the phone.*)

DUDLEY (*on the phone*): Look, Bernard, if the lengths aren't with you, you do understand that's all we can do – get on to Dorian.

PETER (*on the phone*): Beryl, would you get me Dorian on Grey, please? Thank you.

DUDLEY (*on the phone*): Oh, did you really? With Daphne? You randy old toerag! (*He laughs.*)

PETER (*on the phone*): Dorian, it's George here. It's re the lengths. I've been through all channels, and there's no sign of them, but Bernard and Alan are getting a bit het up, and we're going mad up here. I wondered if you could pull all the stops out your end.

DUDLEY (*on the phone*): I know, Bernard. It's not fair on us and it's not fair on you, is it? Anyway, I can't talk cos he's here. I love you too.

PETER (*on the phone*): I'd appreciate that, Dorian, cos we are in a bit of a bind. The consignment should have been off to Montevideo. Haile Selassie's screaming blue murder on Green. Oh . . .

DUDLEY (*on the phone*): Oh, hello, Barbara. How are you? Good! (*To Peter.*) It's Barbara.

PETER: Barbara who?

DUDLEY: Your wife. Do you want to speak to her?

PETER: No, I'm talking on Grey.

DUDLEY: Oh. (*On the phone.*) Er, Barbara, I'm afraid George can't speak at the moment. He's out at lunch. I can't really talk to you cos he's here. I love you too.

PETER (*on the phone*): No, Barbara's on Red. I'll call you back.

(*Peter hangs up.*)

PETER: Hold on, Barbara.

DUDLEY: Yes.

PETER: I'll take it on Red.

(*Peter picks up the phone.*)

PETER: Look, you've come through on Red again, love. How many times do I have to warn you about this? Don't come through on Red. We're up to our eyes. We've got lengths missing. Put yourself in my position, love. Well, untie him and replace the strawberry jam. Yes, and you.

(*Peter hangs up.*)

PETER: That was Barbara on Red. She came through.

DUDLEY: Yes, I think Daphne's the weak link in the chain here, you know.

PETER: D'you know what I think, Reg?

DUDLEY: What?

PETER: I think Bernard is mixing business with pleasure. I mean, a forty-eight-inch bust is all very well, but it doesn't get the dockets in, does it?

(*Dudley picks up the phone.*)

DUDLEY (*on the phone*): Hello. Alan, look, we're doing our best. No one is contesting that, Alan.

(*Dudley hangs up.*)

PETER (*on the phone*): Alan, I've looked through filing and there's no trace. Look, we'll be back. We're working like beavers up here, love.

(*Peter hangs up.*)

(*Dudley picks up the phone.*)

DUDLEY (*on the phone*): Hello, Sybil?

(*Peter picks up the phone.*)

PETER (*on the phone*): Sylvia, I've just sneezed. Would you get that roneoed, photostatted and circulated at once? I don't want any more controversy. Thank you, love.

(*Peter hangs up.*)

PETER (*to Dudley*): Who's that?

DUDLEY: It's Sybil Thorndike.

PETER: Sybil Thorndike?

DUDLEY: Yes.

PETER: What does she want?

DUDLEY: It's about the cider commercial.

PETER: Stall her.

DUDLEY (*on the phone*): Sybil, we'd love to use you for the cider commercial, but we can't really promise anything at the moment. Wouldn't be fair to you, wouldn't be fair to us, would it? Eh? OK? Good luck with St Joan. Yes.

PETER: Is that Fernando?

DUDLEY (*on the phone*): I can't really talk to you cos he's here at the moment. Yes, I love you too. Bye.

(*Dudley hangs up.*)

PETER (*on the phone*): Oh, Claudia, you've got a very bad line. Call me back on Blue.

(*Peter hangs up.*)

PETER: I got through to Fernando – very bad line. I said I'd call him back on Blue. There's no trace of the dockets and no sign of the lengths. I don't know where to turn.

DUDLEY: No, it looks pretty black, doesn't it?

PETER: We might try Lengths, I suppose.

DUDLEY: It's a shot in the dark, isn't it?

PETER: Still, give it a whirl.

(*Peter picks up the phone.*)

PETER (*on the phone*): Brenda, give me Lengths, would you love, on Purple?

Yes.

(*Dudley picks up the phone.*)

DUDLEY (*on the phone, to Peter*): Hello, Reg, Lengths, here.

PETER (*on the phone, to Dudley*): Good. Well, if you could get those up to Transport, we could get Shipping on to it and they'd be in Montevideo by Thursday.

DUDLEY (*on the phone, to Peter*): Fine. Er, I can't really talk to you at the moment cos he's here, but maybe in about half an hour.

PETER (*on the phone, to Dudley*): Yes, I love you.

DUDLEY (*on the phone, to Peter*): I love you too.

PETER (*on the phone, to Dudley*): Thank you, Reg, for your co-operation.

DUDLEY (*on the phone, to Peter*): Bye-bye.

(*Peter and Dudley both hang up.*)

PETER: I've just talked to Reg on Purple.

DUDLEY: Yes.

PETER: And he's got the lengths, down there.

DUDLEY: You're joking!

PETER: No, he's had the lengths all the while.

DUDLEY: Well, why weren't they sent up to Alan?

PETER: Oh, I don't know. I think Daphne's the weak link.

DUDLEY: Yes.

(*Both phones ring. Peter and Dudley both pick up.*)

PETER (*on the phone*): Flora, look, I'm a bit tied up at the moment.

DUDLEY (*on the phone*): Hold on a minute, Basil.

PETER: I'm on Green to Flora.

DUDLEY: Blue for you.

PETER (*on the phone*): Alan . . . Look . . . Trying to sort things out . . .

DUDLEY (*on the phone*): Hold on a minute . . . Oh, blimey . . . Look – I can't speak to you . . .

PETER (*on the phone*): Look, Sybil is on Green and Basil is on Blue . . . Look . . . um . . . Sorry, love . . . Just talk amongst your-selves, would you?

(*Peter and Dudley put all the receivers down together.*)

PETER: There we are.

DUDLEY: Yes, we'll be back in an hour – or two.

DUDLEY (*exiting*): Yes, I think Daphne's the weak link.

PETER (*exiting*): Why do you think Bernard hired her?

DUDLEY (*exiting*): Well . . .

(*Exit Peter and Dudley.*)

CONMAN
(BBC2, 1970)

(*Dudley walks up the driveway of an elegant house and rings the door-bell. Peter answers.*)

DUDLEY: Michael, how wonderful to see you! How are you? Remember me, Brian?

PETER: Brian . . . Er . . .

DUDLEY: Yes, Brian Beavis. I used to come down and wash your car in Pavilion Road when you used to live there. Remember me and my little boy, Tony?

PETER: It's rather a long time ago. I don't remember, no.

DUDLEY: No. You probably don't recognise me because I had my hair cut. They made me have it cut when I was in the . . . er . . . last position I held. Nice to see you.

PETER: Nice to see you. I'm sorry about not recognising you.

DUDLEY: I know your time's very precious, but I wondered if I could have, like, five minutes with you?

PETER: Oh, what about?

DUDLEY: Well, it's a bit personal in nature. I wondered if we could, you know, just pop inside for a couple of minutes?

PETER: Well, the thing is, my wife is rather busy inside, preparing dinner. We've got some people coming round. Talk to me here.

DUDLEY: All right. Well, the thing is . . . this has never happened to me before . . . I don't really know how to put it.

PETER: Well, just tell me what's the matter.

DUDLEY: Last Sunday, my father died.

PETER: I'm very sorry.

DUDLEY: As I say, it's never happened to me before. I remember you saying to me, you said, 'Brian, anybody can get in a spot of bother. You should not be afraid to turn to someone for help.'

PETER: I said that?

DUDLEY: You know me. I wouldn't turn to you unless I was really desperate – I swear on my father's life.

PETER: I thought he was dead.

DUDLEY: Yes, well, he's living in Cardiff – or rather, he died in Cardiff. He wants to be buried there because he spent all his life there – as a youngster. I'm sorry, I don't want to bother you with all my bloody trouble. Anyway, I just wanted to get £50 for the burial and the fare to go down there, you know. I've had to pawn my wife's wedding ring, my dear wife's wedding ring. Look, here's the ticket.

PETER: This is for a transistor radio, in fact.

DUDLEY: Yes, well, we had to pawn that as well, you see – to get the cash to bury him, and that. I just wondered if you could just help us – tide us over?

PETER: Do you have a job?

DUDLEY: Yes, well, that's the point. I had this job as a truck driver, you know, taking away and delivering – mainly taking away. I had this accident and they took my licence away from me. But I was innocent – I had a witness.

PETER: Who was the witness?

DUDLEY: My mother. She was there, on the spot. I ran over her – broke her leg in fourteen places.

PETER: Your mother's broken her leg?

DUDLEY: That's the tragedy, cos she's a professional ice-skater – and she had this tour fixed up in South Africa, and of course she can't fulfil it now, you see. I haven't got a job. They won't let us back in the flat because we're fourteen weeks behind with the rent. My wife's down the launderette. It's the only warm place we can go to now.

PETER: I'm afraid I haven't got much cash, but I could let you have a fiver, if that's any use – but that's really all I can give you.

DUDLEY: I don't want to take it. I really don't want to take it. I really thank you, from the bottom of my heart, and I know my old lady would love to thank you. My mother would be delighted to thank you.

PETER: There's no need for her at all.

DUDLEY: Oh, she'd love to. She's just down the drive.

PETER: I can come down with you, and –

DUDLEY: No. No, please – she's too proud. We walked all the way from Norwood.

PETER: On a broken leg?

DUDLEY: Yes, she's a very proud woman. She wanted to come, just to meet you. You stay inside, in the house, in the warm, and I'll go and get her.

PETER: If you could make it rather brief.

DUDLEY: Yes, certainly. Thanks very much. I won't be a second.

PETER: Thank you.

(*Dudley exits, and returns dressed as an old woman.*)

DUDLEY: Oh, Mr Crane, I'm so sorry to bother you. I told Brian not to come round pestering you, but he's so overwrought, what with my father dying.

PETER: I thought it was your husband who died?

DUDLEY: Yes, well, that was the terrible thing – my father died within minutes of my husband. They say things come in threes – God knows what's round the corner for me. I expect I'll go next.

PETER: Shouldn't you be in hospital?

DUDLEY: Yes, I'm on the critical list – the critical list, but I had to come and see Brian when I heard that my husband and father were dead. I climbed out of the window on knotted sheets. The doctors say . . . they say I may never skate again – and I just had this wonderful tour of New Zealand all fixed up.

PETER: I thought it was South Africa, the tour?

DUDLEY: Yes, that's what makes it even worse. I've got the contract here – skating-tour contract.

PETER: It seems to be a hire-purchase agreement for a hairdryer.

DUDLEY: Yes, well, they insist on tidy hair when you're skating, you know. It's part of the rink rules. I suppose Brian told you about the funeral.

PETER: Yes, you need £50, I understand.

DUDLEY: Well, £75, actually – it's a double burial.

PETER: I'm afraid I haven't any more cash. I'm sorry.

DUDLEY: Well, a cheque will do – anything. I mean, we could move in here for a couple of weeks – we wouldn't make any fuss.

PETER: Mrs Beavis, I think I might be able to make out a small cheque – just to tide you over with the rent, if that's all right. Who do I make it out to?

DUDLEY: Oh, that's wonderful! Make it out to Alan Beavis.

PETER: I thought it was Brian?

DUDLEY: Brian, is it? Yes, Brian Beavis.

PETER (*making out a cheque*): Brian Beavis.

DUDLEY: He's much better at handling the money than I am.

PETER: Yes, well, there we are, and I hope that will tide you over.

DUDLEY: Thank you so much. It's the little boy I'm so worried about, really, you know.

PETER: Which little boy?

DUDLEY: Well, Brian's Tony. He's such a lovely little boy, but he can't go to school – he hasn't got the bus fare, poor little love. Those wide, innocent little eyes – one look at them and they'll have your heart pulsing. I wonder if you'd like just to say hello to him? I know he'd like to say thank you.

PETER: Well, look, I could take you down to the gate and see him there.

DUDLEY: Mr Crane, I may be eighty-four, with multiple fractures, but I do have my pride. I'll go and get him. I'll go and get my little Tony. He's the spitting image of his dad. You'll love him.

I'll bring him up here. Please don't trouble yourself any further. You've been too good already.

PETER: Thank you.

DUDLEY: Thank you. I won't be a sec.

(*Dudley exits, and returns dressed as a little boy.*)

DUDLEY: My granny said that I should come and say thank you.

PETER: I see you've got a broken leg, like your granny.

DUDLEY: Oh. Yes, well, we all have to sleep in the same bed, and I caught it off her. Things have been terrible since my father died.

PETER: Your father, Brian Beavis, has just died, has he?

DUDLEY: I mean my grandfather – but he was like a father to me.

PETER: I'm sure he was.

DUDLEY: Anyway, I just thought I'd come along and say thank you for what you've done, however little it was.

PETER: Would you kindly go and get your father and bring him here as soon as possible. I'd like to talk to him.

DUDLEY: Yes, I will. Thank you very much indeed.

(*Dudley exits, and returns dressed as Brian. Peter exits, and returns dressed as a woman, weeping.*)

DUDLEY: Oh, is Mr Crane in?

PETER: Yes, he's in – he's in. He's just had a heart attack. The doctors are with him now – they've given him one and a half minutes to live. We've lost all our money. We're going to have to sell the house. My grandmother's on fire upstairs. The children are going mad. What can I do? Mr Beavis, Mr Beavis – please help me.

(*Exit Dudley. Peter removes his wig.*)

PETER: Thank God for that.

THE LUNCH PARTY
(BBC2, 1970)

Like 'In the Club', there's a tipsy flavour to this sketch which was increasingly prevalent in Peter and Dudley's comedy, and a whiff of decadence too. Three men and three women are sitting around a dining table, at the end of a long boozy lunch. One of the men is slumped over the table.

DUDLEY: So the chap went up to the policeman and . . . er . . . wait a minute . . . I must get the last bit right . . . No, the policeman went up to the Archbishop . . . have you heard this one before?

PETER: No, no.

DUDLEY: I always get this end mixed up . . . can't tell a story to save my life . . . there was a dog involved somewhere . . . have I mentioned the dog?

PETER: You mentioned a mad dog.

DUDLEY: Blast! That's the whole joke gone. Anyway, it's a good one. Jinks could probably tell it better than I could, but he's passed out.

PETER (*to the butler*): Antonio, would you clear all this stuff away? Now, why don't you girls slip into your swimming togs, and we'll join you outside? The pool's up to eighty. Fiona, show everyone the way. Anyone want to go to the boys' room? More brandy? Or will you stick with vino?

DUDLEY: A little brandy. It's all from the grape. That was a most delicious bird.

PETER: Yes, we're very pleased with Maria. She's very good on roasts and things. Wouldn't let her near a soufflé, though.

DUDLEY: Same as Charlotte. She's all right on boiled potatoes and toast, but you can't expect a Sardinian to whip up a zabaglione. She's jolly, and not too much strain on the pocket – so she's ideal, really.

PETER: I must say it's awfully nice to see a new face in this neck of the woods. Can I call you Freddy?

DUDLEY: Yes you can, by all means. I can't promise to answer – I was christened Teddy.

PETER: Fair enough, Freddy. In that case, I'll call you Teddy – save any confusion. Unless you'd rather be called Freddy – it's all the same to me.

DUDLEY: If it's all the same to you, I'll plump for Teddy.

PETER: Teddy it is, Teddy – and all my friends call me Jumbo.

DUDLEY: Jumbo it is.

PETER: By the way, I sent out some beer and sandwiches to your chauffeur.

DUDLEY: That's very kind. He'll be as happy as a sandboy. Cheers. I must say, it's such absolute heaven being in the country. We've been longing to make the move for years.

PETER: I think we really get the best of both worlds. You've got peace and quiet, but if you want a bit of excitement, forty minutes down the M4 and you're in the West End. Fiona loves the theatre, so we're always popping up. You a theatre man?

DUDLEY: Not really. The last thing Verity and I saw was *Bless the Bride* in 1948 – loved it.

PETER: That was a lovely show. I wonder why it came off? Have you seen that *Hair* thing?

DUDLEY: No, I'm not really a rock and roll man. My two think I'm as square as a coot – but frankly, I had enough noise in the war. You've got two kids, haven't you?

PETER: Yes, Varian's coming up to twenty-eight and young Glenda's three months.

DUDLEY: Quite a gap.

PETER: Thanks. Yes, we decided to have another so Varian could have a bit of company.

DUDLEY: How long have you been married?

PETER: Let's see – Varian's twenty-eight . . . Coming up to two years. Fiona and I met in Mombassa.

DUDLEY: What an extraordinary coincidence! I met Verity in Tangiers!

PETER: It's a small world. Met her in Harry's Bar. She was out there trying to forget about . . .

DUDLEY: Oh, yes.

PETER: I told you about how she . . .

DUDLEY: Yes, frightful business.

PETER: Anyway, Fiona came in, we had a few drinks and a bit of a chinwag, and I suddenly thought, 'Why don't we make the whole thing legal?'

DUDLEY: Damn good brandy, this. Who do you go to?

PETER: Well, I'm very lucky, cos I've got this little man who gets it for me very cheap.

DUDLEY: One of those wholesale johnnies?

PETER: No, what he does is sort of steal it for me.

DUDLEY: Steals it?

PETER: It works out very economical. I must have enough here for about four years – which is about what he got.

DUDLEY: Four years.

(*Noises off.*)

DUDLEY: The girls sound as if they're having a good time.

(*Peter and Dudley go to the window.*)

PETER: The pool's a tremendous boon. Have you met Gerry Butterfield? He's got a lovely pool. Mind you, I think he fills it full of gin and tonic. (*He laughs.*)

DUDLEY: Gerry Butterfield? No.

PETER: Hell of a nice chap. Bit of an alco . . . Wife's very good value, if you're interested in that sort of thing?

DUDLEY: What sort of thing?

PETER: His wife. Get a few G & Ts down her and she's very accommodating.

DUDLEY: Doesn't Gerry mind?

PETER: No, Gerry's very civilised.

DUDLEY: Well, Verity and I have a very honest relationship. She knows perfectly well that, from time to time, I may have a bit of a fling – but she also knows that I'll never get seriously involved with another woman.

PETER: Yes.

DUDLEY: I mean, I've never got involved with her.

PETER: Saves anybody getting hurt. Why don't we pop out and join them? Swim off the lunch. Then, if you fancy a wander through the shrubbery, then fair enough.

DUDLEY: I must say after a lunch like that, and the country air, one does feel a bit Harry Randers.

PETER: Well, let's leave Jinks here to sleep it off, and go and throw all the girls into the pool. Take some brandy with you.
DUDLEY: How very civilised.

THE MAKING OF A MOVIE
(BBC2, 1970)

Having written a brilliant film – Bedazzled – that never received the critical acclaim it deserved, and appeared in several others which failed to make full use of his talents, Peter was entitled to feel rather grumpy about the movies. Dudley didn't need to feel quite so fed up, but like Peter, he still hadn't been cast in a film that utilised his talents to the full, and with his transformation into Hollywood star a decade away, he could be forgiven for feeling similarly frustrated about the big screen's indifference to his charms.

As well as ripping the piss out of portentous arts documentaries, 'The Making of a Movie' satirises several stars of British cinema, particularly playwright Robert Bolt, whose A Man For All Seasons *had won half a dozen Oscars a few years before. Bolt's play, about Henry VIII's marital dispute with Sir Thomas More, featured Paul Scofield as More and Robert Shaw as Henry. Peter and Dudley recast their remake with caricatures of Peter O'Toole and Richard Burton. The period language presented no problems. Although this stuff was scripted, they could improvise in iambic pentameter virtually at will – as they proved at a restaurant during the shooting of this series, swapping soliloquies over the heads of bewildered but delighted fellow diners. No surprise, really, since cod Shakespeareana had been a core part of their repertoire ever since 'So That's The Way You Like It' – their brilliant Shakespeare skit with Alan Bennett and Jonathan Miller in* Beyond the Fringe.

Since this sketch was shot on film, it escaped the BBC's passion for recycling, and ended up on The Best of What's Left of Not Only . . . But Also . . . – the greatest hits video that Peter and Dudley compiled themselves in 1990. However, this version, from the original script, contains a few good gags that didn't make the final cut. Several of the scenes below were trimmed in the eventual broadcast, and a couple disappeared altogether, although there's no sign here of Peter and Dudley ordering lunch in blank verse in the BBC canteen, in full Elizabethan dress.

(*Peter, aka Robert Neasden, is walking his dogs in the country*)

NARRATOR (*voice-over*): Robert Neasden. Author, poet, playwright, a man with a string of successful plays and films behind him – *A Man For All Neasdens*, *A Lion in Neasden* and *Anne of a Thousand Neasdens*.

PETER (*voice-over*): I've always been fascinated by words. I suppose words were the first words I heard. I need solitude to work. That's why I left London and came here, back to my roots, alone with my wife and dogs and the occasional television crew.

(*Cut to Robert Neasden's sitting room.*)

NARRATOR (*voice-over*): Neasden describes how the idea for his new film came to him.

PETER: I was in the cinema at the time – just me, my wife, dogs and children. And I was watching this film, and suddenly I felt 'That's it! A film! A film!' It was so simple, I wept.

(*Cut to a restaurant, where Robert Neasden, played by Peter, is lunching with Fred Neasden, played by Dudley.*)

NARRATOR (*voice-over*): Robert Neasden took his idea to famed producer director, Fred Neasden.

PETER: Basically, Fred, I suppose I want to do a film.

NARRATOR (*voice-over*): Fred Neasden warms to the idea.

DUDLEY: A film! I like it! That's what the industry needs!

NARRATOR: (*voice-over*): They decide to meet again.

PETER: I see it as a film about people.

DUDLEY: Yes.

PETER: People who need people.

DUDLEY: People who need people – yes.

PETER: Big people with universal emotions – a king, a queen, a bishop, locked in a noble conflict. Pageantry, horses, fine language, cathedrals.

DUDLEY: Posed against a rumbustious bawdiness – seething passions and wenches in the straw.

PETER: In a way, King Henry was the world's first hippie. He fore-shadowed the permissive society. For him, mead was the equiv-alent of LSD. He dropped out.

DUDLEY: A historical drama with echoes of *Easy Rider* and *Midnight Cowboy*. OK, Bob! You've got yourself a deal!

(*Cut to a swimming pool. Robert Neasden is floating on an inflatable rubber armchair, sipping champagne and typing furiously.*)

NARRATOR (*voice-over*): Neasden works furiously on the first draft, long into the night. For him, writing is exhilarating, exhausting – agonising.

(*Cut to Fred Neasden's office.*)

NARRATOR (*voice-over*): Months later, he delivers his first draft.

(*Fred Neasden weighs Robert Neasden's manuscript on some scales.*)

DUDLEY: I like it! Maybe a few ounces too long, but terrific!

NARRATOR (voice-over): Fred Neasden shelves his other scheduled spectacular, *When Diana Dors Ruled the Earth*, to concentrate on Robert Neasden's project. Now it's a question of casting. His mind clicks into action. Why not Peter O'Neasden as the Archbishop, and Richard Neasden as the King? Two giants of the box office, who could set the screen alight.

DUDLEY (*on the phone*): Peter? . . . Hello love, how are you? . . . As you know, Richard's committed to play the King, and I wondered if you'd like to give us your lovely Archbishop? . . . Yes, I'll rush you a script in a cab.

(DUDLEY *picks up the other phone.*)

DUDLEY (*on the phone*): Hello, Richard! . . . How are you? . . . Good . . . Down to the nitty . . . Peter's committed to do the Archbishop . . . He's over the moon about the scripts . . . And I thought, who else for handsome Henry but you? . . .

NARRATOR (*voice-over*): Peter O'Neasden and Richard Neasden leap at the chance of playing with each other. But who will be the Queen?

PETER: Look, love – this is way out of left court, but what about Sidney Poitier?

DUDLEY: I like it. I know he wants to break away from this whole black man image. It would be a challenge to play a white woman. But I tell you an even better idea. What about an unknown?

PETER: Do you know any?

DUDLEY: Not that I know of, but I'm sure there must be some about.

NARRATOR (*voice-over*): Weeks of auditions follow.

(*Cut to audition room. Girls get out of crate marked 'Unknowns'.*)

DUDLEY: Jill's got a nice quality. I saw her in *The Caucasian Chalk Circle* last season. She takes direction very well.

PETER: She's not regal, though.

DUDLEY: No, but I think we could use her in the barn.

(*Cut to Peter O'Neasden's bedroom. Peter O'Neasden, played by Peter, is fast asleep.*)

NARRATOR (*voice-over*): Shooting begins. It's five in the morning. London slumbers, but for Peter O'Neasden, the day has already begun. He gets his alarm call.

(*A bucket of water is thrown over Peter O'Neasden.*)

NARRATOR (*voice-over*): Richard Neasden has had a small place built near the studios.

(*Cut to still of Buckingham Palace.*)

NARRATOR (*voice-over*): Here in tranquillity he can study his part in private.

(*Cut to make-up room. Peter O'Neasden, played by Peter, and Richard Neasden, played by Dudley, are both being made up.*)

DUDLEY: I've always wanted to work with Fred, and when I heard that Robert had written the script, I didn't need to read it. The money's neither here nor there – it's in Geneva.

NARRATOR (*voice-over*): How does Richard Neasden feel about working with Peter O'Neasden?

DUDLEY: Peter and I are mates from way back. We spark off each other. I mean, a Welsh miner and a Paddy – what do you expect? There's no rivalry as such. We feel we're just tools in the hand of the director. Wouldn't you agree, Peter?

PETER: Yes.

(*Cut to the interior of a cathedral. Bishop Neasden, played by Peter, is arranging flowers on the altar. Enter Lord Neasden, played by Dudley, in clanking armour. He speaks with a pronounced lisp.*)

DUDLEY: My Lord Bishop.

PETER: Lord Neasden, what ist?

DUDLEY: I ist, My Lord.

PETER: My Lord Neasden – when I say what ist, I mean what is it?

DUDLEY: 'Tis my teeth, My Lord Bishop of Beacontree. This is why I issed.

PETER: I'll start again. My Lord Neasden, what ails thee?

DUDLEY: A mild and bitter – how very kind, to ease my parched throat.

PETER: Defile not this holy house with thy drunken appetites.

DUDLEY: Forgive me, Lord – like a humble snail, I kneel silent at your feet. (*Dudley kneels, with much clanking.*)

DUDLEY: And crave thy holy indulgence – and could you possibly extend the episcopal hand and bear me up again? (*Peter helps Dudley to his feet.*)

PETER: What is thy news, Neasden?

DUDLEY: Grave news, I fear, My Lord. Your cousin, Hal, the King, God's instrument upon this earth, dost bear down upon this holy haven like some black falcon upon his prey, the lowly vole.

PETER: Get on with it.

DUDLEY: I crave thy pardon and kneel like a cringing spaniel that has his master much offended.

PETER: What will the King, Lord Neasden?

DUDLEY: No, Hal the King, My Lord, for Good King Will was murdered most foully by Lord Kilburn and Earl Court – and now King Hal would be unfettered from his Queen.

PETER: Divorce?

DUDLEY: Aye, My Lord. E'en now, he frivels with his fancy maid – the strumpet Nell.

PETER: There can be no divorce.

DUDLEY: He says the Queen is barren, and he yearns for a son. My Lord, Nell is big with child. But hist, methinks I hear his kingly footsteps now. I must away.

(*Exit Dudley.*)

PETER: And I must pray.

(*Enter Dudley, as King Hal.*)

PETER: This is God's house. It is time for vespers.

DUDLEY: Let God wait, for do we not read that His patience is infinite? But patience is a commodity most absent in my nature. Most pressingly, I need a favour from your hand.

PETER: Aye, Hal – you want a son. The taverns hum with rumours of your impetuous adultery.

DUDLEY: I love her, John. Each time I see her, my heart becomes a thousand fluttering larks.

PETER: What of your Queen, and the honour of England?

DUDLEY: My barren Bess can give me neither princeling, nor a king's comfort.

PETER: Then I shall pray for you.

DUDLEY: Good John, dost not recall those times when we were young – hunting and whoring together? Where is the John I used to know that wassailed and rutted like a mountain stag?

PETER: That John is dead.

DUDLEY: And dead shall be the other John, unless there is annulment of my sterile bonds. Wouldst have me spawn a bastard? Just one stroke of a pen is all I crave, to legitimise the fruits of my loins.

PETER: Hal, this is thy twelfth divorce. The Pope wearies of thy constant inconsistencies. But should the Queen agree, then one more time my quill will spill thy will upon the scroll – and then to Nell with you. But now God calls me.

(*Exit DUDLEY, laughing.*)

(*Cut to the King and Queen's bedroom. The King, played by Dudley, and the Queen, played by Peter, are quarrelling.*)

NARRATOR (*voice-over*): In this climactic scene, the King has asked Bess for a divorce, and they hurl insults at each other.

PETER: Bastard.

DUDLEY: Slut.

PETER: Adulterer.

DUDLEY: Bitch.

PETER: Whoremonger.

DUDLEY: Fishwife.

PETER: Pig.

DUDLEY: Cow.

PETER: Milk.

DUDLEY: Please.

(*Peter pours some milk into Dudley's goblet.*)

(*Cut to Fred Neasden's house. Enter Robert Neasden, played by Peter, and Fred Neasden, played by Dudley.*)

DUDLEY: Oh God, it's marvellous to be home! Help yourself to a drink. I'll go and get Vera and the kids.

(*Dudley goes upstairs and shouts. There is no answer. He returns.*)

DUDLEY: That's peculiar. She was here three years ago.

PETER: There's a note here.

DUDLEY (*reads*): 'Goodbye for ever, love Vera.' (*To Peter.*) My God! What a fantastic title for a film!

PETER: Yes, I see it as a very contemporary film.

DUDLEY: A film! A film!

PETER: Young people in revolt against society.

DUDLEY: *Easy Cowboy!*

PETER: Here's to it.

DUDLEY: Marvellous!

PSEUDOLENE
(Australian Broadcasting Commission, 1971)

With its blend of simple slapstick and sophisticated social satire, this shrewd, sadistic sketch really should rank among Peter and Dudley's greatest hits. Yet compared to a lot of their head-to-heads, it's actually relatively unknown. The fact that it was filmed on the other side of the world makes it something of a rarity, but it's because of this that the original broadcast has survived intact – unlike so many of their domestic sketches, which were wiped by the BBC. And it's great that the Australians hung on to it, because the contrast between Peter's cruel, condescending autocrat and Dudley's bright, insecure everyman has rarely been put to better use than in this vicious observation of the imbalance of power between employer and employee.

(*Peter is sat at a restaurant table. Enter Dudley.*)

DUDLEY: I'm very sorry I'm so late. I got lost on the Inner Circle. I'm very sorry. I'm not used to it here.

PETER: I don't know why you came by Underground. It's much

simpler to take a taxi. I just got my chauffeur to drop the car and leave me here. He's gone off for a sandwich. Anyway, now you're here, sit down.

DUDLEY: Thank you.

PETER: Since you are a bit late, I took the liberty of ordering for you. I hope that's OK.

DUDLEY: No, that's very kind of you. Thank you very much.

PETER: We're having minestrone to start with. Does that suit you?

DUDLEY: That's marvellous.

PETER: They do a really very wonderful minestrone here. Quite nice little place, isn't it?

DUDLEY: Yes, very nice. It's not the sort of place I can really afford to go to, being a research chemist. It's not the sort of place I can get around to much.

PETER: No, I'm afraid we treat you research people rather badly, don't we? It's the only compensation being in top executive management – at least you eat well and rather often. Ah! Here comes the minestrone. Thank you, or rather, *grazie*, Antonio. I think you'll like this. It's a delicious minestrone and I think you'll like it.

DUDLEY: Jolly good.

PETER: Right! Let's get down to brass tacks. Why exactly do you want to join Foster, Blackett & Bignell?

DUDLEY: Well, I've heard of your firm for so many years and I've really wanted to join it and be associated with your projects because I admire them so much.

PETER: Yes, well, we do have the most marvellous research facilities, possibly the greatest in Europe for a chemist of your type, so it is the ideal opportunity for a chap like you, isn't it?

DUDLEY: Yes, I mean, I think your firm is fantastic and what's so exciting is the expanding export market, and –

PETER: Yes, yes, yes. I find exports very exciting. We have that little phrase, you know, in my office – export or die. And, of the two, I prefer to export. Rather than die, you see? I've had many a laugh over that.

DUDLEY: Very good.

PETER: It is quite good, isn't it? Yes, I believe you saw our personnel manager, Mr Sprogitt, the other week, didn't you?

DUDLEY: Yes I did, yes. He was . . . I got on very well with . . .

PETER: He was very enthusiastic about you, actually. He said you were the ideal person for the job, in fact.

DUDLEY: Oh, that's marvellous. That's very kind. I was very pleased to talk to him because he said this vacancy had come up and, er, it looks as if it was 100 per cent certain that I could take over. I was delighted.

PETER: Yes. You realise that Mr Sprogitt works entirely in an advisory capacity. He advises me. I can accept – or reject – his advice. Unfortunately, the final decision – and this is what is so agonising about my job as chairman of the board – I have to make the final decision. Not Mr Sprogitt. I have to make the final decision. Enjoying the minestrone?

DUDLEY: It's absolutely delicious.

PETER: It's very good, isn't it?

(*Peter picks up Dudley's bowl and tips it down Dudley's shirt.*)

DUDLEY: Oh, I'm sorry. I seem to have spilt my soup. I'm awfully sorry.

PETER: It's all over your lap, isn't it?

DUDLEY: Yes, I'm terribly sorry.

PETER: Would you like some more?

DUDLEY: No, I won't have any more. No thank you. I'll go on to the next course. I'm so sorry.

PETER: Really? You're sure you won't have any more?

DUDLEY: No, really. That's very nice of you.

PETER: Next course then. Antonio! *Per piacere*, Antonio. The next course. He doesn't speak English, poor devil. Thank you very much. The spaghetti is very good here. It's all hand-woven and I think you'll enjoy it very much indeed.

DUDLEY: Thank you.

PETER: Use a spoon and whirl it round, get it into your mouth. Or a knife and fork, if you like. I just wondered if you could tell me your qualifications for the job.

DUDLEY: Well, I was at Sheffield University for three years and I got a BA – a first, actually. Not a BA. What am I talking about? A BSc. A first in Science, and I specialised in nylon fibres – and things. And, er, that's about it, really, regards qualifications.

PETER: What about your thesis?

DUDLEY: Oh, my thesis! Well, of course I had to write a thesis, and I wrote it, in fact, on your product Pseudolene, and its uses in modern materials.

PETER: Yes, we manufacture Pseudolon.

DUDLEY: But it's Pseudolene, isn't it?

PETER: Well, as we manufacture it, I think I can call it what I bloody well choose.

DUDLEY: Sorry about that.

PETER: I understand you've given up your job in Millwall?

DUDLEY: Yes I have, actually. I've more or less burnt my boats there, really. I came down here to London about four weeks ago with the wife and four children. Moved into a little place in Catford. It's a bit poky. We've got another child on the way, probably. And I've severed my connections because of the children, and –

PETER: And I assume you're rather short of cash, having sort of given up your job, come here and sold everything?

DUDLEY: Yes, a bit short. Yes, a bit on the short side for cash.

PETER: I imagine, Mr Moore, that rather a lot depends on my decision, vis-à-vis the cash.

DUDLEY: Well, more or less everything, really.

PETER: Everything depends on me and my decision.

DUDLEY: It's an important moment in my career, really.

PETER: Are you enjoying the spaghetti?

DUDLEY: Yes, it's absolutely delicious.

(*Peter tips Dudley's plate of spaghetti over Dudley's head.*)

DUDLEY: Oh, I'm so sorry. I seem to have spilt my spaghetti.

PETER: That's quite all right. Would you care to have a little wine to wash it down?

DUDLEY: No, it always goes to my head.

PETER: It's really very good wine.

(*Peter pours a glass of wine over Dudley's head.*)

PETER: Are you enjoying that? Very good. There we are.

DUDLEY: I seem to have split my wine.

PETER: Yes, you seem to be in a terrible mess.

DUDLEY: Yes, I'm sorry about that.

PETER: I hope you're not like this in the laboratory. It's all very well chucking food and wine over yourself when you're in a restaurant, but when you're in a laboratory, one trusts one will try to be a bit more careful.

DUDLEY: Oh, well, up in Millwall they used to call me Meticulous Moore.

PETER: Meticulous Moore?

DUDLEY: Yes, I'm not normally as messy as this. I'm so sorry.

PETER: 'Not normally as messy as this.' Yes. Would you like some more spaghetti?

DUDLEY: No, no, thanks all the same.

PETER: Let's go straight on to the next course, shall we?

DUDLEY: Yes – well, no, I won't have anything more, thank you very much.

PETER: Oh you must have. Antonio! Antonio, my dear chap, bring on the lemon meringue pie, would you please?

DUDLEY: Oh, not for me thanks.

PETER: Won't you have it?

DUDLEY: No, thank you all the same.

PETER: I insist you have the lemon meringue pie. It is the *spécialité de la maison*. It really is superb.

DUDLEY: Well, I've really had quite sufficient.

PETER: Do you think so? This lemon meringue pie, I can tell you, is quite out of this world. It's fluffy on top, crusty on the bottom. You'll never taste anything like it.

(*Peter plants the pie in Dudley's face.*)

DUDLEY: Oh, I'm so sorry. I seem to have spilt my lemon meringue pie! I'm so sorry. I don't normally do this sort of thing.

PETER: You are in a bit of a mess, aren't you?

DUDLEY: Yes, I don't know what came over me.

PETER: Try not to spit at me, Mr Moore. It was lemon meringue pie that came over you. Anyway, I think I've learnt all I need to know from you. It's been very interesting talking. I've got a rather

important business meeting to go to, so if you'll excuse me I'll
have to dash off. Would you settle up the bill?

DUDLEY: I haven't got any cash on me, sir.

PETER: I'm sure they'd accept a cheque from you.

DUDLEY: I don't have an account here.

PETER: Or Diner's Card, Green Stamps, something like that.

DUDLEY: By the way, when do you think you'll be making your
decision?

PETER: Well, this isn't the sort of decision one enters into lightly,
but I'd say within the next two to three weeks in any case.

DUDLEY: Oh, well, I had better give you my phone number, hadn't
I?

PETER: I think I've got it. Or my secretary's got it, certainly.

DUDLEY: No she hasn't.

PETER: Hasn't she? Well then, she can give you a ring and find out
what it is. Anyway, very nice to meet you. Help yourself to coffee
and feel at home.

(*Peter stands up, shakes hands with Dudley, and departs.*)

DUDLEY: I hope I didn't make a mess of that.

SHIRT SHOP
(Australian Broadcasting Commission, 1971)

*Although it was new to the Australians who saw it on Australian tele-
vision, in February 1971, and most of the British viewers who saw it
on BBC1 a few months later, this was actually a reworking of a sketch
which Peter wrote for Kenneth Williams way back in 1959, when he
was still an undergraduate at Cambridge. Originally called Balance of
Trade, it appeared in Williams' West End revue, Pieces of Eight, at
London's Apollo Theatre, with Williams playing the part taken up by
Peter twelve years later. Nevertheless it was the first time it had been
on television, it had aged reasonably well, and Dudley certainly brought
something extra to the role of irate customer.*

(Peter is the shopkeeper in a shirt shop. Enter Dudley. Peter speaks in a posh but supercilious tone of voice. Dudley speaks with a gruff Scots accent)

DUDLEY: Excuse me.

PETER: Hello.

DUDLEY: I wonder if you can help me.

PETER: I wonder if I can.

DUDLEY: I hope you can. I bought this shirt from you two days ago.

PETER: You bought that shirt from me two days ago, didn't you? Yes, I remember. I never forget a chest. It was a blue Gazytex with the built in deodorant. Very necessary in your case, I dare say. *(Peter laughs)* Forgive me.

DUDLEY: No, certainly not.

PETER: What's the matter?

DUDLEY: This shirt is coming apart at the sleeves.

PETER: Coming apart at the sleeve is it? Oh yes, look. One rip . . .

(Peter wrenches the shirt until it rips)

PETER: . . . And the whole sleeve comes apart. You notice, the rest of the shirt isn't in terribly good condition, is it?

(Peter wrenches the shirt again. It rips again)

PETER: Look at this! This is really a most appalling shirt! Woeful!

DUDLEY: I think you could say this shirt is a bit on the weak side.

PETER: Yes, yes, it is on the weak side. This, of course, is the great weakness of our shirts. Their great weakness is their great weakness, if you see what I mean.

(Peter laughs, Dudley doesn't)

DUDLEY: I see what you mean, yes. What about your other shirts? Have you got anything at all that's not weak?

PETER: Yes, we've got plenty of shirts, but they're all much worse than that one. Look at that one over there. That's a very hard-wearing shirt. In fact, nobody's managed to wear it for more than half an hour. It gives you a very nasty . . . Don't touch! It gives you a very nasty rash up the tummy. You don't want a nasty rash up the tummy, do you?

DUDLEY: No, I do not.

PETER: I was going to say, if you do want a nasty rash up the tummy, that's just the shirt for you. And this one here, you see this one here?

DUDLEY: That looks very nice.

PETER: It looks very attractive, doesn't it? The only one problem is, it tends to shrink terribly rapidly. Ten of our customers were strangled last week. It was a tragic business. I had to write to all their mothers and so on.

DUDLEY: Why are your shirts so bad?

PETER: Well, there is a very good reason for all our shirts being so bad, and that is, we employ terribly old men and terribly old women in awful conditions, working underground by a guttering candle, with no wages at all. It's positively Dickensian down there, so you can understand why our shirts tend to come out a bit on the tatty side. I suppose you'd like your money back?

DUDLEY: Well, I certainly would, thank you very much.

PETER: There's only one tiny little snag. That is, we never refund money. It's our strictest rule.

DUDLEY: That's absolutely ridiculous!

PETER: Well, look at it from my point of view. There's no need to take me quite so literally. You see, we have a policy of trying to get excessive profits, and so far we have. You should see our balance sheets. They're really beautiful.

(*Enter another customer*)

PETER: Ah! Here comes another gentleman! I served you yesterday, did I not?

CUSTOMER: Yes, you did indeed. I was in here yesterday. I bought this shirt from you. Look! Already, it's fallen apart!

PETER: It's got a nasty hole up the back, hasn't it, this shirt? Yes, very nasty, in this weather, with a lot of snakes about. (*To Dudley*) Look at that. Look at that! It's almost worse than yours!

DUDLEY: I think the very least you can do is to refund our money. That's the very least you can do.

PETER: I think you'll find that for you, I can do even less. For example, I could lie on the counter, fall fast asleep and ignore you completely. But as you're two very nice gentlemen and I've got nothing against you personally at all, I tell you what I'll do. I'll be perfectly willing to exchange the faulty goods.

DUDLEY: Oh well, that's fine.

PETER: It's fine if I exchange the goods, is it? Everybody happy? (*To customer*) Now, yours was the red one with the hole at the back, wasn't it? (*To Dudley*) Yours was the blue with the faulty sleeve? So why don't you have the blue, you have the red. Fair exchange, no robbery.

DUDLEY: You're just swapping them over!

PETER: Yes, you're not stupid, are you? I'm swapping them over.

DUDLEY: This is the most outrageous behaviour! This is appalling behaviour!

PETER: You're so right, you know. We have a little motto in this shop: the customer is always right.

Chapter Five
Behind The Fridge

The invitation to tour Australia came at just the right time. Peter was in the throes of a divorce from Wendy Snowden, his first wife and the mother of his two young daughters. Dudley's first marriage, to Suzy Kendall, was heading the same way. Australia had always adored Peter and Dudley's humour, with its potent cocktail of erudite and bawdy banter. Where better to escape your problems than on the other side of the world, doing your own stage show, surrounded by admiring fans? Unlike movie-making, they'd be beholden to no one, and the accolades would be immediate. It was an offer that neither of them was in any mood to refuse.

Peter and Dudley wrote the show together in London in the summer of 1971. The writing proved heavy going, but after the last-minute improvisation of the third series of *Not Only . . . But Also . . .* , it was none the worse for that. The show comprised a dozen sketches, plus three of Dudley's piano pieces. It was far darker than anything they'd done before, but it was also more sustained. The darkness was understandable, given the difficulties in their private lives. The longer sketches stemmed partly from Peter's growing indifference to easy laughter, and partly from Dudley's increased input. His logicality grounded Peter's wordplay, and channelled his surreal wit. 'Peter had a very unusual improvisational air to him,' says Clive Anderson. 'Things just sort of tumbled out of him. He'd have a thought and go with it. Somebody like that almost always needs somebody else to give some structure or to spark up against or to react to, otherwise it just becomes completely uncontrolled.'[1] In Peter's case, increasingly, that somebody was Dudley.

The title was Dudley's idea, and harked back to the New York run of *Beyond the Fringe*. 'The whole point of calling it *Behind the Fridge* was to disassociate it from *Beyond the Fringe*,' explained Dudley, in a joint interview a few years later. 'I've never been able to follow your reasoning on that,' interjected Peter. 'No,' admitted Dudley. 'Neither have I.'[2] But it was an excellent title, nonetheless.

They played Canberra, Melbourne, Sydney and Perth, plus Auckland and Wellington in New Zealand. 'There were nights when I couldn't think of anything more enjoyable,' recalled Dudley. 'It was such tremendous fun, and you came off absolutely ecstatic and jumping about the place.'[3] The show was very well received, and there were some fun times offstage, but this wasn't the whole story. Peter's escalating drinking was making life increasingly difficult for Dudley, especially onstage.

'Dudley once said to me that the start of the break-up of the relationship was the *Behind the Fridge* tour,' recalls Michael Parkinson, who saw the show in Australia. 'I think that was the beginning of the end of the partnership.'[4] 'I realised that it was up, that we had to go our separate ways,' Dudley told Parkinson. 'I couldn't go on any more doing this because I loved him so much.'[5] They had to go on for several months, and would go on for several years, but from now on it wasn't a case of if the break would come but when.

Thankfully Australian audiences tend to be a pretty accommodating bunch – certainly more lenient than punters in London or New York. In critical and commercial terms, the tour was a great success, and led to an offer to bring the show to London's West End. In the long run, *Behind the Fridge* may have pulled their partnership apart, but in the short term, it bound them together. In

February 1972, they returned to London. Their Australian tour had been a private disaster and a public triumph.

The West End show wasn't due to open until the autumn, and during the spring and summer, Peter and Dudley went their separate ways. It was one of the oddities of their relationship that although they were inseparable while working together, between projects they rarely met. On the personal front, Dudley and Suzy Kendall divorced, while Peter set up home with the actress Judy Huxtable, who would become his second wife. On the professional front, Peter filled in time with a few fairly undemanding film and telly roles, while Dudley appeared in a BBC show with Lulu. Dudley had to write a sketch for this show, and he hated doing it. Nor was he terribly pleased with the result. Dudley enjoyed working without Peter, but he didn't enjoy writing without him. Whatever his private feelings, he was still tied to his old partner – for the time being, at least.

Behind the Fridge opened at London's Cambridge Theatre on 21 November, half an hour late, since Peter was drunk. 'I thought we weren't going to get the curtain up at all,' says Joe McGrath, whom Dudley had invited to direct the show. 'The review the next day, by one of the leading "crickets", as Peter called them, said "a strangely nervous Dudley Moore was overruled by a magisterial performance by Peter Cook". It wasn't a magisterial performance. Dudley was cueing Peter all the time beneath his breath. Peter didn't know the next line, and Peter would walk into the wings, and I would tell him the next line, and he'd walk back onstage and these "crickets" didn't notice this.'[6]

The rest of the reviews were mixed. 'There is a terrible dearth of punchlines,' wrote Sheridan Morley in *Punch*. 'In search of them, sketches are prolonged far beyond their natural life, occasionally bolstered by irritating fits of giggling.' However, as Peter had predicted, the public didn't care what the 'crickets' said. The show sold out, Peter sobered up and Alexander Cohen, who'd produced the Broadway run of *Beyond the Fringe*, offered them $7,000 per week to bring it to the States. The London show closed on 25 August 1973. In September, Peter and Dudley flew to America.

Shorn of its Idi Amin and Ted Heath numbers (too parochial

for transatlantic tastes) and renamed *Good Evening* by Peter after Alexander Cohen said he didn't like Dudley's title, the American run opened in Boston on 12 October and transferred to the Plymouth Theater in New York on 10 November. The critics loved it and celebs flocked backstage to meet them. The show took more money than any previous performance at the Plymouth Theater and went on to become the longest running two-man show on Broadway. 'We did it rather lazily in the West End,' said Peter. 'We didn't work hard enough at it. When we took it to the States we had Alexander Cohen producing, and he made us work. It was a much, much better show on Broadway.'[7] Peter and Dudley won a Tony and a Grammy. The Broadway run finally ended in November 1974. In February 1975, Peter and Dudley set out on tour.

Good Evening travelled to Washington, Detroit, Montreal, Philadelphia and Chicago, eventually winding up in Los Angeles, where it ran until August 1975. It was nearly four years since it had opened in Canberra. Its success had endured, but so had Peter's drinking. By now, Peter and Dudley had both remarried – Peter to Judy Huxtable, Dudley to the American actress Tuesday Weld, who was now expecting his baby. Dudley decided to stay in Hollywood, with his new family, and make a living as a movie actor. Peter flew home without him. Their partnership wasn't over – not quite – but they would never work so closely together again. Indeed, they might never have worked together again at all if it hadn't been for their two new alter egos, a pair of expatriate toilet cleaners called Derek and Clive.

FOREIGN OFFICE
(Network Nine Television, Sydney, 1971)

(Sir Alec, the Foreign Secretary, played by Peter, is behind a desk, on the telephone)

PETER: Miss Varney? Foreign Secretary here. I've just had this note in from the Chinese and I wondered if there was anybody left in the translation pool . . . Yes, I realise it's half past five. It's just I would appreciate it very much indeed . . . Thank you, Miss Varney. That's very good of you . . . Hello? Ah, Reg. Foreign Secretary here. I've just had this note from the Chinese, in Chinese, and I wondered if you could pop up for a . . . Yes, I realise you knock off at nine minutes to five. It's just that I would be very grateful . . . Thank you, Reg. Thank you, thank you. (*Peter hangs up*) Bloody Chinese. No sense of time whatsoever. Come in all hours of the day.

(*Enter Reg, a civil servant, played by Dudley*)

DUDLEY: Hello, Sir Alec.

PETER: Ah, hello Reg.

DUDLEY: You were very luck to get hold of me. You know we knock off at nine minutes to five.

PETER: Nine minutes to five, yes.

DUDLEY: It's well gone half past now.

PETER: Yes, I realise that, Reg. I'm sorry.

DUDLEY: I just happened to be catching up on a bit of paperwork with Daphne.

PETER: Oh, yes. You often catch up on a bit of paperwork with Daphne, don't you?

DUDLEY: Yeah. Do you know Daphne?

PETER: Yes, I do know Daphne. If we could get on to somewhat, er, weightier matters.

DUDLEY: I don't think you could get much weightier than that.

(*Dudley laughs*)

PETER: (*deadpan*) What a lively sense of fun you do have, Reg. I've just had this note from the Chinese and I can't make head or tail of it.

DUDLEY: Yeah. Well, is it really urgent sir, cos it's almost twenty five to six, you know. Gladys will be expecting me.

PETER: I'm sure Gladys will, but it does say 'very urgent' on the cover of the envelope so I think it could possibly be, as they say, very urgent.

DUDLEY: Yeah. Well, seeing as it's you Sir Alec, I'll have a decko.

PETER: Bless you Reg.

DUDLEY: Not at all sir.

(*Dudley reads the note*)

DUDLEY: Oh blimey! It's Cantonese!

PETER: Is that a problem?

DUDLEY: Well, I'm a Pekinese specialist.

PETER: Of course. It's Reg, Pekinese Sector, isn't it?

DUDLEY: Yeah. Well, I got a smattering of Cantonese. I'll have a go for you.

(*Dudley reads out loud, indecipherably, in Cantonese*)

DUDLEY: Kwong ming haja din, haja for kaja. Don't half give your teeth a go, that.

PETER: Yes, what was that again? Kwong ming haja din, something, something, kaja.

DUDLEY: Yeah. Bit more of a glottal stop on the kaja. Ka Ja.

PETER: Ka Ja.

DUDLEY: Yeah.

PETER: That's where it gets your teeth.

DUDLEY: That's when the teeth go a bit. Yeah.

PETER: Yes.

DUDLEY: Of course, all the Cantonese, all their teeth drop out when they're about twenty.

PETER: I didn't know that.

DUDLEY: Well you're lucky. It's quite straightforward, actually, sir. It means 'if the gnat lies down with the whale, the sheep will dance tomorrow.'

PETER: (*writing it down*) 'If the gnat lies down with the whale . . .'

DUDLEY: The sheep . . .

PETER: 'The sheep will dance tomorrow.'

DUDLEY: That's it, sir. Hope that solves your little problem. Better be off now. See you tomorrow sir. Bye-bye.

(*Dudley starts to go*)

PETER: 'If the gnat lies down . . .' Reg? This doesn't totally solve my problem. You see, it doesn't really make any sense – all these gnats lying down with whales and dancing sheep.

DUDLEY: That's the Chinese for you, ain't it sir? They've been talking in riddles ever since Confucius' time. No, you see what you really need here is George from the Cantonese Riddle Interpretation Pool. Course, he knocks off at nine minutes to five. I'd leave it until tomorrow if I were you.

PETER: But Reg, if these sheep are going to be dancing tomorrow, whatever they are, don't you think we ought to get hold of George tonight at home? Could we give him a ring at home?

DUDLEY: He'll be well into his fish fingers by now.

PETER: Well, give him my apologies, but it does sound rather threatening – these gnats lying down with whales and, er, dancing sheep. Don't like the sound of it.

DUDLEY: See what we can do, sir.

(*Dudley picks up the phone and dials*)

DUDLEY: Oh, hello Alice. It's Reg, Pekinese Sector, here. Is George there? Thank you, love. (*to Peter*) That was Alice.

(*into phone*) Hello, George. It's Reg, Pekinese Sector, here. Look, son, I'm sorry to have to buzz you at this late hour of the gloaming, but we've got a bit of a Cantonese riddle interpretation problem up here at the office . . . Yeah, I realise it's twenty to six. Yeah, I know. That's what I told him . . . No, I can't talk cos he's here. Anyway, I'll give you the message, OK? Is as follows: Kwong ming haja din, haja for kaja.

PETER: Ka Ja.

DUDLEY: Do you mind, sir? We're trying to work.

PETER: Sorry, Reg.

DUDLEY: (*into phone*) Yeah, that's right – the usual gnat, whale, sheep conundrum.

PETER: What does George say?

DUDLEY: He says his fish fingers are getting cold.

PETER: About the note.

DUDLEY: About the note – he's just working on it. (*into phone*) Yes, George. Yeah, that's what I thought. Yeah, OK, I'll do that. Thanks very much, son. See you tomorrow. Bye.

(*Dudley hangs up*)

DUDLEY: Well, both George and I are in agreement. The gnat is a reference to the United Kingdom, sir.

PETER: The gnat equals us, yes.

DUDLEY: Er, no. UK, not US, sir.

(*Dudley laughs at his own joke*)

DUDLEY: Sorry, sir. The whale is a reference to Europe.

PETER: Yes.

DUDLEY: But we're both a bit woolly about the sheep.

(*Dudley laughs at his own joke, again*)

DUDLEY: George actually suggested I get on to Dorian, who is a sheep riddle specialist.

PETER: Oh, good.

DUDLEY: Mind you it's almost ten to six, now. He's probably tucked up in bed.

PETER: See what you do with Dorian.

DUDLEY: See what I can do with Dorian.

(*Dudley picks up the phone and dials*)

DUDLEY: Hello, Dorian. It's Reg, Pekinese Sector, here. How's Natalie? . . . Jolly good. (*to Peter*) Apparently, Natalie, Dorian's wife-to-be, is in the pink. (*into phone*) Dorian, look, I'm sorry to buzz you at this late hour, but I've just been on to George about a Cantonese riddle interpretation problem, which his nibbs is a bit concerned about here at the office . . . Yeah. I realise it's a bit strong, ten to six. Yeah, I know . . . Well, that's what I bloody told him. No, I can't talk cos he's here. Anyway, I'll give you the message. OK? If the gnat lies down with the whale, the sheep will dance tomorrow . . .

(*Dudley laughs, long and loud*)

DUDLEY (*into phone*): You bloody fool, Dorian. I don't think he's up to it, but I'll ask him. Hold on. (*to Peter, still laughing*) I'm going to have an accident. Please excuse the rather personal nature of the question, but have you been to bed with any Oriental ladies recently?

PETER: I haven't been to bed with anybody apart from myself for several years, and you can tell Reg that.

DUDLEY: Dorian, sir.

PETER: Dorian, is it?

DUDLEY: (*into the phone, still laughing*) Much as I thought, Dorian.

You bloody fool. Hold on. (*to Peter*) No, it's just Dorian thought the gnat might be a reference to yourself, and the whale to some Oriental lady spy . . .

PETER: No.

DUDLEY: . . . And if there were any compromising photographs about, the dancing sheep would be the world press. (*into phone*) Bloody fool. It's an ingenious theory, Dorian, but it won't work.

PETER: I'll just have a word with Dorian.

(*Peter picks up another phone*)

PETER: Hello, Dorian.

DUDLEY (*into phone*): Dorian, that is Sir Alec on the extension, now.

PETER Reg, there was no need to tell Dorian that was me on the extension.

DUDLEY: Oh, Dorian, apparently there was no need for me to tell you that that was Sir Alec on the extension.

PETER: There was no need for you to tell Dorian that either.

DUDLEY: Dorian, apparently there was no need for me . . .

PETER: Dorian, Reg rather, would you please shut up and get off the phone.

DUDLEY: Dorian, Dorian, I can't talk cos he's here.

(*Another telephone begins to ring*)

PETER: Would you get that, Reg?

DUDLEY: Yes.

(*Dudley picks up the other phone*)

PETER: Hello, Dorian? Yes, yes, I see.

DUDLEY (*into phone*): Hello? Hello, George.

PETER (*to Dudley*): Who's that?

DUDLEY: It's George, sir.

PETER (*into phone*): Sorry, Dorian – that's George getting Reg back on the other phone.

DUDLEY: Yes, we're on to Dorian now. We're wrestling with the problem. It's bloody bedlam up here, mate.

PETER (*into phone*): Yes, I see. So they could be the sheep? Yes.

DUDLEY (*into other phone*): Oh, now that sounds more like it, George. Yes, that's the ticket. Yeah, of course. Why didn't we think of that before?

PETER (*into phone*): Are you sure, Dorian?

DUDLEY (*into other phone*): Well thank you very much indeed, squire, for working – especially at this late hour.

PETER (*into phone*): Yes, yes.

DUDLEY (*into other phone*): Thank you very much. Got a few words to tell you about old Daphne later on. I'll see you tomorrow, anyway. Ta ta, cock.

(*Dudley hangs up*)

PETER (*into phone*): Thank you, Dorian, and sleep tight. Thank you.

(*Peter hangs up*)

PETER (*to Reg*): What did George make of it all?

DUDLEY: Well, George has been going through his past papers, which is pretty nice of him, pretty nice of him given that it's almost quarter past six now, you know . . .

PETER: Yes, yes.

DUDLEY: . . . When most god-fearing people are in their beds.

PETER: Yes, Reg, but what did he say?

DUDLEY: He said that the message probably means that unless the Chinese are admitted to the Security Council they will sink Taiwan.

PETER: They will sink Taiwan?

DUDLEY: Mmm.

PETER: Good god. Um . . .

DUDLEY: Was that Dorian's interpretation too?

PETER: No, Dorian came up with a very different point of view. He seemed to think that the sheep was some sort of reference to Australia, which could hold water, and it was some sort of veiled threat to supply the aborigines with boomerangs with nuclear warheads – rather a self-destructive device if used carelessly. Buzz, wallop – there you are.

DUDLEY: Could backfire, couldn't it, sir?

(*Dudley laughs*)

PETER: Reg, neither of these two alternatives are particularly funny.

DUDLEY: No sir, it's just a nervous laugh . . .

PETER: Oh, I see.

DUDLEY: . . . In the circumstances. No, well here you have your two alternatives, you see, sir. I'm afraid we can't get much closer because, as I say, the Chinese do tend to talk in riddles.

PETER: Well, Reg, as Foreign Secretary, I suppose I ought to, um, do something.

DUDLEY: That's a good précis.

PETER: I ought to do something about it.

DUDLEY: I think if these sheep are dancing tomorrow, you ought to give Mr Heath a tinkle.

PETER: There's only one problem there, Reg. He's on his yacht, and he hates to be disturbed when he's at sea. And he's been at sea rather a lot recently.

DUDLEY: I won't tell him what you said, sir.

PETER: Be very careful, will you?

DUDLEY: Don't worry, sir. I'll get him on the scrambler.

(*Dudley picks up another phone*)

PETER: Have you got the right code?

DUDLEY: Oh, yes sir.

PETER: Looks as if you're getting through to Chairman Mao.

DUDLEY: Him or my mother. All right, sir, any moment. (*into phone*) Hello, Craig. Craig? Yes, it's Reg, Pekinese Sector, here. I wonder if you could possibly tear Ted away from the wheel for a sec . . . Oh, he's there beside you, is he? Oh, fine. Put him on, would you. Ta, love . . . Hello, sailor! How are you, squire. Long time no talky talky. Look, got Sir Alec on the other end. Would you hold on for a moment, sir? Thank you very much.

PETER (*into phone*): Hello, Prime Minister. I'm sorry to disturb you, but I've had this rather alarming note from the Chinese about dancing sheep and gnats lying down with whales and . . . (*To Dudley*) Reg, go away – this may be secret.

DUDLEY: Sorry, sir.

(*Dudley hangs up*)

PETER (*into phone*): It's either something to do with sinking Taiwan, or else possibly supplying the aborigines with nuclear boomerangs . . . Yes, I see. Well, thank you, sir. Thank you for that advice. I'll do that immediately.

(*Peter hangs up*)

DUDLEY: What did he say, sir?

PETER: Well, it's a bit tricky to translate, Reg, but in layman's terms, the gist of what he said was 'Bugger off! Do you realise it's half past six?'

PARTY POLITICAL BROADCAST
(Network Nine Television, Sydney, 1971)

(Peter is sat behind a desk, dressed in the besuited garb of a typical Tory MP)

PETER: Good evening. The first thing that we in the Conservative Party would like you to do is to relax. Just sit back and relax and listen very carefully to every word that I am going to tell you. Look deep into my eyes and relax. Relax in your armchairs. Feel comfortable. That's right. Relax. Relax with the Conservatives. Your eyelids are getting very heavy. Your whole body is becoming sleepier and sleepier and sleepier. And now you're almost dozing off. And now that you're very very relaxed and very very sleepy, you're all fast asleep and in the morning you will remember nothing of what I have said tonight. But you will all get up. And vote Conservative. Goodnight. Sweet dreams.

CONSERVATIVE
(Network Nine Television, Sydney, 1971)

(Peter is wearing a blue rosette, standing on a town hall stage)

PETER: Naturally I'm very disappointed to have lost this crucial by-election, especially so close to a margin. But politics is an up and down business at the best of times, and one learns to accept these defeats philosophically. Bloody wasps! I think it was a fair campaign, fought evenly on either side. My opponent said various harsh things about me and I said one or two things which might be interpreted as harsh about him. But this is politics. This is politics and one has to learn to take the rough with the smooth. All in all, I'd like to congratulate my opponent on his victory and, furthermore, to thank my many, many supporters who made it such a very close verdict. All I really have to add is Shit! Shit! Goodnight and thank you very much.

PRESTISSIMO
(Network Nine Television, Sydney, 1971)

(*Dudley is seated at the piano, playing Beethoven's 'Ode to Joy' – badly. Enter Peter, as a policeman.*)

DUDLEY: Ah, good afternoon, officer.

PETER: Good afternoon, sir. I've been listening to you for quite a while. You ignored two double bars, went straight through a coda sign and had a very nasty glissando when you were speeding up your fugato passage.

DUDLEY: Are you suggesting that I've been driving incautiously, officer?

PETER: Mmm?

DUDLEY: I mean playing incautiously? According to my metronome, I've only been going andante molto moderato.

PETER: Andante molto moderato? Very strange, sir. I had to go prestissimo possible to keep up with you, sir.

DUDLEY: Well, I might have gone allegro con fuoco for a couple of bars, but I'm sure I didn't get up to prestissimo.

PETER: Do you know this is a built-up area, sir?

DUDLEY: Yes, officer. (*Sings.*) 'This is a built-up area.'

PETER: (*deadpan*) Ho ho ho, as we say in the force, sir. May I see your licence, please?

DUDLEY: Yes, officer.

(*Dudley passes Peter some sheet music.*)

PETER: Bit of trouble here, aren't you? Ludwig van Beethoven? This expired in 1827. Judging from your playing, sir, I would say you are a trifle Mozart.

DUDLEY: Pardon, officer?

PETER: Rhyming slang, sir. Mozart and Liszt. To put it bluntly, sir, prestissimo out of of your bleeding head.

DUDLEY: Officer, at lunchtime I only had one Handel's largo.

PETER: One Handel's largo?

DUDLEY: Yes, officer.

(*Peter takes out a trumpet.*)

PETER: Then you'll have no objection breathing into this trumpet voluntary. I would hate to have to make it obligato, sir.

DUDLEY: No need for that, officer.

(*Dudley plays 'Ode to Joy' on the trumpet – badly*)

PETER: Oh dear. Oh lord. I'm afraid the result is positive, sir. It is my duty to arrest you for being drunk in charge of a grand piano and conduct you to the station, sir.

DUDLEY: Officer, surely there's some amicable way we can come to a, er, some way of resolving it without litigation? I mean, we don't have to resort to this sort of unpleasantness, do we?

PETER: Are you attempting to bribe me, sir?

DUDLEY: Er, yes, officer.

PETER: Thank God for that. I thought you'd never get round to it. We are having our ball at the end of the month. I don't know if you're interested in policemen's balls?

DUDLEY: Fascinated.

PETER: I should not say that, sir. It could be a further offence. But I do happen to have fifty spare tickets about my personage, if you'd like to turn up on the night. It's the 29th. They're a guinea apiece. Pay on the door, bring along forty-nine of your friends, and bring the Steinway as well.

DUDLEY: Well, thank you very much indeed, officer.

PETER: Thank you, sir. I'm glad we could clear this up amicably, as you said.

DUDLEY: Yes.

PETER: By the way, in the next few hours, could I suggest you play rather carefully? Stick, for example, to Chopin's 'Funeral March'.

DUDLEY: Thank you very much indeed, officer.

PETER: Goodnight, sir, and safe playing.

(*Dudley plays Chopin's 'Funeral March'. Exit Peter.*)

DUDLEY: Bloody police. They're all on the fiddle.

PETER COOK BY DUDLEY MOORE
(Cambridge Theatre, London, 1972)

Peter Cook was born in 1937. Two years later war broke out. Educated at Radley College, and Pembroke College, Cambridge. Here, ostensibly, he read French and German, but already driven relentlessly by a lust for power, he concentrated obsessively on seizing the Presidency of the Cambridge Footlights Club in 1959. Revue material gushed from his rancid pen. While still at Cambridge, he wrote two London revues – *Pieces of Eight* and *One Over the Eight*. Peter was thus the only real professional in the four-man cast of *Beyond the Fringe* when we performed it first in Edinburgh in 1959. He consequently received a fee of £110, as opposed to £100 allotted to the three amateurs. We learned later that 10 per cent of his £110 went in agent's fees, bringing his net earnings to £99. The meek shall inherit the earth.

In 1962, Peter opened London's first satirical nightclub, the Establishment, and took over the magazine, *Private Eye*.

Interesting facts. He would like to be Elvis Presley. He pretends to hate fashionable restaurants, and drives a battered Citroën with the front seats ripped out to show his simple tastes. He is a fanatical horse gambler and golfer. He uses me as a bank – £5 I lent him two years ago was returned recently on a cheque inscribed '£5 and not one penny more'. His solo films are *Dandy in Aspic* and *The Rise and Rise of Michael Rimmer*. He was invited to be a poof in Fellini's *Satyricon*, and refused.

He pretends that under his glassy exterior is a heart of gold. The exterior is just the tip of the iceberg. Rumours that we have split up are true.

ON LOCATION
(Plymouth Theatre, New York, 1973)

'I can only work from my direct experience in life,' [8] *Dudley told Mavis Nicholson, in a remarkably raw and revealing TV interview in 1973. And few of Dudley's performances are more revealing, or more directly related to his life, than 'On Location'. 'It was a turnaround of an experience of my father dying,' explained Dudley, in the same interview. 'When somebody close to you dies, or whatever, you go through a lot of extraordinary reactions. And one reaction was I felt I could write a play about the whole thing. Instead, the idea for the sketch emerged, and it was a way of exorcising the event.'* [9] *His father, Jock, had died of colon cancer just two years before.*

Exorcism it may have been, but as autobiography, 'On Location' is extremely self-critical – quite unjustifiably so, in light of Dudley's impeccable behaviour during his father's death. Like the character in the sketch, Dudley was abroad when he heard the news (on holiday in the Far East with his wife Suzy, rather than on location in Yugoslavia), but unlike the character, he flew straight home, and spent the last few weeks of Jock's life with his mother at home in Dagenham. He wasn't with Jock when he died, but that was at his mother's instigation. 'When the call came that he was about to go,' Dudley told his biographer, Barbra Paskin, 'my mother said "Don't let's hurry. Please don't let's hurry. I don't want to see him die. I don't want to see him struggle." Neither did I – I couldn't bear to see him that way.' [10] *Jock's last words to Dudley were: 'Dudley, my boy, don't let it pass you by.'*

Dudley had no reason to berate himself (he played his father's favourite music on the organ at his funeral) but guilt is the soulmate of bereavement, and 'On Location' portrays that parental separation which was particularly acute for Dudley's post-war generation – the working-class lad who fulfils all his parents' aspirations, and finds the success he sought on their behalf has come between them. 'Dudley felt a lot of regrets when my father died,' said his sister, Barbara Stevens. 'He would have liked to have taken him out more often and done more for and with him.'[11] Dudley had done a lot for both his parents, but the achievements of which they were so proud had transported him into a world that was utterly foreign to them. 'I wish we'd talked more,' he told Paskin. 'I wish I could have found out who he was.'[12]

PETER: Hello, Dad.

DUDLEY: Hello, Roger.

PETER: Hello, Dad.

DUDLEY: How's my famous film-star son then, eh?

PETER: I'm fine, Dad. How about you?

DUDLEY: Ah, not so bad, son. Here, come on in and sit down.

PETER: Oh, thanks, Dad.

DUDLEY: Let's have a look at you. Let's have a look at you. Yeah, you're looking a bit more healthy than you did in your last film, I'm glad to say.

PETER: Oh, thanks, Dad.

DUDLEY: Yeah, how about a nice cup of tea and a piece of fruit cake?

PETER: That'd be great, Dad. Terrific.

DUDLEY: Right. Might take a little while.

PETER: That's all right, Dad.

(*Dudley almost falls over tea trolley.*)

PETER: You all right, Dad?

DUDLEY: Yes, I'm all right. You all right, son? No bones broken?

PETER: Yes, I'm all right. You all right, Dad?

DUDLEY: OK, son.

(*Dudley spills the milk.*)

DUDLEY: Sod it. You don't mind your tea black, do you, son?

PETER: I like it Continental.

DUDLEY: Continental it will be. Ooh la la!

(*Dudley staggers precariously towards Peter, carrying two cups of tea.*)

PETER: Can I help you, Dad? You all right?

DUDLEY: Of course I am. You sit yourself down.

PETER: You OK, Dad?

DUDLEY: Nothing like a nice cup of tea, is there?

PETER: No, Dad, it's great. I feel terrible about not being able to get here earlier.

DUDLEY: Oh look, son – it's your life. You can't play silly buggers with your career.

PETER: Did Mother understand that, Dad?

DUDLEY: I told her every time I went to that bloody hospital, I said, 'Ada, you can't expect a film company to stop a multi-million-dollar production in Yugoslavia just because you're feeling a bit under the weather, dear.'

PETER: You know, Dad, I tried to get away, but we were shooting this snow sequence and the snow was melting, and the director just refused to release me.

DUDLEY: Of course he refused to release you, Roger. I would have refused to release you. Now then, I kept on saying to your Mother, I said, 'Ada, what is Mr Omar Sharif going to say if his co-star – our only son – suddenly does a midnight flit out of Yugoslavia just to see his mother? They'd call him Mummy's Boy. He'd never hear the last of it in the profession.'

PETER: So Mother understood the situation, did she, Dad?

DUDLEY: Well, I can't vouch for that, son. She went on and on. 'Where's my little son? Where's my little Roger?' I said, 'Ada . . .'

(*Dudley shakes Peter's arm, spilling his tea.*)

PETER: It's all right, Dad. I've got enough here.

DUDLEY: Try to be a bit more careful.

PETER: Yes. I'm sorry, Dad, I don't know what came over me.

DUDLEY: I said, 'Ada, he's on location in Yugo – bloody – slavia!' I couldn't get through to her.

PETER: It must have been rather tricky for you, Dad.

DUDLEY: She started screaming and hollering. 'Where's my little son? Where's my little Roger?' In the end, they had to move her to a little ward all by herself. Well, she was disturbing the trans-plants, you know. And then she kept on complaining about that. She said, 'I hate this new ward. I want to go back to the old ward.' You know, stubborn and wilful to the last, your mother.

PETER: Yes, that's Mum all over.

DUDLEY: Just like with this lovely new house you bought us. She never really got used to it. Not, of course, to be quite fair, that she had that much time to appreciate it, because no sooner had she walked in through that door, she started feeling strange and then it was downhill all the way.

PETER: Oh, Dad, you don't think moving to the new house had anything to do with her getting ill, do you?

DUDLEY (*indecisively*): . . . I don't think so, Roger.

PETER: I thought she'd like it here, you know, with the garden and everything like that.

DUDLEY: Oh, it's a lovely garden, Roger. Those roses are going to be really nice when I get to them.

PETER: They're lovely roses, Dad, aren't they?

DUDLEY: Oh yes, and don't think I don't appreciate it, son. No. Quite honestly, the thing with your mother was, she missed some of her old friends, like Mrs Stringer and Mrs Booth from 112.

PETER: Yes.

DUDLEY: But I'm sure she'd have made new friends, given time. I'm sure I'll make new friends, given time.

PETER: So . . . so you like it here, Dad, do you?

DUDLEY: Oh yes. Oh, yes. Well, it's much more spacious than Mansfield Road.

PETER: More room for you to sort of dash around in.

DUDLEY: Yes. Not, of course, that I need quite so much room now – with your mother gone.

(*Dudley sobs, Peter pats his head.*)

DUDLEY: Thank you, Roger. The way I look at it, what you lose on the swings, you gain on the roundabouts. Mind you, it's nice having an indoor toilet at my time of life. But your mother would never go within two feet of that indoor toilet.

PETER: I thought she'd like it, Dad.

DUDLEY: I thought she'd revel in it. But you can't change the habits of a lifetime. Directly we moved here, she bought a chamber pot and put it down the bottom of the garden. I think that's how she contracted the pneumonia. Sitting out there on those frosty nights, the wind howling up her nightie. The complaints we had about the noise out there – like Guy Fawkes Night every night.

PETER: I see part of the greenhouse has been broken.

DUDLEY: Yes. She shattered it.

PETER: She what, Dad?

DUDLEY: She shattered it.

PETER: Oh, yes. Well, the delphiniums have come up nicely.

DUDLEY: Yes. Everything's come up huge down there.

PETER: Must be about twelve-foot high.

DUDLEY: Yes, well, your mother had green fingers . . . or something like that.

PETER: Dad, did you consult that specialist I told you about in London?

DUDLEY: No.

PETER: Well, why not, Dad?

DUDLEY: I'll tell you why not, son. I don't want to offend Dr Groarke. Now you must understand, Roger, that Dr Groarke has always been very good to us.

PETER: I know that, Dad, but –

DUDLEY: I mean, he saw you through your German measles.

PETER: Yes, Dad, but that was thirty years ago.

DUDLEY: It might have been thirty years ago but Dr Groarke has lost none of his acumen. He was absolutely right about your mother. You need have no fears about that, because I asked him. I said, 'Dr Groarke, you've got to be quite frank with me – what is the situation concerning my wife, Ada?' He looked me straight in the eyes. He said, 'Norman, your wife is dying. There is no hope.' And he was absolutely spot on. Ada died. Now, how can you grumble with that sort of expertise?

PETER: Very accurate diagnosis, wasn't it, Dad?

DUDLEY: Yes. Dr Groarke is a staggering diag . . . diag . . . diagnostician.

PETER: Dad, is there anything I can do for you at the moment? You know, can I get you anything? Anything you need? Any little luxury?

DUDLEY: Roger, what more could I need? I've got this lovely new house, lovely new colour TV you gave me and your mother. I couldn't be more comfortable. Oh, blimey, here's me rattling on – I nearly forgot. Some bits and pieces your mother set aside she wanted you to have especially. Good job I caught sight of them. She'd never have forgiven me if I'd forgotten. Must get this right, for her sake. Yes, these first. Here are all your old exercise books and school reports from the County High.

PETER: Oh, thanks Dad. That will come in handy. Oh, here's an essay I wrote about Spot. 'He is a mongrel. We got him from the Dogs' Home. My dog is called Spot.'

DUDLEY: 'He was a stray dog and he was starving to death. Someone found him and took him to the Dogs' Home, where they gave him some dinner and a bath because he had fleas . . .' It's a bit boring.

PETER: Not bad for seventeen, Dad.

DUDLEY: And here, here is the illustrated Bible Mum gave you in 1948 – you forgot to take it up to town with you when you moved up to your penthouse.

PETER: Sorry, Dad. I forgot it in all the excitement.

DUDLEY: Don't think I don't understand, my boy. I've been young myself, haven't I? And er . . . here is the . . . er . . . (*He starts to sob.*) I mustn't . . . I mustn't let go . . . Roger, here is your mother's signet ring. She wanted you to have and wear for her. Took me two hours to get it off her bloody finger.

PETER: Well, thanks, Dad. I'll wear it everywhere.

(*Dudley points at Peter's finger.*)

DUDLEY: Just there'll be all right, son. And if you wouldn't mind wearing this black armband, in memory of your mother. I know she'd be pleased, because she sewed it especially for you.

PETER: Dad, the one thing I really wanted to know was, in the end, did Mother die peacefully?

DUDLEY: Roger, your mother left this life as she lived it – screaming her bloody head off. I remember it very well. It was a Wednesday afternoon, Uncle Ralph had come in for a cup of tea – we hadn't seen him for twenty years – and we were, you know, talking about when we used to walk over the cliffs at Leigh-on-Sea watching the boats come in. He's a boring bugger, that Ralph – once every twenty years is good enough for me.

PETER: Yes, Dad.

DUDLEY: Anyway, Mother was lying very quietly, very still, almost at rest, and suddenly, without a word of a lie, she sat bolt upright in bed, she went 'Agh!' Her false teeth hit the ceiling and that was it.

PETER: Oh, Dad, I just wish I could have been there.

DUDLEY: Your mother never did anything by halves. Both sets. Pow! Hit the electric light bulb, the bulb fell to the floor, smashed, Matron came running in, slipped on the broken glass, hit her head on the bedpost, killed outright . . . Nurse Oviatt, hearing the commotion, came roaring in from the President Roosevelt Memorial Ward, tripped over Matron and went flying out the window. She fell five storeys on to a car that was coming into the forecourt. It was an open car, she killed herself and the two passengers. The weight of the three dead bodies on the accelerator took that car roaring into the catering department, killed seven nurses, knocked ten orderlies into a huge vat of boiling potatoes. Well, naturally, the valve on the vat got stuck and there was a tremendous explosion – and the first floor collapsed. Well, you can imagine what that did to the second and third floors. Anyway, son, I won't bore you with details. Suffice it to say, that I was the sole survivor. Nine hundred and eighty-seven people wiped out in a flash of your mother's teeth.

PETER: Oh, Dad, I just feel so guilty that I couldn't have been there.

DUDLEY: There's nothing for you to feel guilty about. There's nothing anybody human could have done. You were on location, Roger. You were on location.

PETER: Dad, I really ought to be getting back to London. I've got this meeting.

DUDLEY: Of course you have, Roger.

PETER: Mr Broccoli has just got back from Brussels, and I've got this rather important meeting with Cubby.

DUDLEY: I'm sorry to keep you hanging about like this, Roger.

PETER: There's just one thing I want to say.

DUDLEY: Here, Roger, your jacket's split.

PETER: No, Dad, that's a vent.

DUDLEY: A what?

PETER: A vent. It's the fashion.

DUDLEY: Well, you get your vent sewn up. You could catch a cold in your pinnie. Look, it's a death trap.

PETER: All right, Dad. I'll get it sewn up. Just one thing I wanted to say before I left, Dad. If ever you need me, at any time, if you're feeling ill or anything like that, just give me a ring and I'll come straight down, whatever I'm doing. OK?

DUDLEY: That's very kind of you, Roger. Oh, just one thing. Are you by any chance on location this Saturday afternoon?

PETER: No, Dad, I'm not working Saturday. Why?

DUDLEY: Marvellous. I just wondered if you'd like to come to the wedding.

PETER: What wedding, Dad? You never mentioned a wedding. Who's getting married?

DUDLEY: Me and Auntie Joan.

PETER: But Dad, you can't. Auntie Joan's already married to –

DUDLEY: Roger, Uncle Ralph died in the hospital catastrophe. We thought we might as well make the best of things.

PETER: Oh. Well, congratulations, Dad.

DUDLEY: Thank you very much, Roger.

PETER: I've always liked Auntie Joan.

DUDLEY: Yes, so have I.

PETER: We all know about that, Dad.

DUDLEY: That's just not bloody true!

PETER: You've always liked Auntie Joan, haven't you?

DUDLEY: Oh, yes. I'm sorry, son. I thought you were implying something else.

PETER: No, it's just something Mother said in passing.

DUDLEY: Yes. Well, your mother had a wild imagination. And some photographs.

PETER: Well, I'll see you Saturday, Dad.

DUDLEY: Righto, Roger. I'll see you on Saturday – 2 p.m., St Thomas's, Beacontree. The Reverend Griffin's doing the service.

PETER: Oh, he's got his frock back, has he?

DUDLEY: Yes.

PETER: Right then, Dad. I'll see you Saturday.

DUDLEY: OK, Roger. I'll see you Saturday – if I'm spared.

SOAP OPERA
(Plymouth Theatre, New York, 1973)

Originally called Resting, this sketch was improvised towards the end of the Australian tour, inspired by Peter's experience of hiring resting actors as his cleaners, and finding that they far preferred talking about acting to actually doing any cleaning.

(A doorbell rings. Peter opens the door. Enter Dudley)

DUDLEY: Hello, blue eyes. (*Sings*) There's no business like show business . . .

PETER: Excuse me. What can I do for you?

DUDLEY: It's more of a question of what I can do for you, isn't it love? I'm your new daily, your new Mrs Mop.

PETER: You're the temporary domestic?

DUDLEY: Yes.

PETER: I'm sorry, I was expecting the agency to send me a woman.

DUDLEY (*Laughs*): Well, you'll have to make do with me then, won't you? Oh, I love your place. I think it's absolutely super.

PETER: Oh, thank you very much.

DUDLEY: You a bachelor?

PETER: Yes, bachelor gay – that's me.

DUDLEY: Me too. You may have guessed, this isn't my normal sort of work.

PETER: Well, I did get an inkling when you came in through the door.

DUDLEY: No, I'm an actor, actually.

PETER: Oh, an actor.

DUDLEY: Yes, I'm resting between engagements, you know. Mind you, not that I don't like this sort of work. I absolutely adore it, because one gets to meet all sorts of interesting people. And I was terribly excited when I was assigned to you, because, do you know, I've never met a barrister before.

(*Dudley sits down on the sofa*)

PETER: Would you mind not sitting on my briefs?

DUDLEY (*Picks up ribbon*): What's this, dear?

PETER: It's the little pink ribbon I tie round my briefs.

DUDLEY: Oh well, that's our little secret. I suppose being a barrister is rather like being an actor, isn't it?

PETER: I don't really see the connection, no.

DUDLEY: Well, you call it 'acting for your client,' don't you?

PETER: In rather a different way.

DUDLEY: Of course you do – dragging up in all those lovely cosies and wigs, swishing round the courtroom, appealing to the jury. Ooh, gentlemen of the jury, I put it to you, my client has a foolproof alibi, on the night of the twentieth . . .

PETER: I can assure you it's nothing like that in court.

DUDLEY: I bet it is. I once played a QC in an Agatha Christie play in Croydon. They used to call me AC QC backstage. You get a lot of giggles in the profession.

PETER: Yes. The washing up is just through there.

(*Peter points to the kitchen*)

DUDLEY: Oh, bonky bonk, down to earth again. Wretch. Have you got any rubber gloves, dear?

PETER: Yes, Mrs Higgins keeps them by the sink.

DUDLEY: It's because I have a very sensitive skin, you know. I've only got to touch a flake of detergent and woosh – I get a terrible rash all over my body. And as an actor, you know, one can't afford that sort of thing in these days of full frontal. Gesture, expression, projection – one can't do all that with a spotty botty! (*Laughs*)

(*Dudley picks up some records*)

DUDLEY: Ooh, I see you like opera.

PETER: Yes, I do enjoy opera.

DUDLEY: (*Looking through Peter's records*) Oh, Bona . . . Bona . . .

PETER: I don't know that one. Is that a new one?

DUDLEY: Silly.

(*Dudley picks out a record*)

DUDLEY: Ooh, Lucia di Lammermoor – one of my favourites. I love that bit where she comes out singing in her nightdress, and she sings that beautiful bit. Remember?

(*Dudley sings from Lucia*)

DUDLEY: I bet your Mrs Higgins doesn't do that for you.

PETER: No, but she does do quite a lot of washing up.

DUDLEY: Oh, touché. Well, sleeves up, gloves on. I'm the boy for liquid Joy.

(*Exit Dudley. The telephone rings. Peter answers it*)

PETER: Hello? What? Oh, I see. Hold on. (Shouts to the kitchen) It's for you.

(*Enter Dudley*)

DUDLEY: Who is it, love?

PETER: It's some woman.

DUDLEY: Oh, wrong number, dear.

(*Exit Dudley*)

PETER: (*Into the telephone*) Hello . . . It sounds very much like him. (*Shouts into the kitchen*) She insists it's for you.

(Enter Dudley)

DUDLEY: Ooh . . .

PETER (*Into the telephone*): He's just coming.

DUDLEY (*To Peter*): Mmm . . . Thank you so much.

(*Dudley picks up the telephone cautiously*)

DUDLEY (*Into the telephone*): Hello, who is this? Oh, Gloria. I thought I was getting kinky phone calls. (*To Peter*) It's my agent, the only woman in my life.

PETER: Well, she shouldn't be ringing you here.

DUDLEY (*To Peter*): I quite agree. (*Into the telephone*) Gloria, we must be brief, otherwise I'll have the law on me. (*To Peter*) Hope springs eternal. (*Into the telephone*) You're joking . . . Fantastico-issimay . . . Do I know the scene, dear? I've been rehearsing it for the last six weeks. When's the audition? Tomorrow morning, love? Oh, I can't possibly . . . Alright, alright love. I'll be there on the dot. Thank you so much. God bless you. Goodbye, sweetheart . . . Mmm . . .

(*Dudley hands up*)

PETER: What on earth was that all about?

DUDLEY: Oh, must sit down. I'm up for Othello. Oh, I say, you wouldn't do me a special favour, would you?

PETER: I very much doubt it.

DUDLEY: No, I mean you wouldn't just give me five minutes of your time and go through my lines with me, would you? Because I've got my audition tomorrow morning.

PETER: What about the washing up? You've hardly started on that.

DUDLEY: I'll work my fingers to the bone if you'll just give me five minutes of your time.

PETER: Just read through a few lines, that's all, then you promise to do some work?

DUDLEY: Cross my legs and hope to die. Have you got a copy of Othello?

PETER: Yes, I've got one somewhere.

DUDLEY: Oh, you are a brick.

PETER: Just a few lines.

(*Peter fetches the book from the shelf*)

DUDLEY: Could we do Act Five, Scene Two?

(*Dudley looks at Peter's book*)

DUDLEY: Oh, you've got the same edition.

PETER: Yes, I rather go for Penguins.

DUDLEY: Mmm, each to his own, dear. Act Five, Scene Two is where Desdemona has dropped her hanky and Iago has been whispering all those awful things in Othello's ear.

PETER: Yes, I know the scene.

DUDLEY: A scene of tremendous jealousy. (*To the audience*) Oh, I know in my bones that I'm going to become Othello. (*To Peter*) When I play a part, love, I really am that part.

PETER: I can't promise to do the same for Desdemona.

DUDLEY: You'll be lovely. Here, why don't you wear your wig? It'll make you feel the part.

(*Peter puts on his barrister's wig*)

DUDLEY: Ooh, you drag up beautifully. Line sixty three. Good Luck.
  Merde. (*Recites, with brio*)
  By heavens I saw my handkerchief in's hand
  O perjur'd woman! Thou dost stone my heart,
  And mak'st me call what I intend to do
  A murder, which I thought a sacrifice.
  I saw the handkerchief.
PETER: (*Recites, deadpan*)
  He found it then
  I never gave it him. Send for him hither
  Let him confess a truth.
DUDLEY: Oh, a bit more life, dear – a bit more vigour.
PETER: Oh, I see. You want something to bounce off, do you?
DUDLEY (*Recites*): He hath confess'd
PETER (*Recites, passionately*): What, my lord?
DUDLEY: Ooh! That he hath us'd thee.
PETER: How? Unlawfully?
DUDLEY: Ay.
(*Dudley bangs his hand against the door*)
DUDLEY: Ooh, bugger!
PETER: I don't have that in my text.
DUDLEY: What, dear?
PETER: I don't have a 'bugger' in my Penguin.
DUDLEY (*Annoyed*): I'll give you a bugger in your penguin, mate.
PETER: Could we get on? I'm just feeling the part of Desdemona.
DUDLEY: Where were we, love?
PETER: Line seventy one.
DUDLEY (*Sing song*): Oh, seventy one, never been done, queen of
  all the fairies.
PETER (*Recites*): He will not say so.
DUDLEY: No. His mouth is stopp'd.
Honest Iago hath ta'en order for't.
PETER: O! My fear interprets. What! Is he dead?
DUDLEY: Had all his hairs been lives, my great revenge
  Had stomach for them all.
PETER: Alas! He is betray'd and I undone.

DUDLEY: Out, strumpet! Weep'st thou for him to my face?

PETER: O! Banish me, my lord, but kill me not!

(*Peter grabs Dudley*)

DUDLEY: Blimey! You didn't half give my left nipple a going over. It's gone all perky!

(*Recites*) Down, strumpet!

PETER: Kill me tomorrow! Let me live tonight!

(*Peter grabs Dudley again*)

DUDLEY: Not the other one! Ooh, I'm all aglow! (*Recites*) Nay, if you strive . . .

PETER: But half an hour!

(*Peter grabs Dudley again*)

DUDLEY: Here! (*Recites*) Being done, there is no pause.

PETER: But while I say one prayer!

DUDLEY: It is too late.

(*Dudley grabs Peter by the throat and chokes him*)

PETER: Oh, Lord!

(*Dudley wrestles Peter to the couch and chokes him*)

DUDLEY: Bloody fabulous! You've acted before, haven't you?

(*Peter is dead*)

DUDLEY: Oh, my God. I went over the top again. Ooh, now I can have my first go at mouth to mouth resuscitation.

(*As Dudley bends over Peter, he observes the audience, watching him*)

DUDLEY (*Into the wings*): Here! Curtain! Curtain!

(*Dudley bends over Peter again, as the curtain falls*)

SPEECH IMPODIMENT
(Plymouth Theatre, New York, 1973)

This sketch was written for the London run of Behind the Fridge, *and included in the script when the show transferred to America as* Good Evening. *Cook & Moore anoraks will recognise distinct similarities with a sketch that Peter wrote for the Establishment Club called 'Appeal on Behalf of the Blond', which later resurfaced as 'Blind' on* Derek & Clive (Live).

DUDLEY: God ovenin. Ee window who manny owf you rollease that lits of popple on this kintry or innubile to pronince the Onglish linguage. It's a bog problem – a vary vary bog problem. Imogen, off you coon, the doffokulties of ovary die loaf, far sich a parson. Bat, spoch impediments kin be carred. Ee missif wince soffared fram sich a dofuct. Bat ifta inly throw wax of tharopoy, aikin mak missif inderstard parfektry. Mich minny is nodded for risich. Plaice guv gonerusly. Sandy notions in the firm of minny or chicks to the fillowing adrifs:

> (*A sign appears*: '*Speech Impediment Fund, 5, Smith Street, London* WI'.)

DUDLEY: Spoch Impodiment Find, Fove, Smoth Strot, Linden Worst Wind.

DEAN OF UNIVERSITY
(BBC2, 1974)

A new sketch for the BBC broadcast of the show, which demonstrated that, whatever else prevented Peter and Dudley from doing a fourth series of Not Only . . . But Also . . . , *it certainly wasn't an inability to write new material.*

PETER: Come in, come in, come in, come in, come in, come in, come along in, come in.

DUDLEY: I'm in, sir.

PETER: You're in? Jolly good, come along in, sit down, relax, and above all come in.

DUDLEY: Thank you.

PETER: Cigarette?

DUDLEY: Oh, thank you very much indeed, sir.

PETER: There we are. And of course matches without which a cigarette will be well-nigh useless. *Olé*. I picked that up in Spain.

DUDLEY: Oh yes, of course, sir.

PETER: Not the only thing. Care for a glass of sherry?

DUDLEY: Oh, well, I wouldn't say no, thank you, sir.

PETER: Why should you say no? A glass of sherry never did anybody
any harm. Except of course Aunt Alice, and that was thrown at
her, many years ago. Neither here nor there and nor is Aunty
Alice . . . Cheers.

DUDLEY: Cheers. Thank you so much, sir. Thank you.

PETER: Now then, tell me precisely why you wanted to come and
see me.

DUDLEY: Oh, well, sir, you asked me to come and see you.

PETER: There's no need to be shy, lad. Get it off your chest. Tell
me, what's bothering you?

DUDLEY: Well, there's nothing bothering me, sir.

PETER: Oh, laddie, laddie, laddie. I'm old enough to be your father,
you can tell me what's bothering you. What's bothering you, eh?

DUDLEY: Well, as I said, sir, there's really nothing bothering me.

PETER: I see. So we've established the fact, have we not, that nothing is bothering you?

DUDLEY: Yes, sir.

PETER: Or put it another way, everything is not bothering you?

DUDLEY: Yes, sir.

PETER: What I think you're probably trying to say, is that you're
not bothered by anything at all?

DUDLEY: Yes, sir.

PETER: In that case, could I ask you rather a simple question?

DUDLEY: By all means, sir.

PETER: Why did you specifically ask to come and see me?

DUDLEY: Sir, you asked me to come and see you.

PETER: That's very well put.

DUDLEY: Thank you.

PETER: I asked you to come and see me.

DUDLEY: Yes, sir.

PETER: Well, you've come in, you've sat down, you've relaxed, you've had a cigarette, you've had a glass of sherry, and in the course of so doing, presumably you have seen me.

DUDLEY: I suppose I have, yes, sir, in a manner of speaking.

PETER: Well, what do you make of it? What do you make of me?

DUDLEY: Why, I really don't know what to say, sir.

PETER: Does that bother you, not really knowing what to say?

DUDLEY: Well, no, sir, not really, no.

PETER: I see, so there is still absolutely nothing bothering you, and you have no worries in the world at all.

DUDLEY: Well, no, sir.

PETER: Well, let me put it to you from a slightly different point of view. Something is bothering me.

DUDLEY: Sir, can I be of any help?

PETER: Can you be of any help? I wonder. You see the thing that is bothering me is the fact that I have a very boring job. Do you realise I have to get up every morning and deliver the identical lectures that I have been delivering for the past thirty years? They never vary, not by a word, not by a jot, or a tittle. And that is bothering me.

DUDLEY: Oh, sir, I enjoy your lectures. I find them terribly interesting.

PETER: That's because you're hearing them for the first time. You wouldn't find them terribly interesting if you'd been delivering the same bloody stupid lectures, week in, week out, for the past thirty years, never varying by a single word now, would you?

DUDLEY: I suppose not, sir, no.

PETER: Just so young people like you can go out into the world, make a success of their lives, drive along in white sports cars.

DUDLEY: Well, I don't know about that, sir.

PETER: Wouldn't that bother you, delivering the same bloody stupid identical lecture, week in, week out, for the past thirty years, never varying by a single word?

DUDLEY: I suppose it might, sir, yes.

PETER: Yes it might. Yes it might. Well, what do you suggest I do about it? What can I do about it?

DUDLEY: Well, sir, I suppose –

PETER: You tell me, lad.

DUDLEY: Well, sir, I –

PETER: Say it off the top of your head.

DUDLEY: Well, sir –

PETER: Don't hold back.

DUDLEY: Well –

PETER: Don't hesitate. He who hesitates is lost, and he who's lost is seldom found. So there's no need to be shy.

DUDLEY: Well, I'm not really, sir, no.

PETER: Don't be uptight, as I believe you younger people call it. So be uploose, hang out or whatever you want to do.

DUDLEY: Well, sir, what I was going to say was –

PETER: I'm not interested in what you were going to say. What you were going to say is all past and forgotten. It's what you are going to say that interests me.

DUDLEY: Well, what I was going to say is what I am going to say, sir.

PETER: You were going to say the same thing twice, were you?

DUDLEY: No, sir, I –

PETER: That's rather ramming it down my throat, lad.

DUDLEY: No, sir, I hadn't really said it yet.

PETER: You've said nothing yet.

DUDLEY: No, I'm sorry to keep you hovering about like this.

PETER: That's all right, lad.

DUDLEY: But what I was going to say – it seems a bit obvious, and I'm sorry – but I was going to suggest maybe you could rewrite the lectures.

PETER: What? It's rewrite the lectures, is it now?

DUDLEY: Well, yes, sir, it seems to be the most –

PETER: Have you any idea of the work involved in rewriting the lectures, as you so lightly put it? Do you realise for a start, for a mere start, it would mean, mean rewriting the lectures?

DUDLEY: Yes, sir, but –

PETER: Having fresh thoughts, new ideas. You ever tried to have a new idea at my age?

DUDLEY: No, sir, I was merely suggesting –

PETER: And who are you to suggest to me? Some pipsqueak undergraduate who comes waltzing in here, helps himself to my sherry
and my cigarettes, and tells me to alter the whole pattern of my
life. You don't have a wife with lumbago, do you?

DUDLEY: No, sir.

PETER: Nor do I. Yet you have the effrontery to come in here fully
clothed and tell me to rewrite my lectures. Good God, they're
perfectly good lectures. I've been delivering them for the past
thirty years with some measure of success.

DUDLEY: Yes, sir.

PETER: And if I remember correctly, you said you found them terribly interesting.

DUDLEY: Well, I do, sir, yes.

PETER: Well, why the bloody hell, should I change them?

DUDLEY: Well, sir, you did ask me . . .

PETER: Could you do me one small courtesy?

DUDLEY: Yes, sir.

PETER: Would you be so good as to get out?

DUDLEY: Yes.

PETER: Get out and take yourself with you.

DUDLEY: Yes, sir, I'm awfully sorry, sir.

PETER: Some people have a little work to do, you know.

DUDLEY: Yes, sir.

PETER: Do you realise I had to prepare all of tomorrow's lectures?

DUDLEY: Yes, sir.

PETER: Well, you're completely wrong. I don't. I've only got to find
them and read them out to a lot of little sods like you. Now get
out, would you?

Chapter Six

Derek and Clive

Like a lot of the best creative endeavours (and quite a few of the worst ones), *Derek & Clive* was inspired by sheer, unadulterated tedium. During a long theatre run, Peter quickly became bored. He hated reciting the same lines night after night, and his restless imagination soon set off in search of less conventional amusements. While performing *Beyond the Fringe* in America, Peter and Dudley amused themselves by recording a series of Gospel out-takes called *The Dead Sea Tapes*. Ten years later, while performing *Good Evening* in America, they amused themselves by recording a series of similarly unholy out-takes that became a best-selling LP, *Derek & Clive (Live)*.

Derek and Clive were the portraits in Pete and Dud's attics – like those flat-capped philosophers, but with a lot less charm or wit. A pair of British lavatory attendants stranded in New York City, the style of their deadpan duologues wasn't all that different from Pete and Dud, though the subject matter was far darker and the vocabulary infinitely more explicit. 'When they were doing Dud and Pete, it was Derek and Clive when we were rehearsing, because they never held back from using four-letter words,'[1] says Joe McGrath, who directed some of their greatest head-to-heads in *Not Only . . . But Also . . .*

Pete and Dud discussed highbrow topics in innocent, lowbrow language. Derek and Clive's language was as unmentionable as the topics they discussed. Dudley called *Derek & Clive* the most obscene thing you've ever heard in your life, and unless you've lived a very full life indeed, it's difficult to disagree with him. 'Mozart had a very scatological sense of humour,' Dudley told his biographer, Barbra Paskin. 'He was always talking about farting and cunts and arses.'[2] But any similarity with the Austrian composer begins and ends right there. Derek and Clive didn't compose symphonies. They concocted curses. At best, these were cheerful Rabelaisian rants. At worst, they were misogynistic howls of rage.

The first *Derek & Clive* LP was the result of three ad hoc recording sessions – first at New York's Bell Sound Studios, then at a Greenwich Village club called the Bottom Line and finally at New York's Electric Lady Studios. At the Bell Sound Studios, without an audience, they recorded 'The Worst Job I Ever Had', the first (and probably the best) sketch in the *Derek & Clive* canon. At the Bottom Line, before a small audience of invited friends, they recorded a few old favourites ('Blind', from the Establishment, and 'Bo Duddley', from *Not Only . . . But Also . . .*) plus five new sketches – 'This Bloke Came Up to Me', 'Squatter and the Ant', 'In the Lav', 'Winky Wanky Woo' and 'Cancer', all of which ended up on the first album. Some of this material was subsequently rerecorded at the Electric Lady Studios, without any friends in tow.

At that time, the idea that any of this material would end up on an LP was the last thing on their minds. They were otherwise engaged with *Good Evening* (not to mention their respective divorces and remarriages) and even if they'd wanted to release it, and found a market for it, it seemed unlikely that any reputable record company would be prepared to distribute it in anything like its current form. Filed and forgotten, these recordings seemed bound for the same oblivion as *The Dead Sea Tapes* ten years before.

However, recording engineers often run off their own private copies of studio sessions, and copies of these copies found their way into the hands of all sorts of people in the record industry, including the Who, the Rolling Stones and Led Zeppelin. As they toured the USA with *Good Evening*, Peter and Dudley were surprised to discover they'd become the favourite comedians of several of the world's biggest rock bands – not as a result of their Broadway show or even their BBC appearances, but on the strength of an unreleased bootleg. When small ads started appearing in *Private Eye*, offering pirate copies for sale, Peter and Dudley decided it was high time they got a slice of the action, and did a deal with Island Records. *Derek & Clive (Live)* was released in August 1976, nearly three years after that first impromptu recording session in New York.

Against all odds, *Derek & Clive (Live)* was a massive international success, selling 50,000 copies in the first few weeks. Being banned by the BBC merely bolstered its illicit appeal. It sold 100,000 copies in Britain, and became their most popular LP in the States. 'This record contains language of an explicit nature that may be offensive and should not be played in the presence of minors,' read a disclaimer on the sleeve, but such warnings are usually as much of an advertisement as a deterrent. The album was especially popular with teenagers, particularly adolescent boys.

On the strength of this lucrative cult hit, Peter and Dudley were offered another movie. They opted for a comic remake of *The Hound of the Baskervilles*, with Peter as Sherlock Holmes and Dudley as Doctor Watson, inspired by the Holmes and Watson skit they'd done on TV in *Goodbye Again*, a few years before. It was Peter's idea, but Dudley was also enthusiastic. 'We both thought it could be the funniest film ever,'[3] he told Barbra Paskin. And by rights it should have been.

The Hound of the Baskervilles promised much, but delivered very little. Barry Took called it one of the worst films ever made. Its American director, Paul Morrissey, adored British humour, but his background was as a member of Andy Warhol's avant-garde US stable, and his UK favourites, the *Carry On* films, harked back to the saucy puns and slapstick of seaside music hall, rather than the literate Oxbridge wit of *Beyond the Fringe*. 'Asking Paul Morrissey to direct English comedy – which he loves – is like asking me to direct an improvised movie about junkies in LA,' reflected Peter, a few years later. 'The script is a very bad compromise between Dudley, myself and Paul.'[4] The 'crickets' were ruthless, but this time Peter had no complaints. 'Paul edited one version of the film,' said Peter. 'I thought it was very bad. Dudley and I edited the version which is out now, which I regard as marginally better, but there's still no making it any good.'[5]

'Paul Morrissey frustrated us at every turn, and we should have dumped the entire idea,'[6] said Dudley. But Morrissey was merely the latest in a long line of directors who'd failed to transfer the magic of their live act to the big screen. Like an awful lot of double acts, Peter and Dudley never found a film style to suit their comic talents. They'd come very close with *Bedazzled*, but when you transplant comedians into motion pictures, a perfect fit is the only one that works. *The Hound of the Baskervilles* was their last chance to crack the movies. It did not succeed. 'Cook and Moore have deteriorated into almost complete reliance on lavatory humour to get laughs,' wrote *Variety*. After that, there was nowhere else to go but back to the lavatorial talents of Derek and Clive.

When people talk about *Derek & Clive*, they tend to lump all three albums together, but there's a world of difference between the filthy, happy first LP and the misanthropic pair that followed. *Derek & Clive (Live)* was a private joke, and that was what made it so appealing. It was made to amuse its makers and a handful of friends. There was never any notion of sharing it with a wider audience, let alone making any money out of it, and its eventual evolution into a best-seller was almost entirely accidental. *Come Again* and *Ad Nauseam* were completely different. Both were straightforward commercial LPs, made for straightforward commercial gain, and the rude good humour of the first LP was replaced by spiteful fury. Willie Donaldson, who produced *Beyond the Fringe*, described it as a scream of pain.

Come Again was recorded in a single day, with scarcely any preparation, and it's painfully apparent. Improvisation and preparation were both integral to Peter and Dudley's comedy. When they were denied the chance to improvise (as they were in movies) the results were awkward and the laughter vanished. When they denied themselves the chance to prepare (as they did on *Come Again*) the results were chaotic and the laughter vanished just as fast. Even their last-minute sketches for *Not Only . . . But Also . . .* were improvised in advance. 'I have listened to this disgusting record with genuine shock and horror,' wrote Peter in the *Daily Mail*, cleverly pre-empting the criticism he knew would follow. 'It is nothing but a stream of obscenities about unpleasant subjects. A learned Australian journalist who had heard the tapes had counted that there were 144 [fucks] and 89 [cunts] in the space of 60 minutes. I urge you not to buy it, unless perhaps as a cheap form of Breathalyzer. If you laugh at *Derek & Clive – Come Again* you definitely shouldn't drive.'[7] More courteous to Dudley in print than he had been on the album, Peter absolved his partner of any blame. 'Dudley claims to have no memory of having made the record at all,' he wrote. 'The last thing he remembers is that somebody handed him a Walnut Whirl.'[8] The record was released on 18 November, by which time they'd wisely left the country.

Ad Nauseam was a bit better than *Come Again*, and also a whole lot worse. Better in terms of quality, in that it benefited from a bit more studio time and prior preparation; worse in terms of content, in that the humour was even more vicious than before. 'Never have two comedians slagged each other off so comprehensively,' said Peter. Still, as Peter also said, anyone who buys a record that comes with its own sick bag can't say they weren't warned. On the second day of recording, a film crew turned up at the studios, invited in by Peter without Dudley's knowledge or consent. The death throes of Britain's greatest double act were captured on camera, in almost pornographic detail, like the home video of a particularly acrimonious divorce.

The result of this day's filming was *Derek & Clive Get the Horn*, a bleak and claustrophobic documentary that must surely qualify as one of the most depressing comic movies ever made. Ghastly yet engrossing, as entertainment it's a disaster – but as biography, it's without equal. What other comedy duo has allowed the world to witness the collapse of their partnership, in all its gory glory? 'I think we were scraping the bottom of several barrels,' recalled Dudley, when the film was finally released, fourteen years later. 'Not so much scraping the barrel,' corrected Peter, 'as incorporating the barrel into the material and going through the floor.'[9]

Neither of them were quite so sanguine at the time. Dudley walked out on Peter while the cameras were still rolling, and though they eventually repaired their friendship, and performed a few brief turns together, this was the last full day's work they ever did.

Ad Nauseam was released in 1979, but *Derek & Clive Get the Horn* was denied a certificate by the British Board of Film Censors. 'The point of this comic exercise is to be as offensive as possible and to break every taboo the performers can think of, however outrageous,' wrote the board's James Ferman, in 1980, in a letter to the producers. 'Cutting would be pointless although we believe that the sequence about Jesus Christ and the sexuality of the lower half of his body is probably blasphemous in the legal sense of the term. If this is so then this brief scene would have to be cut. The offensive references to the Pope and the Holocaust are not, in our view, illegal, though they will certainly prove deeply offensive to some people.' The film's failure to get a cinema certificate was no great loss to Dudley, on the brink of Hollywood superstardom. 'Dudley wasn't too keen on it being released in America,' said Peter, 'but then America wasn't too keen on it being released there either.'[10]

Undeterred, Peter pressed ahead with a video release, but some copies were seized by the police, the distribution company went out of business and the remaining copies were impounded. *Derek & Clive Get the Horn* didn't resurface until 1993. By now, Dudley's Hollywood star had risen and fallen, and Peter was happily married, to his third and last wife, Lin. Lin helped Peter and Dudley to patch up their relationship, and Dudley helped to publicise the video's belated release. A film that had helped to prise Peter and Dudley apart helped to bring them back together, and the spectacular all-night launch party was one of the great finales of Peter's life. In the end, some good came out of *Derek & Clive Get the Horn*, after all.

A quarter of a century later, friends and fans remain divided by

Derek and Clive. People who discovered Peter and Dudley in the seventies tend to think they're brilliant. People who discovered them in the sixties usually aren't so keen. Yet whether you like them or not, Derek and Clive were undoubtedly immensely influential, inspiring alternative comedy in much the same way that *Not Only . . . But Also . . .* helped to inspire *Monty Python*. 'It's the language of utter frustration and impotence, and it's funny, and it has a cumulative effect,' says Germaine Greer. 'You think, 'Where will the next Fuck come in?' Well, the point is, in the end, that Fuck becomes like The and And.'[11]

In the end, you may disapprove of Derek and Clive, but that doesn't mean you won't find them funny. 'At that time, I was quite right on,' says the actress and comedienne Jackie Clune. 'I was studying feminist theatre and I fancied myself as a bit of a sort of socialist feminist. I remember thinking, "This really should not make me laugh. I should really be quite cross with these two fairly privileged white middle-class men, just using cunt as a term of abuse." But actually, I couldn't stop myself from laughing.'[12]

THE WORST JOB HE EVER HAD
(*Derek & Clive (Live)*, 1976)

Dudley's ad hoc response to Peter's celebrated lobster-up-the-bum routine. This version includes material that was cut from the finished album, indicated by square brackets, for the benefit of anyone obsessive enough to care.

CLIVE: What's the worst job you had?
DEREK: The worst job I ever had?
CLIVE: Yeah.
(*Derek coughs.*)
CLIVE: What? Was it just that? Coughing?
DEREK: Well, I had to collect up – this was a very difficult job – I had to collect up, every year, financial year, you know, April –

CLIVE: Every ear? Whose ears did you collect up?

DEREK: No, wait. No, year – April to April.

CLIVE: Yeah.

(*Derek belches.*)

DEREK: Pardon. All the phlegm what Winston Churchill had gobbed out into his bucket by the bed.

CLIVE: Oh God, yes. I was offered that job but I said no. I said, 'I'm not going through all that phlegm.' Because he has so many cigars, so much brandy. 'I am not, as a human being, going to go around with buckets collecting that fucking phlegm.' I said, 'I'm not going to touch it.' I said, 'I won't touch it –'

DEREK: No.

CLIVE: '– I'd rather be a destitute.'

[DEREK: The problem was, what constituted one piece of phlegm, because, as you can imagine . . .

CLIVE: This is the problem.

DEREK: The fucking stuff was all in different shapes and sizes.

CLIVE: Yeah. Some green, some blue, some brown.

DEREK: You used to get a well-defined bogey here and there – nice and crisp, you know, streaky, and you knew where you were. But then you used to get like a six-inch green one, which was sort of umbilically tied to another one or two. It was like, you know, a fucking myriad.

CLIVE: This is what put me off the job, frankly.

DEREK: Well, I went insane, you know.

CLIVE: For how long?

DEREK: Well, for about a fortnight. I went completely off my head. I went on aspirin.

CLIVE: But Winston Churchill's bogeys, I mean, have turned many a man to aspirin, which is a lethal drug. It can turn a man to bogeys, which Winston Churchill was on.]

DEREK: The trouble was he used to take bogeys in secret, you see.

CLIVE: What? He had them in a cupboard which no one could see?

DEREK: He was a secret bogeyer. He used to have bottles of the stuff. I used to collect it up for him. I never realised that he was in fact taking it of a night.

CLIVE: And then just blowing it out?

DEREK: And then blowing it out in the fucking morning. I mean, you didn't know where you fucking were. I come in, in the morning, there was the same fucking bogey on the bedspread. I thought, 'Fuck me – I only collected this one last night,' and yet there's the cunt lying on the fucking bedspread again, you see. I thought I was seeing things. I had a feeling of déjà vu.

CLIVE: Well, it must have been tricky for you, because I remember hearing stories about Winston's bogeys which were unbelievable because, you know, he could produce a bogey as big as the *Titanic*. Oh, it was dreadful.

DEREK: You know why?

CLIVE: He threatened Hitler with it.

DEREK: You know what happened?

CLIVE: He threatened Hitler with it.

DEREK: Well, the bogey that was as big as the *Titanic* was in fact the *Titanic*. Did you know that?

CLIVE: Well, this is what I heard. I've never had it confirmed.

DEREK: Now keep it, like, very quiet.

CLIVE: I'll keep it very quiet.

DEREK: But the bogey that Winston had that was like the *Titanic* was in fact – there was no such fucking thing as the *Ti-fucking-tanic*.

CLIVE: So people went to sea . . .

DEREK: People thought it was the *Titanic*, but it wasn't. They went to sea on Winston's bogey, and the fucker sank. And fucking why not?

CLIVE: And they played on. They played on.

DEREK: They fucking played on.

CLIVE: The violinists keep playing as the bogey sank.

DEREK: The trouble is, you see, bogeys are not really seaworthy.

CLIVE: I've always said this. You cannot float on a bogey. Don't try to cross the ocean on a bogey, otherwise you're sunk. And who took any notice? Fucking nobody took any notice. I'll tell you who took notice.

DEREK: Who?

CLIVE: Fucking nobody took notice.

DEREK: Right. You're fucking right, mate.

CLIVE: Yeah. Nobody took fucking notice.

DEREK: Fucking no one.

CLIVE: No one took notice.

DEREK: All those cunts.

CLIVE: All those cunts putting out to sea on Winston's bogey. And what happened to them?

DEREK: SS fucking *Bogey*.

CLIVE: They fucking sank, didn't they?

DEREK: Right fucking cunts.

CLIVE: Yeah. So the next time you see a travel brochure saying Go To Majorca On A Bogey, forget it mate. Forget it, because that is the fucking end of the world.

SQUATTER AND THE ANT
(*Derek & Clive (Live)*, 1976)

This creepy sketch was a continuation of Peter's lifelong passion for creepy crawlies – a fascination that dated back to his boyhood in Torquay. Peter's early childhood coincided with the Second World War, and with most men away (his father included) the gardener was one of his few male role models. Poignantly, in a home movie, Peter can be seen following the gardener around the flower beds, imitating his spadework with his own tiny trowel. This may account for Peter's unusual fondness for insects (on the other hand, it may very well not), but either way, 'Squatter and the Ant' is far darker than most of his anthropomorphic fantasies. Again, this version contains material cut from the record, indicated by square brackets for hardcore fans.

(*PETER and DUDLEY play a couple of upper-class old buffers.*)

PETER: Have you heard anything recently of Squatter?

DUDLEY: No.

PETER: No, I wouldn't think you would have heard anything of Squatter.

DUDLEY: What's he up to at the moment?

PETER: Squatter Madras? Well, he tends to lie a bit low, you know.

DUDLEY: Really? Why's that?

PETER: Well, that's the way he lies – a bit low, which is the best way to lie, I think, in my view. But Squatter was one of my very best friends, which was him and, um, and him. He is in fact my only best friend. But Squatter had this incredible quality, which was, um, I don't know how you can define it, but I would say it was stupidity, which very few people I've known have got, to quite the same extent that Squatter has. I don't know if I've ever told you the story about Squatter and the ant.

DUDLEY: No, no, no.

PETER: Have I told you about Squatter and the ant?

DUDLEY: No, no, no.

PETER: Well, Squatter was in a terrible position. He was in Bahrain, which is a pretty bloody place to be, and there was this ant, which had only one leg.

DUDLEY: God.

PETER: And only one eye.

DUDLEY: God.

PETER: And was about two miles away from Squatter.

DUDLEY: God.

PETER: So, a pretty bloody menacing position for Squatter.

DUDLEY: Yes.

PETER: Who was equipped only with a hydrogen bomb.

DUDLEY: God.

PETER: Six grenades.

DUDLEY: God.

PETER: And a few rifles.

DUDLEY: Yes.

PETER: And this bloody ant, with one eye and one leg, was advancing towards Squatter, at I'd say about a mile every century, you know.

DUDLEY: God.

PETER: Really speeding up. I think the animal was on drugs.

DUDLEY: Yes, or heat.

PETER: Or heat, yes, as you may say. And Squatter, with his extraordinary calm, took it very smoothly. And do you know what he did?

DUDLEY: No.

PETER: Nothing.

DUDLEY: Good God.

PETER: He immediately did nothing. And this stupefied the ant. It stopped in its tracks. It didn't move an inch for about three and a half years. But still Squatter was very much aware of the problem of the ant, with all of one leg and all of one eye, advancing towards him. So he took up a strategic position – about five thousand men on one side, and seven thousand men on the other side, all equipped with various kinds of guns and so on. The ant was fairly pinpointed, but what was odd –

DUDLEY: Yes, go on – go on.

PETER: I will – was the ant understood Squatter. The ant realised he was up against somebody as good as he was.

DUDLEY: Some sort of understanding between them. They knew they were equals.

PETER: Equals in a struggle, yes. So Squatter, with a tremendous display of courage, put up his hands and surrendered. And the ant, five years laters –

DUDLEY: Five years laters?

PETER: Yes, five years laters – crept into the hole, and Squatter was gone. And this is the extraordinary thing about Squatter. He was never there when he was wanted. And Squatter told me later that he had gone because he'd had to go. That sums up Squatter for me.

DUDLEY: Yes, it's a sort of very simple approach to life.

PETER: The ant these days is writing its memoirs, you know, in the *Sunday Telegraph*, but Squatter . . .

DUDLEY: Squatter refuses to come out.

PETER: He refuses to comment on the whole situation. He just won't. He just won't. And I think he's quite right.

DUDLEY: I think he retains his dignity.

[PETER: He retains everything, including himself, which I think is only right.

DUDLEY: How is his arsehole these days?

PETER: Squatter's? Oh, why, it is in terrific form. Oh, he's got an enormous great party going on down there at the moment – Twiggy, Dustin Vulverne, John Prompt. Do you know John Prompt?

DUDLEY: Oh yes!

PETER: You do? I'm surprised. I never heard of him. John Prompt is down there, and apparently he is making the whole party go with a tremendous swing. That's what a party needs to go with – a tremendous swing.]

DUDLEY: Yes. What I think is the tragedy about Squatter is that you know that one of these days . . .

PETER: Yes, one of these days.

DUDLEY: One of these days, he's going to let fly with the most enormous fart.

PETER: Well, this is the tragedy about Squatter. I mean, one has tried to hush it up. One has attempted to put cushions up his arse, one has attempted to do many things. But Squatter, taken unaware, may give fly to the most enormous fart, and this will be his undoing.

[DUDLEY: But not only his – also his arsehole's. I think there's going to be a frightful scene. You know, he has been eating solidly, let's face it, for sixty-four years, and without ever giving vent to his, er, things.

PETER: The necessary thing. He is, as the Spanish put it so quaintly, *constipado*.

DUDLEY: Yes, I think that's it.

PETER: *Un poco constipado.*

DUDLEY: *Conquisita pat chipata.*

PETER: Sixty-four years without ever letting forth a single . . .

DUDLEY: And the terrible thing is, one of these days he's going to crack – or his crack is going to.

PETER: One of these days, his crack is going to go, as you say.

DUDLEY: And there is going to be the most almighty Madras.

PETER: Well, this is Squatter's terrible problem.

DUDLEY: And you know, of course, what Madras is like. It is no fun at all!

PETER: It is no fun at all.

DUDLEY: Once that starts, or stuff, rather, starts coming out, it's going to burn his arsehole right off – it's going to take the lining off.

PETER: One thing I told Squatter about four years ago, I said, 'Squatter, if you allow yourself to be bunged up for another four years, you're going to go into orbit.' And Squatter turned to me, looked me straight in the eye, and he said, 'Fuck off.'

DUDLEY: Well, I pleaded with him. I said, 'Look, for God's sake,' I said. 'Let's have a look at your crack. For God's sake, let me line it with some Fairy, because otherwise it's going to be the most unholy mess.'

PETER: Or the most holy unmess.

DUDLEY: No, the most unholy mess. But he goes on and that's what –

PETER: But he doesn't go on. This is the problem. He never goes. He never goes on. He never starts. This is the trouble with Squatter. He has got, what, about sixty-five years of pent-up fury in his arsehole.

DUDLEY: Well, you know he is living in Blackpool now?

PETER: Well, it's a good place to –

DUDLEY: Very near the tower, and I was crossing the Atlantic –

PETER: Exploring North Sea Gas, I imagine.

DUDLEY: Air India, and I heard this faint rumbling and I knew it was from Blackpool and I thought, 'God! You know, it is not long, and that tower . . .'

PETER: Well, it's not long. It's reasonably long.

DUDLEY: That tower is going to be the first thing to go.

PETER: Yes, well, that's what I keep pleading with him.

DUDLEY: The whole of the British Isles is going to be covered with Madras. You know, with old Madras.

PETER: But how do you put this across? After all, he is an old friend.

DUDLEY: I don't know.

PETER: He is going to cover the world in a shower of shit.

DUDLEY: One has to tread very carefully here.

PETER: Yes, well, one will be unable to tread.

DUDLEY: Well, one will be. The situation will be out of one's hands. One will be presumably either floating or sinking, depending on the –

PETER: But what does one say to Squatter?

DUDLEY: On the texture of his expelling, expiring –

PETER: Build a hole and bung it in.]

DUDLEY: Well, I just wish him luck.

PETER: I wish him luck. At the same time, I wish him a strange sort of happiness – death.

DUDLEY: Yes, I think that would be the best thing for Squatter.

PETER: I think if death could come to Squatter now.

DUDLEY: Rather than the other way round.

PETER: Yes.

DUDLEY: I think we'd all be very happy.

PETER: I think so.

WINKIE WANKY WOO
(*Derek & Clive (Live)*, 1976)

OK, so there was no Internet or video or cable television, and if you wanted to see a dirty movie, you had to sneak into a seedy cinema with a bunch of sad old men in dirty macs – but when it came to comedy, the seventies was much more permissive than the noughties. Some of Peter and Dudley's gay gags and racial references wouldn't be so acceptable today, and in the current climate, this sketch about a couple of furtive perverts seems far more sinister than it did at the time. Nowadays, we call them exhibitionists or voyeurs, but back then we simply laughed them off as flashers or peeping toms. Again, there's some stuff in here that isn't on the record, indicated by square brackets.

DUDLEY: Excuse me? Would you be, um, I wonder if you would be interested in a, um, sex crime?

PETER: Er, could you speak up a bit? I can't really hear you. I thought I heard the words 'sex crime', but I didn't hear anything else.

DUDLEY: Well, um, you got the gist of what I said. Um, I wonder if you'd be interested in, um, er, playing with my thing.

PETER: Oh, I see – sort of playing with your doodahs.

DUDLEY: Yes, with my willy winkie.

PETER: Erm, well, this depends rather on the terms – and indeed the lengths. What are the lengths of the doodah?

DUDLEY: My doodah is about, um, four foot nine by three and a half.

PETER: When you say, er, four foot nine by three and a half, do we take the three and a half as being accurate, or could that be possibly three and three-quarters?

DUDLEY: Probably more in the region of five and a half.

PETER: Oh, five and a half? Well, that's rather more interesting. You see, um the problem with me is that my, um . . .

DUDLEY: Winkie wanky.

PETER: Thing tends when . . .

DUDLEY: Willy winkie wanky.

PETER: Aroused, which is very seldom.

DUDLEY: Oh.

PETER: About once every century.

DUDLEY: Yes.

PETER: To be about a thousand miles long.

DUDLEY: Oh, fucking arseholes. Well, I wonder if we could come to some arrangement?

PETER: Well, I don't see any reason why not. I mean, you're a fine man.

DUDLEY: Well, that's very kind of you, you fat –

PETER: Well, I'm a very kind person.

DUDLEY: – Cunt.

PETER: And I'd just like to say that mine being about a thousand miles long . . .

DUDLEY: Oh God.

PETER: Which is quite a length in this day and age . . .

DUDLEY: Oh God, oh God, oh God . . .

PETER: Given the inflation which surrounds us, I'd like to get to grips with something, you know, on a sort of par with mine.

DUDLEY: You know, um, I think you'd be quite pleased with the, um, this particular winkie wanky woo.

PETER: When you say it's a winkie wanky woo, it's a winkie – yes?

DUDLEY: Well, mainly it's on the wanky side.

PETER: And where does the woo come in?

DUDLEY: Wherever you like, dear.

PETER: Well, I'd prefer you to do the wooing before you do the winkie and the wanky.

DUDLEY: Well, um . . .

PETER: I may be a bit old-fashioned, but I like to see a bit of wooing before the winkie and the wanky, you know.

DUDLEY: Oh, right, you smooth-talking fucker.

PETER: Er, where do you live? Earls Court?

DUDLEY: Erm, er, no.

PETER: Nowhere?

DUDLEY: Pardon?

PETER: Do you live nowhere at all?

DUDLEY: Well, you're getting near the truth.

PETER: Why don't you come back to my place and perhaps we could sort things out?

DUDLEY: That would be wonderful.

PETER: Did I ever tell you before that I love a man who has no convictions?

DUDLEY: Oh.

PETER: How many convictions have you got?

DUDLEY: Well, depends what you mean by convictions.

PETER: How many times have you been in prison for offences against, erm, Anna Neagle?

DUDLEY: Forty-four times, Your Honour.

PETER: Well, come back and see me and we'll see if we can sort things out.

[DUDLEY: Can't we do it here?

PETER: I see no reason why not. Oh, you beautiful creature, my love, my darling.

DUDLEY: Fuck off.

PETER: You sweet little thing.

DUDLEY: Now come over here and do that.

PETER: I'm sorry. I was doing it to the tap.

DUDLEY: You silly old fool.

PETER: I'm a bit short-sighted.

DUDLEY: Well, you certainly make up for it.

PETER: Thank you, darling.

DUDLEY: Um . . . um . . .

PETER: What is it?

DUDLEY: I want to go to the lavatory.

PETER: Yes, well, I'm sitting here, so just go ahead.

(*Dudley whistles for a while.*)

DUDLEY: Thank you.

PETER: You have a wonderful singing voice. I never knew someone could sing like that.]

DUDLEY: You're too kind.

PETER: I am what?

DUDLEY: You're getting fainter.

PETER: I'm getting Fanta? Yes, I should go off and get some Fanta.

DUDLEY: No, you're getting fainter.

PETER: Oh, I'm getting fainter. Yes, yes, because, do you know, in forty-five years in the British Army, I've never met anyone who really cared?

DUDLEY: How very sad.

PETER: It is, isn't it? When one has fought two wars, beaten the Boche twice, one ceases to care. One only hungers for where it's at.

DUDLEY: Well, get your willy wanky woo over here, darling.

PETER: I wish I could. It was shot off in the First War.

DUDLEY: Well, fuck off, you silly old poof.

[PETER: Goodbye, darling.

DUDLEY: Goodbye, darling. See you at the same time next week.

PETER: Goodnight.

DUDLEY: That was an extract from –
PETER: *Winnie-the-Pooh*.
DUDLEY: By ee cummings.
PETER: Once again.]

BO DUDDLEY (AGAIN)
(*Derek & Clive* Live), 1976

PETER: Ladies and gentlemen, we're very pleased to have with us this evening the famous coloured singer Bo Duddley. Take it away, Bo.

DUDLEY: (*sings, in a thick African American accent, self accompanied on the piano*)
Mama's got a brand new bag!
Mama's got a brand new bag!
We're going to groove it the whole night long!
Mama's got a brand new bag!
Right on baby!
Get down baby!
Let's get it on now, baby!
Lay it on me, brother!
Later! Out of sight!
Far out! Ugh!

PETER: Thank you very much indeed, Bo.

DUDLEY: (*in an upper class English accent*) Thank you.

PETER: I think it can be truly said that the Americans have their soul singers and we English have our soul singers and Bo is one our leading soul singers.

DUDLEY: Arsehole singers, yes.

PETER: Bo, I wanted to ask you first of all, this is obviously sort of boogie jive stuff, is it?

DUDLEY: This is a jive boogie-woogie song, and it is a story . . . Well, shall I sort of go through it?

PETER: Yes, I was thinking that some of the lyrics for English speaking audiences might be a little obscure.

DUDLEY: Absolutely.

PETER: I wonder what it really is all about.

DUDLEY: Well let me just go through it for you.

(*sings*) Mama's got a brand new bag! (*speaks*) Mama's got a brand new bag.

This means that the Harlem mother has gone out into the bustling markets of Harlem to buy a gaily-coloured plastic bag. There's a certain amount of pride in this. Mama's got a brand new bag.

PETER: I suppose a gaily-coloured plastic bag is a bit of a status symbol in Harlem.

DUDLEY: Yes, it certainly is. Obviously a sign of a birthday, or something like that. Anyway, it goes on . . . (*sings*) She's gonna to groove it the whole night long!

PETER: (*repeats, deadpan*) She's going to groove it the whole night long.

DUDLEY: Yes, she's going to groove it the whole night long – meaning she's going to do the traditional Harlem decorating on the bag with a groover. This grooving process, grooving grooves . . .

PETER: Sort of indentations on the bag?

DUDLEY: On the bag.

PETER: To make it even more attractive?

DUDLEY: Even more attractive.

PETER: Than it was?

DUDLEY: Than it was.

PETER: And it's going to take her the whole night?

DUDLEY: This is going to take her the whole night. Therefore, the indication that she's going to groove it the whole night long. I must point out that grooving goes back a long way into darkie history. They used to have groovers going round the streets in the old days . . .

(*sings*) Mississippi groover!

And people used to bring out their bags. Of course, they weren't plastic in those days, but anything they wanted grooved, they went out into the street to give it to the groover. And then we hear the words . . .

(*sings*) Right on, baby!

PETER: This seems a little puzzling, 'right on, baby.'

DUDLEY: Well, let me explain. The father of the house has just walked into the wigwam, and he says, 'Right on, baby' to the mother, meaning, 'Write the shopping list on the baby for tomorrow morning.'

PETER: They actually use babies as shopping lists?

DUDLEY: Well, paper is scarce, plastic is very difficult to write on, so the baby comes in very handy for the shopping list.

PETER: What would they use to write on the baby?

DUDLEY: Well, ordinary white paint.

PETER: Ordinary white paint, yes.

DUDLEY: Which accounts for the fact that very little is bought, because, you know, one can't write very much with a big brush. And then we have the line (*sings*) Get down, baby!

This is a panic signal. The baby, realising that once again he's going to be written on, has climbed the wall, and this is one of those instinctive boogie Harlem instincts and talents that the infant has. They are able to climb walls.

PETER: I believe many small Harlem children are in fact able to cling to the ceiling by their feet, hence the phrase, isn't it, In The Gecko.

DUDLEY: Exactly. Now, they want the baby to get down for the shopping list, but the baby is in a mood of panic, and so the father of the household says . . . (*sings*) Let's get it on, baby!

PETER: Get what on, baby?

DUDLEY: Well, I'm coming to that. Let's get the plastic coloured, er gaily-coloured, er plastic bag coloured gaily, on to the baby.

PETER: They have difficulty with words, don't they?

DUDLEY: They do. And they see that the baby's panic stricken. They're using the same sort of system that they use with the budgerigar. They put a carrier bag over the cage to keep it calm.

PETER: To keep it quiet, yes.

DUDLEY: And they feel, if we put this gaily-coloured plastic bag

over the baby – it's got a dark lining, so that will calm the child
– we'll bring it down to some sort of normality.

PETER: And then the line comes up?

DUDLEY (*Sings*): Lay it on me, brother!

Now this is the first sign of jealousy in the family. The mother
is saying to the husband, 'Lay it on me, brother!' She wants the
gaily-coloured plastic bag.

PETER: She wants the bag on her head, rather than the baby?

DUDLEY: Exactly, and she says 'brother', which is an indication of
the amount of confusion that is rampant in these boogie house-
holds – calling the father brother. But of course it is a possibility that he is indeed her brother.

PETER: Well, they are extraordinarily difficult to tell apart, aren't they?

DUDLEY: Absolutely. And then he replies . . .

(*sings*) Later!

Later meaning what it says, really. She then comes back with
'out of sight' and 'far out' which is her explanation to us, the
audience, that she has hidden the bag.

PETER: In her sort of voodoo rage?

DUDLEY: Yes, she hurtles round the wigwam, looking for a dark
corner to hide this gaily-coloured plastic bag, for her own devices,
because she's very jealous of the baby. And then finally we have
'ugh!'

PETER: Could you do that with the music? I think it works better
with the music.

DUDLEY (*sings*): Ugh!

This is the grandmother of the house, the black widow, sitting
on a bucket in a hamper in the corner of the old wigwam. She's
having a bit of trouble. She had rather a lot of grits the night
before, and she's trying to expel them.

PETER: Basically, let's not mince words, she's trying to shit a grit.

DUDLEY: Well, it's fascinating you picked up on that phrase 'shit
a grit' – of course very like the phrase we know over here,
'shit a brick'. And in fact, the nature of grits is to coagulate in
some way, so that in fact when she does expel the grits they
are in the form of a brick, which is a wonderful sort of recy-

cling process, because this is how they build the wigwams in the first place.

PETER: Yes.

DUDLEY: With grit bricks, you see. In fact, George Formby wrote a song around the last part of this boogie ditty . . .

(*sings, in a Lancashire accent*) Sitting on a bucket in the hamper in the corner of the old wigwam . . .

But I think basically you have the idea.

PETER: The gist of it is, mother goes out, gets a brand new bag, she's going to spend the whole night grooving it, she starts writing on the baby – the shopping list – the baby gets upset and leaps to the ceiling, and he wants to get it on the baby – the bag, that is – and then she wants to lay something on him.

DUDLEY: No, no. She wants the bag on her.

PETER: The bag on her, yes, sorry, and then she, in a rage, hides the bag.

DUDLEY: Yes.

PETER: And then grandmother winds the whole thing up with a 'ugh!'

DUDLEY: Yes, showing that the process of life is going on, that there's going to be an extension to the wigwam very soon – possibly a front porch or a patio of grit shit bricks. Have you ever tried to say that very fast? Grit shit bricks.

PETER: I never have. Bo, thank you, and play us out with some more of your delightful darkie boogie rhythms.

DUDLEY: Yes, thank you so much.

TOP RANK
(*Derek & Clive (Live)*, 1976)

CLIVE: I was down the Top Rank ballroom the other day.

DEREK: Oh yeah?

CLIVE: Yeah. You know, with the lads, and brought the wives along.

DEREK: Social occasion?

CLIVE: Made it social, you know. Nice to have the birds there, you know. Got things to talk about, haven't they? You know, women's talk.

DEREK: Nice.

CLIVE: I was talking with the lads. I'd been up the football, you know.

DEREK: Which? Norwich and Tottenham?

CLIVE: Norwich Tottenham, yeah. Fucking awful game, that. Norwich are a team of fucking wankers, aren't they?

DEREK: Yeah, right.

CLIVE: Fucking wankers, those Norwich. Did you see the game?

DEREK: No, I was wanking that afternoon. I didn't have time.

CLIVE: Oh, couldn't make it, yeah. I was down to be wanking, but I got a call from a friend and thought it was best to go along. Anyway, I was down at the Top Rank ballroom, any case. I was talking to Sid. You remember Sid? Married to Doris. And I suddenly turned around, fuck me, I saw the wife.

DEREK: Well, was that surprising?

CLIVE: No, no. It's not surprising. What was happening to the wife was surprising. I turned round, saw the wife, fucking great gorilla fucking her arse off. I thought, 'Fuck me.'

DEREK: Fucking hell.

CLIVE: I said, 'What's going on?'

DEREK: Yeah, well you would.

CLIVE: I said, 'Who do I turn to?' You know, 'Who do I fucking get in touch with?' I pay five shillings to come to the Top Rank ballroom, have a civilised conversation, I turn round, there's a fucking gorilla fucking the arse off my fucking wife. I thought, 'Fuck me.' I mean, who do I get in touch with?

DEREK: Right, yeah. You must have been in a state of near panic.

CLIVE: Yeah, well, you know – I've got pride. I'm not going to allow anybody, let alone a gorilla, just to fuck the arse off me wife like that.

DEREK: Yeah. So what d'you do?

CLIVE: Well, I turned to Sid. I said, 'Sid! Look! There's a fucking gorilla, fucking me fucking wife!' He said, 'Fucking hell! She fucking is being fucked by a fucking gorilla! Fuck me!' He said, 'You should get in touch with the top man, the manager.' So I went straight up. I stormed up, because let's face it – I've got a temper. I'm human.

DEREK: Well, I wouldn't like to be on the end of it.

CLIVE: I'm human. I knocked on the manager's door. No reply. Well, I wasn't taking no reply for an answer. So I stormed straight in and there he was, stark naked, on the floor, with an ant sucking his left nipple.

DEREK: Oh no. Oh fucking hell.

CLIVE: And I said to him, with all the dignity I could muster, I said, 'Is this a way to run a fucking ballroom?'

CANCER
(Derek & Clive (Live), 1976)

Say what you like about Derek and Clive, but at least you can't accuse them of double standards. They could dish it out, but they could take it too, and this brief taboo-busting flurry is all the more remarkable for the fact that Dudley's father had died of cancer a few years before. 'I was dreadfully upset and I just couldn't stop sobbing,' Dudley told his biographer, Barbra Paskin. 'It was very difficult when I lost my first parent and I was very unnerved by it.'[13] There's something almost masochistic about Dudley's stoic refusal to quash Peter's cancerous references, a trend that continued on their second Derek & Clive *album,* Come Again. *Radio journalist John Junkin suggested to Peter and Dudley that this sketch was Pinteresque. 'Yes,' joked Peter. 'Pinter stole a lot of Derek and Clive material.'[14]*

CLIVE: I heard that George Stitt had moved away from the Willesden area and gone up round Chadwell Heath.

DEREK: Cancer?

CLIVE: Yeah.

DEREK: Oh my. It's funny you should say that, because you remember Enid, who used to live across the road, at number 104.

CLIVE: Yeah, just next to 105.

DEREK: Right. She's now working at the United Dairies, down Green Lane.

CLIVE: What, cancer?

DEREK: Yeah.

CLIVE: Christ. You remember the Nolan twins?

DEREK: Oh yeah.

CLIVE: Fifi? Fifi Nolan?

DEREK: And Ronnie.

CLIVE: And Ronnie Nolan, yeah. They've taken up darts.

DEREK: Cancer?

CLIVE: Yeah.

BACK OF THE CAB
(Derek & Clive – Come Again, 1977)

Like the lobsters up Jayne Mansfield's bum in 'The Worst Jobs They Ever Had', this sketch actually bore a vague resemblance to a real-life occurrence, recounted to Peter by Kenneth Williams, who'd met a taxi driver who'd had Bertrand Russell in the back of his cab, and recounted by Peter to the readers of the Daily Mail *in his weekly column, 'Peter Cook's Monday Morning Feeling'. 'The brilliant philosopher was quite surprised when the cabby turned around and said, "Hello, Bertie, I've read a lot of your books. What's life all about then?" Apparently the aged sage was speechless. "Would you believe it?" the cabby said to Kenneth. "I asked the world's greatest philosopher a simple question, and he didn't know the [fucking] answer.'*[15]

CLIVE: How you doing, 4105?

DEREK: What?

CLIVE: I said how you doing, 1045?

DEREK: Oh, not so bad, 305/z.

CLIVE: I've had a fucking terrible day.

DEREK: Yeah?

CLIVE: You know that, what's he called, that philosopher?

DEREK: Philosopher?

CLIVE: Philosopher. The one who knows words and everything like that.

DEREK: Des O'Connor?

CLIVE: No, not Des. No, Des is clever, but he's not quite as reputed to be as clever as is, um . . . Russell, Russell!

DEREK: Oh, Jane Russell!

CLIVE: No, Bertrand! Bertrand Russell!

DEREK: Oh, Bertrand! Russell!

CLIVE: I had fucking Bertrand Russell in the back of my cab!

DEREK: Yeah, right.

CLIVE: I looked round – you know, I recognised him – and I said, 'Hello, Bertie.'

DEREK: Yeah, right.

CLIVE: He was a bit surprised because, you know, he's not used to it.

DEREK: Well, he was pissed out of his head, wasn't he?

CLIVE: Yeah, pissed out of his fucking head, the old fucking dwarf – wide-headed cunt.

DEREK: Yeah.

CLIVE: So I said, 'Here, Bertie, you've written the history of the fucking Western World.'

DEREK: Right.

CLIVE: I said, 'What's the fucking answer?'

DEREK: Yeah.

CLIVE: He looked round. He didn't fucking know.

DEREK: Probably farted, didn't he? Knowing him, mate.

CLIVE: He farted twice. He clouded up the windscreen.

DEREK: Yeah, right.

CLIVE: And I said, 'Look, Bertie – Bertie, Bertie.'

DEREK: Yeah, right.

CLIVE: 'Get out of the cab!'

DEREK: Right.

CLIVE: 'Get out of the cab!

DEREK: Right, right.

CLIVE: I always use those words when I've got some cunt in.

DEREK: And you want to get him out of the cab.

CLIVE: I said, 'Get out of the cab!'

DEREK: 'Get out of the cab!'

CLIVE: He said, 'What is the meaning of getting out of the cab?' I says, 'No fucking meaning. It just means get out of the cab.' And he went into some philosophical argument about whether getting out a cab was the same as getting in a cab, and all that crap, and I thought, 'Fuck it!'

DEREK: Yeah, fuck, all that dualistic world crap.

CLIVE: And you know what I got for a tip?

DEREK: What?

CLIVE: Nothing. Absolutely nothing.

DEREK: I suppose that was his philosophical joke.

CLIVE: Yeah. You get a philosopher in the cab and you get nothing. The same with Picasso.

DEREK: Yeah. You had Picasso in your cab?

CLIVE: Picasso. I knew him once because he was enigmatic.

DEREK: Yeah.

CLIVE: And I said, you know, just as a friendly joke, I said –

DEREK: You have a paintbrush out of his arsehole.

CLIVE: You have a fucking oil painting coming out of his arsehole. And a neolithic-style abstract on his –

DEREK: On his knob.

CLIVE: On his knob.

DEREK: On his knob. Yeah, I know. He paints his knob.

CLIVE: He paints his knob different colours, then photographs it, then sells this to other people.

DEREK: Yeah, dirty fucking cunt.

CLIVE: So I said, 'You know what I call you, Mr Picasso?'

DEREK: Yeah?

CLIVE: I said, 'I call you Mr Picarsehole.'

DEREK: Right, fucking right.

CLIVE: 'Because as far I'm concerned, you take shit out of other people's arseholes, shove it on the canvas and sell it to other cunts.'

DEREK: Right.

CLIVE: And he was nonplussed.

DEREK: Yeah, well, I had the same experience. I opened the cab door for somebody who hailed me on the corner.

CLIVE: Who's hailed you?

DEREK: Richard Wagner.

CLIVE: Richard Wagner? But he's been dead two hundred years.

DEREK: That's what I thought. But no, he was large as fucking life, in the King's Road.

CLIVE: You're not confusing him with Robert Wagner?

DEREK: Er . . .

CLIVE: No, cos he's been alive been alive for years.

DEREK: No, he's been alive for years. You'd know the difference.

CLIVE: Yeah.

DEREK: No, Richie came into my cab, humming, you know, snatches of, er, *Tristan and Isolde*. I thought, 'Fucking hell! I thought you was dead!' I thought, you know. Anyway, he sat in the cab, whistling away, you know. I said, 'Hello! I recognise that leitmotif!'

CLIVE: Yeah.

DEREK: Yeah, and he recognised, you know, another soul on his wavelength, and he said, 'Fuck off, cunt!'

CLIVE: In German, or English?

DEREK: No, in English. I said, 'You speak very good English for a cunt.' Anyway, I pulled over, I looked round, I said, 'What was that all about?' I says, 'You can fucking get out the cab as far as I'm concerned.' I said, 'Get out the fucking cab!' I said, 'You may be Richard Wagner, but you can't come in my fucking cab and tell me to fuck off.'

CLIVE: No.

DEREK: So I said, 'You just fuck off out the cab.' I never saw him again. He didn't give me nothing.

CLIVE: He gave you no tip whatsoever?

DEREK: Nothing. No tip, no fare.

I SAW THIS BLOKE
(Derek & Clive – Come Again, 1977)

DEREK: I saw this bloke the other day.

CLIVE: No! Did you?

DEREK: Did I tell you?

CLIVE: No, you didn't. I don't fucking believe it. Don't come that with me. You saw this bloke the other day? You don't you expect me to believe that, do you?

DEREK: I don't, no.

CLIVE: No! It's outrageous, that is! That's outrageous!

DEREK: No, it's true, though.

CLIVE: You saw this bloke the other day!

DEREK: No, it's true, though. It's true.

CLIVE: Oh, come off it, you cunt. You saw this bloke the other day!

DEREK: I saw him.

CLIVE: You cunt.

DEREK: I saw him.

CLIVE: Of course you didn't. You never saw a bloke the other day.

DEREK: I saw him.

CLIVE: How could you have done?

DEREK: I don't know. That's what defied description.

CLIVE: All right, then.

DEREK: I saw him and I don't know how. I don't know how I saw him, but I saw him. I was going along the street and I saw this bloke.

CLIVE: Nah, come on! What proof have you fucking got that you saw this bloke?

DEREK: I've got no proof.

CLIVE: What proof have you got?

DEREK: I've got no proof mate.

CLIVE: Well, without proof there's no fucking point in talking, is there?

DEREK: Well, there is.

CLIVE: I can prove that I'm here cos I've got a witness.

DEREK: Who?

CLIVE: You!

DEREK: Where are you?

CLIVE: I'm here, cunt! Can't you see me? You talk about some bloke you saw the other day.

DEREK: Yeah.

CLIVE: Yeah, OK. You've seen the bloke, have you? So what's so good about that?

DEREK: Nothing.

CLIVE: What's so interesting about this particular story?

DEREK: Nothing. I just wanted to tell you, I saw this bloke.

CLIVE: You saw a bloke. So what? You saw him. So what happened?

DEREK: Nothing happened.

CLIVE: Any happier. Are you any happier? You feeling better for seeing this bloke? Course you aren't!

DEREK: I didn't say I feel better.

CLIVE: Why raise it in the first fucking place, then?

DEREK: I thought you might be interested.

CLIVE: I wasn't in the least interested. I was sitting here, quietly wanking.

DEREK: How would I know?

CLIVE: How would you know? By fucking intuition, mate – can't you have something intuitive?

DEREK: All right. I saw this woman.

CLIVE: That's better.

DEREK: Right.

CLIVE: Now you're talking.

ENDANGERED SPECIES
(*Derek & Clive – Ad Nauseam*, 1979)

CLIVE: Did I tell you about Damien?

DEREK: No?

CLIVE: Damien down 112?

DEREK: No, you didn't, no.

CLIVE: Well, he had a terrible blow last Tuesday.

DEREK: I had a lovely blow last Tuesday.

CLIVE: Well, I know. You told me all about that. But Damien was in terrible trouble, because the people from the ecology – you know, the environmental people – come round, and he was just off to the launderette to take his Y-fronts down there.

DEREK: Oh yeah, I know. He does that of a Wednesday, doesn't he?

CLIVE: No, not every Wednesday – every two years. He's been wearing these Y-fronts for about two years, and every two years he thinks, 'Well, I might as well get them cleaned up, you know – get a proper job done on them.'

DEREK: Get them scraped.

CLIVE: Precisely. Anyway, these people from the Ministry of the Environment come round, and they said, 'Excuse me. Before you take these Y-fronts down to the laundromat, we'd like to inspect them.'

DEREK: Why not? They've got every right.

CLIVE: He thought it was something to do with Britain going decimal, but it wasn't, and they looked in his Y-fronts and, fuck me, they discovered this endangered species. They found the only two living examples of the barking toad.

DEREK: The barking toad?

CLIVE: Yeah, everybody thought the barking toad was extinct, but no – there was two of them in Damien's Y-fronts.

DEREK: Was it the Barking and Romford toad?

CLIVE: No, it's not called the barking toad because it lives in Barking. It's called the barking toad because it goes woof. And they said, 'This is an endangered species.' And they'd been flourishing there because it was exactly the right environment, you know. Because they like it humid, they like plenty of humidity and sort of body temperature, which Damien has. His body is usually body temperature.

DEREK: Well, if he's got anything, mate, it's body temperature.

CLIVE: He's got body temperature – I'll grant him that. And he said, 'Well, I've got these barking toads in me Y-fronts. What do I do?' And they said, 'Well, we want them to breed, and you'll have to keep these Y-fronts on for at least four years, because we're hoping these two toads will get the horn and get in the mood and, you know, spawn some more. You know, they was hoping that they'd spawn in his socks, and he has to keep his socks on for the next two years. The man from the Environment Ministry, he thought the reason why all these barking toads were taking refuge in Damien's Y-fronts was because of the similarity of the bollocks that were hanging there in the first place.

DEREK: Oh, maybe they'd gone there thinking they could mate with the bollocks.

CLIVE: With the bollocks. And indeed they had been trying to mate with the bollocks. You know, Damien used to wake up in the night thinking, 'Hello? What's going on?' It was barking toads up his bollocks. But he's got to keep them in there for another two years, in the hope that they'll spawn, and the spawn will trickle down to his socks.

DEREK: Do you think it's possible that the barking toads could mate with his bollocks? Because I must say, that would be interesting, wouldn't it?

CLIVE: Well, then you'd get a species called the web-footed barking bollocks – which would be a new thing, wouldn't it? But still, if it's an endangered species I say, 'Fuck 'em.'

DEREK: Right.

CLIVE: I'd like to see every endangered species wiped off the fucking face of the earth. People, they're all moaning on. They say whales are more intelligent than human beings. Are they? Do you think whales and dolphins are more intelligent than human beings?

DEREK: Oh yeah.

CLIVE: Why?

DEREK: Say-so.

CLIVE: Yeah, but they're not. Whales are fucking stupid. Can you mention one whale in the history of mankind that has had a record in the top ten? Can you? Can you mention one whale who has written the equivalent of *Othello*? Shakespeare? Health and Efficiency? They've produced nothing in the way of literature. All they've fucking produced is a load of other whales, and all they eat is fucking plankton, and they call them intelligent. Can you imagine, drifting along in the sea with your mouth open, and a lot of fucking plankton going in?

DEREK: Yeah, I can imagine that.

CLIVE: You'd like it, would you? Just drifting around in the sea. They're such cunts, they can't even breathe underwater. They have to keep coming up the whole fucking time and spouting. Then some cunt comes on telly and he says, 'Oh, the whale is being wiped out by mankind. Save the fucking whales.' Well, during the War, did we notice a lot of whales rallying round and saying, 'Save England'? I didn't notice many down my part of the world. I didn't see whales coming up with the Union Jack, saying, 'We'll fight the Bosch.' No. They do fuck all. Swim around in the fucking sea, sucking fucking plankton down.

DEREK: The whales were all Nazis. They were at the Nuremberg rallies, mate. They were all whales.

CLIVE: What? They were tried in the Nuremberg Trial?

DEREK: No! They were whales at the rallies. Hitler was talking to whales.

CLIVE: Well, that doesn't make them more intelligent because Hitler lost, didn't he?

POLITICS
(*Derek & Clive – Ad Nauseam,* 1979)

CLIVE: I tell you what the Conservative Party should do in the next General Election.

DEREK: Yeah, go on, then.

CLIVE: I tell you what would really get the electorate going, is if that Maggie Thatcher just flashed her tits about. No, don't laugh, because I mean, frankly, they're firm, they're hard and they're fucking beautiful. I've never seen them, but you can see from the, er, you know, from the pictures in the papers and on television, she's got a lovely, lovely pair of tits, and if she just flashed her tits, you know, if she even gave, you know, just a brief tasteful glimpse of her vag, you know, it would get a lot of the horny voters in, you know. You could say the same for Jim Callaghan, because he's got huge tits, hasn't he? What would you do for the Liberals?

DEREK: Nothing.

CLIVE: I think it would be nice if the Liberals went round with, you know, flowers up their arseholes.

DEREK: Yeah. That's nice. It's a good idea, that.

CLIVE: And, er, got back to the Sixties, when they had a lot of seats, you know. And there'd be this subliminal connotation between flowers up their arseholes and a lot of seats, and people would identify with that, I think. I mean, if I saw Clement Freud with a posy up his arse . . .

DEREK: Well, you'd vote, wouldn't you?

CLIVE: I'd vote for him, and all he stood for.

THE WORST JOBS THEY EVER HAD
(*Derek & Clive – out-take*, 1973)

A special treat for Derek & Clive *obsessives – a rare out-take from the ragbag of recordings which formed the first album, never released on any of the three* Derek & Clive *LPs. It's a variation on a theme – Peter's Worst Job and Dudley's Worst Job, dovetailed together, and as with rival versions of their other sketches, it's hard to say whether this one's worse or better, since there are some good gags in here that don't appear elsewhere and vice versa. With Peter and Dudley (and especially Derek and Clive) you never got precisely the same sketch twice.*

CLIVE: How's it going?

DEREK: Well, not too bad, considering the way the fucking job problem is.

CLIVE: Well, the economy is to blame, isn't it?

DEREK: It's up the spout, basically. I'm amazed they got anything to offer down at the fucking Labour Exchange at all.

CLIVE: Oh, they've got nothing for me at all. I went down there yesterday, they've got nothing that I'd touch with a barge pole, and I've had some bad jobs in my time.

DEREK: Oh, I know, you've told me. I was going to ask anyway, cos when I was down there I thought to myself, actually, 'What was the worst job I ever had?' And I was going to ask you that, because I've had some bummers in my time. And what I'm trying to say –

CLIVE: Well, to be frank, Derek, and I have to be frank about this, don't I? It would be silly to evade the issue. The worst job I have ever had is getting lobsters out of Jayne Mansfield's arsehole. That was a really bad job. I mean, it was twenty-four-hour call, you know. I had no time off.

DEREK: Why was that?

CLIVE: Because she was a star. She was a star, wasn't she? And she insisted on a twenty-four-hour service, to retrieve the lobsters from her bum.

DEREK: What happened, then? How did they get up there in the first place?

CLIVE: Well, they got up there the normal way. How do you expect a lobster to get up somebody's bum? Jayne used to go swimming in the sea off Malibu, like all the starlets – skinny-dipping off Malibu, totally nude, and then boing! She'd have a lobster up her arse. I don't know whose fault it was. I don't think it was Jayne's fault. I don't think it was the lobster's fault.

DEREK: Probably fifty-fifty. She probably led them on as much as they wanted to get up there.

CLIVE: Yeah, and it was my job, at all hours of the day, to retrieve these fucking lobsters.

DEREK: Oh, God. Well, how did you . . .

CLIVE: Well, there was one method, and that is to plunge your arm up the arse. And the worst aspect of the job, apart from the hours, and the arse – she had a spacious arse, you know, she used to be able to get twenty lobsters up there, you know, with a good day's swimming – and the problem was the lobsters were not asleep. They were comatose.

DEREK: Well, you would be, wouldn't you, up there? I mean, I can't imagine really falling asleep.

CLIVE: No, no – they were comatose, and a bit, you know, carried away with the old fame thing of being up a famous lady's bum.

DEREK: They were probably wild.

CLIVE: Well, I think they felt a bit overcome. And you would put your arm up, and they could give you a nasty nip, those fuckers, the lobsters. That was a bad job, and in the end I says to Jayne, 'You know, Jayne, enough's enough.' And you know, being the star she was, she said, 'Fuck off, cunt.' And I left on that note. That was a pretty bad job. What was the worst job you ever had?

DEREK: Oh, the worst job I ever had, I don't know, that's going back a bit now, but I think, frankly, the worst job I ever had was cleaning up Winston Churchill's bogeys.

CLIVE: You had that job? I turned that down. I got a letter through the mail, offering the job, and I said, 'No fucking thank you very much.' I wrote back, you know, on the government stationery. 'No thanks. You got that?'

DEREK: I took it on cos, you know, I figured –

CLIVE: My country, 'tis of thee?

DEREK: Well, something like that. And the problem was, I used to take a couple of bogey buckets into his bedroom. And you know, he used to drink a lot and smoke a lot, and of course there were a lot of bogeys. I used to come in of a morning and pick up his bogeys and take them down to the workshop.

CLIVE: Were they analysed by forensics?

DEREK: I used to send some along to the forensics boys. Course, in those days, he was very afraid that the Nazis would use them against him. But they were sort of tucked away. But I must admit, he was an amazing bogey producer.

CLIVE: He was a big bogeyer?

DEREK: Yeah. He had all types, you know. He had sort of crispies, and, you know, moist green ones.

CLIVE: I remember reading about the long green ones, yeah.

DEREK: And, of course, he was very proud of his bogeys, which I can understand because they were magnificent. In fact, in his later years, the only thing he could produce were his bogeys.

CLIVE: Well, apart from a history of the English-speaking world.

DEREK: And, of course, he was very good at painting lobsters. But he used to produce some really huge ones – staggering.

CLIVE: I read a story somewhere, you know, the underground press somewhere, that he once produced a bogey the size of the *Titanic*.

DEREK: Well –

CLIVE: Now, you don't have to listen to me.

DEREK: Well, listen –

CLIVE: But it would help if you did.

DEREK: Well, you've touched on a sore point here, because, um, it's fascinating you should bring this up, about the *Titanic*. Because the bogey that he produced that was as big as the *Titanic* was, in fact, the *Titanic*.

CLIVE: You're telling me there was no fucking *Titanic*?

DEREK: There was no fucking *Titanic*. The *Titanic* was one of Winston Churchill's bogeys. Of course the fucker sank! I mean, people going out on a bogey? And of course, bogeys are not seaworthy.

CLIVE: They are not seaworthy. The poor fuckers were doomed!

DEREK: The regular bogey does not float. You know how to test if a substance is a bogey? You put a bogey in a glass of beer. If it floats, it is not a bogey. If it goes down to the bottom, it is a bogey. Well, I mean, I think it's cruel but there you are . . .

CLIVE: And the band played on.

DEREK: The band played on and the bogey went down.

CLIVE: So, if you see a poster saying Go To Majorca On A Bogey . . .

DEREK: Forget it, mate.

GENERAL EISENHOWER
(*Derek & Clive* – out-take, 1973)

CLIVE: I tell you what's the worst job I ever had.

DEREK: Oh fucking hell.

CLIVE: That was gathering General Eisenhower's dandruff, one by one, every single fucking flake, and having to count them night after night.

DEREK: Oh fucking hell.

CLIVE: Oh, that was terrible, cos, you know, he was almost bald towards the end.

DEREK: Oh fucking hell.

CLIVE: He only had about four strands of hair, but he could generate such an amount of dandruff, you know.

DEREK: What a fucking cunt.

CLIVE: No, don't. Be fair. He won the war, didn't he? No, he didn't win the war, but he took credit for half winning it.

DEREK: Yeah, all right.

CLIVE: And I had the misfortune to apply for the job of getting his dandruff and counting it. It used to be about 353 per day, on average. You couldn't distinguish. Half of the dandruff fell apart. A bit of dandruff fell on the floor and you thought you had one bit and suddenly you'd be struck with this vision of two bits. You didn't know whether it was one bit of dandruff or two.

DEREK: What the fuck did you do?

CLIVE: Well, I used to fiddle the books. I used to say he had about 353 bits of dandruff per day. Whether it is truth or lie I don't know.

DEREK: I don't think you should fucking worry about it. I mean, you know, what's two bits of dandruff amongst friends?

CLIVE: Well, quite a lot, actually. Because I remember the day Hedda Hopper came round, and she was doing her Hollywood column, you know, asking about Eisenhower's dandruff, and I was asked on the spot how much dandruff falls off his head, and I said, you know, I said 353. And she took me up on it. So I sat on this pile of dandruff and it amounted to 354, and Hedda went berserk.

DEREK: I bet you felt a fool on top of that.

CLIVE: I felt an idiot. I thought, 'What am I doing?' I should have a decent job.

VIETNAM
(*Derek & Clive* – out-take, 1973)

CLIVE: That plaster you've got on your finger – how did you get that? Did you nick yourself?

DEREK: Did I what?

CLIVE: Did you nick yourself? Did you get a cut?

DEREK: Did I fucking nick myself, did you say?

CLIVE: Yeah. How did you get it?

DEREK: Fuck me, mate. No, er, it's a long story. Well, a lot of people think that I just nipped myself on a doorknob or something.

CLIVE: Yeah, that's what I thought. Frankly, that's what I thought. Thought you caught yourself on a doorknob – something like that.

DEREK: Like, to put a plaster on? Well, er, what happened was that I sustained this when I was fighting in Vietnam.

CLIVE: Oh, you were fighting in Vietnam, were you? Yeah?

DEREK: And –

CLIVE: Mate of mine was fighting out there. Forget which side.

DEREK: Yeah, well, I was out there.

CLIVE: Which side were you on?

DEREK: Well, I don't know. At the time, everything was confused.

CLIVE: Yeah, well, any yellow fucker you kill, don't you?

DEREK: Yeah, right. And we were making a sortie, and suddenly I was grabbed by the Vietcong – and quite honestly, Clive –

CLIVE: Wait. They are the yellow fuckers who, er, grab you?

DEREK: Yeah, right.

CLIVE: I know them. Fucking arseholes. They were down my place the other night.

DEREK: Well, they got hold of me and they fucking done me over, and that's how I got this fucking plaster on my finger.

CLIVE: What? They actually attacked your finger, did they – physically?

DEREK: They done my fucking finger over.

CLIVE: Oh, fucking hell. These fuckers, they don't know where to leave off, do they?

DEREK: No.

CLIVE: Because I was down –

DEREK: Yeah, suck us off, Clive.

CLIVE: What?

DEREK: I said suck us off.

CLIVE: Yeah, well, when I've told you what I was going to tell you about. You know, get the knob up ready. You know I can't stand fucking flaccid . . .

DEREK: No.

CLIVE: If there is one trip I don't want to be on it's fucking flaccid. You know, it really turns me off.

DEREK: Yeah. No, I think I'm gonna get a stalk-on in a moment.

CLIVE: It's like fucking Doris Day singing those ballads. When I suck flaccid, mate, I can't stand it. But a good hard knob – now there's something different. You're talking now.

DEREK: Yeah.

CLIVE: Yeah, you know. You know, get a big – you're doing well. Go on, my son – get it up, that's right. That's right. That's better now.

DEREK: Oh my God. Oh!

CLIVE: Did you see him.

DEREK: No.

CLIVE: When you said, 'Oh my God,' I thought you'd seen God for a second.

DEREK: No. No, that was purely theatrical.

CLIVE: Oh, it's a bit of saline, this, isn't it? Anyway, I was telling you, I had the same trouble with the fucking Vietcong. You see this scar I got on the side of my face?

DEREK: Where?

CLIVE: Just on the left cheek, there.

DEREK: Where?

CLIVE: Just here – a little nick. A lot of people come up to me and say, 'I see you nicked yourself shaving.' And I say to them the truth. The fact is, I've not nicked myself shaving, because I never nick myself shaving, because I shave careful. You know, you've seen my knob.

DEREK: Yeah, of course.

CLIVE: And it's spotless, mate. There is not a hair amongst it. So they say, 'You nipped yourself shaving.' And I say, 'Fair enough. You think I nip myself shaving.' I say, in the end, 'You cunt.'

DEREK: 'What do you fucking know,' eh?

CLIVE: I was imprisoned by the fucking Japanese in Dresden, when they were dropping all those fucking bombs. When the Nips got into Dresden.

DEREK: Yeah.

CLIVE: Sir Winston Churchill, of his own accord – and I bless him for this, I thank God that he was alive and he made the decision.

DEREK: Yeah.

CLIVE: Cos otherwise I would have been against it.

DEREK: You would have been 'dead' against it. Ha ha ha.

CLIVE: He decided to drop . . . Yeah, right. Ha ha ha. You've got a sense of humour. Fuck off, cunt. Anyway, he said to the top people, to the GPO, whoever drops the bombs . . .

DEREK: Yeah. Give us a suck, Clive.

CLIVE: Yeah. I'm sorry. I thought you'd had it. Fucking arseholes. That was a bit of saline! Anyway, Winston Churchill dropped fucking bombs and my whole body was blown into five thousand bits.

DEREK: Fucking hell.

CLIVE: And I thought to myself, 'Fucking hell, what am I fighting for?'

DEREK: 'What a fucking mess I'm in,' eh?

CLIVE: You know I was on the wrong fucking side. I should be on the British side instead of German, but who's to tell in this, you know, troubled time, and I was blown to bits.

DEREK: What happened then? What did you do?

CLIVE: Well, I went to the nearest doctor – or part of me went – and he pieced me together, and the next thing that happened, oh, it was terrible. I was assigned to a leper colony on Kathmandu. Have you been there?

DEREK: Yeah. Oh yeah.

CLIVE: Just off the bypass, then turn left.

DEREK: Down the banjo.

CLIVE: Down the banjo, fucking leopards everywhere, and I thought, 'Fucking hell,' you know.

DEREK: 'What the fuck are you doing here,' eh?

CLIVE: What am I doing here? But they are nice people.

DEREK: Yeah. Suck us off, Clive.

CLIVE: Yeah, sure. Oh, Jesus Christ! You been swimming again? But I . . . oh, sorry – it's on your shoe.

DEREK: Oh, it's all right.

CLIVE: Would you like me to suck your shoe? Shall I suck the shoe?

DEREK: Oh all right.

CLIVE: Fucking hell! What boot polish do you use? If that's fucking Kiwi, I'm a Dutchman!

A MILLION POUNDS
(*Derek & Clive* – out-take, 1973)

(*Peter talks like a hysterical woman, Dudley talks like Dudley.*)

DUDLEY: Darling, darling. Yes, darling, yes. Get it all out. Oh, my darling.

PETER: It's so miserable.

DUDLEY: Darling.

PETER: No one understands me.

DUDLEY: Darling.

PETER: No one understands me.

DUDLEY: Darling, darling – I try.

PETER: You were so sweet to me. It makes me feel awful.

DUDLEY: Oh darling – not over my jersey, dear.

PETER: I'm sorry. It's just that all my life I've been treated by people as some kind of object. Yes, that's the word for it – it's object. Just used me. People just used me.

DUDLEY: No, darling. You know I look upon you as a human being – somebody with feelings.

PETER: What makes you so different from everyone else? I know every man I've known has just treated me as if I'm some kind of whore.

DUDLEY: Oh my darling, oh my darling – let it pass.

PETER: Oh, I'm so unhappy.

DUDLEY: Darling, tell me what's wrong. Tell me.

PETER: I want something I don't like.

DUDLEY: I know, darling. We're all looking for that, darling.

PETER: I know.

DUDLEY: It's so difficult.

PETER: I know. I want . . . I want a million pounds. I always wanted a million pounds and nobody has given me a million pounds and I'm so miserable.

DUDLEY: Darling, I don't see why anybody could resist giving you a million pounds.

PETER: How much have you got?

DUDLEY: Well . . .

PETER: How much have you fucking well got? How much have you got? You're just like all the rest of them. You just use me – use my body.

DUDLEY: Oh darling, please. Oh, don't – don't shout at me.

PETER: Well, you're a stupid little prick that's no use to me at all. I want a million pounds and nobody, nobody will give it to me. You're all alike.

DUDLEY: Shut up.

PETER: What?

DUDLEY: I said shut up!

PETER: Nobody has ever said that to me before.

DUDLEY: Fuck me. I'm sorry, darling. I couldn't hold it.

PETER: How much have you got?

DUDLEY: I've got three pounds in fifty pees.

PETER: Oh, what use are material possessions? Just give it to me.

TOP RANK (AGAIN)
(*Derek & Clive* – out-take, 1973)

CLIVE: I had a funny thing happen to me the other day. I was down, you know, the Top Rank ballroom, Tottenham.

DEREK: Oh yeah.

CLIVE: I was down there with a few of the lads and the wife.

DEREK: Yeah.

CLIVE: You know, I just went down there for a bit of a drink and, you know, a social evening.

DEREK: Did they have their birds with them, and that?

CLIVE: Yeah. Yeah, it was a social evening. You know, just having a drink and the wife. You know, just the usual chat. And I was there for half an hour, you know – just chatting to the ladies, and the wife was chatting to the, you know, the birds.

DEREK: Yeah. Well, they do that.

CLIVE: Yeah, and talking about, you know, the match. Fucking Norwich. What a team of fucking wankers they are.

DEREK: Yeah. Cunts.

CLIVE: Right cunts they are. Anyway, we won three-nil so it didn't matter.

DEREK: Fuck 'em.

CLIVE: They are very physical, you know.

DEREK: Oh yeah?

CLIVE: You know they've got no bite in the midfield, and I think they're lacking up front. But, you know, with three-nil you can't grumble.

DEREK: You can't fucking grumble.

CLIVE: You can't grumble. You know, Gilly done a good job up front with his side headers and Pearcey got a nice goal.

DEREK: Must have been an exciting match.

CLIVE: No, it was fucking boring, actually.

DEREK: I'm sorry I missed it, actually, but I was wanking that afternoon.

CLIVE: Yeah, well, you have to, don't you? Anyway, as I was saying, we were down the Top Rank, having a drink, and I was chatting to Les. I turn around, you know, almost instinctively, and –

DEREK: Almost?

CLIVE: No, completely. I turned around completely.

DEREK: Yeah, I see.

CLIVE: And there was my wife, you know, standing there. And this fucking great gorilla, huge great gorilla, was fucking the arse off her.

DEREK: You're joking.

CLIVE: I am not.

DEREK: A fucking gorilla?

CLIVE: A fucking gorilla. God knows where it came from. You know, you don't expect a fucking gorilla down the Top Rank on a Saturday night, do you? Fucking great gorilla fucking the arse off the fucking wife.

DEREK: Fuck me.

CLIVE: And I thought, 'Fuck me.' My words exactly. I thought, 'Fuck me.' If I can't go down, you know, to drink –

DEREK: Quiet drink.

CLIVE: – without your wife being fucked by a gorilla, what can you do? I thought, you know, what the fuck can I do?

DEREK: Right.

CLIVE: I mean, who do I get in touch with?

DEREK: Right.

CLIVE: Who's the top man?

DEREK: Right.

CLIVE: And our Sid – you know Sid?

DEREK: Yeah.

CLIVE: Sid comes up to me and I said, 'Sid, there's this fucking great gorilla, don't look now, but there is this fucking great gorilla, fucking the arse off my fucking wife.'

DEREK: Fucking hell.

CLIVE: And he said, 'Fuck me, you're joking!' I said, 'I am not joking.'

DEREK: Yeah.

CLIVE: 'I am being deadly serious.'

DEREK: Well, fuck me, you wouldn't joke about something like that.

CLIVE: I wouldn't joke about somebody fucking my wife whether he be gorilla or not.

DEREK: Right.

CLIVE: I've got my pride.

DEREK: Exactly.

CLIVE: And Sid said, we have to hand it to him, 'If there's a fucking gorilla fucking your wife, you fucking well get in touch with the top man.'

DEREK: Yeah.

CLIVE: 'Don't piss about. You go straight to the manager.' So I rushed up to the manager's office, knocked on the door, no fucking reply. So I stormed in. I wasn't taking no for an answer.

DEREK: Yeah.

CLIVE: I went in and there was the fucking manager, lying on the fucking floor, with a fucking ant sucking his nipple. I said, 'You fucking cunt.'

DEREK: Yeah.

CLIVE: 'Is this the way to run a ballroom?'

THE WORST JOBS THEY EVER HAD (AGAIN)
(*Derek & Clive* – out-take, 1976)

CLIVE: I've had some terrible jobs, you know. Yeah, I think the worst actually was in the States.

DEREK: Oh, you've been over there?

CLIVE: Yeah, I've been Stateside. And I was working for Jayne Mansfield.

DEREK: Jayne Mansfield, eh?

CLIVE: Yeah. You know, she was very big in her day.

DEREK: She was very big in her day. Is that what you said?

CLIVE: She was very big all day and, you know, all night. But the point I'm coming to was that my job was to retrieve lobsters from Jayne's arsehole. Cos Jayne, like a lot of Hollywood starlets at the time . . .

DEREK: Wait, wait – let me get this straight. You retrieve lobsters from Jayne's arsehole?

CLIVE: Did fucking retrieve them? Yeah, I've got the marks to prove it.

DEREK: I'd have thought that was a job with a lot of interest.

CLIVE: No. Well, you're forgetting various factors, you see. Jayne had a huge bum and an enormous capacity for lobster. And she used to go swimming every day off the beach at Malibu. You know, like the starlets did in those days. It was the fashionable thing to be seen with Hedda Hopper topless. And Jayne used to go out swimming, and what happened was inevitable, really. The lobsters flocked up her bum. I mean, I'm not blaming Jayne. I mean, she had her personal problems, and I'm not going to drag those in . . .

DEREK: Especially in the water.

CLIVE: Especially in the water, no.

DEREK: Well, from what you say, it sounds like a fifty-fifty thing. I'm sure that she led the lobsters on, and I'm sure the lobsters got a sort of . . .

CLIVE: Got a kick from going up her bum. Yeah, and, er, the problem with the job was . . .

DEREK: Sort of I'll scratch my arse, you scratch mine . . .

CLIVE: Yeah, that was the sort of thing. And the problem with the job, basically, was that I was on twenty-four-hour call, you know. There was no let up. I mean, Jayne being a star, being temperamental – I mean, all the accoutrements for being a star . . .

DEREK: Big tits.

CLIVE: Big tits, yes. I mean, she was very demanding. If she had several lobsters up her bum, be it three o'clock in the morning or midnight, whatever time, she'd come screaming on the telephone. 'Come up and get the lobsters out!' Which, of course, I did. And the pay wasn't bad, but the problem was once the lobster was lodged in her bum.

DEREK: They must have been buggers to get down.

CLIVE: Oh, they were buggers to get out, because a lobster, once in a crevice, likes to stick there. That's built into the lobster from, you know, nature – a self-protective device. And she wore a heavy perfume.

DEREK: They used to back in, apart from that, because of their claws, didn't they?

CLIVE: No, they used to zoom up her bum backwards. Because the claws . . .

DEREK: They couldn't get out, because, you know, although the arsehole is spacious, the entrance was, you know . . .

CLIVE: Well, you know, it was not tiny, and you'd have to – no you didn't have to – I had to put my hand up, you see, and get these lobsters out, and they were comatose, sort of dozy. They were stupid, overcome by the fame of it all. Any lobster worth its salt is going to have a story to tell. 'I've been up Jayne's bum!'

DEREK: Do you think they're that aware of things?

CLIVE: Lobsters? Oh, they're like dolphins. They're more intelligent than Joe Levine. And I used to get my hand right up, and Jayne was not co-operative. She used to say, 'Oh, come on, move on.' But all the time she was relishing the movement. So it was a tricky job, but it had its perks, because a lot of the job – and I use the word with a certain amount of forbearance – sort of rubbed off on you. And in the fashionable bistro scene in

Hollywood in those days, you know, you could walk into a restaurant with a brown forearm, and they knew where that came from, you could pick up a few birds, mate, I'll tell you that. What's the worst job you've ever had?

DEREK: Oh, I've had some fuckers. Well, I think all things considered, the worst job I ever had was towards the end of the war. I used to collect Winston Churchill's bogeys.

CLIVE: You? You had that job?

DEREK: Yeah. I used to clean up after his bogeys.

CLIVE: I turned that one down.

DEREK: You did?

CLIVE: Yeah. I wasn't taking that one for all the money in the world.

DEREK: Well, I was a bit, you know, skint at the time, and I thought it would be fascinating to be so close to greatness. And, well, the basic procedure – I used to leave a bucket by the bed, and Churchill would, after an evening of brandy and cigars, he used to . . .

CLIVE: He was a great leader.

DEREK: A great leader and a great cougher, and used to have a lot of bogeys, and the buckets were filled to the brim by the morning, and I used to take them down to the workshop . . .

CLIVE: Did you actually have to go up his nose with pincers?

DEREK: No, no. He did the work himself. He was decent enough to use the bogey bucket. Well, we had to be very careful. It was a closed shop. He was afraid that the Nazis would use the bogeys against him in the war. I mean, if they got hold of one of these bogeys and analysed it, Christ knows what would have happened to him. And anyway, I must say that despite the drawbacks of the job, he was a great bogey boy. You know, tremendous variety. Great colour, textures.

CLIVE: Enormous range.

DEREK: You know, from your basic streaky crisp to the green . . .

CLIVE: Long slimy one.

DEREK: Yeah, some of them were wonderful.

CLIVE: I understood that Winston used to hoard his bogeys.

DEREK: Right. He was a great bogey hoarder. I used to find a spare bucket in his wardrobe on the weekends when I used to clear up, and sometimes, after a party, the whole room would be full of bogeys. I mean, the whole floor – and I used to go in there with a face flannel and, you know, mop them up.

CLIVE: I imagine it's a lot like what Freud says, like a child with its hoarding – thinks it's valuable.

DEREK: Well, I think Churchill has a point. His bogeys were spectacular. And I think if I'd been him, and producing that line of bogeys, I'd have . . .

CLIVE: Opened an exhibition? Didn't he produce that legendary bogey, the one the size of the Titanic?

DEREK: Well, you see, the unfortunate thing was, that story leaked out shortly after the Titanic tragedy. It shouldn't have leaked out. In fact, only a few people knew about it. I'm going to tell you something that is very, very private, and I want you to keep it under your hat.

CLIVE: What, the bogey?

DEREK: No, not the bogey. Don't be silly. The bogey that Winston produced, that was as big as the Titanic was, in fact, the Titanic.

CLIVE: You mean there was no fucking Ti-fucking-tanic?

DEREK: No.

CLIVE: Just a big fucking bogey?

DEREK: The Titanic was a bogey.

CLIVE: And the poor fuckers who went on the Titanic, well, what happened?

DEREK: Well, they sank.

CLIVE: And the fucking band played on.

DEREK: Well, of course. They went to sea on a bloody bogey. They didn't go on a boat. They went on a fucking bogey, and everybody knows a bogey is not seaworthy. I mean, a bogey will not float! I mean, you know how to test whether a substance is a bogey or not? You put a bogey in a glass of beer. If it sinks to the bottom, it is a bogey. If it floats, it is not a bogey. Those poor fuckers, they streamed onto the Titanic, and they were streaming onto a bogey. And off they went to sea, and of course it wasn't long before the inevitable happened.

CLIVE: Hit another iceberg. Another rule, isn't it?

DEREK: Don't mix bogeys with icebergs.

CLIVE: Steer clear of bogeys on the rocks. So, if I see one of those ads, Go To Majorca On A Bogey, I'm going to . . .

DEREK: Oh, forget it mate.

CLIVE: You haven't by any chance got one? Not for me. It's just for the kids.

DEREK: Listen, let me explain. And really, if anyone knew about this I'd get skinned. I mean, during the whole time, I was very closely inspected and I couldn't get away with any of his bogeys. People were continually asking me and I had to refuse, because, I mean, the whole war effort could just go out the window if one of these bogeys got into the wrong hands. But, towards the end, I was able to get hold of a very small one, about a quarter of an inch, and it was a jewel. A very beautiful one, sort of rainbow coloured, and I thought to myself, 'Where am I going to put this?' Now, if you look up here – you see the way the light plays on it?

CLIVE: That is the most fantastic nostril I ever saw in my life. It's like the Hanging Gardens of Babylon up there.

Chapter Seven
Pete & Dud

Older fans may prefer *Beyond the Fringe*. Younger fans may prefer *Derek & Clive*. But if Cook and Moore are still remembered in a hundred years, it will be for Pete and Dud. With their flat caps and flasher's macs, and their Estuary English accents, and their half-baked opinions about everything from fine art to the afterlife, they're not only a great double act, but also an iconic one, like Laurel and Hardy. Onstage or on television, from *Goodbye Again* to *Not Only . . . But Also . . .* , from *Behind the Fridge* to the Royal Variety Performance, Pete and Dud were always the highlight of the show. Maybe they should have made a Pete and Dud movie after all. Yet they might never have existed if it hadn't been for a Canadian broadcaster called Bernard Braden and a show called *On the Braden Beat*, which immortalised Peter's wise fool, E.L. Wisty.

'Dudley invited me to appear on his TV show,' recalled Peter, 'and I wrote a sketch about an old man who was always being rung up by film stars like Jane Russell who wanted to go to bed with him.' This would have made an ideal monologue for E.L. Wisty – but Wisty was already appearing in *On the Braden Beat*, at Braden's invitation, so Peter wrote it as a two-hander and Pete and Dud were born. 'Pete is a slightly more active extension of E.L. Wisty,' explained Peter. 'Pete is the informed idiot and Dud is the un-informed idiot. They're both idiots, but Pete is always slightly supe-rior. In fact, he knows nothing either. They discuss the same lofty subjects as E.L. Wisty.'[2] Wisty was destined for comic immortality, but although he was immensely popular, he was like an idiot savant who'd floated in from a parallel universe. Pete and Dud were every-day idiots – well-meaning, dim-witted know-alls propping up the public bar down the road.

Peter had Dudley to thank for this welcome injection of comic realism, which extended Pete and Dud's shelf-life, and broadened their appeal. Pete and Dud may have started out as a pair of E.L. Wistys, but in the sketches that followed, Dudley quickly brought his own attributes to bear. He decorated his dialogue with refer-ences to his Essex upbringing (a subsequent book of Pete and Dud scripts was called *The Dagenham Dialogues*) and based Dud on a hapless congregant at his childhood church. 'I never knew his name but he was a strange sort of cloth-capped individual who was obvi-ously very down on himself,' said Dudley. 'He almost made me cry because he was so pathetic and didn't know anything about anything.'[3] Dud almost made his audience cry, the way he let Pete push him around. As well as the Dagenham details, which litter these scripts like confetti, there was also a potent strain of auto-biography in Dud's unequal partnership with Pete. These authen-tic elements made Pete and Dud plausible and compelling – even when Dudley collapsed in fits of helpless giggles, as he so often did.

Corpsing is usually a sign that something isn't working, but Dudley got the giggles in some of Pete and Dud's greatest head-to-heads, and it was always genuine, whether Peter was trying to make him laugh or not. 'The laughter in the Dud and Pete sketches, between Dudley and Peter, was never rehearsed,'[4] says Joe McGrath, who directed the first Pete and Duds, in the first series of *Not Only . . . But Also . . .* McGrath likened Peter's ploys to make Dudley laugh to a Spanish matador tormenting a wounded bull. 'The sword had hit Dudley right between the shoulders,'[5] he recalls, of the numerous occasions when Peter delivered a ruthless comic *coup de grâce*.

'If Dudley makes a mistake, Peter would instantly pick up on it and hone in on it,' says Dick Clement, who directed the second series of *Not Only . . . But Also . . .* 'You can see Dudley desperately trying to hold it in and failing, and of course that became part of the act.'[6] The reason Dudley's corpsing was charming rather than irritating was because he was laughing with the audience, not at them. Usually, performers corpse out of sheer embarrassment, because things are going so badly. Dudley usually corpsed out of sheer enjoyment, because things were going so well.

When Dudley wasn't giggling, the acting was of a remarkably high standard – achieving a level of naturalism quite unusual for an era when comic sketches were still commonly regarded as glorified seaside turns. This was the result of a unique writing process. Peter and Dudley employed this process throughout their partnership, but they never put it to better use than they did as Pete and Dud. They began by improvising into a tape recorder, refining their efforts over the course of several takes. The final take would be transcribed, and memorised by Dudley, who copied his lines out by hand, so as to learn them off by heart. Dudley played the sketch word for word, while Peter improvised around the script he read off the autocue. The result combined inspiration and preparation, spontaneity and polish.

The characters soon took on a life of their own. 'They would just sit down and start doing Dud and Pete when they came into the office or during rehearsals or when they were in the BBC canteen,' remembers McGrath. 'It didn't stop. It just went on. I mean, they could just have gone on doing Dud and Pete for the rest of their lives.'[7] The reason they didn't was due to Dudley's growing confidence, both as a performer and a person. Their comedy was all about the lopsided nature of their relationship – Dud's willingness to be bossed about by a fellow imbecile who knew no more than him. As soon as Dud started standing up to Pete, and Dudley started standing up to Peter, that imbalance levelled out. 'I drew my own character from various inoffensive compliant men I'd known, including myself,'[8] said Dudley. 'Once during the *Beyond the Fringe* days I observed that Dudley went from being a subservient little creep, a genial serf, to become an obstinate bastard who asserted himself,'[9] said Peter. Dudley's intrinsic subservience was the perfect foil for Peter's very English wit. His growing obstinacy was better suited to America, and the movies.

THE FORK IDIOM
(*The New London Palladium Show*, ATV, 1965)

(Pete is sat at a kitchen table, making tea. Dud is sat at an upright piano, playing a one-fingered version of Glenn Miller's In The Mood)

DUD: Red blue green, red blue green, red blue green, red blue green. Red red green, red red green, red red green. Yellow ochre white, yellow ochre white, yellow ochre white, yellow ochre white. Red blue green, red blue green, red blue green, red blue green.

PETE: Tea's up.

DUD: Oh, thanks, Pete.

(Dud joins Pete at the table)

PETE: Nothing like a nice cup of tea.

DUD: Nothing like a nice cup of tea.

PETE: The beverage of queens. How many sugars would you like?

DUD: Eight.

PETE: Heaped?

DUD: Partially.

PETE: Only partially, Dud?

DUD: Yeah. I don't want to overdo it. I'm on a diet.

PETE: You don't want to get Euphrates of the blood – too much sugar in the blood, Dud, do you? How's it going with your music – the piano lessons?

DUD: Oh, you mean the Ephraim Bag Teach Yourself Piano By Colour method?

PETE: Yes. How does that method work, the Ephraim Bag method?

DUD: Oh, it's quite easy. In layman's terms, Pete, you have a different colour for each note on the piano. You have the colours laid out and you learn the tunes like that. For instance: you have C, you have red; D, you have yellow; E, you have green, and so on, up the scale.

PETE: You know Titian?

DUD: B flat.

PETE: That's a lovely colour, Titian. It sounds a wonderful method.

DUD: Oh, it is wonderful. You know Stravinsky used it?

PETE: I remember seeing that on the advertisement. Except I thought it said, 'This is the method that Igor Stravinsky does not use.'

DUD: Oh, yeah. That's right.

PETE: That's what made it famous.

DUD: Yes, and Beethoven didn't use it either.

PETE: No musician has ever used it. That's why it's got such a following.

DUD: Yes, exactly.

PETE: What was that you were playing there?

DUD: Er, Red Blue Green.

PETE: No, what's the title of the song?

DUD: The song was called In The Nude. That's a boogie-woogie version of In The Mood that Claude Debussy wrote forty years previous.

PETE: Oh, yes. Debussy wrote In The Nude, didn't he?

DUD: It was very hot in Tahiti, where he used to compose. He had a wonderful ear for music though, didn't he?

PETE: Debussy has a wonderful ear for music. His left ear – a wonderful ear. His right one was terrible. And eventually, he had to bite it off and send it to Queen Victoria.

DUD: That's right. And she sent back a bag of old tennis balls with a covering note saying 'We are not amused.'

PETE: She had a wonderful sense of humour. Why are you learning, actually?

DUD: Well, I'm learning because I want to go into showbiz and get a few birds.

PETE: What kind of act were you thinking of doing?

DUD: Well, I thought of doing an act like Mrs Mills, you know?

PETE: Oh, yes. Lovely.

DUD: Start off with a song like Bye Bye, Billy Bumblebee.

PETE & DUD (*singing*): Bye bye, Billy Bumblebee, bye bye. Bye bye, Billy Bumblebee, bye bye.

DUD: Play it cool, boy!

PETE: It's a wonderful song, that. Course, if you really want to succeed today, Dud, I think you ought to adopt the fork idiom.

DUD: Yeah?

PETE: The fork idiom is very popular now – the songs of protest which are so justified.

DUD: Yeah.

PETE: Cos when you look round you, Dud, and you see all the way all the awful lunatics – the politicians, the hydrogen bomb and the injustice – it makes you absolutely furious.

DUD: Makes you sick, doesn't it?

PETE: Somebody could take his finger, put it up in the air, put it down on a button – and the whole world is blown up in a nuclear hollyhocks.

DUD: Yeah, a mushroom cloud of terror.

PETE: A toadstool of death. It makes me furious! I wrote that song about it, remember? I was so angry once, I wrote that song – Come Off It Mr Menzies.

DUD: Come off it Chou En Lai.

PETE: And end the nuclear lunacy.

DUD: Or else the world must die.

PETE: He's nine foot one.

DUD: He's five foot three.

PETE: He plays for Spurs.

DUD: Does he really?

PETE: Yes. Inside left.

DUD: Oh.

PETE: That's a wonderful way of doing it. You know that one – Peter, Paul and St Joan's? They make over five quid a night with that stuff.

DUD: Really?

PETE: They do 'The answer, my friend . . .'

PETE & DUD (*together*): '. . . is blowing in the wind. The answer is blowing in the wind.'

DUD: Lovely.

PETE: I was listening to that one day in the kitchen. It was a lovely sunny day. I looked out the window, the sun was beautiful there, little clouds scudding across it.

DUD: Little children playing with their hoops in the meadows.

PETE: Precisely. Birds twittering in the sky. There was a bit of a wind going, and I heard this: 'The answer, my friend, is blowing in the wind.' So I thought I'd pop outside and see if it was. And sure enough, fluttering from over the horizon came a strange white piece of paper blowing over Chadwell Heath. Well, naturally I pursued it. It alighted in a gooseberry bush and I found it and took it out. Do you know it said?

DUD: What?

PETE: It said McWhirter's Raspberry Style Ice Lolly.

DUD: 'The answer, my friend, is McWhirter's Raspberry Style Ice Lolly.' Not a very good answer, is it?

PETE: It's a rotten answer. Of course, if you're thinking of entering the ephemeral world of show business, Dud, you must beware to keep hold of your values.

DUD: Yeah.

PETE: Cos it's a strange, artificial world. Behind the glamour and the glitter lurks heartbreak.

DUD: Yeah, behind the clown's happy mask lurks the tear of tragedy.

PETE: The continual tear of tragedy, for everything's so artificial and false. I mean, take Kirk Douglas. What d'you think of when you think of Kirk Douglas?

DUD: Dimple.

PETE: Dimple. Dimple springs to your lips.

DUD: Springs to his chin.

PETE: Do you know what that dimple is?

DUD: What is it?

PETE: That dimple, it's a wart.

DUD: No it's not. It's a dimple. It goes in.

PETE: No, it's a wart – it goes out. But what they do in Hollywood is they photograph it in double reverse triple negative, and it comes out – or goes in – like a dimple.

DUD: Oh, yeah.

PETE: It's the same with his nose. His nose goes in as well.

DUD: He's got an ingrowing nose, has he?

PETE: Yeah. He nearly kills himself every time he sneezes.

DUD: Of course, you know the same sort of artificiality can be found with Sonja Henie the skater.

PETE: Oh, Sonja Henie.

DUD: She couldn't skate a note. They used to stand her up on one leg and move the ice rink underneath her. Mind you, Pete, she had a wonderful smile.

PETE: No, she had a horrible smile. What they did was, they took Myrna Loy's smile and dubbed it on to Sonja Henie.

DUD: Oh. But that's strange, cos I can't stand Myrna Loy's smile, but it looks lovely on Sonja.

PETE: It's lovely on Sonja, lousy on Myrna. That's show business.

DUD: Well, of course another example like that is Laurence Harvey's legs. They're played by Marlene Dietrich.

PETE: Yes, and beautifully played at that. Of course, Dud, if you're going to get on in show business, you've got to have a good name – something to catch the public. What are you thinking of calling yourself?

DUD: I thought of calling myself Gregory Peck.

PETE: That's a good name. It's got a certain ring, hasn't it? The only trouble is, I think it's already being used by somebody.

DUD: Oh, wait a minute!

PETE: Who's that bloke who used it? Um, what's his name? It's on the tip of my tongue.

DUD: Gregory . . .

PETE: Gregory . . . Palmer?

DUD: Palmerston? Peck! Peck! Gregory Peck's used it.

PETE: Gregory Peck! He's the one! He's been flaunting it all over the place. Of course you know the secret about Peck – Gregory Peck?

DUD: No.

PETE: He can't sit down.

DUD: Really?

PETE: He can't sit down, Dud. He has an ailment of what can only described as the . . . er . . .

DUD: Bottom?

PETE: Of the bottom, yes. And he doesn't sit down, so he has this bloke to do all the stand in work for his bottom.

DUD: Or the sit in work, you mean.

PETE: The sit in work, yes. It's all done by George Noades of Dagenham.

DUD: Dagenham Dye Works?

PETE: Dagenham Dye Works.

DUD: Oh yeah?

PETE: He sits down for Gregory Peck.

DUD: Really?

PETE: You must have seen it at the end of The Guns of Navarone. 'Starring Gregory Peck, with the active participation of George Noades' bottom.' And now Noades is getting very uppity about it. He's asking for better billing. He's asking for the next one to be 'starring George Noades' bottom and introducing Gregory Peck.' He's getting very big headed about his bottom.

DUD: His bottom's gone to his head, hasn't it?

PETE: Best place for it, Dud.

DUD: Did I tell you about the very strange experience I had last night, Pete?

PETE: No, Dud. What was it?

DUD: Well, Pete, I was sitting down. I was in bed at the time, drinking a cup of cocoa . . .

PETE: Course you were, Dud.

DUD: Course I was, Pete. And I was flicking through Sophisticated Screen Secrets – the wonderful magazine for the film connyskinny. And I was drinking my cocoa . . .

PETE: Course you were, Dud.

DUD: Course I was, Pete. It was the June 1930 edition.

PETE: Oh, yes.

DUD: And I'm flicking through the yellowed pages, you know . . .

PETE: Steeped in history.

DUD: And coffee stains. And I came across this picture of Jane Russell.

PETE: The busty beauty.

DUD: But this is the point. Jane Russell – flat as a pancake. It was a still from a film called *The In Law*. I thought to myself, 'Funny.' You know, busty beauty – nothing there. I thought, you know . . .

PETE & DUD (*together*): Funny.

PETE: Busty beauty – nothing there. Funny.

DUD: Famous for the, er . . .

PETE & DUD (*together*): Doo dahs.

PETE: Nothing there.

DUD: Nothing there.

PETE: Busty beauty.

PETE & DUD (*together*): Nothing there. Funny.

PETE: Well Dud, I'll tell you the answer to that.

DUD: What's that, Pete? Blowing in the wind, is it?

PETE: No, it's not that. The answer to that is that Jane Russell was indeed extremely flat-chested and they made a film, *The In Law*, and it was a terrible failure. Nobody went to see it. I didn't go to see it. I remember that.

DUD: I didn't either. No.

PETE: I remember you not going to see it. Anyway, Metro Goldwyn Paramount Mayer did an audience research to see why no one had gone, and back came the answer – lack of busty substances. Well, what they did was, they persuaded this bloke, Sabu . . .

DUD: Oh, the Indian elephant boy?

PETE: You remember Sabu? Lovely little bloke. They asked Sabu to climb into her blouse and stick his fists out – stick his fists out like this to stimulate the busty substances – and that's how they made it. They changed the name to *The Outlaw*, and it was a tremendous success.

DUD: Yeah.

PETE: Of course it was dreadful conditions in there, inside the blouse.

DUD: Sweated labour, really.

PETE: Sweated labour. That's why they had to get an Indian to do it. You'd never get a white bloke doing that – terrible conditions. And it was this busty beauty that gave her wonderful BO appeal.

DUD: I don't think I'd go for BO appeal, Pete.

PETE: No, BO is the Hollywood term, Dud, for box office.

DUD: Box office?

PETE: That's what they whisper to each other in sophisticated circles on Malibu beach, Dud, yes.

DUD: Well I must say, Pete, the film industry sounds a very shoddy affair, doesn't it?

PETE: It is. I should stick to your music, Dud.

DUD: Stick to the music. Did I tell you, I've almost learnt that song those two blokes sing?

PETE: No.

DUD: I'll play it you. It's very good.

PETE Yes. You do that.

(*Dud goes to the piano, sits down, and begins to play Goodbyee*)

DUD: It's the one that goes – blue red green, blue yellow green, red . . .

PETE: He's got it. By George, he's got it!

DUD: (*sings*) Now is the time to wend our way, until we meet again some sunny day . . .

BY APPOINTMENT
(Royal Variety Performance, London Palladium, 1965)

Three years after her royal night out at Beyond the Fringe, *Peter and Dudley entertained the Queen again, with this specially written sketch. Aptly, it's all about the vagaries of aristocratic ancestry and the duties of constitutional monarchy, but its cheeky topicality proved a bit too risqué for the show's producer, Bernard (Lord) Delfont, who requested several cuts. Consequently, there was no reference to the*

Queen's brother-in-law, Antony Armstrong-Jones (Lord Snowdon) or 'the former underwater wrestler, Strong-Arm Jones,' as Pete and Dud erroneously called him, and no truth whatsoever in Pete and Dud's assertion (also cut) that before he could marry Princess Margaret, he'd been forced to 'run from Land's End to John O'Groats in a rubber diving suit to get his weight down'. It's hard to imagine any member of the royal entourage objecting to these harmless jokes, which might have given this performance a more subversive edge. 'The mink and bow tie audience at the London Palladium hooted like schoolkids,' reported the Sun, *'for wasn't it, after all, a college rag show when just the mention of the headmaster's name has them falling about?' However, even without these irreverent quips, Peter and Dudley were the stars of the show, outshining far more established stars like Peter's childhood heroes – Spike Milligan and Peter Sellers. Incredibly, it was only a decade since Peter had feigned illness every Friday, in order to listen to Milligan and Sellers in* The Goons *on the school sanatorium radio.*

PETE: Tea's up, Dud.

DUD: Nothing like a nice cup of tea, is there? Nothing like a nice cup of tea.

PETE: Nothing like it.

DUD: What's that you're reading, Pete?

PETE: Oh, this is a wonderful book, Dud. It's steeped in history and everything else. It's *Burke's Peerages*.

DUD: *Burke's Peerages*? What's that?

PETE: It's a brilliant idea. It's a book which contains the names of the twenty thousand most noble people in the realm.

DUD: Who'd want to read that?

PETE: Well, the twenty thousand most noble people in the realm for a start. It's a superb idea, it all dates back to the eighteenth century, Dud – the Age of Reason. There was this Burke, you see.

DUD: What was his name, Pete?

PETE: Burke, that was his name, one of the great Sussex Burkes – and he was wandering about his palatial parkland, you see,

Dud, on a fine eighteenth-century summer morning, a lovely scene, as you can well imagine – the sun dappling through the trees.

DUD: His beautiful peacocks flaunting their exotic feathers in the sunlight.

PETE: Precisely, emitting a strange birdlike cry, which sometimes comes from them. Suddenly it come to him.

DUD: What come to him, the peacock?

PETE: No, this wonderful concept come to him. He thought, 'Why don't I get hold of the names of the twenty thousand most noble people in the realm and flog it for two quid a time?' He made a fortune out of it.

DUD: Course he did. I could do exactly the same thing, couldn't I? I could go up Baron Road and knock on every door and say, 'Excuse me, Mrs Taylor, I wonder if you would give me your name and I'll put it in a book and flog it back to you.'

PETE: You'd do very well, the *Baron Road Gazette*.

DUD: Yeah.

PETE: Could do very nicely with that sort of thing. Course the whole business of ancestry is extremely fascinating. I've been into my past, you know, I've traced myself back at Somerset House and do you know, in primordial times my great-great-great-grand-father come over with the Druids.

DUD: Oh, the Druids of Lymington Crescent.

PETE: George and Phoebe's ancestors.

DUD: I had a bit of bother, I went to Somerset House one morn-ing – it was a nice morning, I thought, 'Go along to Somerset House, pop down, look at the birth certificate – makes a change.' I went down there – I said to the gentleman behind the counter, 'Can I have a look at my birth certificate?' And so he got it out and I had a look and it said . . . it had my mother's name down there but where my father's name is supposed to be there was nothing there. I thought to myself, 'Funny.' You know – mother's name here, father's name not here.

PETE: Funny.

DUD: Very peculiar. So I tackled my mother on this point but she was very evasive about it.

PETE: It was probably a foggy evening that magic night. But the wonderful thing about it, the ancestry business, is we've all got a bit of noble blood in our veins.

DUD: It's the best place for it, isn't it?

PETE: Yes, it's a wonderful place for blood, that.

DUD: Let's keep it that way.

PETE: Do you know that we're all in line for succession to the throne?

DUD: Really?

PETE: Well, if forty-eight million, two hundred thousand, seven hundred and one people died I'd be Queen.

DUD: Where would I come in that, Pete?

PETE: I think three-quarters of the world has to pass away before you get there.

DUD: But what would you do if you were Queen, Pete?

PETE: I'd turn the job down. I wouldn't do it – too much like hard work.

DUD: I'd rather like to be Queen. I tell you what I'd do. I'd give the MBE to Mrs Woolley and I'd give Aunt Dolly the Order of the Garter for services rendered to humanity.

PETE: Your Aunt Dolly could do with a bit of decoration, couldn't she?

DUD: Why wouldn't you like to be Queen, Pete?

PETE: The trouble is, you see, you're always being looked at. Wherever you go you're in the public eye. You go to the theatre, nobody looks at the stage, they're all looking at you. And it's like living in a goldfish bowl, Dud.

DUD: Well, I wouldn't mind living in that goldfish bowl, Pete. I mean, that palace is at least twice the size of Dagenham Dye Works.

PETE: It's a nice area too. It's very handy for the West End.

DUD: West End? They don't need the West End! They got their own shops in there – their own cinema. I mean it's the only place in the West End where they don't play the national anthem after the film.

PETE: That's an advantage, isn't it? Mind you, think of all the extramural expenses they have, the upkeep of the children, the clothing, the food for the pets.

DUD: I mean, those royal corgis eat like horses.

PETE: Not to mention the royal seals all jumping up and down in the fountains. The money for their food has to come out of her pocket, you know. I mean, it's a very busy life, you know. You only have to look at the royal diary to realise what a busy life it is.

DUD: Have a peep in the diary, boy – you get the message.

PETE: Yeah, you get an indication, Dud. Seven thirty: got up, cup of tea. Got into long car, waved, opened Parliament.

DUD: Got back, had lunch with Mr Wilson, got into long car, waved, cut ribbon, launched oil tanker.

PETE: Got back, Mr Wilson still there, looking round for his briefcase containing secret measurements of C.P. Snow, posed for Battle of Britain stamp, had tea with three thousand people, tried to meet them all.

DUD: Five o'clock, soaked right hand in methylated spirits. Six o'clock: practised sitting on horse sideways. Seven o'clock: got into long car, waved, went to Commonwealth Dance Festival.

PETE: Eleven thirty: come home, cup of cocoa. Goodnight, diary.

DUD: Terrible, isn't it?

PETE: Very, very busy life.

DUD: Very busy life that, Pete. Mr Wilson seems to hang about a bit, doesn't he?

PETE: Well, he's always creeping round there, Dud. Course, being a socialist he's fascinated by all the trappings of royalty. Before becoming Prime Minister, the grandest building he'd ever seen was the Hampstead Golf Club. He's always sniffing round there, fingering the gold lamé curtains.

DUD: Casting covetous eyes on the tapestries. On the other hand, Her Majesty has the chance to meet some interesting people.

PETE: The trouble is, you see, although they're very interesting, when they get round the Palace they're so nervous they become boring. They're overawed by the occasion. Now the other day,

Albert Einstein, the bloke who invented gravity, went round to collect his OBE.

DUD: His what?

PETE: His OBE for inventing the gravity – a very interesting person and a fine mind. The Queen was looking forward to meeting him, asking him a few questions, you see. So Einstein was waiting there, all tense, waiting for his medal. Her Majesty come up and stuck one on him and said to him, 'Hello, Mr Einstein, how does all this gravity business work?' And Einstein was so nervous his teeth dropped out on the floor. Mind you, Her Majesty passed it off very nicely and said, 'Aha, Mr Einstein, I see gravity is at work today,' and with a tinkling laugh moved on to Tony Curtis who was picking up a baronetcy.

DUD: That's marvellous.

PETE: A wonderful thing to do.

DUD: What's the time, by the way?

PETE: It's about quarter past nine, Dud, and do you know, at this very moment, Her Majesty is probably exercising the royal prerogative.

DUD: What's that then, Pete?

PETE: Don't you know the royal prerogative? It's a wonderful animal, Dud. It's a legendary beast, half-bird, half-fish, half-unicorn, and it's being exercised at this very moment. Do you know that legend has it that e'er so long as the royal prerogative lives, happiness and laughter will reign throughout this green and pleasant land.

DUD: And the yeoman will stand tall upon this sceptred isle, Pete.

PETE: The Archers will look out o'er the dales and see happy laughing children. Flaxen-haired Anglo-Saxon youths will scan the foam-flecked waves for marauders.

PETE / DUD (sing): Rule Britannia, Britannia rule the waves . . .

PETE: Course it does, Dud.

DUD: Course it does, Pete.

CHRISTMAS
(*Radio Times*, 1965)

They don't make television listings magazines like they used to. Nowadays, the Radio Times *is a fairly standard mid-market entertainment mag, but back in that civilised, restrictive age before any old rag could publish TV listings, it commissioned original illustrations from artists like Edward Ardizzone and even original scripts from artistes like Peter Cook and Dudley Moore.*

PETE: All right, Dud?

DUD: All right, Pete, nothing like a nice cup of tea, especially when it's laced with a splash of VP Five Star – it warms the cockles of the heart, warms you right through.

PETE: Yes, in the Festive Season, what could be more appropriate?

DUD: Wonderful, isn't it, Pete, in the Festive Season, when the Robin Redbreast sings his roundelay of cheer.

PETE: Robin Redbreast symbolises the Christmas spirit to me.

DUD: And he does for me, Pete.

PETE: The trouble is that you don't see any robins in England at Christmas time.

DUD: You see them on Christmas cards though, don't you?

PETE: Yes they're all drawn by Australian artists because that's where the robins go for Christmas. Australian Christmas must be wonderful, with all those people surfing in with the Christmas pudding on trays.

DUD: Marvellous that, ain't it?

PETE: But do you think we're going to have a white Christmas this year?

DUD: I hope so, Pete, because I'm looking forward to making the traditional snowman, and throwing a few snowballs at Greenlane Primary School windows.

PETE: Lovely crisp snow, it's part and parcel of a wonderful Christmas, isn't it?

DUD: It certainly is, Pete – holly looking lovely and green.

PETE: Yes, I can never find any holly with berries on it. Course, it's largely due to the robins, cos it's a long flight to Australia, and they usually take a few berries with them . . .

DUD: . . . to keep them alive on the way . . .

PETE: . . . strapped to their legs. As you know, the spider weaves his gossamer threads through night and day and the robin, when he sees a berry in mid flight, well, he feels like a berry and so he sees a berry on a holly and he can't carry it in his beak all the way, so he gets the spiders to tie the berries to his legs with their webby substances.

DUD: It's wonderful the way those spiders help out, you know, when robins are in need of a bit of help, there they are weaving away –

PETE: If only human beings, Dud, could behave towards each other the way spiders do to robins.

DUD: If only that could happen, Pete, then peace would reign on earth.

PETE: And U Thant would be out of a job again.

DUD: Exactly, Pete. Well, anyway, Christmas, as you know, comes but once a year.

PETE: And when it comes it brings Aunt Dolly.

DUD: Yeah, that is the only thing I dread about Christmas, that it brings Aunt Dolly.

PETE: Well, you have these seasons and have to extend your charitable facilities.

DUD: Yes, but after a few glasses of light ale she starts extending her charitable facilities along Lymington Crescent at the top of her voice.

PETE: Well, of course, you know it is the season of goodwill to all men and she takes a somewhat literal attitude towards this old saying.

DUD: Last year I thought she was a bit of a disgrace. I mean, she came out of the Royal Oak reeking of stout and I didn't get a look-in at the chicken.

PETE: Well, she is a voracious woman, Dud, there's no doubt about that . . .

DUD: What are you going to do this year, Pete? Are you going to put some decorations up?

PETE: Well, you know I don't like buying things. You know I like to make my own decorations. Cos if you use your imagination you can get wonderful things like, er . . . well, if you take some potatoes and dip them in silver paint and you stick some . . . stick some . . .

DUD: A couple of berries in for eyes . . .

PETE: Yes, a couple of berries in for eyes and you take a carrot for the nose and you cover that with frosting . . .

DUD: It's wonderful, Pete. I do a very similar thing with corn flakes. What I do is I dip them in some tinsel, which I have smeared with seasonal honey, and when I bring the Christmas pudding in and set light to it with paraffin, I throw the cereals over it.

PETE: What a lovely thought.

DUD: It is a lovely thought, Pete, but it ruins the taste of the pudding, that's the only thing.

PETE: Yes, well, you know you can't have everything.

DUD: You can't, Pete, you can't. I think you've either got to have the colour or the tastiness – not both.

PETE: The thing I like is the Christmas crackers you get, some of those jokes they have in the crackers. Whoever does those, he's a wonderful wit.

DUD: And it's the work of one mind, Pete. It isn't a group of people. It's the work of one mind because they've all got the same stamp of hilarity.

PETE: I'm told it's the Duke of Edinburgh does it.

DUD: I wouldn't be at all surprised, Pete.

PETE: What are you going to give for presents this year?

DUD: Well, I've given you a pen and pencil set . . . Whoops, I've let it out.

PETE: Where? You haven't let it out. It's in the cupboard upstairs. I've seen it.

DUD: Oh, you've seen it. I put it behind the apricot jam. I didn't think you'd see it there.

PETE: Well, I was looking for a place to hide my gift to you.

DUD: Is it hankies again?

PETE: It's not the same hankies, no. No, I bought you some underpants with the wines of the world all over them. You know, they have pictures of bottles of Beaujolais on and bottles of champagne and it gives you a sort of festive feeling under your trousers.

DUD: Are you sending any cards this year, Pete?

PETE: No, I'm taking out an advertisement in the *Dagenham Advertiser*, saying that I am not sending cards this year, but instead am making a small contribution to the Clean Up TV fund.

DUD: A very wonderful idea, Pete. Well, I think I'd better be getting back.

PETE: If you look out of the window you can see the first flakes of snow.

DUD: It's going to be a white Christmas, Pete.

PETE: Or perhaps it's Mrs Woolly shaking her head out of the window again.

DUD: Well, whatever it is, it's settling, Pete.

DISEASES
(*Not Only . . . But Also . . .* , BBC2, 1966)

DUD: Here, Pete, take this thermometer out my mouth will you?

PETE: Has it been in the full half hour?

DUD: Yeah.

PETE: Under the tongue?

DUD: Yeah.

PETE: No cheating?

DUD: No, honest.

PETE: You've not been breathing in rapidly and cooling it?

DUD: No, of course not.

PETE: All right, let's have a look. Oh dear, oh dear, oh dear.

DUD: What does it say, Pete?

PETE: It's ninety eight degrees point four.

DUD: That's normal, isn't it?

PETE: That's normal, Dud. That's a dreadful thing to be at this time of the year.

DUD: Very suspicious, innit?

PETE: Very few people are normal at this time of the year.

DUD: Yeah.

PETE: Should be about ninety eight point three is normal temperature.

DUD: Yeah. I do hate having a cold, don't you? I mean, why does God have to plague us with germs and things?

PETE: How dare you say that? How dare you accuse God of plaguing you with germs? It's nothing of the sort! The germs are plagued by you – far more! Do you know the germs were the first things to be invented? The first thing which was created was the germs.

DUD: Really?

PETE: He said, 'Let there be germs'; and there they were – millions of them, covering the face of the Earth, having a wonderful time, swimming about, going for picnics, having a marvellous time. And then, after a few million years, God become a bit bored with the germs being so small. He couldn't see them from his lofty stance, you see. And so He invented the human being. And then the poor old germ had to start flying up people's nostrils and creeping all over the place. They don't like doing it. Not one bit.

DUD: No, I'm sure they don't actually. But there are a lot of them about, aren't there, Pete?

PETE: Well, they're omnipresent, Dud – they're omnipresent.

DUD: They're in the air, they're in bed, they're in your socks, they're everywhere. I mean, only the other day Mr Rigby, he sat on a germ-ridden radiator, and he contracted polaroids.

PETE: They're the things what develop in eight seconds, aren't they? Very quick moving disease – the worse kind. But you know, whatever you say about disease, it is a wonderful thing. Because if it wasn't for disease and suffering and all the ghastly tornados and things that happen like that, ordinary life wouldn't be happy. You wouldn't enjoy yourself when you're having a good time if you didn't have disease to fear and look back on.

DUD: Yeah, that's true enough. Mind you Pete, I've had my toll of disease.

PETE: Have you had your toll?

DUD: I've had my lot of suffering in this world, mate.

PETE: When did you have it?

DUD: Well when I was three, Pete, I nearly died, you know.

PETE: I had no idea.

DUD: When I was a mere babe, my face was all blue and I could hardly breathe, you know, and my mum didn't know what was wrong, and Doctor Armstrong didn't know what was wrong. Nobody knew what was wrong, and then finally a great surgeon found the solution to it all.

PETE: What was the cause of it?

DUD: The cause of the disease was my father holding me under water for ten minutes.

PETE: It was a hereditary disease, was it?

DUD: Yeah, that's right.

PETE: You know, in the family – there's a lot of those about.

DUD: But yeah, what I don't understand, Pete, is in this world of scientific advance, technological miracles, when man is reaching out into the unknown, and into space with loony probes, why there's no cure for the common cold?

PETE: Ah, the common cold was cured a few years back, by a Mr Wainwright. Mr Wainwright of Harlesden invented the cure for the common cold. He come across it in some fig jelly – a terrible mould of one kind or the other, so he wrote up to Boots about it, but during that same night, two burly men come from the British Handkerchief Association, and they bunged him two million pounds in used notes, and he's off in the Bahamas now with some blonde floozy I dare say. Terrible that, ain't it?

DUD: Mind you, you know, there are some wonderful cures about. I mean, I was, I was reading in Revel the other day, in the medical section, I read that the Chinese have got this wonderful system of agriculture.

PETE: No, it's aquapuncture – the science of the pin, and what a wonderful science that is.

DUD: What a wonderful science.

PETE: The Chinese! For example, if you've got toothache in China, you ring up a Chinese doctor, all he comes round with is a little pin. That's all he has, in a black bag, you see. And he says, 'So you've got a toothache?' Takes out his pin and with uncanny Chinese precision, Dud, he bangs it right into your lumbar regions.

DUD: Where's that Pete?

PETE: Well, lumbar region is technical medical word for the bum. And so he bangs the pin in the bum and of course, you forget about the pain, in your jaw, and you start thinking about the pain in your bum, Dud. The toothache's gone.

DUD: Toothache's gone, but bum ache.

PETE: No, what he does then, the Chinese doctor, before the ache can develop in the bum, he bangs it in the knee, so he's got knee ache.

DUD: And then he goes round the body

PETE: He goes round the whole body.

DUD: One step ahead all the time.

PETE: One step ahead of the pain. And as soon as he's run out of the whole human body, then he gives the pin to the patient and says, 'Go out and stick it in other people.' And you go out and stick in it other people and get a good laugh when you see them jump up in the air. And you stop thinking about your own disease and you start enjoying other people's.

DUD: Wonderful.

PETE: Beats medicine.

DUD: Yeah. Mind you we had some wonderful folk cures our side of the Atlantic.

PETE: Oh, the gypsy cures.

DUD: Yeah, as you know my mum is a part-time gypsy.

PETE: She is a Romany is she?

DUD: Yeah, but she wasn't built in a day.

PETE: Of course she wasn't. She took nine months like everyone else.

DUD: No, it was a joke, Pete. Never mind. I'll tell you about it later. When I used to get earache when I was a mere suckling, and still at my mother's breast, she used to put a threepenny bit . . .

PETE: Where did she put the threepenny bit?

DUD: She used to put a threepenny bit under my pillow, and tie my ears to the door with a bit of string, and slam the door very hard.

PETE: What effect did this somewhat primitive treatment have on the ear, Dud?

DUD: It nearly tore my ear off.

PETE: And to the door?

DUD: Well, the handle fell off, normally.

PETE: Sounds like a rather useless cure.

DUD: Oh, it was – totally useless.

PETE: A useless folk cure.

DUD: But mind you, Pete, I think half the complaints and diseases in the world are in the mind you know.

PETE: That's where they have their origins, Dud – in the human mind. That's where it all begins. Psychopathetic things come up, and in the sebaceous glands everything starts moving. It's all in the mind. Just tell yourself 'I've not got a cold' and you won't have a cold.

DUD: Really?

PETE: Yeah.

DUD: I have not got a cold.

PETE: There, you're cured.

(*Dud sneezes*)

DUD: I sneezed, Pete.

PETE: No, you didn't sneeze. You thought you'd sneezed.

(*Dud sneezes again*)

PETE: There. You thought you'd sneezed again, didn't you?

DUD: Yeah.

PETE: Yeah. Well, be careful. I don't want to catch your mind.

MUSIC
(*Not Only . . . But Also . . .* , BBC2, 1966)

Thanks to the parsimony of the BBC, this classic sketch has only survived in script form. However, even on the printed page, it still provides an intriguing insight into the men beneath the macs. Dudley's music was his greatest gift, which had flourished despite his humble beginnings and the considerable handicap of a club foot. Peter, on the other hand, would have loved to have been a pop star – but despite his unique comic talent, and his flair for foreign languages, he was triumphantly tone deaf. Hence, the subject of this sketch was close to both their hearts, and hinted at the shifting balance of power between them. 'I often wish my mother had forced me to learn the piano when I was young,' says Pete. 'Me too,' replies Dud. 'If only she'd forced me to play, forced me to be a genius.' It was merely bluster, as both men knew full well. Just as Dudley never matched Peter's way with words, Peter never could have matched Dudley's musicality, even if his mother had forced him to practise the piano night and day throughout his youth.

Apart from all the familiar place names, borrowed, as usual, from Dudley's childhood, the sketch also contains several other autobiographical references. 'Rustle of Spring' became the title of a benefit gig (organised by Peter), at which both men performed, to raise £8,000 for Lord Russell of Liverpool, who'd won £5,000 damages and £3,000 costs from Peter's Private Eye *in a libel trial against the magazine that year. And ironically, Ravel's 'Bolero' later became the tune to which Dudley attempted to seduce Bo Derek, in Blake Edwards' '10' – the film that finally made Dudley a Hollywood star.*

PETE: Isn't it wonderful?

DUD: Oh, it's absolutely glorious, this music.

PETE: Debussy is so brilliant at conjuring up a whole scene with the use of his instruments.

DUD: Yeah.

PETE: You can almost see the scene, can't you?

DUD: Yeah.

PETE: 'La Mer'.

DUD: Yeah.

PETE: There she is – Debussy's mother, comes into the room, a silver tray covered with a silver teapot, silver cups.

DUD: Silver hair.

PETE: Silver hair on the mother. She comes in – Debussy sitting there on the sofa in his little blue smock – she pours the tea. D'you hear the tea being poured?

DUD: Yeah, you can almost hear the cream going into the cup.

PETE: Not too little.

DUD: Not too much.

PETE: Just right. And outside – what is it?

DUD: A bird – a bird twittering its roundelay of summer mirth, Pete.

PETE: The flute takes up the theme of the bird – it's wonderful.

DUD: You can almost see the myriad hues of his feathers.

PETE: Beautiful.

DUD: And Mum gets on with the ironing.

PETE: Beautiful.

DUD: The bread baking in the oven.

PETE: Well, I think that's enough of that. Turn it off. I can't hear myself think. D'you know I often wish – I often wish my mother had forced me to learn the piano when I was young.

DUD: Yeah, me too. If only she'd forced me to play, forced me to be a genius.

PETE: You wouldn't be here now, would you?

DUD: No, exactly.

PETE: You'd be in Vegas with some blonde girl.

DUD: Playing that Latin American boogie. But you know I remember when I was a nipper, I used to hate people who played the piano, like Enid Armstrong.

PETE: Oh, Enid, she had a gift for the piano, didn't she?

DUD: Yeah, she did, that was about all she had a gift for. I mean, I used to go round to Goodmayes Park to play football, and I remember I used to see her playing in her window, and she used to pretend that she didn't know that everyone could see her through the curtains. She always used to have the window open even if it was freezing cold just so people could hear her playing 'The Rustle of Spring'. Showing off, y'know.

PETE: Mind you, Enid had a wonderful ear for music.

DUD: Yeah, oh wonderful.

PETE: Her left one.

DUD: Left one, yeah, the right one was completely useless.

PETE: A terrible ear, her right one.

DUD: Blocked up with wax.

PETE: She could have been a professional, y'know – she was toying with the idea of becoming a professional.

DUD: Concert pianist . . .

PETE: Concert pianist at the Wigmore . . . er, Auditorium. And unfortunately her musical career, as you know, came to an end when she fell under the bus.

DUD: Yeah.

PETE: She never played another note after that.

DUD: Never breathed another breath either, did she?

PETE: That's right actually, I remember now, she stopped breathing at the same time as she stopped playing the piano.

DUD: Died under the influence of bus.

PETE: But suffering can be a wonderful boon to the musician, you know. Take an example – Beethoven. Beethoven as you know was born in – er, Flanders, and er, it was a nice family, y'know, fairly well-to-do. His mother was a weaver, and er, his father was a weaver.

DUD: Yeah.

PETE: And Beethoven was a happy young child, you know. Did a little light composing in the lovely town of Bruges, where the tapestries caught on so well during the fourteenth century – you know, hawks on the wrist and everything – and he wrote a few light-hearted tunes.

DUD: Jingles.

PETE: Jingles, basically, for the sales conferences of the tapestry-makers. He did one, what was it? Er, 'Come and see our tapestry, No better one you'll see.' It wasn't, y'know, brilliant, competent but . . .

DUD: Not brushed with the stamp of genius.

PETE: But one day, as good fortune would have it, he suddenly became struck down with pleurisy, lumbago and athlete's foot.

DUD: And lightning.

PETE: Yeah, lightning.

DUD: Cos there's always that picture of him shaking his fist at the thunderstorm.

PETE: And suddenly he was plunged into the most miserable state. He sank to the bottom and peered over the abyss of insanity. But he crawled back from the pit.

DUD: Over the hard rocks of endeavour . . .

PETE: A new man. He saw what life was all about – misery and suffering, and suddenly this wonderful music began to pour out of his fingers, and he locked himself away and composed like a demon.

DUD: Yeah, but, of course, while he did that, Pete, he forgot everything else. He forgot to feed himself, clean himself, his toilet habits went to pot, the laundry used to come round every week, knock on the door, but they could never get any laundry out of Mr Beethoven. 'Mr Beethoven, Mr Beethoven, open up and let us have your laundry.'

PETE: Too busy composing. As soon as he'd worn out one lot of clothes he'd pull them off and shove on the next lot of clean ones.

DUD: Exactly. And the laundry used to pile up at the door, on the window, shelves, and on the piano muffling all the strings so that he thought he was going deaf. He couldn't hear himself.

PETE: And the good people of Bruges outside – they couldn't hear through all the piles of linen that wonderful Fifth Symphony.

DUD: Yeah.

PETE: All they heard was a very muffled, 'Da-da-da-Dah . . .'

DUD: 'Da-da-da-Dah.' 'I can't hear.' 'Da-da-da-Dah.' 'What's the matter with my ears?' cried Ludwig.

PETE: And then eventually he passed away, and they found him . . .

DUD: Lying in a heap of manuscript and old baked-bean tins, and apricot slices . . .

PETE: And his underwear, cos when he ran out of paper Beethoven used his underwear in his frenzy of composing and all over his underwear is written his last symphonies – his string concerto on his Y-fronts and his organ concerto on his string vest.

DUD: Yeah.

PETE: And all the underwear is preserved to this day – seventeen tons of it – in the Munich Museum of Beethoven's undies. A wonderful sight. The very stuff on which he composed. It would be wonderful, wouldn't it, to write a tune which would linger on for centuries?

DUD: Yeah, and you'd know that when your bones have gone to clay and your dust had gone to something or other, whatever it is, that you'd written a tune like 'Robin's Return' and people would be whistling it.

PETE: I'd like to have done that 'Gypsy Flea' by Leroy Anderson.

DUD: Yeah, wonderful.

PETE: Isn't it amazing how music can conjure up a whole era of the past which you'd forgotten about? Just a tune will suddenly bring back a whole scene.

DUD: Like when I cycled up Chadwell Heath to get some bananas for my mum. On the way back down Wood Lane, I could hear Mrs Woolley's gramophone blaring out Caruso singing 'Oh, For the Wings of a Dove' and I was so carried away with it that I didn't see a small orange in the road and I fell off my bike and squashed my bananas. And every time I see squashed bananas, immediately it comes to mind. 'Oh, For the Wings of a Dove.'

PETE: Like me whenever I hear Ravel's 'Bolero' I think of Eileen Latimer. I can't think why I keep thinking of her whenever I hear that tune. I think it may be due to the fact that she came round to tea one day and smashed the record over my head.

DUD: That could be the link.

PETE: Let's hear the other side of 'Debussy's Mother'.

IN HEAVEN
(*Not Only . . . But Also . . .* , BBC2, 1966)

DUD: In the midst of life, Pete, we are in death, as the poet says.

PETE: No, he didn't say that. You're thinking of Coleridge. What he said was 'In the midst of life we are in debt', referring to his own financial plight, brought about by spending too much on opium, what he took intravenously to do his poems.

DUD: Oh, I see, yeah. But what I was meaning, Pete, was, are we really alive, you know? Or are we merely figments of our own imagination? But if we're not alive, then we haven't got no imagination – so whose figments are we, then? I don't like the idea of being somebody else's figment, boy. Or are we, in fact, merely a reflection of ourselves, as seen in a pool at twilight?

PETE: What you're saying is if the imagination of an imagined being imagines that life itself is imaginary, how can the imagined life of the being who is himself imagined be imagined by the being who is imagining himself through a glass darkly. That's what you mean, isn't it?

DUD: Yeah. That's it, yeah – of course.

PETE: I thought that was what you were getting at.

DUD: And if we are merely figments, Pete, and we're not really alive here, then perhaps we come alive after death. But as we're not alive we can't really die, can we? But it seems to happen that way. So, when we come alive after death, I wonder what it's like up in heaven. I mean, I wonder what it's really like up in heaven.

(*Celestial music.*)

DUD: Is it through here, Peter?

PETE: I don't know. I've never been here before.

DUD: I wasn't talking to you. I was talking to the bloke at the gates.

PETE: Well, I think it's this way. He said turn left at the plinth and carry straight on until you hear some spherical music or something coming down.

DUD: Is this it, then? Is this heaven, Pete?

PETE: Bloody hell. Is this what I've been good for all my life?

DUD: Is this what the Reverend Griffin promised us, Pete?

PETE: It's very vulgar, isn't it? It's more like Liberace's bedroom. Oh dear, oh dear, oh dear, oh dear. That bloke at the gate, he's a gloomy old devil, isn't he? That Peter, jangling his keys at you the whole time. Who does he think he is?

DUD: Well, he's got all that bookkeeping and gatekeeping to do, Pete – all the administration of the place.

PETE: Well, I don't know why he worries about that. It's a steady job, isn't it? He should be very pleased he's employed continuously on that basis. He don't even keep the gates up. Those pearls could do with a going-over with a bit of Duroglit. They're in terrible condition – all ropy and musty. It's awful. I wonder actually, Dud, what is the procedure when somebody dies. What is the administrative procedure, do you suppose?

DUD: Well, I think what happens Pete, is that St Peter sees you die on his radar screen, and he gets in touch with the authorities above, Pete.

PETE: I suppose he uses the hotline to get on.

DUD: The white-hot line.

PETE: The white-hot line. He rings up God, I suppose. He says, 'Excuse me, God, sorry to disturb you at this hour, but grave news – Dud's dead.' And then God tells His secretary, because I shouldn't think He does all the work Himself, especially with unimportant people like you. I imagine when the Pope dies or royalty or film stars He does, but with somebody just like you, the secretary looks up in the ledger, the ledger of life, all your deeds.

DUD: Yeah, of course they always put a tick for every good deed you do, Pete, and a cross for every bad one, and then the secretary tots the ticks up, and if you've got more ticks than crosses, then you go up. And if you've got more crosses than ticks mate, down you go, boy.

PETE: Must be difficult deciding between ticks and crosses, because sometimes your motives are a bit mixed. For example, suppose you help an old lady across the road, but the only reason you help her is because you fancy her daughter like mad.

DUD: No, they see through all that up here, Pete.

PETE: Do they?

DUD: You can't get away with it, you know.

PETE: I suppose not. He knows, you know.

DUD: He does, yeah. I reckon we've only just scraped through, don't you?

PETE: Well, I think I was about one tick ahead when I went. I think this is why we've been put in this particular bit of heaven. This is obviously not the best bit of heaven at all. I can see that. We've been shoved in the suburbs. We're miles from the centre. In the centre, in the bestest street, the Mayfair, you get all the really good people, all the saints where the cherubim and seraphim continually do cry, Dud.

DUD: I don't blame 'em crying, Pete, with all them goodie-goodies about.

PETE: Yeah, be a bit overpowering. Wouldn't it?

DUD: Yeah. D'you know it's very strange, because I haven't had anything to eat for quite a while now and I should think I'd be feeling hungry. But I feel no pang.

PETE: Well, you feel no pang, Dud, because when you die, you kiss goodbye to every bodily function and feeling. That's all in the past now. You'll never eat again. The only food what is ever produced is for ceremonial purposes about every three thousand years. Doubting Thomas comes round, he's the chef up here – not a very good one because he can never make his mind up what to put in the saucepan – but he comes round with a trayful of ambrosia.

DUD: Not that creamed rice again.

PETE: No, it's a heavenly substance, Dud. It's made out of honey and flowers and all things bright and beautiful.

DUD: Yeah, but once every three thousand years, boy – that's no bloody good to me, is it? Wash my mouth out with soap and water.

PETE: That's another thing you won't be able to do, Dud – wash your mouth out with anything. There's no soap and water up here – there's no facilities. This is the realm of utter hygiene. There's not a speck of dust anywhere. Every cloud has a silver lining with an air-conditioning plant inside it. There's no need to wash. You never will.

DUD: No, and one thing I have noticed, Pete, is there's no toilets – there's no angelic conveniences.

PETE: Well, of course there isn't, Dud. The toilet is behind you now. That's a thing of the past. You'll never see it. You could wander throughout the whole of heaven and you'd never see a toilet, because you don't want to bring down the tone of the place with a sign saying Heavenly Gents, Heavenly Ladies. It wouldn't go, you see. They've had to abolish all that kind of thing.

DUD: Here, I wonder if we have the opportunity to glimpse any of the great names of the past, Pete. Like, you know, Napoleon, Hannibal and all them.

PETE: Boadicea. Will we ever see the all-time greats – Wellington, King Henry the First, all those people? Will we ever see them?

DUD: Will we, I wonder?

PETE: No we won't, because we only just scraped in by about one tick, so we won't see anybody interesting. We'll just sit around here, and if we're lucky we'll see a long-distance shot of Stanley Baldwin. Not a chance. Who'd you like to see actually?

DUD: I'd like to see Nell Gwynn, flaunting her Jaffas, Pete.

PETE: That would be a sight for sore eyes, wouldn't it? The trouble is, all the good ones like Nell Gwynn haven't got up here. They've gone done into the infernal foyer, down below, where they have to wait for ever and ever and ever. And even if she did get in, I mean, she died about, what was it, five hundred years ago. I find it very difficult really to get romantically involved with anything what had been dead for four hundred years. I mean, she wouldn't be the same type of beauty who used to flaunt her wonderful busty substances.

DUD: I suspect they're more like musty substances.

PETE: What, what were we meant to do with these? (*He waves his lyre.*)

DUD: Pluck 'em, I suppose.

PETE: They're very useless, aren't they?

DUD: They don't work, do they? I've tried pulling them already.

PETE: That's all we've got to do up here – sit here, plucking these lyres. Not much of a way to spend eternity, is it?

DUD: Not much cop, is it, really? In fact, I'm rather bored already.

PETE: It's a very boring place. You'll find that, over the millions of years – over the aeons, over the centuries stretching out ahead of you, Dud. It's one of the most boring places in the world – and what's more, you're here for ever. Here today, here tomorrow – that's the saying in angelic circles.

DUD: I think we ought to get in contact with people on Earth, Pete, and tell them it's death up here.

PETE: We ought to pierce the veil and warn humanity of what they're letting themselves in for. Get on to Aunt Dolly, tell her to let rip in her last years.

DUD: Shall I get on to her?

PETE: Get on to her. See if you can pierce the veil.

DUD: Hello, Dolly!

PETE: Hello, Aunt Dolly, this is Pete speaking to you from beyond the grey veil of death in the other world. Don't bother living good, let rip – it's lousy up here . . .

(*Back down on Earth.*)

PETE: Here, wake up.

DUD: What?

PETE: That's the last time I get caught up in your thoughts.

DUD: Oh, sorry.

THE UNEXPLAINED
(*Not Only . . . But Also . . .* , BBC2, 1966)

The second series of Not Only . . . But Also . . . *was the only one of the three to be awarded the BBC accolade of a Christmas Special, and this was Pete and Dud's festive offering. For anyone who's followed the recent adventures of the Beast of Bodmin, and other unexplained big cats roaming the British countryside, this thirty-eight-year-old Surrey puma has a surprisingly topical air.*

DUD: Tea's up, Pete.

PETE: Nothing like a nice cup of tea.

DUD: Nothing like a nice cup of tea.

PETE: Nothing like a nice cup of tea.

DUD: Yeah.

PETE: I see they caught that Surrey puma at last.

DUD: Really?

PETE: The Surrey Puma Captured, it says here.

DUD: That ferocious mammal that has been terrorising the Surrey commuters with its unpredictable sallies?

PETE: Precisely. That furred beast that has been terrorising that lovely part of the Surrey wolds. Do you know what it turned out to be?

DUD: What?

PETE: Sheep.

DUD: Sheep?

PETE: It was a sheep.

DUD: Really?

PETE: A sheep what had got hold of some drugs, become crazed, gone berserk and gone around biting people. It just shows you how incredibly gullible and naive people can be. They see something flitting through the laurels, they immediately assume it's a puma, whereas in fact there is a perfectly logical, rational explanation – namely, that a sheep had broken into a chemists, got hold of some Benzedrine, and is rushing through the countryside in a state of excitement.

DUD: There is always a logical explanation for everything.

PETE: There is always a logical explanation, Dud, for everything.

DUD: Take, for example, a not dissimilar case – the case of the Loch Ness Monster, something that has mystified the bearded Celt for trillions of years, Pete. I mean, as far as I can see, there's a logical explanation. The Loch Ness Monster is none other than –

PETE: A sheep.

DUD: A sheep? No, it is obviously a Venusian submarine that has been lurking beneath the Lochy surfaces for . . . quite some time.

PETE: You've been reading that *Astral Digest* again, haven't you?

DUD: Yeah. Professor Kelper's interesting articles on space and its implications.

PETE: What a load of rubbish!

DUD: What do you mean?

PETE: It's a load of rubbish. There's no such thing as all these things he talks about.

DUD: Don't you believe in people on other planets?

PETE: Course I don't. Let me phrase it this way – I have no reason to believe that life exists of any kind on any other planet because I see no scientific explanation for it. It's all a projection of people's own psyche. Their own sort of inner feelings and conflicts are made forward in a phantasmagoria in the mind, which takes the shape of the extraterrestrial things what people claim to have sighted. For example, take the case of the woman in Arizona.

DUD: Mrs Wainwright.

PETE: Mrs Wainwright. She was in Arizona – one day, in the kitchen, she heard a tapping at the door, she goes out to see what it is, she opens the door, and there it is – a horrible green, long creature, covered in green scales from head to foot, with long green fingernails and bulging eyes.

DUD: A Venusian!

PETE: Far from it – nothing more or less than the Arizona frozen pea salesman. He is a gentleman who travels around Arizona knocking on doors, and if a housewife happens to have a couple of frozen peas in the house, he gives her a free packet and a night out with Dermot Stringer.

DUD: Well, that's as maybe, Pete – but I mean, as far as I'm concerned, that was a Venusian who came banging on Mrs Wainwright's door that sunny afternoon. I mean, you've always been a septic, Pete. I mean I had an experience last Tuesday –

PETE: You didn't tell me you'd had an experience.

DUD: No. Well, I've been bottling it up.

PETE: That's the worst thing you can do with an experience is bottle it up. You bottle it up at your own peril.

DUD: Well, I didn't tell you in case you laughed me to scorn.

PETE: Well, I probably will laugh you to scorn, but go on in any case.

DUD: I'll tell you anyway. I was cycling along last Tuesday night, about ten o'clock at night, beside the Willesden Common.

PETE: Course you were, Dud.

DUD: Course I was, Pete. And I was going along, and it was a balmy night.

PETE: Barmy cyclist.

DUD: That's a good joke. I like that.

PETE: It's not a joke. It's a truth.

DUD: Oh, sorry, Pete. Anyway, I was going along and the clouds were scudding across the moon and I could hear a tiny owl hooting from a distant cathedral.

PETE: Twit twoo.

DUD: A sound not dissimilar to the one that just emanated from your mouth, there. I was going along, whistling this tune, 'Oh, For the Wings of a Dove'.

PETE: A lovely tune – what an oldie, but a biggie.

DUD: A biggie but an oldie. And suddenly, as I was going along I saw this light flashing on the Common. I thought to meself, 'Who's flashing on the Common this time of night?' I thought to meself, you know, I thought, 'Funny,' I thought.

PETE: Flashing on the Common?

DUD: Flashing on the Common.

PETE: This time of night.

DUD: This time of night.

PETE: Owl hooting in the cathedral.

DUD: Owl hooting in the cathedral.

PETE: Clouds scudding across the moon, and you thought to yourself . . .

PETE / DUD (*together*): Funny.

DUD: And I thought . . . well, I thought I'd investigate. I leant my bicycle on the country stile.

PETE: In the country style.

DUD: A bit of both, Pete. In and on the country stile. And I started to pick my way across the spongy surface of the Willesden bog. As I was approaching this light I heard a strange 'woo!'

PETE: That's the air coming out of your tyres.

DUD: Would that it had been, Pete – but no. I approached the light and I parted the fronds and there, horror of horrors . . .

PETE: Aunt Dolly.

DUD: . . . I saw this saucer-like object. And I heard this strange, hypnotic voice coming from within. (*Sings, to the tune of* The Magic Roundabout.) Dud climb up the saucer, and fly away with me / Oh please come up to Venus, and have a cup of tea.

PETE: A Wordsworthian outburst.

DUD: A Shakespearean strain, Pete. So I delved my way into the illuminum Venusian depths of the saucer, and suddenly I blacked out – just like that. And then the next thing I knew I was waking up and I could hear the sound of rockets and I was descending on to this strange, illuminated surface – a planet I had never seen before in my life, Pete, and people I'd never seen before.

(*Pete and Dud's living room disappears, to be replaced by an alien planet. Pete is dressed in a silver mac and cap.*)

PETE: Welcome, earthling.

DUD: Where am I? And who are you?

PETE: This is the planet of Dudpeter, and I am a superior being – so watch it.

DUD: For what scientific purpose am I here?

PETE: We brought you here for one reason. Superior beings though we be, we are a dying race. We are becoming extinct because, you see, the larger our brains have got, so have our other powers diminished. This is why we brought you up here, for reproductive purposes. You are to be a stud, Dud.

DUD: My talents are at your disposal. Convey me, or most of me, to those fabulous females who lie trembling for my terrestrial tap. Allow me to tamper tenderly with their outer spaces.

PETE: You're out of luck, mate – completely. We have only two forms of life up here. There are Duds and there are Petes. Lo, the survivors of our race.

(*A crowd of doleful Duds surround them.*)

DUD: Cor blimey.

PETE: Right. Are you ready to breed?

DUD: Yes. Let the reproduction commence.

PETE: Right.

(*Pete claps his hands. A glass bowl descends towards them.*)

DUD: Here! How did you do that?

PETE: Well, we've got two little bits of wire, there, you see, and a bloke up there with a fishing rod. That's what makes it possible.

DUD: Oh, I see.

PETE: Right. Now for the breeding purposes, place the nose against the bowl and concentrate on a little Pete, right?

(*Dudley presses his face against the bowl.*)

DUD: Right.

PETE: Go.

DUD: Concentrate. Concentrate.

PETE: Do you feel anything coming yet?

DUD: My nose is starting to twitch.

PETE: Contractions are beginning.

DUD: Oh dear.

(*A little Dud appears inside the bowl.*)

PETE: You bloody idiot! That's another Dud! That's not a Pete! I asked for a Pete – I get a Dud! A fat lot of bloody use you are! Destroy it!

DUD: What are you talking about?

(*Dud seizes the bowl.*)

PETE: Get back to the planet where you belong, earthling! We've no room for twits like you up here! Get back to Willesden! Get off into your saucer! Take you away from here! Go on, then!

DUD: I should coco, you inhuman monster.

(*Dud returns to his flying saucer.*)

PETE: How dare you say that to a superior being! Well I never! Ready for take-off . . .

(*Dud's flying saucer lifts off. The alien planet disappears, to be replaced by Pete and Dud's living room.*)

PETE: What a load of unmitigated cod's udders.

DUD: What d'you mean? You didn't believe me?

PETE: Course not. The only thing that rung true was that I was a superior being. The rest of it was obviously a projection of your disturbed psyche.

DUD: Well, I have proof.

PETE: Proof? Let's see it, then.

DUD: It's a big one. The original Venusian breeding bowl.

(*Dud produces the glass bowl.*)

PETE: That's a goldfish bowl you bought last Tuesday. It's still got the one and six on it. You got it down the market.

DUD: I didn't.

PETE: Where's the Dud, then? Show me the Dud.

DUD: Well, the Dud had to go invisible – otherwise he would have perished with, er, the noxious gases on the earth's atmosphere.

PETE: What a ludicrous explanation! There's nothing in there.

(*Pete seizes the glass bowl.*)

DUD: No! No!

PETE: Pour the tea on it. See what happens then.

DUD: No! No!

(*Dud seizes back the bowl.*)

DUD (*to the bowl*): Sorry about that, Dud. (*To Pete.*) He's feeling a bit peckish now. I'll give him a bit of tapioca pudding or something. (*To the bowl.*) Come on, Dud, you come along with me, mate.

(*Exit Dudley.*)

PETE: Blimey! I've got a loony in the house!

THE BEESIDE
(Decca, 1967)

In the summer of 1965, Peter and Dudley released their signature tune, Good-bye-ee, *as a single, and Peter relesed a solo single called* The Ballad of Spotty Muldoon. *They reached number 18 and number*

*34 in the same Top Forty – an unprecedented double chart success for
a comedian. Two subsequent singles,* Isn't She A Sweetie (1966) *and*
The LS Bumblebee (1967) *didn't have the same impact; but the B
side of* The LS Bumblebee *was a brand new Pete and Dud duologue,
about the perils of alcohol and narcotics.*

PETE: All right, Dud?

DUD: All right, Pete?

PETE: Nothing like a nice cup of tea.

DUD: Nothing like a nice cup of tea, Pete. Ladies and gentlemen,
may we take the opportunity of these few grooves at our disposal
to give you a solemn warning against the dangers of the drug
traffic.

PETE: This peril that lurks in teenage haunts, where beat music
pulses out into the night, keeping vicars awake and old ladies
jumping out of their beds continuously.

DUD: Ghastly business, Pete. Well, without more ado, over to you
for ghastly example number one.

PETE: Of the perils of drugdom.

DUD: Exactly, Pete.

PETE: There was a famous man who shall be nameless . . .

DUD: Mr A. Woolley of 31 Wainwright Road, Willesden.

PETE: Precisely. Mr Woolley was a very nice family man, with a
lovely wife and two beautiful children what he used to dangle
on his knees, when he come home from the office to his little
house with lovely little roses poking up through the trellis.

DUD: And the cucumbers and radishes growing peacefully on the
allotment at the back.

PETE: One evening he come home and looked around and said,
'Nice though this be, I seek yet further kicks.' And he moved
inexorably towards the mantelpiece, where he kept his dolly
mixture. Seizing hold of some of the mixture, he plunged it into
a glass of cherry brandy, quaffed it down with one draught and
he was, of course, on cloud lucky one an a half, swinging away
right up, and grooving tremendously.

DUD: Freak out, baby.

PETE: Freaking out completely. Well after that, the kicks got ever stronger. His craving got worse and worse. He got more and more drugs down his face and eventually he became so irresponsible, he left his lovely wife and kids and home behind, and went to Hollywood and lay on a beach all day with a lovely busty starlet with blonde hair what come down to her knees.

DUD: That doesn't sound too bad, Pete.

PETE: No. I don't think that's a very good example of the perils actually. Have you got one?

DUD: I've got a worse one Pete, yes. One that concerns a brain scientist who used to do interesting experiments on the curdling of milk. One day, when he was pouring milk over a live mouse, to see the effect of it on it, he suddenly was consumed by an enormous depression, and without more ado he flung himself at the medicine cabinet and got an aspirin down his throat.

PETE: Ooh!

DUD: Before you could say Swiss Family Robin . . .

PETE: Swiss Family Robinson!

DUD: You said it before I done it. However, worse was to come. Within minutes he was at the blackcurrant pastilles and Vaseline.

PETE: Mescalin, innit? The sacred mushroom drug.

DUD: Oh, sorry. Mescalin. His plight went from worse to worse, and now he leads his life as a rake, nestling in burnt leaves and compost at the bottom of the garden.

PETE: The only time he moves is when somebody treads on him, and he jumps up and bangs them in the eye. A used gourd, a hopeless shard, useless to man, woman or beast.

DUD: A great scientist and nudist gone to the dogs, or drugs if you like. Of course you cannot deny, Pete, the magnificence of the psychedelic achievements in the past, let it be said.

PETE: As exemplified by the A side of this record, which of course is written under drugs.

DUD: Exactly, Pete. Which means, of course, we are the B side.

PETE: Are we the B side?

DUD: We are. However, as the old age says, 'I do like to be B side the A side.'

(*Dud laughs*)

PETE: Shut up.

DUD: Sorry.

PETE: Of course Coleridge, T.S. Coleridge, used to write some of his best poetry under the influence of the poppy. He used to cram poppies down his face, in order to make his poetic imagination come out better. That's how he wrote that one about in Xanadu the Aga Khan did an aerodrome decree, while Alf the sacred Ramsey ran through caverns spacious to man down to the cider sea.

DUD: Phantasmagorical, Pete.

PETE: Phantasmagorical, Dud.

DUD: But despite this we cannot rule out the fact, the burning fact, ladies and gentlemen, that Frankie Vaughan still tops the Palladium on crystallised fruits and weightlifting.

PETE: Exactly. A glass of milk and a walk over the heath is far better than any druggy druggy druggy can achieve, Dud.

DUD: Exactly, Pete. And now the commercial. Beware psychedelic drugs.

PETE: Steer clear of LSD.

DUD: That type of thing is for the mugs. Stick to a cup of tea.

PETE: A very moving plea.

DUD: Wonderful piece of propaganda, Pete.

PETE: Wonderful, Dud. How many lumps?

DUD: Six please. And while you're about it, would you dip them in that colourless fluid, Pete?

PETE: Oh, right you are.

DUD: Thank you very much. Druggy druggy!

IN PRISON
(*Goodbye Again*, ATV, 1968)

(*Pete & Dud are languishing in a prison cell*)

PETE: I wonder what's keeping Aunt Dolly?

DUD: I suppose she's been unavoidably detained, Pete.

PETE: By Mr Prendergast, I dare say.

DUD: Yeah. Well, of course she's getting to that frisky age. You know, the Naughty Forties.

PETE: More like the Filthy Fifties, as far as she's concerned.

DUD: Well, the way she's looking these days, it's more like the Sexy Sixties.

PETE: Or the Sensual Seventies, Dud, but I don't think we need concern ourselves at which particular stage of decline Aunt Dolly is at. The fact remains that we, the only two innocent people amidst this crowd of riff raff and hoodlums, are the ones without outside succour.

DUD: Deserted by our own kith and kin.

PETE: Arrested on a trumped-up charge which won't hold water. I mean, why did they arrest us?

DUD: I don't know why. I mean, when I saw that crowd of people, you know, shuffling along quietly, I thought it was a queue for Sex In The Swamps at the Continental Cinema Club.

PETE: An extremely controversial film, Dud.

DUD: Yeah, exactly – extremely controversial.

PETE: I suppose our suspicions should have been aroused when they all sat down and started singing 'We shall not be moved.'

DUD: Yeah. Well, I mean it struck me as pretty peculiar because I had heard that Sex In The Swamps was a very moving film.

PETE: It's a tearjerker, Dud, yeah.

DUD: So when I heard the crowd sing 'We shall not be moved,' I thought to myself, 'Funny.' Tearjerker. Sex in The Swamps. Crowd shouting 'We shall not be moved.' Funny.

PETE: A film designed to move people, yet they shouted 'We shall not be moved.' You think to yourself, 'Funny,' don't you? It's a bit odd.

DUD: That's the irony, as I was being bundled by two policemen into the Tia Maria.

PETE: A disgraceful episode in the annals of law, Dud.

DUD: Yeah. But what I must say, Pete, is that I do admire the way you've handled things ever since we've been here. You know, the way you've asked for everything we are entitled to.

PETE: Well, Dud, as a citizen of the realm, I know my rights. And this is why I asked for Habeas Corpus at once.

DUD: Yeah.

PETE: I said 'Give me Habeas Corpus at once!'

DUD: Quite right.

PETE: Because if they don't give you Habeas Corpus, Dud, they haven't got a case against you.

DUD: Yeah. Er, what is a Habeas Corpus, Pete?

PETE: A Habeas Corpus, Dud, is something which is everybody's inalienable right to have.

DUD: Inalienable right?

PETE: It's your inalienable right to have a Habeas Corpus. And so I asked for me Habeas Corpus. As for what it is, I don't know exactly. But unless it's a glass of water, they haven't given it us.

DUD: D'you think that by some chance they might have slipped a Habeas Corpus in the cell and we haven't recognised it?

PETE: There is always the possibility, Dud, that the fuzz have covertly planted bits of Habeas Corpus upon us. But I imagine it's a fairly bulky object, and this is out of the question.

DUD: I tell you the humiliating thing about this incarceration to which we have been subjugated, Pete, is the fact that my previous brushes with the law have been of a most sympathetic kind. I don't know if you remember, but fifteen years ago we lost my little dachshund, Twinkie. I went up to the Chadwell Heath constabulary, and I said to Sergeant Facker, I said, 'Excuse me, Sergeant Facker, but have you seen my Twinkie?' And he said, 'No, have you lost it, Dud?' So I said, 'Yeah' and he says, 'Oh dear.'

PETE: A sympathetic response from the man in blue.

DUD: Yeah. And he got onto squad car forty-five, which was patrolling Mortigrave Crescent at the time, and he said, 'Keep a look out for Dud's Twinkie.'

PETE: Are they still combing the area?

DUD: Well, they found what they thought to be a few traces of

Twinkie on the pavement, and they sent it across to the forensic boys for analysis.

PETE: I understand that at the time of the Great Train Robbery,
Dud, Facker was forced to pull two of his men off the Twinkie
file, in order to concentrate on the location of the Mr Big behind
that enormous snatch.

DUD: Oh yes.

PETE: And also, Dud, I think you should remember that Twinkie was
seventeen years of age when she disappeared. Fifteen years have
elapsed, which makes her four hundred and ninety one dog years
old. So I think you've got to face up to the possibility, Dud, appalling
though it may seem, that Twinkie has passed off this mortal coil.

DUD: And is now in that heavenly kennel where winged Corgis
float blessedly and happily amongst clouds of aniseed.

PETE: At all events, I think you can stop putting out that bowl of
Fido meat every evening.

DUD: But Twinkie might come back, Pete.

PETE: And so might Colonel Fawcett. But we're stuck here in a
dilemma. We've got to get out of here. I mean, if we don't get
a defence together, we'll be incarcerated, pending Her Majesty's
pleasure. And goodness knows when that's going to be.

DUD: But, I mean, as we haven't got our own solicitors or our own
PVC, who's going to defend us, Pete?

PETE: Well, I think in the absence of our own Silk, Dud, we should
defend each other. I'll act for you and you act for me. It's a
simple case of Mens Rea and Habeas Corpus, you see. We just
rise before the judge, looking as dignified and respectful as you
can. Adjust your dress for the occasion, you see. And I shall make
a moving plea for the defence.

(*Pete & Dud are now in court*)

JUDGE: Do you plead guilty or not guilty?

PETE: M'ludship, gentlemen of the jury, in the case arraigned before
you here, of Dud versus Regina, I have only this to say. If it is
wrong to stand by that which you believe to be right, why then
indeed my client is guilty.

DUD: Guilty.

PETE: If it is wrong to fight for those principles that have made this great country the great country it is today, why then indeed my client is guilty.

DUD: Guilty.

PETE: If it is wrong to resist all outside tyranny and oppression, why then indeed my client is guilty.

DUD: Guilty.

PETE: If in short, gentlemen of the jury and my judgeship, it is wrong to be right, why then my client is guilty.

DUD: Guilty!

PETE: But if however, gentlemen of the jury, it is right to stand firm for all those things which you hold most dear in this sceptred isle against all tyranny and oppression then, gentlemen of the jury, my client is . . .

DUD: Guilty!

PETE: Innocent!

DUD: Innocent!

JUDGE: Where were you on the afternoon of the alleged offence?

PETE: My client refuses to answer that question, on the grounds that he has forgotten.

JUDGE: I must ask you to remember where you were!

PETE: And I must ask you, your ludship, to remember where you were on the afternoon of the alleged offence, for I put it to you, gentlemen of the jury, beneath the wig and the powder, there lurks none other than the Streatham Nude Strangler, who has put every housewife's wife and life in jeopardy!

JUDGE: Will you please plead guilty or not guilty!

DUD: Objection m'lud!

JUDGE: On what grounds?

PETE: On the grounds of Mens Rea and Habeas Corpus, as exemplified in the case of Diblock versus Harris 1947, with which your holiness is doubtless familiar.

JUDGE: I beg your pardon?

PETE: And if your holiness is not familiar, perhaps he will be gracious enough to cast his learned eyes on to page seven million and one of the lawyers' gazette!

(*General hubbub from the gallery*)

JUDGE: Clear the court! Clear the court! Clear the court!

PETE: The defence rests.

(*Pete & Dud are back in their prison cell*)

DUD: I think you were marvellous, Pete. I don't know how you do it.

PETE: I think it's very good. You heard what you said, didn't you?

DUD: Yeah. Clear the court.

PETE: Clear the court. That means we all get off scot free. That's a way of saying you're let off, you see.

AT THE DOCTOR'S
(*Goodbye Again*, ATV, 1968)

DUD: Excuse me. I have an appointment with Doctor Watson for a complete medical check-up.

NURSE: Doctor Watson will see you within four hours.

DUD: Blimey! I might not last that long.

PETE: Here we are, let's get a good seat up the front. I don't know why you wanted to come here in the first place. You're a perfect physical condition for a person in your physical condition and age.

DUD: Well, I've never really felt the same ever since Mrs Woolley made those astrological predictions.

PETE: You shouldn't take any notice of Mrs Woolley. She's the only palmist I know who predicts the future by looking at the soles of your feet.

DUD: Well, she says your left foot is what you're born with and your right foot is what you make of it.

PETE: What a lot of rubbish, you're born with both feet. You're not just born with your left foot and then the baby has to make his right foot up on the spot. That's a stupid idea.

DUD: I don't think Mrs Woolley meant it in quite the naively literal way you are intimating, Pete.

PETE: Oh, in what brilliantly sophisticated unliteral way did she mean it in then?

DUD: What she meant was that your fate's on your feet.

PETE: Your fate's on your feet?

DUD: Yeah. And when she had a look at my left foot, she staggered back.

PETE: Well, I don't blame her. I think any human being would, from your left foot, Dud.

DUD: No, she didn't mean that at all. When she was feeling my foot, she had a look at it. She was holding it in her hand. She had those rubber washing-up gloves on, you know.

PETE: Oh, I know them – yeah.

DUD: Keep it sanitary and all that. And she said, 'Dud, your fate's on your feet.' And do you know what she said? 'You're not long for this Earth.'

PETE: Well, this seems a very fair statement of fact. I mean, what-ever your many virtues may be, Dud, and let's not minimise them – length is not one of them. You are not, let's face it, you are not long for this Earth. You're on the short side for this Earth. Perhaps on another planet you might tower over the extraterrestrial beings, but down here, Dud, you are a bit on the short side.

DUD: Point taken, Pete, but what I think she meant was, that most people's lifelines go from their big toe to their heel, but mine was cut off in the middle.

PETE: That's when you trod on that razor blade, wasn't it, in the sitting room?

DUD: You see? All you have to do is leave one of your rusty old razor blades in the living room on the floor and my life is cut in half. But what I think is worse than that is that I think she's put a curse on me.

PETE: What makes you think that?

DUD: Well, when she was feeling my foot, to look at the lines you know, she tickled my instep, and I jumped you know, because I'm a bit ticklish on the feet, and I bunged her up the nose with my big toe.

PETE: And you think she's holding it against you?

DUD: Well, I was holding it against her at the time – but now I think the situation's drastically reversed. I think she's holding it against me. I think she's put a curse on me, I think she's made an effigy of me. She's sticking pins up my effigy.

PETE: And you think this is the reason why you're getting pains in the chest is she's sticking pins up your effigy?

DUD: Yeah.

PETE: Well, if you believe all this mumbo jumbo, Dud, and let's face it – that's all it is, mumbo jumbo. If you believe this mumbo jumbo, all you have to do is make an effigy of Mrs Woolley, then just before you feel a pain coming on – now, this is important – just before you feel the pain coming on . . .

DUD: Just before.

PETE: Just before. Stick a pin in her effigy. If you stick a pin in her effigy first, she won't be able to stick it. You stick before she can stick you, you see.

DUD: I've got better things to do with my time, mate, than stick pins up Mrs Woolley's effigy.

PETE: Like what, for example?

DUD: Well, I mean I'm growing that mustard and cress in the shape of the Union Jack on my flannel.

PETE: Well, this is a very vital part of the Backing Britain movement, I admit, Dud. I suppose she also asked you what star you were born under?

DUD: Yes, she said, 'What star were you born under, Dud?' So I said Mickey Rooney, because my mum had a picture of Mickey over her bed when she was having me.

PETE: Oh yes, she used to worship the ground he walked on, didn't she?

DUD: Yes, she loved him – loved Mickey. And she wrote to him. She said, 'Dear Mick, send us a bit of the earth you walk on because I love you. I worship the ground you walk on.' And he sent her a bit of the earth he walked on. We had it in the living room.

PETE: Really?

DUD: Yeah. But my dad bunged it out the window.

PETE: Threw it right out of the window?

DUD: He bunged it out the window. He said, 'We're not having that sod in here.'

PETE: Well, you can't blame him really, can you?

DUD: No, you can't. But then she said, 'No I don't mean that sort of star. I mean what sign are you?'

PETE: What astrological sign?

DUD: What astrological sign are you born under? So I said, 'I am the ram.'

PETE: Aries.

DUD: Aries – mercurial, quixotic.

PETE: Tempestuous – given to sudden flights of fancy.

DUD: For Valerie Pearson at four in the morning.

PETE: Exactly.

DUD: Outgoing, ingoing, avoid brunettes, lucky number four.

PETE: And steer clear of steamrollers.

DUD: Yeah, all that.

PETE: Load of rubbish in fact.

DUD: Well, I don't know, you see. With all this information she had about me, and all the things she was telling me, it was uncanny. I think she is occult. I think she is occult. I think, in fact, she had second sight.

PETE: I think she's got double vision, the amount of beer she puts back of an evening. I went down there the other Friday for one of her combined bingo and black magic sessions.

DUD: Oh what, down her basement?

PETE: Yeah, she has them down the basement. It's quite cosy. I went down there with a group of people, including Mr Prendergast, you know, just as curious human beings, just to see if there was anything in it. And sure enough there was something in it.

DUD: What was that?

PETE: Mrs Woolley, sitting in the end of the basement, at the table you see. She had a tea cosy all over her head.

DUD: All over it?

PETE: Not all over it. Just the eyes peeping out, just down to here, you see. And in her left hand she had a fish fork. And in her right hand, she had a frozen fish finger – for sacrificial purposes, you see, for summoning up the devil. Normally she slits a cockerel's throat over an upturned tea chest and says 'Land of Hope and Glory' backwards. But she'd been out on the booze a bit the night before and she's a bit short of cash, so she made do with a fish finger.

DUD: Sacrificial fish finger.

PETE: A sacrificial fish finger.

DUD: Say that six times quickly.

PETE: I'd rather you didn't, if you don't mind. And suddenly, she switched off the lights.

DUD: Click.

PETE: Very similar to the noise you just made then, and a strange chill came over the room – due to no small measure to the fact she'd left the fridge door open when she's going for the fish finger. And the room was lit only by a guttering candle which flicked eerie shadows everywhere.

DUD: Gutter, gutter.

PETE: Gutter, gutter. And suddenly she began to moan and tremble as if seized by alien force.

DUD: More like Mr Prendergast. He gets a bit iffy at night, doesn't he?

PETE: She was sitting next to Mr P. And she moaned and she trembled and suddenly out of her mouth come a strange tongue.

DUD: Somebody else's tongue, Pete?

PETE: No. Her own tongue came out, but she spoke in a strange, ethereal, mystic voice that was not her own. And suddenly she said . . .

NURSE: The doctor will see you now.

DUD: Blimey! That's uncanny! I didn't see your lips move.

PETE: Well, as in most of these cases, Dud, there is a rational explanation for that fact. The reason my lips didn't move was I wasn't speaking. You were, in fact, being addressed by a lovely nurse – behind you.

NURSE: The doctor will see you now.

DUD: Oh, thank you.

PETE: If we could get going. Thank you very much. I don't know what's the matter with you, Dud, but we're going to the ante-natal clinic.

AT THE GYM
(*Goodbye Again*, ATV, 1968)

(*Pete and Dud are hanging from the rings in a gymnasium, still dressed in their trademark caps, scarves and macs*)

PETE: All right, Dud?

DUD: All right, Pete?

PETE: How are you feeling?

DUD: All right. A bit tired, you know.

PETE: Are you in agony yet?

DUD: On the verge.

PETE: That's a very good sign, because agony is the body's way of telling you something.

DUD: Telling you you've had enough.

PETE: No, Dud. Agony is telling you it's doing you good. The more agony you're in, the more good it's doing you.

DUD: How much we got up here?

PETE: Another fifteen seconds rope work, Dud.

(*Dud drops to the ground, Pete drops down after him*)

PETE: And now we follow it up with a little toe touching, to get our trapezoids moving.

(*Pete bends to touch his toes*)

PETE: One two, touch down, one two, touch down. Now you have a go.

(*Dud tries, and fails, to touch his toes*)

DUD: I can't get down there, Pete. D'you think you could touch my toes? I'll touch yours next time.

PETE: Well, it's not really getting the full benefit of the exercise, Dud, but as this is your first workout, I'll touch them this week.

(*Pete touches Dud's toes*)

DUD: Here, your knees bent. That doesn't count.

PETE: Come on, let's go and have a sauna bath. That'll do you good.

DUD: Hold on. I want to rest a bit. I'm exhausted.

PETE: You see, the only way you're going to get physically fit, Dud, is through perseverance.

DUD: Oh yeah, the Percy Verence physical culture method.

PETE: What a wonderful man Percy was. Mr Universe, 1912. Superb deltoids.

DUD: What amazing pectorals, too.

PETE: What amazing pectorals, Dud. But even with a course like the Percy Verence course, you've got to be extremely careful. Because let's face it, the body is a very, very delicate instrument. Remember what happened to Mr Wainwright?

DUD: Tragic business.

PETE: A tragic business. He saw this advertisement, you see, which said tick off which parts of the body you wish to improve, you see. Do you want a chest like a barrel? If so, tick. Do you want legs that never tire? If so, tick. Do you want arms like rods of steel?

DUD: If so, tick.

PETE: Precisely. And it was two guineas for each part of the body. Now, Mr Wainwright only had four guineas to spare.

DUD: Oh yeah, cos he'd been off work for a fortnight with a carbuncle, hadn't he?

PETE: He had a very nasty carbuncle upon him. And so he wrote away for the two part of the body he thought needed building up most. Namely, his extremely puny chest – for puny it was, Dud – and namely, his very puny arms. So back come the brochure, and he exercised away for months on end. And eventually, he built up this magnificent chest, just like a barrel, just like the advertisement. Wonderful arms. Arms like lengths of steel, they were. He had a superb great big torso. But the tragic thing was, that due to lack of funds, he had not built up the legs that never tire, with the result that one day, he's running for a Green Line bus, and they snap like twigs beneath him.

DUD: Terrible business, that.

PETE: A terrible business, Dud.

DUD: Can we go to the sauna now, Pete?

PETE: I think a sauna would be a very refreshing thing to do after such a wonderful workout, Dud.

DUD: Is it through here?

PETE: It's through here, yeah.

(*Pete and Dud enter the sauna, still wearing their caps, scarves and macs*)

DUD: You know the one thing I don't understand with a sauna is what it does to you apart from making you hot, sweaty and uncomfortable.

PETE: The point of a sauna, Dud, is manifold – but mainly, it's to enable your pores to breathe.

(*Pete points to a large gentleman, clad only in a towel*)

PETE: There you have an example of pores breathing. D'you see? Breathing very nicely. This is why nudists throw off their clothes, to allow the oxygen to get to their pores, and allow them to breathe.

DUD: I suppose that's why you get all that heavy breathing down the Sunny Glade nudist camp.

PETE: A possible explanation of this phenomenon, Dud. But even more important than the pores breathing, and everything like that, is the diet. Because we intake so many poisons and starches into the system, you see.

DUD: Yeah, course we do.

PETE: Course we do.

(*Dudley pours some water on the hot coals, engulfing them in a cloud of steam*)

DUD: Tea's up, Pete.

PETE (*deadpan*): Very humorous, Dud. You see, the less you eat the healthier you get, and the more your mind begins to work. The less you eat, the more your mind works – and this explains why so many of the fakirs and swamis in India go on these prolonged fasts.

DUD: And on these prolonged nails, Pete.

PETE: They go on prolonged nails for mortification of the flesh, Dud.

DUD: For mortification of the flesh.

PETE: Mortification of the flesh, nothing more or less. And once they're sitting there, mortifying their flesh as best as they can, they become aware of things they weren't aware of before.

DUD: Like how hungry they are.

PETE: Precisely, and the fact they're sitting on nails. But more than that, they become aware of great thoughts. They have transcendental thoughts. They glimpse God, and think of wonderful new things. This is why you'll find, throughout the anals of history, all the way down from Bertrand Russell to the tiny sheeted form of Ghandi, the great thinkers have tended to be rather skinny and meagre.

DUD: Yeah, thin people tend to have big brains.

PETE: This is right, Dud.

DUD: Well, by that token, Twiggy should have one of the greatest minds in the western world.

PETE: Well, rumour has it she was a contender for the Brain of Britain, '68.

DUD: A hot contender, Pete.

PETE: Ably guided by Justin de Villeneuve, of course, her shrewd business manager.

DUD: Yeah. Of course, to take the whole point to its logical conclusion, God, who has the greatest mind of all, and God, who in His ineffable wisdom embraces us all, with His mind . . .

PETE: Er, yes.

DUD: And everything – He must be as thin as a rake.

PETE: He's thinner than a rake, Dud. Hence the hymn – Immortal, Invisible.

DUD: Yeah.

PETE: And this is why God is so hard to see, and why people go to such lengths to see Him. This is why all these people are going over to India, you see, to study under the Maharishi de Sade, out at his transcendental meditation centre by the Ganges, you see.

DUD: Yeah.

PETE: Many people, some of the world's greatest thinkers – Mia Farrow, along with pop luminaries . . .

DUD: Pop loonies?

PETE: Pop luminaries.

DUD: Oh, I thought you said . . .

PETE: Leading lights of the pop world – Donovan, Beach Boys, Beatles, that type of thing – are going over to that part of the world to try and get a glimpse of God. For example, when the Beatles arrived over there in Nepal . . .

DUD: When the Beatles arrived over there in Nepaul, Negeorge, Nejohn and Neringo.

PETE: What d'you mean?

DUD: When the Beatles arrived over there in Nepaul, Nejohn, Negeorge and Neringo.

PETE: No, they only arrived in Nepal. I've not heard of these other places you mention.

DUD: It's a joke, Pete.

PETE: Oh, I see. A play on words, based on the Christian names of the Beatles – John, Paul, George and Ringo, adding the prefix 'Ne' to make the somewhat ludicrous pun.

DUD: Yeah.

PETE: An amusing sally, Dud, but scarcely germane to the rather serious discussion we have in hand about God at the moment.

DUD: My apologies for introducing such a flippant note into the conversation.

PETE: Apology accepted, Dud, but don't do it again.

DUD: Point taken.

PETE: Shut up. Anyway, when they arrive there by the Ganges, you see, the Maharishi de Sade comes over to them, the wonderful bearded mystic, and he hands them some flowers with a wonderful, warm greeting giggle.

(*Dud cackles*)

PETE: Very similar to the noise you uttered, but slightly more warm and human and wonderful. And then takes them off to their tent, and comes over to them, and whispers a mantra in their ears.

DUD: What's a mantra?

PETE: A mantra, Dud, is a secret word you've got to remember.

DUD (*sings*): Remember a mantra . . .

(*Pete beats Dud with birch twigs*)

DUD: Here, what d'you hit me with that bunch of old twigs for?

PETE: This was to get your nerve ends tingling, and to shut your face.

DUD: Oh.

PETE: A mantra is a very important thing, which is geared to the individual psyche and personality trait of the undergo-ee.

DUD: Oh.

PETE: You see, they choose a word which suits everybody. The Maharishi chooses it, and then you say it to yourself endlessly, and you go into a trance, and think transcendental great things, using the two thirds of the mind what are not used usually. You could do it now, if you could choose a mantra for yourself.

DUD: What, it makes you go calm, does it, when you repeat it?

PETE: Exactly, it makes you extremely calm and very sort of lucid. So if you could choose one to suit your psyche, what kind of word would suit your psyche?

DUD: A word for me . . . Er, Jane Russell.

PETE: Jane Russell might well be a very suitable mantra. Right. Let your mind go blank.

DUD: All right.

PETE: Have you done it?

DUD: Oh, yeah.

PETE: Not a very difficult step for you, I imagine. Now your mind's blank, repeat your mantra.

DUD: Jane Russell, Jane Russell . . . Is it supposed to make you go calm?

PETE: This is the desired effect, Dud, yes.

DUD: It's not working with me. I'm coming over all unnecessary.

A SPOT OF THE USUAL TROUBLE
(*Goodbye Again*, ATV, 1969)

PETE: All right, Dud?

DUD: All right, Pete?

PETE: Nothing like a nice glass of beer.

DUD: Nothing like a nice glass of beer, Pete.

PETE: I had a terrible time last night, you know.

DUD: What? The usual trouble?

PETE: Usual trouble. I got home feeling a bit tired, you know. I got into bed, thought I'd get an early night. And I was, you know, just about to drop off –

DUD: You got to get that bed seen to. It sounds dangerous.

PETE: I was about to enter the realms of slumber when suddenly my peace was shattered by an insistent bring-bring, bring-bring.

DUD: What's that?

PETE: That's my peace being shattered by the telephone going bring-bring.

DUD: Oh.

PETE: So I picked up the receiver and said, 'Hello.'

DUD: Best thing to do in the circumstances.

PETE: I thought so. I said, 'Hello,' and the operator said – I'm the operator, you see – would I accept a long-distance call, reverse charge, from St Tropez? I said, 'I don't even know the fella.'

DUD: Well, I mean, can't go on paying for calls from impoverished saints, can you?

PETE: Exactly. But it turned out that what he meant was St Tropez, the Riveera – haunt of the rich and famous.

DUD: Oh yes, where the busty beauties sun themselves on the golden beaches.

PETE: International playground, yes. And there was a Miss Brigitte Bardot on the line, you see?

DUD: Not again?

PETE: Yeah, Brigitte was on the line again! And, er, you know, er, don't you? Roger Vadim's former protégée.

DUD: The Gallic symbol.

PETE: Yeah, the well-known Gallic symbol, you see. Asked, 'Could you talk to me?' So I said, 'All right, put her on if you must,' you know. Her voice came on the phone, wailing, saying, '*Oh ma chérie, oh ma chérie.*'

DUD: Omar Sharif? He lives in Saudi Arabia, don't he?

PETE: No, I'm not talking about the dusky charmer of *Funny Girl* fame and fortune, so much as French for 'Oh my darling.' '*Oh ma chérie.*'

DUD: *Oh ma chérie.*

PETE: Anyway, Brigitte was coming out with the usual Continental rubbish. You know, would I catch a night flight to Cannes. She'd meet me at the airport in a Rolls-Royce, we'd go back to her yacht and dance and drink and make love and everything like that. The usual empty boring show-business claptrap.

DUD: The normal rampant frog patter.

PETE: Exactly. I said, 'Look, Brigitte, we've had our laughs, we've had our fun, we've had our kicks, we've had our thrills. We've quaffed deep of the cup of love.'

DUD: Right.

PETE: 'But now it's over. *C'est finis!*'

DUD: *C'est finis.*

PETE: But she wouldn't take that for an answer. She went mad, wailing and moaning on the phone, beating her breasts against the receiver. I had to hang up on her. I had to bang the phone down.

DUD: Well, it's odd you should say that, because I had much the same trouble last night.

PETE: Really?

DUD: I had a hard day watering the cucumbers.

PETE: Takes it out of you, doesn't it?

DUD: Takes it out of you. And I was feeling a bit tuckered out. You know, a bit on the tired side, so I thought I'd get an early night. You deserve an early night, Dud. And I thought I'd make meself a cup of cocoa, go to bed and pore over the *Harmsworth's Universal Encyclopaedia.*

PETE: You pour your cup of cocoa over the encyclopaedia, do you, last thing at night?

DUD: No, I'm using pore in the sense of inwardly digest.

PETE: Oh, I see. Read.

DUD: Read. Yes.

PETE: Quite right.

DUD: Anyway, I made me cup of cocoa – nice and hot and sweet and strong – and I started up the stairs and, er, just about the third rung I smelled this headily sophisticated perfume.

(*Pete and Dud both sniff.*)

DUD: You know, I thought, you know – funny.

PETE: Heady sophisticated perfume on the third rung.

DUD: Yeah, funny. I thought, 'Mrs Woolley was in last Thursday for a cup of sugar, but it couldn't be hanging over from then, could it?'

PETE: It wouldn't linger on. It wouldn't.

DUD: Anyway, I cast it out me mind. Went upstairs to bed. Got into bed. And I was just settling down nicely and I heard a tinkle from the bathroom. I thought, 'I've left the taps running!' So I trot along to the bathroom and blimey! This perfume's getting stronger and stronger . . .

PETE: Stronger.

DUD: Terrible whiff. And I burst open the bathroom door and there she was – Esther Williams and five aqua lovelies frolicking in my suds!

PETE: Esther at it again, was she? At it again?

DUD: At it again. Of course, once she clapped eyes on me, she made a pathetic attempt to impress me by doing backflips off the shower attachment.

PETE: Sad, really, isn't it?

DUD: Sad, pathetic. Pathetic! I said, 'Esther, Esther baby doll, aqua love,' I said. 'We've had our thrills, we had our kicks . . .'

PETE: Said much the same as what I said, did you?

DUD: 'We've quaffed deep at the cup of love . . .'

PETE: Yeah.

DUD: 'But,' I said, 'as the tide runneth out, so does love, and I wish you lot'd get the hell out too!'

PETE: You used a watery metaphor for her, did you?

DUD: Well, she's been in the water all her life, and I knew it'd get through to her. Course, she went berserk.

PETE: Course she did.

DUD: She started gnashing her legs together and wailing. She tore her rubber bathing cap to shreds! Course, I threw 'em out, and they're dripping all over the place. Ruined the wallpaper.

PETE: You threw 'em out?

DUD: Yeah.

PETE: That's the only thing you can do, you see.

DUD: Well, of course, you have to be cruel to be kind, Pete.

PETE: That's the point. You have to be very cruel to be very kind as well. Well, what are you doing this evening?

DUD: Well, I thought I'd go to the pictures. You know, take in a movie.

PETE: That's a good idea. There's a Myrna Loy revival at the Roxy. I always enjoy her.

DREAMS
(*Not Only . . . But Also . . .* , BBC2, 1970)

If you think this Pete and Dud sketch is a bit tighter than some of the others they made that year, you're probably not mistaken. Due to the tight schedule of the third series of Not Only . . . But Also . . . , *it was the only flat-cap duologue they actually had time to rehearse.*

DUD: Where am I?

PETE: You're in bed.

DUD: Who are you?

PETE: I am me and you are Dud. You've just been sleepwalking again.

DUD: I've just had the most extraordinary dream. I keep getting it every night in colour.

PETE: Lucky old you.

DUD: It's a nightmare. It always starts the same way. I'm feeling very cold and then suddenly I'm walking down this endless corridor, opening door after door.

PETE: Just one moment, I'll jot this down.

DUD: Finally, I come to a staircase.

PETE: Oh dear.

DUD: And there's this lady at the top.

PETE: Scantily clad?

DUD: No, discreet twin set and pearls – and it's always Mrs McDermott.

PETE: That friend of your mother's?

DUD: Yeah, and she's beckoning me with her finger.

PETE: Good way to beckon.

DUD: So I go up the stairs and she vanishes and I find myself in this room, confronted by a wardrobe, just like this one.

PETE: Mahogany wardrobe confrontation.

DUD: And I've got this terrible urge to get inside it and yet I have this dread of being trapped inside and as I stand there the wardrobe starts to get bigger.

PETE: It's not you getting smaller?

DUD: Could be a bit of both.

PETE: Either, or.

DUD: Anyway, it seems to get bigger and bigger and then when it's just about to overwhelm me I wake up in a cold sweat.

PETE: Going 'Agh'.

DUD: What does it all mean?

PETE: Well, this is a very simple dream to interpret. I don't know whether you're familiar with the works of Freud?

DUD: I do have a cursory knowledge of his theories. I recently skimmed through his lectures to the students of Heidelberg on the phallic implications of the penis.

PETE: An interesting, if superficial, study. Did you read it in the original German?

DUD: No, I read it in précis form on the back of a box of Swan Vestas.

PETE: I'm afraid it loses a lot in translation. Freud's basic theory – to which in general I adhere – is that every human action, conscious or unconscious, is motivated by the sex drive.

DUD: Ah, the sex drive. You mean when you get girls in the back of the car and drive up the M1 and bung 'em one.

PETE: The serious German doctor was not referring to sexual shenanigans in the back of a Volkswagen.

DUD: Sorry, Pete.

PETE: He maintains that sex is behind everything we do.

DUD: You mean everything we do is based on sex? What about reading a newspaper?

PETE: Exactly, the opening of a newspaper in Freudian terms is a symbolic rape.

DUD: I gave the *Radio Times* a right going-over this evening then.

PETE: Shall we preserve a serious tone? Freud says you have your conscious mind and your subconscious mind – in your case the division is marginal. When you go to sleep your subconscious takes over from your conscious and releases your hidden fantasies and desires – the inner you.

DUD: Does that mean that because I feel cold in my dream, deep down I'm frigid?

PETE: No, you were probably just feeling cold in bed and this became part of your dream. Fact can trigger off fantasy.

DUD: And, vice versa, fantasy can trigger off fact.

PETE: I don't catch your gist.

DUD: Like when a dream comes true. You dream you're going along to the bathroom and then you wake up and find that you haven't been to the bathroom – except that you have, in a manner of speaking. Not that it's ever happened to me, but a friend told me about it.

PETE: He was incontinent.

DUD: No, it happened right here in England.

PETE: I would prefer not to dwell on your friend's nocturnal mishaps.

DUD: Exactly his feelings, Pete. He spent the rest of the night drying off on the radiator.

PETE: In your dream you're going through a number of doors. Now, as any fool knows, doors represent years in your life.

DUD: I didn't know that.

PETE: As most fools know, a door represents a year in your life, so you are subconsciously returning to your childhood.

DUD: I then come to the staircase.

PETE: An obvious phallic symbol.

DUD: Mrs McDermott is standing at the top of it.

PETE: You climb up the staircase.

DUD: Up my phallic symbol.

PETE: And Mrs McDermott vanishes.

DUD: I don't blame her.

PETE: Then you're alone in a room with a menacing wardrobe. Now what do you think the wardrobe represents?

DUD: Er . . . a wardrobe?

PETE: Good guess. No, the wardrobe represents your mother and your desire to get into it shows an infantile yearning to return to the warmth and security of your mother's womb.

DUD: You're wrong there, Pete. I have absolutely no inclination to get back into the confines of my mother's womb.

PETE: Not consciously. I'm not suggesting that you go round to 439 Beacontree Avenue and ask your mum for readmission – it's three o'clock in the morning and anyway it's illegal. But I think that something traumatic occurred when you were being born that causes this yearning.

DUD: A yearning mingled with dread.

PETE: What happened that rainy night in Ward 10 in the Charing Cross Hospital that so profoundly scarred your psyche?

DUD: I don't know. I can't remember being born.

PETE: But your subconscious does. Now, the only way we can free your subconscious, with its obsession with the womb, is to recreate symbolically the circumstances of your birth.

DUD: And through self-knowledge emerge a wholer man, a more whole man – feel better.

PETE: The wardrobe is your mother.

DUD: It's nothing like her.

PETE: But in your unconscious dream state it stands for your mother. I want you to imagine that this old brown mahogany wardrobe is your mother.

DUD: That's a bit tricky. But I suppose those two knobs at the top ring a bell and those huge creaky drawers are reminiscent.

PETE: Let's get you conceived. Be upstanding, please. It's nine months before you are born. You are nothing.

DUD: Not even anything?

PETE: Put it this way – you're a tiny little microscopic cell eager to meet up with your cellmate. It's Saturday night. Fulham have won the Cup. Your dad's been at the Green Chartreuse. Suddenly, the miracle of life occurs. Kindly enter your mother's womb.

(*Dud enters the wardrobe. Pete slams the door.*)

PETE: You are now in your mother's womb. How does it feel?

DUD: Dreadful. Full of old socks and mackintoshes.

PETE: There are nine months to go before you are born. We won't take that literally otherwise we'll be here all night. Nine months to lift out. Beginning countdown. Zero minus eight, Dud – looking good.

DUD: Feeling dreadful, Pete.

PETE: Zero minus seven, zero minus six.

DUD: Arms and legs forming, Pete.

PETE: Zero minus five, zero minus four – heart and pulse satisfactory.

DUD: Zero minus three – beginning to kick about a bit.

(*Dud kicks at the door.*)

PETE: Zero minus two.

DUD: Facial characteristics forming.

PETE: God help us! Zero minus one.

DUD: I like it here.

PETE: Zero. We have lift out.

DUD: I don't want to. It's nice and warm here.

PETE: Zero plus one. Come out.

DUD: The door's jammed, Pete.

PETE: Come out, you little sod. You're a month overdue.

(*Dud pushes the door open.*)

DUD: That's it, that's what the doctor said. 'Come out, you little sod, you're a month overdue.' No wonder I wanted to get back in.

(*Pete hits him on the backside with a cricket bat.*)

DUD: What did you do that for?

PETE: To get you breathing, of course. You can thank your lucky stars you're not Jewish.

DUD: Does this mean that I won't ever have that dream again?

PETE: No danger, Dud. You are cured of your recurrent nightmare cycle.

DUD: That's marvellous. Now perhaps I can get back to dreaming about Debra Paget.

(*Pete and Dud get into bed.*)

PETE: Oh, the sheets have got chilly. I think I'll put a pullover on.

(*Pete goes to the wardrobe.*)

DUD: Here, leave my mother alone. Stop tampering with her drawers.

PETE: It's not your mother. It's a wardrobe.

DUD: Are you telling me I can't recognise my own mother? You never liked her, did you?

PETE: Not particularly. I think she could do with a boot up her side panels.

DUD: Leave her alone. She's eighty-four and very frail. It's all right, Mum, don't worry. I'll look after you.

DOUBLE O DUD
(*Not Only . . . But Also . . .* , BBC2, 1970)

Then, as now, the identity of the next James Bond was a subject of intense press interest. Sean Connery had stepped down in 1967 after You Only Live Twice, *and George Lazenby did just one tour of duty as Ian Fleming's suave secret agent, in* On Her Majesty's Secret Service *in 1969. In 1971, Connery returned to play Bond in* Diamonds Are Forever, *before handing over to Roger Moore in* Live and Let Die *in 1973. Yet in 1970 the part was vacant, and naturally Dud considered himself an ideal candidate for the role.*

(*Dud is sitting at a table, brandishing a toy gun. A toy panda is trussed up, on the table. On the chair beside him is a teapot.*)

DUD (*to the panda*): So, Blofeld, you thought you could outwit James Bond! I'm afraid your little ruse of the hand grenade in my oyster soup at dinner did not quite come off. Or go off, shall I say? (*To the teapot.*) Come, Pussy Galore, my dear. Let's away to my Aston Villa in my Martin . . . Er, let's away in my Aston Martin to my villa, for a candlelit soirée. (*To the panda.*) Goodbye, Blofeld.

(*Dud pretends to drive.*)

The brakes! That villain Blofeld has sabotaged my discs!

(*Enter Pete.*)

DUD: Agh! Agh! It's all right, Pussy. Agh!

(*Dud sees Pete, and pretends he's merely coughing.*)

PETE: It's all right, Pussy? What are you on about?

DUD: I thought I heard the cry of a cat in distress.

PETE: So you thought you'd tie up a panda and make love to a teapot?

DUD: I was rehearsing for an edition I'm about to have.

PETE: An edition or an audition?

DUD: An audition. I'm afraid I pronounced the word rather badly.

PETE: That's due to your bad background. You're going to have an audition? Are you going for the part of a second-hand car?

DUD: I don't really want to discuss it, as everything is a bit hush-hush. Nothing has, as yet, been settled.

PETE: I can imagine. Are you going to play the part of the dead body in *The Mousetrap*?

DUD: It's a film, actually – a rather more demanding role. Perhaps the name Fleming gives you an inkling.

PETE: You'd like to play in a film with Rhonda Fleming.

DUD: I would do, actually, yeah – but that is completely by the by. I was referring to I. Fleming, the creator of the legendary 707.

PETE: Since I think it's a little unlikely, Dud, that you'll be selected for the part of a bulky Boeing jet-airliner, I presume that, in your fumbling fashion, you're probing towards referring to 007, the legendary James Bond.

DUD: Correct, yes. As Sean Connery and George Lazenby have

both vacated the role, I thought it was time for a new face to step in.

PETE: You don't think that your lack of acting experience might stand in your way?

DUD: I've acted. I played the part of a troll in the Wood Lane Primary production of *Peer Gynt*. And in any case – *de toute façon* – that's just an ad lib I threw in. You can throw it out again, if you like.

PETE: I'd rather ignore it altogether, frankly.

DUD: Well, what I was going to say is that film is a director's medium. The actor is there to be moulded like putty.

PETE: Yes, I think you'd have to be moulded like putty. Have you done anything about securing a screen test?

DUD: Naturally. I got on to the Saltzman Broccoli Organisation and I asked to speak to Mr Broccoli.

PETE: And did you speak to Mr Broccoli?

DUD: No. Mr Broccoli was in Brussels.

PETE: Who, in that case, did you speak to?

DUD: I spoke to Mr Broccoli's secretary, who most kindly referred me to the switchboard operator, who put me on to the hall porter.

PETE: And what was his response?

DUD: Well, he was very encouraging. He said, 'It's a very bad line. Is it raining at your end?'

PETE: Did he ask you about previous screen exposure?

DUD: No, but I volunteered the information that my last screen appearance was on *Match of the Day*, April 1968, Fulham v Chelsea – slightly obscured by goal post, netting and flying bronco rolls.

PETE: I somehow doubt, Dud, whether this brief glimpse of your, albeit distinctive, features will have been picked up by many film moguls.

DUD: Be that as it may, the hall porter said that Mr Broccoli would be on to me once he got back from Brussels.

PETE: Oh, I see. You left your address, did you?

DUD: No.

PETE: But you gave him his name, did you?

DUD: I didn't give him his name, no.

PETE: But you gave him your name?

DUD: No.

PETE: Very shrewd thinking. I imagine the entire Broccoli Saltzman Organisation are, at this moment, combing the countryside for your whereabouts. I expect the police have been taken off normal duties to take part in this intensive search for an anonymous phone caller.

DUD: Shoot me down in flames if I err, Pete, but do I detect a note of sarcasm?

PETE: Only in your own mind, Dud. Far be it from me to stamp on potential talent. It's just that I think you should be fully acquainted with the Bond phenomenon before you expose yourself to Mr Broccoli.

DUD: I was trying to do the very same thing when you interrupted me.

PETE: I'm sorry about that. Let's see if you've thought your way into the role by a series of improvisations, Stanislavsky style.

DUD: Right.

PETE: Now then, think of a typical Bond situation. You, Bond, have just been having a sauna bath with some Geisha girls. You return to your hotel bedroom, well sated, little suspecting –

DUD: Well what?

PETE: Well sated. Little suspecting that in your room there is lurking Blofeld, the villain, who has a Luger, this gun, trained upon your vitals. Now then, I'll be Blofeld, you be Bond. Let's see how you cope with this situation.

DUD: Right.

PETE: Now remember, you're all relaxed form the sauna. You're not expecting Blofeld to be here.

DUD: Right.

PETE: Bit of a dilemma for Bond.

(*Exit Dud.*)

PETE: Ready!

DUD (*offstage*): Right.

(*Enter Dud, singing the James Bond theme.*)

PETE: Mr Bond! The very man I was expecting!

DUD: Ah, Mr Blofeld! What a surprise! Why don't you bung your Luger out of the window and let's discuss this rationally over a cup of tea?

PETE: Absolutely hopeless. Bond is a man of action, not words. He never loses his cool, as Dilys Powell said. He's never surprised by anything. Now you be Blofeld, I'll be Bond, and I'll show you exactly how it should be done.

DUD: Right.

PETE: OK?

DUD: OK.

(*Exit Pete.*)

DUD: Ready!

(*Enter Pete.*)

PETE: Ah, Mr Blofeld. Just the man I was hoping to see. Why don't we celebrate our reunion with a glass of Don Partidgeon 49, shaken not stirred?

DUD: Thank you very much.

PETE: And by the way, I should put your revolver down. Miss Moneypenny, my secretary, has already removed the cartridges.

DUD: What do you mean?

(*Pete snatches the gun from Dud.*)

DUD: Oh, no! Don't shoot! The flag'll come out!

PETE: You're dead, Dud – completely dead. Useless.

DUD: Not a very good start.

PETE: Not a very good start. Perhaps you'll fare better with the amorous side to Bond. Do you know anything about that?

DUD: Well, I know that he is a ruthless lover.

PETE: He is a ruthless sexual animal, Dud, who uses women for their bodily pleasures but never becomes emotionally involved.

DUD: Stirred but not shaken.

PETE: An aphorism worthy of Wilde on his deathbed. Now then, let's assume the table is your bed.

DUD: Right.

PETE: So, would you get the crockery out of it, for a start? You, as

Bond, are lying exhausted after a protracted struggle with a tarantula spider.

DUD: Right.

PETE: Pussy Galore – I shall essay this particular role – enters your room clad only in a black PVC bikini, her harpoon still blood-stained in her hand.

DUD: Yes, her suntanned frame heaving from the efforts of her moonlight dip.

PETE: Exactly.

DUD: Sweating profusely.

PETE: Yes, don't go on. In she comes. Seductively, she enters. (*Playing Pussy, badly.*) James, I had to see you.

DUD: Pussy! Oh, how wonderful to see you! You must be tuckered out after your dip. How about a nice cup of tea?

PETE: My dear Dud, Pussy Galore has not entered Bond's bedroom at 3 a.m. in the morning for a cup of Typhoo. Her purpose is more basic – sexual. Bond's response should be a mix of international suavity combined with direct sexual invitation. Remember Pussy wants it. You want it.

DUD: She'll get it!

PETE: In she comes. (*As Pussy.*) James, I had to see you.

DUD: Pussy, how nice to see you. Kacks off and cop this!

PETE: I don't think there's any doubt about the directness of the sexual invitation. I do think it lacked some of Fleming's suavity and subtlety. Still, you showed a certain fire, a certain passion – and that's good.

DUD: Yeah. It gives you an idea what I can do.

PETE: It certainly does give me an idea, and I hope you get the chance. I must say, I was favourably impressed by your range as an actor – emotionally and dramatically.

DUD: So you think I've got it in me?

PETE: I certainly think you've got something in you, Dud, yes. And I'd be willing, if it's your wish, to further negotiations between yourself and the Saltzman Broccoli office.

DUD: Oh, that'd be marvellous, because I think you can do it better on the phone that I could.

PETE: I have got a rather better telephone manner. Don't be surprised if I seem a little ruthless – something of a hard sell. That's what you have to do in this business.

DUD: Yeah, well, I'll just top up the pot while you make the call.

PETE: Thank you very much. I like two lumps – stirred but not shaken.

(*Dud makes the tea. Pete picks up the phone.*)

PETE (*on the phone*): Hello? I'd like to speak to Mr Broccoli, please. This is Titanic Globular Modular Productions speaking – managing director here. Yes, this is rather urgent, so would you interrupt Mr Broccoli's call to LA? Thank you. (*To Dud.*) They're putting me through. (*On the phone.*) Hello, Cubby. Pete here. It's re your Bond dilemma. I think I may be able to help you out of your hole. I agree, I think Lazenby's conduct has been disgraceful throughout. I only wish you'd seen my client before committing, but that's all water under the bridge. Yes, he's tall, dark, handsome and an expert at judo.

DUD: Ludo! It's ludo I'm good at!

PETE (*to Dud*): I know. (*On the phone.*) I thought you'd take my word for it, Cubby, yes. Now, the only possible fly in the ointment is the question of my client's availability. I'll just check that out for you. (*To Dud.*) Are you available in the latter half of 1970?

DUD: Er, well, I've got a weekend in Margate pencilled in for August.

PETE (*on the phone*): There is a slight availability problem here, Cubby, but I think we'll be able to work around it. Now, let's get down to the question of money . . . £25,000? My dear Cubby, the fact that you paid Lazenby peanuts is of no interest to me whatsoever.

DUD: I'll do it for nothing.

PETE: (*on the phone*): Let's be sensible about this – $250,000 against 10 per cent of the gross and I must insist on a no-garlic clause.

DUD: I'll do it for nothing!

PETE: I'm sorry, Cubby – $250,000, or the deal's off. It's not worth messing about with this. Goodbye, Cubby. I'm sorry.

(*Dud tries to snatch the phone.*)

DUD: Let me talk to him! Let me! (*On the phone.*) Mr Broccoli, Mr Broccoli, don't take any notice of what he said. Now, er . . . Yes, I'm sure it is 7.14 and 50 seconds . . . No, but what I wanted to say . . . Or 7.15 precisely, if you want to put it . . . Now what . . . 7.15 and 10 seconds?

RACIAL PREJUDICE
(*Not Only . . . But Also . . .* , BBC2, 1970)

(*Pete is playing Solitaire. Enter Dud, blacked up*)

DUD: Hello.

PETE: Hello.

DUD: What are you playing?

PETE: Solitaire.

DUD: Quite a nice day.

PETE: Is it? I haven't been out.

DUD: I have.

PETE: Yes, I saw you come in.

DUD: I expect you're wondering what I've been doing this afternoon.

PETE: No, I haven't given it much thought, really.

DUD: Don't you notice anything peculiar about me?

PETE: No more than usual.

DUD: Doesn't my face look a little odd?

PETE: Yes, but I've learned to live with that.

DUD: Do I detect a stubborn resistance on your part to acknowledge the fact that I am sitting here in front of your nose, blacker than the ace of spades?

PETE: Am I expected to react differently because of the colour of your skin? I have been guided by the principle that every man, irrespective of his race, colour, kith or kin, should be treated in exactly the same way.

DUD: Granted, a worthy sentiment. But aren't you mildly surprised that, in the space of an afternoon, I have changed from lily white to jet black?

PETE: Not in the least. By the way, did you find time to replenish our supply of Kiwi nut brown shoe preservative?

DUD: You saw me at it, then?

PETE: Well, I was seeking some rational explanation for you spending eight and a half hours in the lavatory when I chanced to see you creeping out with two empty tins of boot polish.

DUD: Why didn't you ask me what I was doing?

PETE: I assumed – correct me if I'm wrong – that you were sneaking out to some fancy dress do from which you saw fit to exclude me.

DUD: Not at all – I was out on some more serious bent.

PETE: You've not been to a party? What serious bent have you been off on?

DUD: I wanted to find out first hand how it feels to be black in a white-dominated society. I can tell you, Pete, until you are black, you have no idea of the hostile currents that riddle our society.

PETE: You ran into some hostile currents, did you?

DUD: Well, it wasn't overt prejudice. I mean, nobody said, 'Get up a banana tree where you belong, wog chops.' It was more of an insidious nature, a bizarre nuance of sophisticated resentment nurtured.

PETE: What happened?

DUD: Well, first of all I went along to a five star restaurant and requested a table in the Grill Room. But the head waiter saw fit to turn me away on the grounds that I was improperly dressed.

PETE: Well, you do look a bit unconventional to the untutored eye.

DUD: Unconventional but correct. I informed him that I was sporting the formal evening wear of a Zambezi chieftain.

PETE: And what was his response to this information?

DUD: He suggested in no uncertain terms that I return to the Zambezi and tuck into some best end of missionary.

PETE: I trust you treated the display of bigotry with the contempt it deserved.

DUD: Certainly. I said, 'My good man, I have no wish to bandy words with a menial. Kindly summon the manager.'

PETE: Bravely spoken.

DUD: But he said the manager is on a trip up the Zambezi and why don't I meet him there. At this I realised I was up against a brick wall, which, indeed, moments later, I was.

PETE: They used physical force upon your person? I trust you took this up with the authorities.

DUD: Certainly. I immediately gave the Race Relations Board a tinkle and informed them of the facts – namely that I, a white person, had been bunged out of a restaurant because I was black, in spite of the fact that I was correctly dressed in the equivalent of white tie and tails up the Zambezi.

PETE: A lucid précis of the situation. Are they taking any action?

DUD: They said they were a bit busy. Apparently, they're investigating the shocking case of a Welshman who was refused Irish coffee in an Indian restaurant.

PETE: Yes, I read about that in the Jewish Chronicle.

DUD: Then, to cap it all, when I came home on the bus – further humiliation. I gave my seat to a lady and she laid out a newspaper on it before she'd sit down.

PETE: Well, of course most prejudice of this kind is caused by ignorance. Naturally there are differences between black and white people.

DUD: They're black and white, for a start.

PETE: Exactly. Both have individual talents. If the white man is good at one thing, then the black man is good at the other.

DUD: Yeah, I heard they was good at that.

PETE: No, Dud. I am not referring to the myth of sexual superiority of the Negro. That is a load of cobblers. There is no reason to suppose that Jomo Kenyatta is any better in bed than you and me.

DUD: Poor sod. I mean, of course not. But you take the field of music, for instance. There is no denying that the blacks have made the blues their own. Show me your white Ray Charles.

PETE: To which I could reply, point out your black Beatle. It's all a matter of taste. They have their soul, we have our soul.

DUD: But their soul is more heartfelt than our soul.

PETE: Perhaps, but during those dark, turbulent years from 1939 to 45 . . .

DUD: The Second World War?

PETE: . . . Auntie Nora's pregnancy, would you have been comforted by the driving rhythms of Muddy Waters or the haunting beauty of Vera Lynn? The argument is meaningless. We could say, 'Where is your sepia Shakespeare? Where is your tinted Tintoritto?'

DUD: To which I would reply, 'Where is your white Al Jolson?'

PETE: Al Jolson was white.

DUD: OK, where is your white Cassius Clay?

PETE: Mohammed Ali, as he prefers to be called. You must admit our own Cooper OBE had Ali in trouble in the fifth, and put him down for seven, and the fact does remain that the African people have never produced a lasting civilisation.

DUD: On the other hand they have never spawned a tyrant of the proportions of thwarted artist Adolf Hitler.

PETE: Not so fast, Dud. There is a theory that Hitler was a black man who whited up for social reasons, using his own paintbrush and watercolours.

DUD: What evidence is there for this theory?

PETE: His moustache is the giveaway. The answer, my friend, is not blowing in the wind.

DUD: What's not blowing in the wind?

PETE: Hitler's moustache is not blowing in the wind in all those newsreel shots. Did you ever once see his moustache move naturally, as if buffeted by a breeze?

DUD: Not that I recall, no.

PETE: And the theory put forward is that his moustache was not a moustache at all but the only piece of his skin that he failed to white up – hence its unnatural lack of movement.

DUD: A persuasive argument.

PETE: Not to mention the so-called Nazi salute, the raising of the right arm, which is in fact the traditional greeting of the pygmy to the giant Masai tribesman. It is his basic attempt at shaking hands.

DUD: Even if Hitler was black, which I'm prepared to take as read, it's still no reason to condemn an entire race.

PETE: Of course not. Would you let your daughter marry a man covered in boot polish?

DUD: I'll cross that bridge when I come to it. The fact remains that I feel beautiful being black. My teeth are whiter and I feel a certain litheliness in my gait, an animal power in my movement.

PETE: This is superficial. Underneath, you still remain a white, sluggish Dud. If Gracie Fields leapt into a vat of tar she would not become Ella Fitzgerald. If I were you, I'd get that polish off at once.

DUD: Say it loud – I'm black and I'm proud.

PETE: Have you read the warning on the underside of the tin?

DUD: No. What does it say?

PETE: It says, 'This polish is long lasting and deep penetrating.'

DUD: I can wash it off.

PETE: No you can't. It's waterproof. It also says here, 'Do not apply to any other part of the body than the shoe.' I wouldn't worry, Dud. You'll have an interesting life with a black head and a white body. You could tour the world. Of course, on your return, you would present a bit of a problem for the Home Office. They would have to repatriate your head and hands and keep your body for medical science. On the other hand, they might of course let your head in as a dependant.

BESTSELLER
(*Not Only . . . But Also . . .* , BBC2, 1970)

(*Pete is watching television, Enter Dud, laden with books*)

DUD: Did you have a nice evening's viewing?

PETE: Fair to middling. I just tuned in to Verdi's Requiem. How did it go at the institute?

DUD: Would you like some of this?

PETE: What is it?

DUD: Have a guess. Taste it.

PETE: No, I don't really know. Is it blancmange, or something?

DUD: It's cauliflower cheese. It's good, isn't it?

PETE: I thought it was Esperanto tonight.

DUD: Well they're combining Esperanto with cookery in a crash course. They give you the recipes in Esperanto.

PETE: Oh I see. Are you keeping up the painting?

DUD: Yes, but Doreen was off with flu so Mrs Amory stripped off, and as I'm half way through Doreen, I thought I'd give it a miss. So I went to the chemistry class and I found out the specific gravity of self-raising flour.

PETE: You certainly seem to have a very broad spectrum of interests. Don't you think you're over-taxing your intellect?

DUD: Not at all, Pete. The more fields the mind can embrace, the better. The mind, like the body, needs exercise.

PETE: But does it need violent exercise? I mean, can you encompass and digest in one evening aesthetic purity and Esperanto and cauliflower cheese?

DUD: Yes, I think so.

PETE: You think you can absorb it all, do you?

DUD: Yes, I do.

PETE: Well, what's Esperanto for cauliflower cheese?

DUD: Er, I think it's one of the few cases where the Esperantos use the same word as we do. Cauliflower cheese.

PETE: There are no such people as the Esperantos. Esperanto is a composite language, Dud.

DUD: There isn't a place called Esperanto?

PETE: No.

DUD: I wrote off for two weeks there in August.

PETE: With a view, no doubt, to catching the spaghetti trees in bloom.

DUD: I know spaghetti doesn't grow on trees.

PETE: Where does it grow?

DUD: I don't know. We're doing spaghetti next Wednesday.

PETE: What's all this rubbish you brought back?

DUD: What? The books? These are my reference books.

PETE: Reference books?

DUD: Yes.

PETE: *Angelique? The Voyeur? The Adventurers? The Nude Ice Murders?* What sort of rubbish is this you're digesting?

DUD: I'm writing a novel.

PETE: What kind of novel are you writing?

DUD: I thought a bestseller would be a good thing, combining the ingredients of sex, violence and money. I thought of calling it *Sex, Violence And Money.*

PETE: A very good title – *Sex, Violence And Money*, brackets, a bestseller by Dud.

DUD: Yes. Tied up with film package possibilities. It's the story of Rip Taggart, millionaire playboy stud. Chapter One: the hot sun-baked parched walls of the Harlem tenement building, a fly buzzing indolently in the humid heat.

PETE: A fly?

DUD: Yeah.

PETE: What's the point of a fly? What's that doing there?

DUD: Setting the scene.

PETE: Well, the fly's got nothing to do with the story. Our story's about Rip Taggart, who is about to be born. We don't want to divert the reader's attention with this fly. I mean, what's it doing?

DUD: Well, I could weave him into the plot. Have the fly land on the sweaty nose of Mrs Taggart.

PETE: Oh, I see. All right. You didn't say you were going to have it land on the sweaty nose of Mrs Taggart. You just had it buzzing indolently.

DUD: Then you get the birth of Rip.

PETE: Yes.

DUD: Heaving thighs ringing across Manhattan.

PETE: *Mamma mia!*

DUD: No, she's not Italian.

PETE: What is she?

DUD: She is of Puerto Rican extraction.

PETE: What do Puerto Ricans of extraction shout in agony?

DUD: I don't know. We can find out later.

PETE: Yeah. We'll ring up the reference library. All right. Go on.

DUD: Rip is born, his mother dies, he becomes a pimp and a drug pusher.

PETE: A puller and a pusher simultaneously.

DUD: He is picked up at the age of eight on 42nd Street by a seductive starlet, Delores Del Carlo.

PETE: (*reads*) 'She takes him back to her penthouse pad and sates her bust on him.'

DUD: 'Sates her lust on him.' Then I've put, like . . . 'she pops his cherry, he thrusts at her like a mountain ram.'

PETE: I prefer something like 'he rammed her like a mountain thrush.' It's a more original image – a thrush coming in than a ram. I think ram has been done to death by Robbins.

DUD: Yeah, that's true. Well we'll decide that later.

PETE: She's exhausted, isn't she? Because he's a sexual machine, even at the age of eight – an unfeeling Don Juan.

DUD: Well, anyway, Rip nicks 500 dollars out of her handbag.

PETE: Rip nicks.

DUD: Yeah. It ties up with Delores' ripped knicks. You could say, 'Rip nicks 500 dollars from Delores' ripped knicks.'

PETE: Yeah. Wonderful wordplay, that – worthy of Lawrence Dureell in *Tunc* and *Nunquam*.

DUD: That sounds dirty.

PETE: It is dirty, but it's intellectual so he can get away with it.

DUD: Starts his magazine empire.

PETE: What do we call it?

DUD: *Mind And Body*.

PETE: *Mind And Body*. A combination of nude ladies and intellectual articles by Jonathan Miller and Kenneth Tynan.

DUD: Rip makes love to countless women but never finds happiness.

PETE: Why the bloody hell not?

DUD: If he finds happiness, I'd just have to end the book after a few pages.

PETE: Oh, I see. It's a plot device. All right. He's unhappy.

DUD: One day, as Rip is on his way to sophisticated cocktails in Acapulco, his private jet encounters engine trouble. Gawd! Rip balls out! Oh, I'm sorry. Rip bails out. Couldn't read me own writing. Rip bails out and lands, ironically, on the patio of his old school friend, Gus Brett. One night Rip is having dinner with Gus's wife, Mary. Gus is out carol singing.

PETE: Is he a goodie, then?

DUD: Yeah.

PETE: Mary clears away the dinner things, trips on the carpet.

DUD: Rip bends down.

PETE: Their arms brush.

DUD: Electricity flows, and their bodies fuse. That's a good bit, isn't it?

PETE: That's a very good bit there, their bodies fusing.

DUD: I like that. Then I thought perhaps some bits in about breasts heaving, fire flickering, and, of course, they're on the floor, cos we had Rip and Delores on the bed last time.

PETE: Yes, you've got to vary locale.

DUD: Keep it moving, keep it moving. Rip, anyway, with Mary, samples true love.

PETE: But of a forbidden nature.

DUD: And at the expense of his old friend, Gus.

PETE: Deeply ashamed, Rip goes out into the night, vowing never to return. He seeks to forget Mary in an endless round of booze and broads.

DUD: He goes to South America, grows a beard and becomes a guerrilla. Mary confesses of their affair to Gus, who hurtles distraught out of the house, goes to the car factory where he works, and, in a fit of pique, bungs himself into molten steel and, ironically, his rendered down remains are incorporated into the car which, by chance, Rip Taggart buys a few months later.

PETE: A rather heavy hand of coincidence here, isn't it? Gus just happens, ironically, to fall in some steel which, ironically, becomes part of the very car that Rip Taggart, by some strange chance, happens to buy. I think your plot mechanism is a little creaky, Dud.

DUD: Life is stranger than fiction, Pete.

PETE: Your fiction is stranger than fiction.

DUD: Rip drives off to visit Gus and Mary. You be Rip, I'll be Mary. This is a very good scene. You'll like it.

PETE: (*as Rip*): 'Knock-knock on the door. Hello, Mary.'

DUD: (*as Mary*) 'Hello, Rip.'

PETE: 'Hello. Where's Gus, my old buddy from reform school days?'

DUD: 'Oh, he went off – never to be seen again.'

PETE: 'Cripes!'

DUD: 'Yes, it was quite a blow.'

PETE: 'What a choker! Well, by chance I've got a new car outside, the ideal thing to go and look for Gus in.' (*out of character*) Electrifying dialogue, this. They don't say 'what a choker' in the United States. They say 'hot dog' and 'gee whizz' and things like that. Not 'what a choker'.

DUD: They could say both. 'What a choker, hot dog, didgeridoo.' Hit the international market.

PETE: What happens after that? It seems to be blank.

DUD: I don't know. I haven't finished it yet.

PETE: You haven't pieced it out yet.

DUD: No.

PETE: Well, they go out and look for Gus.

DUD: Yeah.

PETE: Unaware that Gus is, in fact, in their big end. They arrive at the beach, the waves flowing. Passions mount. They make passionate love on the back seat, their necks and legs intertwined like maddened snakes. Having made love, they go to sleep – like you do when you've made love.

DUD: You do? Oh, yes.

PETE: They fall asleep, and whilst asleep, the waves lapping over them, they are drowned – are dead.

DUD: Ironically, brought together as dead bodies – Gus, Rip and Mary, at the bottom of the sea.

PETE: And the biggest irony of them all – Rip and RIP.

DUD: Rip and rip?

PETE: Rip and R – I – P.

DUD: Ah, that's marvellous.

PETE: And furthermore, to take him to the beginning of the novel, why not have the same fly you so cleverly incorporated in the first chapter, why not have that fly . . .

PETE & DUD (together): Ironically . . .

PETE: Buzz over the sea and land on the aerial of the wireless which is still playing Andre Kostelanetz beneath the waves?

DUD: Knockout! Knockout!

PETE: It's good, isn't it?

DUD: It's a knockout!

PETE: Yeah. I think we do a bit of work on this, we'll have something on our hands.

DUD: That's marvellous!

THE ART OF SEDUCTION
(*Not Only . . . But Also . . .* , BBC2, 1970)

(*Dud is drawing at an easel – Enter Pete*)

PETE: I thought you were meant to be down the institute tonight.

DUD: Yeah, I was, but Doreen's off with flu, so Mr Atkins said we'd abandon the real life class and we'd go home and do a subject of our own choice.

PETE: Oh, I see. What's this? (*Peter reads the title of Dud's painting*) 'World War Two.' What's it all mean?

DUD: Well, this is flak, heavy flak.

PETE: Heavy flak over there, yeah?

DUD: Same over here. There's a Nazi.

PETE: A Nazi, yeah.

DUD: A Nazi. And there's one of our ships.

PETE: I see. Who's that?

DUD: That's the pilot

PETE: Well, why's he wearing a bowler hat?

Dud: It's Winston Churchill.

Pete: Well, you can't tell that's Winston Churchill. Put in a distinctive emblem of some kind.

(*Dud adds a cigar*)

Pete: A cigar. Yeah, that's a good distinctive sign. That could still be Lew Grade. I think we should add a little thing. Why not add a monogram to him, like that, you see. Put WC on his shirt, like that. Identifies him as Winston Churchill.

Dud: Yeah. Do you like it?

Pete: What's this? Is this Winston Churchill's eyebrows fallen off?

Dud: It's two seagulls.

Pete: Seagulls? Well, why is this ship firing at Winston Churchill? It's a British ship!

Dud: It shows the horrid irony of war.

Pete: 'The Irony of War', by Dud.

Dud: Yeah, it's good, innit?

Pete: Well, it has a certain primitive charm, worthy of the early Mozart.

Dud: Thank you. I didn't know he could paint.

Pete: No, he couldn't.

Dud: Very funny. I suppose you could do better.

Pete: I could scarcely do any worse. Could I have a bit of charcoal?

(*Dud drops a pencil on the floor*)

Pete: Thank you for dropping to the floor in that nice fashion. I have a more linear approach to art. Now then . . .

(*Pete draws an outline of a female breast, driving Dud into a lustful frenzy*)

Pete: What's that?

Dud: Urgh!

Pete: What is it?

(*Dud pulls himself together*)

Dud: It looks like one of my seagulls flying sideways a bit.

Pete: I see, seagulls get you going a bit. You're wrong, actually. Let me fill in a little more detail, to give you a hint of what it is.

(*Pete adds a nipple, driving Dud into an even greater frenzy*)

DUD: Urgh! Urgh!

PETE: Tell me, what's that?

(*Dud struggles to contain himself*)

DUD: I don't want to say.

PETE: Why don't you want to say?

DUD: It's dirty – specially cos there's only one.

PETE: Well, would you rather have two?

DUD: Yeah. No!

PETE: I'll fill in two of them.

(*Pete draws another breast*)

PETE: There. Does that tell you what it is? Come on. What's that?

DUD: It's a lady's things.

PETE: A lady's things? Is that all you ever think about? How can you say that's a lady's things, when anyone could see it's two lovely little doggies going out for a nice stroll?

(*Pete adds eyes and ears, transforming the breasts into doggies*)

PETE: You see? If that's a lady's things, I'm a Dutchman.

DUD: Very clever. All right then, clever drawers – what's this?

(*Dud writes WOO WOO WWW*)

PETE: Woo, woo, double u, double u, double u? That's just a word that doesn't make any sense. It says woo, woo, wu, wu, wu.

DUD: No it doesn't. It says bum titty, bum titty, bum bum bum.

PETE: (*sarcastic*) I see – what a wonderful visual pun.

(*The doorbell rings*)

DUD: I'll get it.

(*Exit Dud*)

DUD: (*offstage*) Oh, Mr Postman, so there's no mail today, thank you for telling us.

(*Enter Dud, concealing a parcel behind his back*)

PETE: Who was that?

DUD: It was the postman. He just called to say there wasn't any mail today.

PETE: What have you got behind your back?

DUD: Nothing.

(*DUD attempts to put the parcel in the drawer of the table*)

PETE: What are you putting in that drawer?

DUD: Nothing.

PETE: You're taking a lot of time to put nothing in the drawer.

DUD: I was just seeing if it would open.

PETE: Could I see in this drawer?

DUD: No! No!

PETE: Excuse me.

(*Pete opens the drawer and removes the parcel*)

PETE: Is this the nothing the postman delivered?

DUD: Well, he said it was next to nothing, so it was nothing for filing purposes.

PETE: I see. I'll open it, in that case.

(*Pete starts to open the parcel*)

DUD: No, it's for me. It's addressed to the occupier. That's me.

PETE: I also occupy this address, if I remember right.

DUD: Yeah, but it's a seed catalogue and I told them to address it to the occupier, so I wouldn't get on the FBI's lists.

PETE: Seed catalogue, you say? Just the sort of thing I like to read about this time of day. Nothing I like better than looking at a good seed catalogue at about this time.

(*Pete opens the parcel, to reveal a book*)

PETE: Seed catalogue? 'Honeymoon Hints by the Reverend Prendergast – Sexual Ecstasy for Practising Christians.'

DUD: Must be a mistake. I'll take it round for Mr Woolley – it's probably his.

PETE: You think it's for Mr Woolley? Mr Woolley has been married for 51 years and had 17 children. I think Honeymoon Hints would be rather shutting the stable room door after the horse has bolted.

DUD: Better late than never.

(*Pete scrutinises Dud's book*)

PETE: I see. It's very thorough. 'The use of the elbow in foreplay, contraceptive methods, locked doors, curry for supper, and leaving the country.'

DUD: Has it got any picture of people kissing?

PETE: It has certain illustrations, but I don't think you should look at this type of thing. You're not even married. Are you getting married?

DUD: I'm putting out feelers, and I want to be prepared. It's no good rifling through the book on the actual night.

PETE: It is rather bulky to bung down your pyjamas on the honeymoon night. Who are you setting your cap at?

DUD: Oh, no one in particular. I thought I'd play the field for a bit. No use in tying myself to one woman at this stage.

PETE: I think tying yourself to a woman is the only way you could keep her. Let's face it – up to now, *The Amorous Adventures of Don Dud* would make a rather slender volume, to say the least.

DUD: I've been saving myself.

PETE: You've been saving yourself to ridiculous lengths. The trouble with your approach to women is that you don't approach them.

DUD: What about Shirley Powell?

PETE: What about Shirley Powell? When did that happen? 1948. And what occurred?

DUD: Well, I said I'd meet her outside the Royal Oak. And I met her, and she said, 'I'll just pop across the road, and see if my friend can come out.' And she went across the road, and five minutes later she came back and said. 'My friend can't come out, so I'm going home.'

PETE: What a torrid night of passion. I think your trouble, Dud, quite seriously, is that you're not assertive and dominant enough. I think you've got to be a bit more masterful. A woman likes to be dominated. You must be like a brute with them.

DUD: Be a monster with them.

PETE: Be a monster! Despises them, you see? Your tactics aren't really right. Take that incident at the harvest supper with Stella Newby. Now, I think it was a tactical error to fall to your knees in front of her, saying, 'Stella, please never leave me.'

DUD: Especially as I'd never even met her.

PETE: That's where you went wrong. You've got to give the impression that you don't want women.

DUD: That's a bit difficult, cos I do.

PETE: I know you do, but you must give that impression. Now,

Stella Newby – have you been in touch with her since?

DUD: No.

PETE: Well, would you like to have her luscious frame moving all around you in sinuous motion?

DUD: Yes. You know, when I first saw her I thought she'd broken both her arms and got them in splints, but they were her things.

PETE: I wish you wouldn't keep calling them things. You'd like to get back in touch with her, would you?

DUD: Yeah.

PETE: Why don't you give her a ring?

DUD: No, I couldn't.

PETE: Well, I'll give her a ring.

DUD: I don't want you going out with her!

PETE: I don't wish to go out with Stella Newby. She's rather too buxom for me. But if you like, I'll give her a ring, and imitate you, and be a bit more assertive and dominant – treat her the way she would like to be treated.

DUD: Treated like dirt.

PETE: Like dirt, Dud. Have you got her number?

DUD: Yeah. It's scratched on the dresser by the phone.

PETE: Right. I'll give her a phone.

(dialling) Grr! Grr! Grr!

DUD: Don't overdo it.

PETE: I'm just getting into the voice of the mannerisms. Grr! Grr!

DUD: Grr! Grr!

PETE: (*on the phone*) Hello? Stella? Dud here. Yes, I was that amusing fellow who fell to his knees at the harvest supper and wept. What an amusing joke that was. Anyway, I was just ringing to say that I'm still at the same number and address, and I never want to see you again. Yes, you get the message, you old rat bag. I can't talk now, cos I've got to go and judge a beauty contest, and pose for some stills for some underwear publicity. Goodbye, Stella. I never wish to see you again.

(*Pete blows a raspberry and hangs up*)

DUD: Knockout. If that doesn't get her going, nothing will.

PETE: I reckon she'll be ringing you up in the next minute. Treat them like dirt. That's the only way.

WOMEN'S RIGHTS
(*Behind the Fridge*, Plymouth Theatre, New York, 1973)

Peter still had more than twenty years left to live, and Dudley nearly thirty, yet this was the last fully-fledged Pete and Dud sketch they ever wrote together. At least they went out with a triumphant bang, rather than a despondent whimper. There's no sense of finale here – merely the latest instalment from a duo who appeared to share an infinite capacity for finding mundanity in the most important topics, and occasionally vice versa. After four years together on the road, in three different continents, their partnership had run its course, but even at the very end, they never ran out of ideas.

(*Pete and Dud are in the kitchen.*)

PETE: 'Ere, Dud, is the tea up yet?

DUD: Yeah, I'll give it another couple of minutes to brew because we don't want to lose any of the flavour, do we?

PETE: No, we don't want to lose any of that delicious flavour bursting forth from the tea bags.

DUD: No. I'm using the larger capacity tea bags now, you know.

PETE: Oh, those bigger bags, as advertised.

DUD: Yes. They're a bit more expensive, you know, but it's worth it in the long run because when you've saved up a hundred labels you send them in to the firm and they send you back a plastic replica of a member of the Royal Family.

PETE: How delightful.

DUD: Terrific. And when you've got all 437 members of the Royal Family you send them in to the firm and they send you back a free tea bag.

PETE: A free tea bag?

DUD: Yeah – a gratis tea bag.

PETE: What a wonderful gesture in this materialistic age.

DUD: Well, it gives you a ray of hope, doesn't it?

PETE: It certainly does, yeah. Well, while you were making the tea I was reading an interesting article about the emancipation of women by Ms Germaine Greer.

DUD: Oh yeah?

PETE: Did you peruse the item aforesaid?

DUD: Well, I got about halfway through the first word and then I had to nip off and check on my rice pudding, cos the pinger was going.

PETE: Well, it was rather an interesting article about the subjugation of women throughout the ages – you know, how they've been held down and dominated by the male.

DUD: Oh, yeah?

PETE: You be Mum, will you, please?

DUD: Yes, certainly.

(*Dud pours the tea.*)

PETE: Not too much milk. You made it a bit wishy-washy last time.

DUD: Sorry.

PETE: And I think Miss Greer, who is not an unintelligent woman –

DUD: No, let's give her that.

PETE: Let's give her that – has raised a number of interesting and salient points.

(*Dud scrutinises the magazine.*)

DUD: Yeah, she raised two on the cover that caught my attention.

PETE: Don't follow you. There's nothing written on the cover.

DUD: No, the points I was referring to were not of a literary nature. They had a certain visual appeal.

PETE: You are referring to her tits?

DUD: Her T.I.T.S. – yes.

PETE: Do you realise you are doing precisely what Miss Greer objects to – namely, you are treating women purely as sexual objects.

DUD: I wouldn't mind it the other way round.

PETE: What?

DUD: I wouldn't mind having ladies use me as a sexual object – having them satiate their lust upon my body.

PETE: But surely you'd rather be respected for your mind than your body.

DUD: No. Well, eventually, yes, but I'd like them to give my body a good going-over first.

PETE: Oh, so you'd like them to start on your body and then gradually work their way down towards your mind.

DUD: Yeah, yeah – that sounds all right.

PETE: Are those scones ready yet?

(*Dud looks in the oven.*)

DUD: Yeah, they should be done now.

PETE: They should be, they've been in there for three days.

DUD: Well, if you want something nice, you have to wait for it.

(*Dud brings the scones to the table.*)

DUD: I think that whatever Miss Greer says, the lot of women has improved since Victorian times, you know.

PETE: For a lot of women.

DUD: I mean, in Victorian times a woman's life was pure drudgery.

PETE: Mind you, there are still countries in the world today where the woman is completely dominated by the male.

DUD: Oh, really. Where?

PETE: Well, take the Far East, for example. Would you butter this scone? There, in the Far East, the woman is treated as a mere beast of burden.

(*Dud butters Pete's scone.*)

PETE: No, not too thick.

DUD: Oh, sorry. Is that OK?

PETE: Yeah.

DUD: Do you want it all around the edges?

PETE: Of course I do. I'm not going to start in the middle, am I?

DUD: Is that OK?

PETE: It'll do. You see, in the Far East, the woman is treated as a mere beast of burden. Do you know the woman has to walk ten yards behind the husband?

DUD: Yeah?

PETE: The only time she is allowed to walk in front of her husband is in suspected minefields.

DUD: Good Lord. That's terrible.

PETE: So is this tea.

DUD: What?

PETE: This tea is terrible. You smell it.

DUD: Oh, bloody hell!

PETE: Like the Ganges in here!

DUD: Oh, look. I've got Princess Anne up the spout. I've never seen her like that before. I'll just throw in a couple of tea bags and drown her out. It's interesting what you were saying about Man's basic hostility to women because I think that God, with His usual perspicacity, has made Man the aggressor in the eternal war of the sexes. I mean, since primordial times, when Diana Dors ruled the Earth, Man has been the hunter. Where did I put those bloody tea bags?

PETE: You usually secrete them in that box by the stove.

DUD: Getting back to what Miss Greer says – I think she overstates her case.

PETE: She blows things out of all proportion.

DUD: There are so many things that ladies have that we men could never share in. I mean, not for us the exquisite pleasure of a baby suckling at our breast – milk and two lumps, as usual?

PETE: Thank you. Yes, I agree. Man, denied this ultimate ecstasy, is forced to channel his mind into the realms of Art and Science.

DUD: Yeah, he's bound to.

PETE: And if you look back through the annals of history, where will you find a female equivalent of say, Ludwig van Beethoven?

DUD: Yeah, Beethoven and his incomparable symphonies.

PETE: Schopenhauer.

DUD: Schopenhauer and his lyrical nocturnes.

PETE: Of course, I think you have to go along with Professor Shockley here and face the fact that the whole thing is tied up in our genes – the Genetic Factor. But these women's libbers will not accept it. Do you know, they regard the brassiere as a symbol of masculine enslavement?

DUD: Oh, but that's ridiculous, isn't it?

PETE: Yeah.

DUD: We didn't push them into their brassieres, did we?

PETE: No, we did not.

DUD: I ask you, did we males force the females into their brassieres?

PETE: No.

DUD: I've been trying for years to get them out of them.

PETE: And who was it that invented the brassiere, for the benefit of ladies?

DUD: Who?

PETE: A man.

DUD: Might have known.

PETE: Dr Otto Titsling, working away in his laboratory in Hamburg, first came up with *der Büstenunterhalter Gesellschaft*. And look at all the other things that men have been coming up with for ladies throughout the centuries. The list is enormous. The kitchen stove.

DUD: A miracle.

PETE: The ironing board.

DUD: And, of course, in recent years, the paper panty.

PETE: An enormous breakthrough.

DUD: Man, you see, has invented the paper panty especially for ladies. They're so economical. Whereas in the past, Mrs Woolley used to have to toil for hours over her knickers in the sink, now all she has to do of an evening is go over them with an eraser.

PETE: Dropping Mrs Woolley's knickers for the moment, I think we have to face the fact that thanks to the Pill, another man-made device for the benefit of ladies of the opposite sex, women are becoming, increasingly, the sexual aggressors.

DUD: Oh, they're bound to.

PETE: I don't know if you're familiar with *Cosmopolitan*.

DUD: What's that?

PETE: It's a ladies' periodical that comes out monthly.

DUD: Ah, no – don't know it.

PETE: You don't know that one?

DUD: No.

PETE: Well, in that magazine, all the stress is laid on the onus of the male – to satisfy the female, sexually speaking.

DUD: Oh, yeah – all that stuff about how it takes longer for the female to feel . . . dirty . . .

PETE: Not quite the scientific term, but how it takes a lady a little longer to become sexually aroused.

DUD: Yeah. It's all that stuff about erroneous zones, isn't it?

PETE: No, it not erroneous, it's erogenous. Erroneous is where you go wrong.

DUD: That's where I go wrong.

PETE: Oh, you go wrong on the erogenous zones?

DUD: Yeah.

PETE: Yeah, well, I'm not surprised, if there's so many of the bleeding things.

DUD: Well, a lady's peppered from head to foot with erogenous zones.

PETE (*pointing to his magazine*): Have you seen these diagrams?

DUD: Of the erogenous zones?

PETE: Yeah.

DUD: I daren't look.

PETE: It's like a map of the Underground.

DUD: A man is hard put to know where to start his sexual voyage.

PETE: Yeah, well, not the Northern Line.

DUD: Yeah, I mean, what may attract one lady, may repel the other.

PETE: This is the dilemma.

DUD: This is the eternal dilemma. You could spend six hours tickling her calves with a Japanese feather device, as advertised, when all she needs to get her going is your hot breath on her . . . on her . . . doodahs . . . her busty substances.

PETE: On her busty substances. I think ladies, having all these many and various erogenous zones about their person – I think the least they could do is to label them.

DUD: Yeah.

PETE: You know, label them in order of preference.

DUD: Yeah.

PETE: Then at least you could be certain of starting off on the right foot.

DUD: That's a daft place to start.

PETE: I was speaking metaphorically. I wasn't suggesting you go crawling round the floor at parties sucking ladies' toes. Though, of course, that might turn them on in these freaky, degenerate days we live in. Have A Go – Suck A Toe. That might be the new slogan for the Salacious Seventies.

DUD: Yeah, count me out.

PETE: Count me out. Anyway, I'm off to the pub for a pint of beer. Are you coming?

DUD: Yeah.

PETE: Might meet a few girls down there.

DUD: Oh, I'd better take the diagram then.

Chapter Eight
Sir Arthur Streeb-Greebling

Sir Arthur Streeb-Greebling was one of Peter's greatest comic creations, but he also benefited greatly from Dudley's selfless comic acting. On the face of it, Dudley's role in these sketches seems pretty marginal, to say the least. All he does is put the questions. Surely anyone could do it, and it would still be just the same? But plenty of other people played Boswell to Peter's Dr Johnson, before Dudley came along – and after he departed – and somehow, it didn't have quite the same magic.

Sir Arthur Streeb-Greebling was the character Peter was born to play, far closer to his own roots than Pete or Clive or E.L. Wisty. From *Behind the Fridge* right back to Footlights shows like *Pop Goes Mrs Jessop*, his patrician caricatures were variations on the same stock archetype, Streeb-Greeblings by a variety of other names. Sir Arthur was the sort of man Peter might have been if he'd joined the Foreign Office, not a million miles away from Harold Macmillan, the prime minister whom Peter parodied in *Beyond the Fringe*. 'My impersonation of Macmillan was in fact extremely affectionate,' said Peter. 'I was a great Macmillan fan.'

And you could tell that Peter was a great fan of Sir Arthur Streeb-Greebling.

Peter knew Sir Arthur inside out, from Radley and Cambridge, and his father's impeccable diplomatic career, and although the things he says are absurd, the way he says them is completely plausible. Sir Arthur is a stranger to his emotions – in that aloof yet amiable way only an English gentleman can be. He's too distracted to be spiteful, too preoccupied with his useless hobbies to indulge in proper healthy human passions, and in this disconnected state, he's capable of absent-minded acts of spectacular cruelty. Sir Arthur is incurably narrow-minded, but although he can be a heartless bastard, at least he's not a hypocrite, and there's something almost heroic in his indifference to the changing world around him.

Sir Arthur speaks in monologues, but men of his age and class are far too self-contained to talk about themselves without concerted prompting, which is where Dudley came in. 'Some disclose information about themselves without knowing they're doing it,' wrote Peter McKay, in a witty and instructive essay on the art of the gossip columnist. 'Aristocrat to diary reporter: "Why are you asking all these questions?" Diary reporter: "This is merely an interview, sir." Aristocrat: "I see. Carry on."'[2]

TAILOR SHOP
(*Not Only . . . But Also . . .* , BBC, 1965)

(*Dudley is a trendy shop assistant in a Swinging Sixties tailors.*)

SIR ARTHUR STREEB-GREEBLING: Good morning. I was recommended to come to you by my son Basil.

DUDLEY: That's very nice, sir.

SIR ARTHUR STREEB-GREEBLING: He's up at Fettes.

DUDLEY: He's where, sir?

SIR ARTHUR STREEB-GREEBLING: He's at Fettes – the Scottish school

– and he suggested I come to you to see you about a suit. I'm going up for his half-term next week, and he thought it might be a good idea if I got a suit that was a trifle more 'gear' than this one. This, he feels, is not quite 'with it'. He thinks it's a little bit, er, without it, and I wondered if you could help me in any way?

DUDLEY: Well, sir, of course, sir, yes, sir. Indeed, you've come to the right place. We do pride ourselves on the fact that we are the only tailors on Savile Row who cater for the hippies.

SIR ARTHUR STREEB-GREEBLING: You have the hippies in here, do you?

DUDLEY: Yes, we get all the ravers in here.

SIR ARTHUR STREEB-GREEBLING: Yes. I noticed one on the way out.

DUDLEY: Yes. Matter of fact, only last week we had the Archbishop of Canterbury in here asking for a pair of topical gaiters.

SIR ARTHUR STREEB-GREEBLING: Really? That is good.

DUDLEY: Have a glass of claret, sir?

SIR ARTHUR STREEB-GREEBLING: That's very civil.

DUDLEY: Not at all.

SIR ARTHUR STREEB-GREEBLING: A disgusting vintage.

DUDLEY: Now I'll tell you what we'll do, sir. To give you that trendy sixty-five look, the first thing we'll do is give you a fourteen-inch bottom.

SIR ARTHUR STREEB-GREEBLING: Er, yes. I think you'll have some difficulty cramming my bottom into fourteen inches. I was with the Camel Corps in the desert and I'm afraid it rather stretched my reserves beyond their natural endowments.

DUDLEY: Yes, well, in fact I was referring to the bottom of your legs, rather than the bottom of your bum.

SIR ARTHUR STREEB-GREEBLING: Oh I see – my ankles in fact.

DUDLEY: Your ankles, sir, yes.

SIR ARTHUR STREEB-GREEBLING: Well, my ankles are a good deal slimmer than my bottom.

DUDLEY: I hope so for your sake. Now, if we have a look here. I think what we'll do, sir, is give you a spot of the Crystals round the lapels, you see – then give you a Beatles tuck in there, a spot

of the Manfred Manns there. Give you a forty-five-inch degree
. . . I mean, a forty-five-degree slant there.

SIR ARTHUR STREEB-GREEBLING: That would be very good. I'd like
a sort of Dave Berry look about the trousers, if you can – a sort
of Tamla Motown excitement about the whole thing.

DUDLEY: Yes. Do you know I had the Stones in here last week, sir?

SIR ARTHUR STREEB-GREEBLING: Really? You're looking very well
now. Now is this the sort of suit one can smoke marijuana in?

DUDLEY: You planning to get stoned out of your mind, are you, sir?

SIR ARTHUR STREEB-GREEBLING: Well, Basil told me it was going
to be a rave . . .

(*Dudley shows Sir Arthur a suit.*)

DUDLEY: I think that's rather nice, sir.

SIR ARTHUR STREEB-GREEBLING: I like it. The only thing that strikes
me is that it is a trifle effeminate.

DUDLEY: Effeminate, sir? Effeminate? I wouldn't say it was effeminate.

SIR ARTHUR STREEB-GREEBLING: I would say it was effeminate, yes.

DUDLEY: I wouldn't say it was effeminate.

SIR ARTHUR STREEB-GREEBLING: I've just said it. It is effeminate.
It is effeminate.

DUDLEY: Well, sir, we had Max Schmeling the boxer in here the
other day, and he went away with a replica of this very suit. And
I wouldn't call him effeminate, would you, sir?

SIR ARTHUR STREEB-GREEBLING: Max Schmeling? No, I wouldn't
call him effeminate. No.

DUDLEY: He's not effeminate, sir. He's never been near a woman
in his life. He wouldn't touch one, you know, sir.

SIR ARTHUR STREEB-GREEBLING: It really worries me, this effeminate thing, because my wife is extremely effeminate, you know.
Ghastly business. I don't know where she picked it up. She sort
of goes flimflamming about the place. It's most depressing.

DUDLEY: Well, we don't want people having difficulty trying to
distinguish between the pair of you, do we?

SIR ARTHUR STREEB-GREEBLING: Certainly not.

DUDLEY: Would you like a vent up the back, sir?

SIR ARTHUR STREEB-GREEBLING: If you have one, yes.

(*Dudley selects another suit.*)

DUDLEY: Now that's rather nice, isn't it?

SIR ARTHUR STREEB-GREEBLING: It's nice colouring, isn't it? I find it a little tight, though.

DUDLEY: Is it really?

SIR ARTHUR STREEB-GREEBLING: It is a little tight. I don't want anything tight, you see, because I want to be able to stuff a couple of birds in my trousers.

DUDLEY: I don't quite follow you, sir, I'm afraid.

SIR ARTHUR STREEB-GREEBLING: I do a lot of shooting and I want to be able to get a couple of snipe in my trouser pockets, you see. These are very voluminous. I can easily get a few birds in here. This, I think, wouldn't be good enough.

DUDLEY: Well, what we could do, of course, is give you a zippable polythene lining in here, sir, in which you could thrust birds until your heart's content.

SIR ARTHUR STREEB-GREEBLING: Yes, I'm allergic to polythene – it brings me out in warts. I think I'll bid a reluctant farewell to this one – much though I like the cloth. If you have something I'd like it with rather large lapels. I need large lapels because I want to be able to get my flies behind my lapels.

DUDLEY: That's stretching it a bit, isn't it, sir? It's a bit of a way to go.

SIR ARTHUR STREEB-GREEBLING: No – not that. I do a bit of fishing – fly fishing – and I like to keep my blue merlins here, you see, for the trout.

(*Sir Arthur picks out another suit.*)

SIR ARTHUR STREEB-GREEBLING: I must say this is rather a pleasant suit, isn't it?

DUDLEY: This is actually very good, sir.

SIR ARTHUR STREEB-GREEBLING: Is this definitely 'pacey'?

DUDLEY: It's very pacey, sir.

SIR ARTHUR STREEB-GREEBLING: I don't want to be laughed at at this function.

DUDLEY: I think it's really rather you.

SIR ARTHUR STREEB-GREEBLING: It seems pleasant enough. Have you got the trousers?

DUDLEY: Which side do you dress?

SIR ARTHUR STREEB-GREEBLING: Nearest the window.

(*Dudley measures him.*)

DUDLEY: Good Lord! You've got an enormous inside leg, sir!

SIR ARTHUR STREEB-GREEBLING: Thank you very much. Have you got a cubicle?

DUDLEY: A cubicle? Certainly, sir.

SIR ARTHUR STREEB-GREEBLING: There's rather a lot of people peering in through the window, and I think I might possibly be observed.

(*Sir Arthur takes the suit into the cubicle.*)

DUDLEY: How are they fitting, sir?

SIR ARTHUR STREEB-GREEBLING: They're not fitting at all yet – I haven't started.

(*Sir Arthur reappears, wearing very tight trousers.*)

SIR ARTHUR STREEB-GREEBLING: They are a little figure-hugging.

DUDLEY: They are what, sir?

SIR ARTHUR STREEB-GREEBLING: A little figure-hugging.

DUDLEY: Well, that's the trend, sir. That's the fashion, you know.

SIR ARTHUR STREEB-GREEBLING: Are 'pacey' people wearing that?

DUDLEY: Most certainly. This is sixty-five gear, sir, you know.

SIR ARTHUR STREEB-GREEBLING: Good. Well, it seems very nice. I think I'll take this one.

DUDLEY: Oh, that's splendid, sir. Look, I'll tell you what. Would you like to wear that suit, and we'll pack your other suit and send it on to you?

SIR ARTHUR STREEB-GREEBLING: Right you are. Send that and the bill to me, would you?

DUDLEY: Certainly.

(*Dudley writes down his details.*)

SIR ARTHUR STREEB-GREEBLING: Sir Arthur Streeb-Greebling.

DUDLEY: Yes.

SIR ARTHUR STREEB-GREEBLING: Flog Hall.

DUDLEY: Flog Hall.

SIR ARTHUR STREEB-GREEBLING: Dumfriesshire.

DUDLEY: New Brunswick.

SIR ARTHUR STREEB-GREEBLING: Thank you very much. Is this the way out over here?

DUDLEY: There is an exit door there certainly. You can get through there.

SIR ARTHUR STREEB-GREEBLING: Thank you very much. This is hard-wearing, isn't it?

DUDLEY: It's very tough wool – yes, sir.

(*Exit Sir Arthur.*)

DUDLEY: Hard wearing? It's practically impossible.

THE FROG & PEACH
(*Not Only . . . But Also . . .*, BBC2, 1966)

DUDLEY: Good evening.

SIR ARTHUR STREEB-GREEBLING: Good evening.

DUDLEY: Good evening.

SIR ARTHUR STREEB-GREEBLING: Good evening.

DUDLEY: Good evening. We're talking this evening to Sir Arthur Greeb-Streebling . . .

SIR ARTHUR STREEB-GREEBLING: Streeb-Greebling.

DUDLEY: Oh, I'm terribly sorry. I thought it was Greeb-Streebling.

SIR ARTHUR STREEB-GREEBLING: No, Streeb-Greebling. You're thinking of Greeb-Streebling. The T is silent, as in Fox. Good evening.

DUDLEY: Good evening.

SIR ARTHUR STREEB-GREEBLING: Good evening.

DUDLEY: Good evening.

SIR ARTHUR STREEB-GREEBLING: Good Greebling.

DUDLEY: We'd like to ask Sir Arthur, actually, about his rather unique restaurant, the Frog & Peach.

SIR ARTHUR STREEB-GREEBLING: Good evening.

DUDLEY: Good evening. If you would tell us something about it, Sir Arthur.

SIR ARTHUR STREEB-GREEBLING: Yes, well, the idea for the Frog & Peach came to me in the bath. A great number of things come to me in the bath, mainly sort of mosquitoes and adders, but in this case a rather stupendous idea. I suddenly thought, as I was scrubbing my back with a loofah, I thought where can a young couple who are having an evening out, not too much money, and they want to have a decent meal, you know, a decent frog and a nice bit of peach, where can they go? Where can they go and get it? And answer came there none. And so I had this idea of starting a restaurant specialising in these frogs' legs and peaches, and on this premise I built this restaurant.

DUDLEY: In these premises, in fact?

SIR ARTHUR STREEB-GREEBLING: These precise premises, yes – these very ones you see around you. Good evening.

DUDLEY: Good evening. How long ago did you start this venture? Was it recently?

SIR ARTHUR STREEB-GREEBLING: Certainly, it was certainly within living memory. Shortly after the First World War.

DUDLEY: Ghastly business, wasn't it?

SIR ARTHUR STREEB-GREEBLING: Oh, absolutely ghastly business. And I started it shortly after that, and ever since then it's sort of been here, you know. Hereabouts, in any case.

DUDLEY: And how has business been?

SIR ARTHUR STREEB-GREEBLING: Well, er, business hasn't been, in the strict sense of the word. Rather, let me answer that question in two parts. There hasn't been any business, and nobody's been. It's been a quiet time, these last fifteen to eighteen years – a quiet time for us, really, in the business.

DUDLEY: But don't you feel that in a way you're at some disadvantage being stuck out in the middle of Dartmoor here?

SIR ARTHUR STREEB-GREEBLING: I think the word disadvantage is awfully well chosen there, yes. This is what we're at. We're at a disadvantage. You see, when I had the idea, I weighed up the pros and cons, and I came to the conclusion, rightly or wrongly, or possibly both –

DUDLEY: Or neither.

SIR ARTHUR STREEB-GREEBLING: Or neither, or neither, as they say in some parts of the country.

DUDLEY: Or Cointreau.

SIR ARTHUR STREEB-GREEBLING: Indeed. I thought that the pros outweighed the cons by about two and a half ounces. And I thought the people in Britain were crying out for a restaurant where there wasn't any parking problem. In fact, I heard somebody in the street, crying out for a restaurant without a parking problem. A Norwegian sailor, I believe, on leave. He was saying, 'Oh, for a restaurant without a parking problem!' And this sort of inspired me to start this one. There's no parking problem here, situated, as we are, in the middle of a bog in the heart of Dartmoor. No difficulty parking – some difficulty extricating your car, but otherwise well situated. Good evening.

DUDLEY: Good evening. Don't you feel, again, you're at a disadvantage, because of your menu? I mean –

SIR ARTHUR STREEB-GREEBLING: The menu? Oh dear! Yes, this has been a terrible hindrance to us, building up a business. The menu is the most . . . have you seen it?

DUDLEY: Well, I have, yes.

SIR ARTHUR STREEB-GREEBLING: It's the most appalling thing. There's so little to choose from. You start with – what's that?

DUDLEY (*reading the menu*): Spawn cocktail.

SIR ARTHUR STREEB-GREEBLING: Spawn cocktail – probably the most revolting dish that's known to man. Then there's only two other dishes, really. There's frog à la peche, which is frog done in Cointreau, and with a peach stuffed in its mouth. And then of course there's peche à la frog, which is really not much to write home about. A waiter comes to your table, he's got this huge peach, which is covered in boiling liqueur, you see, and then he slices it open to reveal about two thousand little black tadpoles. It's one of the most disgusting sights I've ever seen. It turns me over to think of it, poor little creatures.

DUDLEY: It is rather nauseating.

SIR ARTHUR STREEB-GREEBLING: Squiggle, squiggle they go.

DUDLEY: Who does the cooking?

SIR ARTHUR STREEB-GREEBLING: My wife does the cooking, and luckily she does the eating as well. An amazing creature. Of course, she's not a well woman, not a well woman at all, and so she very much resents having to go down the well every morning to swoop on the toads. An amazing creature, my wife, an amazing creature. I met her during the War, actually.

DUDLEY: You did?

SIR ARTHUR STREEB-GREEBLING: Yes, she blew in through the drawing-room window with a bit of shrapnel, became embedded in the sofa, and, you know, one thing led to her mother, and we were married in the hour.

DUDLEY: I suppose, actually –

SIR ARTHUR STREEB-GREEBLING: Would you like some pond water?

DUDLEY: No, I won't.

SIR ARTHUR STREEB-GREEBLING: It's two shillings.

DUDLEY: No.

SIR ARTHUR STREEB-GREEBLING: It is revolting stuff. I wouldn't touch it.

DUDLEY: No . . . um . . .

(*Dudley is lost for words.*)

SIR ARTHUR STREEB-GREEBLING: Good evening.

DUDLEY: Good evening.

SIR ARTHUR STREEB-GREEBLING: What are you about to ask me about?

DUDLEY: I'm about to ask you . . . I suppose this sort of menu could in fact appeal to the French.

SIR ARTHUR STREEB-GREEBLING: It could appeal to the French and I've tried appealing to the French over Radio Streeb-Greebling which, as you know, is situated in the moat, not a stone's throw from here, but the response has been . . . Oh, it's not been excessive. Nil, I think, would be the word.

DUDLEY: Well, it all sounds rather disastrous.

SIR ARTHUR STREEB-GREEBLING: Disastrous. Catastrophic, I think, would be a better word, really, for it.

DUDLEY: Do you have any other plans for other business ventures?

SIR ARTHUR STREEB-GREEBLING: Yes and no. I thought of starting a sort of sophisticated restaurant, with kind of sophisticated music, somewhere up in Peeblesshire. Somewhere where a young couple who are out for the evening, you see, who've got about eighty-five guineas to spend, could have a really decent meal.

DUDLEY: What are you going to call it?

SIR ARTHUR STREEB-GREEBLING: The Vole & Pea.

DUDLEY: What sort of food?

SIR ARTHUR STREEB-GREEBLING: Well, I was thinking largely simple English roast vole, you know, and a decent British pea. Get the two together and I think you're on pretty good ground.

DUDLEY: Yes, indeed. Do you feel you've learned by your mistakes here?

SIR ARTHUR STREEB-GREEBLING: I think I have, yes, and I think I could probably repeat them, almost perfectly. I know my mistakes inside out.

DUDLEY: I'm sure you will repeat them. Well, thank you very much, Sir Arthur.

SIR ARTHUR STREEB-GREEBLING: Thank you very much.

DUDLEY: And goodnight.

SIR ARTHUR STREEB-GREEBLING: Would you like one for the toad?

DUDLEY: No thank you.

THE FUNNEL-WEB SPIDER
(Australian Broadcasting Commission, 1971)

DUDLEY: Good evening. I'm talking once again with Sir Arthur Greeb-Streebling.

SIR ARTHUR STREEB-GREEBLING: Good evening.

DUDLEY: If you recall, Sir Arthur, seven years ago I was interviewing you about your project to get ravens to fly underwater.

SIR ARTHUR STREEB-GREEBLING: Yes.

DUDLEY: Did you have any luck with this?

SIR ARTHUR STREEB-GREEBLING: No, I didn't really have very much luck or success. In fact, I'd say total failure with a capital F as a result of it.

DUDLEY: Well, I'm amazed at that, because –

SIR ARTHUR STREEB-GREEBLING: No, you shouldn't be amazed at it, because the project never really got off the ground. Never got off the ground at all. The ravens never got out of the water so I jacked it in after fifty-three years. I wouldn't go on for ever.

DUDLEY: Sir Arthur, what is the porpoise of your visit to Australia?

SIR ARTHUR STREEB-GREEBLING: There is no porpoise involved in my visit to Australia. I've never got involved with a porpoise. One of my strictest rules – never get involved with a porpoise. Whatever you may have read in the sensational tabloids, I have never become involved with a porpoise. What I think is happening is you're misreading the word 'purpose'.

DUDLEY: Oh yes.

SIR ARTHUR STREEB-GREEBLING: You see, the word 'purpose', is a totally different kettle of fish, although of course, ironically enough, the porpoise is a mammal. It suckles its young.

DUDLEY: Like a whale.

SIR ARTHUR STREEB-GREEBLING: Yes, I'd love a whale. Have you got one on you? Have you got one about your person? Must be a very tiny whale if you've got one on you. Big things, whales – big things.

DUDLEY: Might be able to pick up a killer whale in the loo afterwards, or something. Anyway, back to the visit, Sir Arthur. What is the purpose of it?

SIR ARTHUR STREEB-GREEBLING: Well, after fifty-three years of unsuccessfully trying to get ravens to fly underwater and finding that, basically, my ravens were chicken, I decided to seek pastures new and come over to a country with fresh opportunities, and the fact that I owed £58,000 to the Midland Bank, Lyme Regis, had nothing to do with my decision to creep away in a small rowing boat with muffled oars. I'm over here, I may say, with the full support of the Australian government, Mrs Ethel Nibbs, 31 Bent Street, Sydney.

DUDLEY: Mrs Ethel Nibbs is the Australian government?

SIR ARTHUR STREEB-GREEBLING: So she tells me and I've got no reason to disbelieve her. She's a very charming woman, gives you a wonderful breakfast, a wonderful fruit compote of fresh fruit and lovely prunes and, this isn't going to be a long interview, is it? Have you got another question?

DUDLEY: Yes, if we could get off your compote for a moment, Sir Arthur, what does your project entail?

SIR ARTHUR STREEB-GREEBLING: Well, I don't know if you've ever heard of a little chappie called the funnel-web spider?

DUDLEY: A very tricky customer.

SIR ARTHUR STREEB-GREEBLING: He is a tricky customer, nasty little beast, and has the unfortunate habit of going around biting people. I don't know where he gets the habit from, probably his mother or his father. Anyway, he picked it up from somewhere. He goes around biting people on the land. So you see, the land is not a safe place for Australians to be because of this funnel-web spider. Nor, unfortunately, is the sea a particularly safe place to be, because of the other things that swim around in there. Have you seen them? With their mouths at the bottom of their stomachs – what are they called?

DUDLEY: Oh, sharks.

SIR ARTHUR STREEB-GREEBLING: Sharks. Yes. Sharks. And they have the same nasty habit of going around biting people. So the Australian is neither safe on the land nor in the sea.

DUDLEY: In fact, you could summarise by saying that the Australian is only really safe in the air.

SIR ARTHUR STREEB-GREEBLING: Yes. That is the only safe place for an Australian to be. And of course the Australian, like anybody else, is unable to stay in the air for more than about half a second.

DUDLEY: What do you propose to do with this creature?

SIR ARTHUR STREEB-GREEBLING: I am attempting to train the funnel-web to swim.

DUDLEY: I see.

SIR ARTHUR STREEB-GREEBLING: If I can get the funnel-web spider to swim, I think we'll be halfway there.

DUDLEY: I think you're halfway there already.

SIR ARTHUR STREEB-GREEBLING: That's very kind of you to say so. Thank you very much.

DUDLEY: How do you propose to teach these creatures to swim?

SIR ARTHUR STREEB-GREEBLING: Oh, I've already started. Wasted no time at all. What I do is, I get these tiny water wings. They're made in Japan – really superb, the Japanese, at miniaturisation. Get these water wings, shove them on their legs and bung them in the bath.

DUDLEY: And then what happens?

SIR ARTHUR STREEB-GREEBLING: Absolutely nothing – unless, of course, you happen to jump in the bath, and then, of course, all hell breaks loose.

DUDLEY: Does the spider float?

SIR ARTHUR STREEB-GREEBLING: Oh yes, they float all right. They go around in circles, having eight legs flailing away with these little water wings on them. They go round in circles, then remain very stationary. They're like horrible little hairy helicopters whirling round and round. Not a pretty sight.

DUDLEY: No. You know, I don't really see what you're driving at at all here.

SIR ARTHUR STREEB-GREEBLING: You don't see what I'm driving at? My dear good fellow, look, if I can induce the funnel-webs to enjoy a swim, they may take to the sea, and then we can attach little winking lights to the top of their heads so we know where the devils are. Then the sharks, the other menace to the Australians, will come up, bite the funnel-webs, and then we kill two birds with one stone.

DUDLEY: But what makes you think the sharks will be attracted to the funnel-web?

SIR ARTHUR STREEB-GREEBLING: It is a problem, isn't it? They're not very attractive creatures.

DUDLEY: Well, couldn't you use some sort of bait?

SIR ARTHUR STREEB-GREEBLING: Would you be willing?

DUDLEY: Probably on Sundays.

SIR ARTHUR STREEB-GREEBLING: No, I was actually working on the theory that sharks are extremely attracted to some forms of after-shave lotion.

DUDLEY: Do you have any reason to believe that this is the case?

SIR ARTHUR STREEB-GREEBLING: No reason at all, no. I'm working entirely on instinct. Archimedes discovered gravity by leaping in the bath when an apple fell on his head. You may remember that? Pure instinct.

DUDLEY: Sir Arthur, a personal thing here –

SIR ARTHUR STREEB-GREEBLING: Where?

DUDLEY: I notice you're wearing gloves.

SIR ARTHUR STREEB-GREEBLING: Yes, I'm wearing gloves. Can't you see the reason why? I'm dealing with a terribly dangerous animal, which might bite me. Therefore I wear these gloves for protection.

DUDLEY: But Sir Arthur, you seem to be rather scantily clad about the rest of your person. I mean, doesn't it occur to you that a funnel-web might nip you on the knee or something?

SIR ARTHUR STREEB-GREEBLING: Do you think they would?

DUDLEY: Yes.

SIR ARTHUR STREEB-GREEBLING: What? Bite you on the knee? Dirty little beasts! Yes, that's a very good thought indeed, isn't it? Yes, I think when I get back home I'll ask Mrs Nibbs to give me a damn good wellington boot. That should obviate the problem. I think she'll come across with a couple of wellies. She's always been mentioning it ever since I've been here. As I was saying, being bitten to death by a spider is the last thing I want.

DUDLEY: It's the last thing you'd get, Sir Arthur.

SIR ARTHUR STREEB-GREEBLING: You're very astute. Would you like to join me on the project?

DUDLEY: I'd love to, yes. That seems to be a very convenient moment for us to slice this programme, to bring it to a halt. So, good luck with the project, Sir Arthur, and thank you.

SIR ARTHUR STREEB-GREEBLING: Thank you very much. I think it's doomed to success.

TERMINATED INTERVIEW
(Australian Broadcasting Commission, 1971)

DUDLEY (*to camera*): Sir Arthur is, of course, President of the World Domination League. (*To Sir Arthur, perfectly friendly, almost ingratiating.*) Sir Arthur, I wonder if I could begin by asking you whether you –

SIR ARTHUR STREEB-GREEBLING: No! Certainly not! Certainly not! I dislike the whole tone of the question and the aggressive way it was phrased!

DUDLEY (*perplexed*): Sir, I hadn't really begun –

SIR ARTHUR STREEB-GREEBLING: You hadn't really begun? You'd begun quite far enough for me, thank you! You can't bully and hector me, you know, like a lot of people you've tried to do it to! No thank you very much! Rephrase the question immediately!

DUDLEY (*tongue-tied*): Er . . .

SIR ARTHUR STREEB-GREEBLING: Come along! Rephrase it! That was no good at all!

DUDLEY (*apologetic*): Well, I'll try again. Sir Arthur, I wonder if –

SIR ARTHUR STREEB-GREEBLING: That's no better! That's no better! The same manner! The same tone of voice! The same sort of sneering undertones in your voice! Oh, I recognise it! I recognise that! I recognise that horrible sneering undertone! You try to undermine political figures like me!

DUDLEY: Not at all. I wasn't being at all impolite.

SIR ARTHUR STREEB-GREEBLING: I think we've gone into this question quite deeply enough! I've answered it fully, you've been very aggressive, you've bullied me and you've been extraordinarily rude, and I would ask you to apologise!

DUDLEY: Well, if you've been offended then I apologise.

SIR ARTHUR STREEB-GREEBLING: Thank God for that. Is that a camera?

DUDLEY: Yes it is.

SIR ARTHUR STREEB-GREEBLING: Is that a camera? Horrible little red light on it, peering at me?

DUDLEY: Yes.

SIR ARTHUR STREEB-GREEBLING: That's a camera, isn't it? You promised me that this was completely off the record! No cameras, no film! Will you get the film out of that camera and give it to me at once!

DUDLEY: There's no film in the camera, Sir Arthur.

SIR ARTHUR STREEB-GREEBLING: Are you refusing to give me the film out of that camera?

DUDLEY: No, of course I'm not.

SIR ARTHUR STREEB-GREEBLING: I realise what you people do with those films! You edit them, you cut them about, you change them round so that decent people, decent political figures such as myself, become ridiculous! I know what you do with film! Are you refusing to give me the film?

DUDLEY: I'm not refusing to give you the film.

SIR ARTHUR STREEB-GREEBLING: You're refusing to give me the film!

DUDLEY: There is no film.

SIR ARTHUR STREEB-GREEBLING: There is no film? I see, another cheap lie! You don't have to tell me where you come from! Yes, I know your political allegiance all right! All that long hair, poofy boots – Communist, homosexual, if ever I saw one!

DUDLEY: Would you like to come back to my place?

SIR ARTHUR STREEB-GREEBLING: No, I am not coming back anywhere! I am leaving here now! I have friends in influential places, and you won't be sitting on this seat tomorrow! You'll have another job, or rather you won't have any job at all!

(*Exit Sir Arthur, fuming.*)

DUDLEY (*to camera, bashful*): Good evening. We did have Sir Arthur Streeb-Greebling in the studio tonight, but he declined to appear –

(*Enter Sir Arthur, still fuming.*)

SIR ARTHUR STREEB-GREEBLING: Are you continuing with this ridiculous performance? I told you to stop the film! Stop all those people cranking round the film!

DUDLEY: I'm just rehearsing for tomorrow night.

SIR ARTHUR STREEB-GREEBLING: You're rehearsing for tomorrow night? You won't be here tomorrow night – let me tell you that much! Now then, I'll be listening to every word you say!

(*Exit Sir Arthur, fuming.*)

DUDLEY (*to camera*): Sir Arthur declined to appear, and so I hand you back to Bill Peach. Thank you very much indeed.

(*Enter Sir Arthur, still fuming.*)

SIR ARTHUR STREEB-GREEBLING: Bill Peach? He's worse! He's worse! I've heard of that Bill Peach!

DUDLEY: He can't be worse.

SIR ARTHUR STREEB-GREEBLING: Where is he?

DUDLEY: I don't know.

SIR ARTHUR STREEB-GREEBLING: I'll find him. Peach! Where are you?

(*Exit Sir Arthur.*)

DUDLEY (*to camera*): I'm so terribly sorry. I've been awfully aggressive. I apologise.

(*Dudley bursts into tears.*)

(*Enter Sir Arthur. Sir Arthur comforts him.*)

DUDLEY: Thank you, Sir Arthur.

SIR ARTHUR: That's all right. Come back to my place.

(*They exit together, arm in arm.*)

Chapter Nine

Goodbye-ee

Peter and Dudley died seven years and several thousand miles apart. Peter died in London in January 1995, aged fifty-seven, of a gastro-intestinal haemorrhage. Apart from a few brief turns, it was more than fifteen years since he'd last worked with Dudley, and almost twenty since they'd last worked together on anything of any note. Peter's solo career was casual and leisurely. He had no further ambitions, other than to enjoy himself. He only worked when he felt like it, or when he felt he needed to. One of the titles of the autobiography that he never got around to writing was *Retired and Emotional.* Another was *Can I Go Now?.* Yet in the last few years of his life, he produced some of the finest comedy of his career, with Clive Anderson on Channel 4, and with Chris Morris on Radio 3 in *Why Bother?.* His final outing as Sir Arthur Streeb-Greebling was just as good as his first one, nearly thirty years before.

Peter never stopped being funny, but he became increasingly bored of being funny in public, in front of anonymous paying punters, rather than in private, for the benefit of half a dozen friends. 'I don't much enjoy being on television,' he said, in his last ever interview, less than two months before he died. 'I'd rather do it for a few people socially, but it would be a bit rude to take up a collection after dinner.'[1] He confirmed his lasting affection for Dudley, and looked back on *Not Only . . . But Also . . .* as the happiest time of his career. 'That was perfect,' he said, fondly. 'I can't imagine a comedy relationship being better. I adore Dudley. I would have been very happy for it to continue.'[2]

Peter found some peace in his final years with his last wife, Lin, who helped repair his friendship (though not his professional partnership) with Dudley. When Peter died, Dudley was the first person Lin called. 'Dudley was the person Peter loved the most, but I think in the earlier years Dudley didn't realise how much Peter felt for him,' said Lin, soon after Peter's death. 'Both of them had difficulty in expressing their love, and it was only in later years that Peter felt more able to express his emotions.'[3] 'I'm a big softy,' confirmed Peter, in his final, tearful interview. 'I've curbed my tongue a bit. I don't like unpleasantness about other people. I get no pleasure out of other people's alleged failure, and comics are probably as bad as anyone else in the envy game. I've just got slightly nicer. Awful, isn't it?'[4]

Dudley died in New Jersey in March 2002, aged sixty-six, from pneumonia brought on by progressive supranuclear palsy. It was an especially cruel disease for a man who'd been famous for his nimble fingers and his nimble mind. His Hollywood career peaked soon after he split with Peter, and by the time Peter died, it was virtually over. He never repeated the triumph of '10' or *Arthur*, although he did score a notable stage success in 1988 with Los Angeles Opera in *The Mikado*, directed by his old friend from *Beyond the Fringe*, Jonathan Miller. The *LA Times* said he flirted shamelessly with the audience, but as Dudley might have said, what's so bad about a bit of flirting between old friends? 'A comedian of the first order,' said *Variety*, who'd been so blunt about *The Hound of the Baskervilles*. 'A brilliant performance,' concurred Miller. 'There are moments when it takes my breath away.'

As Dudley's film career waned, he revived his first love, classical music, and his melodic renaissance really blossomed after he met fellow pianist and former child prodigy Rena Fruchter. With Rena's empathic help, and the support of her husband, Brian Dallow, Dudley finally became the virtuoso he surely always would have been, if comedy hadn't intervened. In 1994, he played Grieg's Piano Concerto in A minor at Carnegie Hall, to raise funds for Rena and Brian's charity, Music For All Seasons. In 1995, this concerto became his first classical CD. Yet by now Dudley was having problems with memory and coordination, and in September 1999 he revealed he was suffering from a rare syndrome related to Parkinson's disease. In November 2002, when he went to Buckingham Palace to collect his CBE, he was already in a wheelchair. He died a few months later, in New Jersey, in the bosom of Rena's family.

Dudley ended his career as he had begun it, as a musician not a comedian. But what other musician could also claim a half-share in the funniest double act in the history of British television, and one of the smartest and most successful two-man shows ever to tour the United States? Not since Stan Laurel has Hollywood inherited such a perfect comic talent. But Stan Laurel found his comic soulmate in America. Dudley Moore left his back in Britain.

THE TOWER OF LONDON
(*To the Queen! A Salute to Elizabeth II*, ABC, 1977)

Fans of Derek and Clive tend to regard Peter and Dudley as anarchic figures, but bad language and bad behaviour was only one side of their story. True, their attitude to sex and drugs was refreshingly relaxed, yet their lifestyle wasn't entirely rock and roll. For all their loose talk and fast living, it would be ridiculous to pretend that everything they ever did was radical or even innovative. In 1977, as the Sex Pistols provoked establishment outrage with their punk version of 'God Save the Queen', Peter and Dudley appeared in this American Silver Jubilee tribute, entitled To The Queen! A Salute to Elizabeth II. In fact, their contribution wasn't nearly so sycophantic as this title suggests, but it was hardly 'Anarchy in the UK', either.

PETER: Yes, you know this is the first time I've ever seen the Tower of London in the flesh, so to speak.

DUDLEY: Yes, me too. It's amazing how you spend your entire life in your own city and you never see the historical monuments, do you?

PETER: You never see the greatness around you?

DUDLEY: Yes, certainly.

PETER: I think the only time I've seen it before, actually, was on that, er . . . what was that programme? *Starsky and Hutch*, I think.

DUDLEY: Oh yes, I remember. Yes, yes. It was very beautifully lit.

PETER: Beautifully lit. The Americans like things beautifully lit.

DUDLEY: Absolutely.

PETER: It was one of David Soul's clues, I think.

DUDLEY: I think he wrestled the Tower to the ground, or something.

PETER: That's right – marvellous scene.

DUDLEY: Good Lord!

PETER: What?

DUDLEY: Over there is a pigeon. Must have come from the North Sea. It's covered in oil.

PETER: No, no. That's not a pigeon. That's a raven.

DUDLEY: Oh, one of the legendary ravens of the Tower.

PETER: That's right.

DUDLEY: Yes, I remember the legend. If the ravens leave the Tower, the Queen flies to Capristano.

PETER: And Prince Philip goes to Greece.

DUDLEY: Yes, wonderful show that, wasn't it?

PETER: Beautiful. Lovely foot-stomping music. Or will he go to pieces?

DUDLEY: Probably a bit of both.

PETER: Bit of both.

DUDLEY: See that chap down there?

PETER: What?

DUDLEY: Looks like he's in fancy dress.

PETER: No, that's not fancy dress. That's one of the official yeomen

– the Yeomen of the Guard. They wear these peculiar red knickers and clothing and things to attract the ravens, to keep them at the Tower.

DUDLEY: The same principle as red rag to a bull.

PETER: Red flags at sunset, yes.

DUDLEY: Red knickers to the ravens, yes. Must cost an enormous amount of money to keep these yeomen and ravens and things.

PETER: Well, the entire Royal Family come out of our pocket.

DUDLEY: They do, yes.

PETER: And the Queen has an enormous retinue.

DUDLEY: Yes, but she conceals it very well. You never see it, do you?

PETER: She hides it. She hides it beautifully. But in these days of inflation, I mean – let's think of a round figure . . .

DUDLEY: The Queen Mother?

PETER: Yes, she'll do. What do you reckon the Queen is worth, so to speak?

DUDLEY: Oh, I think in these days of inflation, as you say, I think the Queen isn't worth the paper she's written on.

PETER: I don't think she is.

DUDLEY: Frankly.

PETER: I tell you, the ultimate security measure they take here is this raven. The yeoman, every morning, glues him to this position, you see.

DUDLEY: Ah.

PETER: So he can't fly away.

DUDLEY: I see. The idea, I suppose, is if the rest of the flock fly off, this little chap's left here to guard the British Empire.

PETER: Absolutely. Yes.

DUDLEY: And the Queen doesn't have to fly to Capristano.

PETER: No, I have to, though. Could you possibly give me a lift?

DUDLEY: Give you a lift in the old banger.

PETER: Yes. Shall we go the same way?

MADAME TUSSAUD'S
(*To The Queen! A Salute To Elizabeth II*, ABC, 1977)

PETER: You've been standing there for four hours and I'm afraid you're still not taller than Princess Margaret.

DUDLEY: Oh really? How very disappointing.

PETER: Nope. You're not.

DUDLEY: I thought I'd be taller than at least one member of the Royal Family.

PETER: Well, you might be taller than Antony Armstrong-Jones, but of course he's been melted down and recycled since the separation.

DUDLEY: I gather he's become part of Margaret Thatcher's tie.

PETER: That's right. A very nice place to be. Yes, a super place to be.

DUDLEY: I must say I do feel the whole idea of Madame Tussaud's, for these wax effigies, is really super.

PETER: Tremendous. She deserves a round of applause, I think.

DUDLEY: I think the Queen must be especially grateful for it because, you know, being so busy she can bung one of these wax effigies –

PETER: In the coach –

DUDLEY: When she can't get round to doing something. Frightfully useful.

PETER: So she just bungs out an effigy.

DUDLEY: Yes.

PETER: One thing that puzzles me. Perhaps you know the answer. You know that radiant smile she has? The only that she uses to win the hearts and minds of people?

DUDLEY: Right.

PETER: How do they get that on an effigy?

DUDLEY: Oh, they do that electronically from the Palace.

PETER: Oh, laser beams.

DUDLEY: Yes, so what you're seeing is really happening twenty years ago.

PETER: Oh, I understand.

DUDLEY: Ingenious device.

PETER: The coach, I suppose, has to be air conditioned.

DUDLEY: Naturally, otherwise the wax melts down to a disagreeable mess.

PETER: Yes. You can't have the Queen flopping in the carriage, can you?

DUDLEY: Floating on the bottom of the coach. It hasn't got the same effect.

PETER: No. And Prince Charles. He's air conditioned as well, isn't he?

DUDLEY: Of course. Being the heir apparent, he has to be.

PETER: Air conditioned to be the heir. Heir today gone tomorrow, as they say.

DUDLEY: Yes. They've got enormous security, as you can see here.

PETER: Oh, those ropes – they're really strong security, aren't they?

DUDLEY: Well, you know, otherwise any Tom, Dick or Harry could climb over and stick a pin in the Queen's effigy. Marvellous attention to detail, isn't it?

PETER: Absolutely superb, yes.

DUDLEY: Rather a lot of wax in the ears, though.

(*Peter and Dudley each inspect one ear.*)

PETER: Can you see me?

DUDLEY: Oh, yes. Hello.

PETER: How are you?

DUDLEY: I'm fine. Are you?

PETER: Well, not too bad. Well, this explains a lot of things, doesn't it?

DUDLEY: Certainly does.

PETER: Well, I'll see you again sometime.

DUDLEY: Yes, same time next year.

HORSE GUARDS PARADE
(*To The Queen! A Salute To Elizabeth II*, ABC, 1977)

PETER: Well, it's a beautiful day, isn't it?

DUDLEY: It's absolutely wonderful.

PETER: Absolutely beautiful day.

DUDLEY: What time does the Queen actually clop by for the Trooping of the Colour?

PETER: The actual Trooping of the Colour? Well, nobody knows that because that's kept a secret for security reasons.

DUDLEY: Oh I see.

PETER: The route and the time.

DUDLEY: That's very wise.

PETER: In fact, they don't tell the Queen.

DUDLEY: Really?

PETER: No, they blindfold her and spin her round four times and put her on a horse sideways. Then they take the blindfold off, cos she'd look a bit stupid with her wandering about with a blindfold on.

DUDLEY: Yes, you like to see the eyes, don't you?

PETER: You like to see the eyes, yes.

DUDLEY: I don't like the blindfolds at all myself.

PETER: No.

DUDLEY: I must say I think England is looking awfully jolly with the Jubilee decorations, don't you?

PETER: Tremendous sort of atmosphere. It's almost like the War, isn't it? Tremendously jolly.

DUDLEY: A few bombs dropping and we could really celebrate.

PETER: I'm very fond of this Jubilee soap. Have you seen it? With the Queen's face on it?

DUDLEY: I've heard about it, yes – awfully good.

PETER: No matter how small the soap gets, her face goes on smiling, you know.

DUDLEY: Isn't that wonderful? It's all that work.

PETER: I wouldn't use the Queen under my arms.

DUDLEY: No. I suppose that would be a bit . . .

PETER: Dodgy. The police came round the house yesterday, saying I'd been using Prince Philip in an unauthorised zone.

DUDLEY: Really? Well, I don't suppose he'd mind. He's a very sort of . . .

PETER: Bluff character – awfully bluff character.

DUDLEY: Did the police nick you for it?

PETER: No. I was lucky. I gave them a million pounds and they told me not to do it again.

DUDLEY: Fair enough, fair enough. I was very lucky. I got one of those inflatable Queen dolls.

PETER: The Queens you blow up?

DUDLEY: Yes.

PETER: Tremendous.

DUDLEY: Damn good value.

PETER: Is she operational? I mean, does she wave?

DUDLEY: Yes. You get the arms up like this, you see. You let a little air out of her left leg and the arm drops like that and gives you a wave.

PETER: Tremendous. So when you need her, you just blow her up and –

DUDLEY: When you don't, you just deflate her, put her in your handbag, take her to a party or whatever – very good.

PETER: You were going to get something for your mother's birthday, weren't you?

DUDLEY: Gosh, I nearly forgot! Thanks awfully, yes.

PETER: What are you going to get?

DUDLEY: Well, I don't know. I must get something without a picture of the Queen on, because she's allergic to the Queen, I'm afraid.

PETER: She's allergic to the Queen?

DUDLEY: Yes, well, my father ran off with the winner of a Queen lookalike contest many years ago.

PETER: Oh, yes. I remember that.

DUDLEY: And Mother's been very dicky about it ever since.

PETER: Has she written to the authorities?

DUDLEY: No. Well, every time she puts a stamp on a letter, she sees the Queen looking up at her, and immediately –

PETER: Another violent attack. Yes. Well, everything's got the Queen on now, as far as I can see.

DUDLEY: Everything's got the Queen on. You're quite right.

ONE LEG TOO FEW

(*The Secret Policeman's Biggest Ball*, Cambridge Theatre,
London, 1989)

*Cook and Moore's most famous sketch, about a one-legged man called
Spiggott auditioning for the role of Tarzan, was one of the first sketches
Peter wrote, when he was just eighteen. Its first real airing was in 1960
in an undergraduate revue at Pembroke, Peter's Cambridge college, and
it reached a wider audience later that year when Cook performed it
in his celebrated Cambridge Footlights revue,* Pop Goes Mrs Jessop,
*directed by John Fortune, of Bird and Fortune fame. A year later, it
cropped up again in Kenneth Williams' 1961 West End revue,* One
Over the Eight. *Yet although the writing was all Peter's, it didn't
become an outright classic until Dudley came along. The BBC turned
it down, and of all Peter's sketches in* One Over the Eight, *Williams
actually liked it least of all. So what did Dudley do to turn this mixed
reception into universal acclaim?*

*'One Leg Too Few' is a joke about English good manners – a man
so polite, he can barely bring himself to tell a cripple he'd be miscast
as the most agile man on earth – but even the daftest jokes require
their own internal logic, and Williams' sardonic playing style was the
complete opposite of what the part of Spiggott required. The joke only
really works if Spiggott is likeable and vulnerable – two qualities that
Dudley could play better than any other actor. Dudley's indefatigably
eager portrayal provided the perfect contrast to Peter's languid reserve,
and Cook found his cruel quips were far funnier if the audience felt
some compassion for their hapless target. Dudley's talent for inspiring
sympathy was practically unsurpassed – and so this sketch became the
basic template for all their best routines.*

*There was also a potent subtext to Dudley's inspired casting, albeit
purely accidental. Cook had actually been inspired to write 'One Leg
Too Few' by his Cambridge friend Peter Bellwood. Bellwood was standing on one leg, Cook began ad libbing, and a great sketch was born.
It was ironic that Bellwood's one-legged role was later adopted by a
man with a club foot. The sketch clearly struck a resonant chord in
Peter, too. He appropriated the name of Dudley's character, Spiggott,*

when he played the Devil in Bedazzled, *and signed his letters to Dudley with the same name.*

Dudley said 'One Leg Too Few' was the funniest sketch they did together, Jonathan Miller called it one of the most masterly humorous sketches of the twentieth century, and more than thirty years later, in 1993, barely a year before his death, Peter still insisted he'd never written anything better. He was right. In the sixties, they performed it on Broadway, in Beyond the Fringe, *and before the Queen, in ITV's Royal Gala Show. In the seventies, they took it back to America in their two-man stage show,* Good Evening. *Unfortunately, it ended up in* The Hound of the Baskervilles, *their dire Sherlock Holmes parody, but thankfully this disastrous movie wasn't its last resting place. They did it again for American Comic Relief in Los Angeles in 1987, and finally for this Amnesty International fund-raiser in 1989, in the theatre where they'd performed* Behind the Fridge. *It was the last time they appeared onstage together.*

(*Peter is alone onstage. Enter Dudley, hopping.*)

PETER: Mr Spiggott, is it not?

DUDLEY: Yes, Spiggott by name, Spiggott by nature.

PETER: Wonderful. Settle down. Mr Spiggott, you are auditioning, are you not, for the role of Tarzan.

DUDLEY: Yeah, right.

PETER: Mr Spiggott, I couldn't help noticing, almost immediately, that you are a one-legged man.

DUDLEY: Oh, you noticed that.

PETER: When you've been in the business as long I have, Mr Spiggott, you get to notice these little things almost instinctively.

DUDLEY: Yeah, well, you're bound to, aren't you?

PETER: Yes, you're bound to. Now, Mr Spiggott, you – a one-legged man – are applying for the role of Tarzan, a role traditionally associated with a two-legged artiste.

DUDLEY: Er, yes.

PETER: And yet you, a unidexter, are applying for the role.

DUDLEY: Yes, that's right, yes.

PETER: A role for which two legs would seem to be the minimum requirement. Well, Mr Spiggott, need I point out to you, with undue emphasis, where your deficiency lies, as regards landing the role?

DUDLEY: Yes, yes, I think you ought to.

PETER: Perhaps I ought. Yes, perhaps I ought. Need I say with too much stress that it is in the leg division that you are deficient.

DUDLEY: Oh, the leg division?

PETER: The leg division, Mr Spiggott. You are deficient in the leg division to the tune of one. Your right leg, I like. It's a lovely leg for the role. As soon as I saw it come in I said, 'Hello! What a lovely leg for the role!' I've got nothing against your right leg. The trouble is, neither have you. You fall down on the left.

DUDLEY: You mean it's inadequate?

PETER: It is inadequate, Mr Spiggott. And in my view, the public is not yet ready for the sight of a one-legged Tarzan swinging through the jungly tendrils, shouting, 'Hello, Jane.' However great the charm of the performer be, they are not ready for it. Mind you, you score over a man with no legs at all. If a legless man came in here demanding the role, I'd have no hesitation in saying, 'Go away! Hop off!'

DUDLEY: So there's still hope?

PETER: Yes, there is still hope, Mr Spiggott. If we get no two-legged artistes in here within, say, the next eighteen months, there is every chance that you, a unidexter, are the very type of artiste we shall be attempting to contact at this agency. I'm sorry I can't be more definite, but you must understand with the Channel Tunnel going ahead, we can't afford to take extra risks.

DUDLEY: Thank you so much. Thank you, goodbye.

(*Exit Dudley, hopping.*)

GOODBYE-EE
(Decca, 1965)

Released as a single by Decca in the summer of 1965, Peter and Dudley's signature tune climbed to eighteenth place, and spent ten weeks in the hit parade, as people were wont to call it in those days. They performed it together on countless occasions, but one of the most moving performances was at Peter's memorial service, when Dudley played it with Peter's old school choir.

DUDLEY (*sings*): Now is the time to say goodbye.
PETER (*speaks*): Goodbye.
DUDLEY (*sings*): Now is the time to yield a sigh.
PETER (*speaks*): Yield it, yield it.
DUDLEY (*sings*): Now is the time to wend our way, (*falsetto*) Until we meet again some sunny day.

DUDLEY (*sings*):
Goodbye, goodbye
We're leaving you, skiddly-dye
Goodbye, we wish you fond goodbye.
PETER / DUDLEY (*singing, together*):
Fa-ta ta-ta, fa-ta ta-ta.
DUDLEY (*sings*): Goodbye.
PETER (*speaks*): Goodbye.
DUDLEY (*sings*): Goodbye.
PETER (*speaks*): Goodbye.
DUDLEY (*sings*):
We're leaving you, skiddly-dum
Goodbye, we wish you a fond goodbye
Fa-la, ta-ta-ta.

PETER (*speaks*): You know there comes a time in everybody's life when they must say goodbye. That time is now, and so with tears in either eye we say goodbye, as people have said throughout the years. We leave this mortal coil on which we strut and fret our weary way, as Shakespeare put it. God bless him. What a wonderful odd chap Shakespeare was, bald but sexy. Oh, take that rhythm away with its wonderful melodies. Oh, goodbye, they say.

PETER / DUDLEY (*singing, together*):
Goodbye, goodbye
We're leaving you, goodbye
Goodbye, we wish you fond goodbye.

Notes

INTRODUCTION

1   *Peter Cook – At a Slight Angle to the Universe*, BBC2, 2002
2   *Dudley Moore – The Authorized Biography*, Barbra Paskin, Sidgwick & Jackson, 1998
3   'Some Interesting Facts about Peter Cook', *Omnibus*, BBC1, 1995
4   *Observer*, 9 December 1979
5   *From Fringe to Flying Circus*, Roger Wilmut, Methuen, 1980
6   *Dudley Moore – The Authorized Biography*
7   *Fame, Set and Match – Beyond the Fringe*, BBC2, 23 November 2002
8   *From Fringe to Flying Circus*
9   Ibid.
10 *Dudley Moore – The Authorized Biography*
11 Ibid.
12 *Peter Cook – At a Slight Angle to the Universe*
13 *Parkinson*, BBC1, November 1978
14 ITV, 22 November 1989
15 *Peter Cook – At a Slight Angle to the Universe*

16 *Dudley Moore – The Authorized Biography*
17 *Fame, Set and Match – Beyond the Fringe*
18 Ibid.
19 *Sun,* 17 March 1982
20 *Beyond the Fringe and Beyond,* Ronald Bergan, Virgin Books, 1989
21 *Fame, Set and Match – Beyond the Fringe*
22 Ibid.
23 *Dudley Moore – The Authorized Biography*
24 Ibid.
25 *Harty,* LWT, 9 October 1975
26 *Peter Cook – At a Slight Angle to the Universe*
27 *Dudley Moore – The Authorized Biography*
28 Ibid.
29 Ibid.
30 *Daily Mirror,* 26 October 1981
31 *Good Afternoon with Mavis Nicholson,* Thames TV, 9 March 1973
32 ITV, 22 November 1989
33 *Beyond the Fringe and Beyond*
34 'Peter Cook – Bedazzled', John Lahr, *The New Yorker,* 23 January 1995, reprinted in *Light Fantastic – Adventures in Theatre,* John Lahr, Bloomsbury, 1996
35 *Independent,* 30 March 2002

CHAPTER ONE

1 Kenneth Tynan, *Observer,* 14 May 1961
2 *Beyond the Fringe and Beyond,* Ronald Bergan, Virgin Books, 1989
3 *Fame, Set and Match – Beyond the Fringe,* BBC2, 23 November 2002
4 Ibid.
5 *Cartoons,* Radio 4, 16 October 1998
6 *Peter Cook – At a Slight Angle to the Universe,* BBC2, 2002
7 Ibid.

8   Ibid.

9   *From Fringe to Flying Circus*, Roger Wilmut, Methuen, 1980

10 *Guardian*, 29 October 1962

11 *Fame, Set and Match – Beyond the Fringe*

12 *Peter Cook – At a Slight Angle to the Universe*

13 *From Fringe to Flying Circus*

14 Ibid.

15 *That Was Satire That Was*, Humphrey Carpenter, Gollancz, 2000

16 *That Was Satire That Was*

17 *Fame, Set and Match – Beyond the Fringe*

18 *From Fringe to Flying Circus*

CHAPTER TWO

1   *From Fringe to Flying Circus*, Roger Wilmut, Methuen, 1980

2   *Beyond the Fringe and Beyond*, Ronald Bergan, Virgin Books, 1989

3   Ibid.

4   *Good Afternoon with Mavis Nicholson*, Thames TV, 9 March 1973

5   *Peter Cook – At a Slight Angle to the Universe*, BBC2, 2002

6   Ibid.

7   *Dudley Moore – The Authorized Biography*, Barbra Paskin, Sidgwick & Jackson, 1998

8   *From Fringe to Flying Circus*

9   Ibid.

10 Ibid.

11 *Daily Mail*, 18 November 1965

12 *Peter Cook – At a Slight Angle to the Universe*

CHAPTER THREE

1   'Some Interesting Facts About Peter Cook', *Omnibus*, BBC1, 1995

2   *From Fringe to Flying Circus*, Roger Wilmut, Methuen, 1980

3 Ibid.
4 *Something Like Fire – Peter Cook Remembered*, edited by Lin Cook, Century, 1996

CHAPTER FOUR

1 *From Fringe to Flying Circus*, Roger Wilmut, Methuen, 1980
2 Ibid.
3 *Beyond the Fringe and Beyond*, Ronald Bergan, Virgin Books, 1989
4 *The Times*, 3 November 1973
5 *Dudley Moore – The Authorized Biography*, Barbra Paskin, Sidgwick & Jackson, 1998

CHAPTER FIVE

1 *Peter Cook – At a Slight Angle to the Universe*, BBC2, 2002
2 *The Times*, 3 November 1973
3 *Beyond the Fringe and Beyond*, Ronald Bergan, Virgin Books, 1989
4 *Peter Cook – At a Slight Angle to the Universe*
5 Ibid.
6 Ibid.
7 *From Fringe to Flying Circus*, Roger Wilmut, Methuen, 1980
8 *Good Afternoon with Mavis Nicholson*, Thames Television, 9 March 1973
9 Ibid.
10 *Dudley Moore – The Authorized Biography*, Barbra Paskin, Sidgwick & Jackson, 1998
11 Ibid.
12 Ibid.

CHAPTER SIX

1 *Offensive – The Real Derek & Clive*, Channel 4, 2002

2 *Dudley Moore – The Authorized Biography*, Barbra Paskin, Sidgwick & Jackson, 1998
3 Ibid.
4 *From Fringe to Flying Circus*, Roger Wilmut, Methuen, 1980
5 Ibid.
6 *Dudley Moore – The Authorized Biography*
7 'Peter Cook's Monday Morning Feeling', *Daily Mail*, 14 November 1977
8 Ibid.
9 *Today*, 4 September 1993
10 *Danny Baker After All*, BBC1, September 1999
11 *Offensive – The Real Derek & Clive*
12 Ibid.
13 *Dudley Moore – The Authorized Biography*
14 *Junkin's Jokers*, BBC Radio Two, 19 October 1993
15 *Daily Mail*, 1 August 1977

Chapter Seven

1 *Daily Mail*, 18 November 1965
2 *From Fringe to Flying Circus*, Roger Wilmut, Methuen, 1980
3 *Dudley Moore – The Authorized Biography*, Barbra Paskin, Sidgwick & Jackson, 1998
4 *Peter Cook – At a Slight Angle to the Universe*, BBC2, 2002
5 *Offensive – The Real Derek & Clive*, Channel 4, 2002
6 *Peter Cook – At a Slight Angle to the Universe*
7 Ibid.
8 *Beyond the Fringe and Beyond*, Ronald Bergan, Virgin Books, 1989
9 Ibid.

Chapter Eight

1 *From Fringe to Flying Circus*, Roger Wilmut, Methuen, 1980
2 *Secrets of the Press – Journalists on Journalism*, edited by Stephen Glover, Allen Lane, 1999

CHAPTER NINE

1 *Daily Mail*, 12 November 1994
2 Ibid.
3 *Dudley Moore – The Authorized Biography*, Barbra Paskin, Sidgwick & Jackson, 1998
4 *Daily Mail*, 12 November 1994